Can We Zoom into God?

Can We Zoom into God?

A Major Critique of New Church Worship—
Causes and Effects

ANDREW HEMINGWAY

RESOURCE *Publications* · Eugene, Oregon

CAN WE ZOOM INTO GOD?
A Major Critique of New Church Worship—Causes and Effects

Resource Publications
An Imprint of Wipf and Stock Publishers
199 W. 8th Ave., Suite 3
Eugene, OR 97401

www.wipfandstock.com

PAPERBACK ISBN: 978-1-6667-4429-3
HARDCOVER ISBN: 978-1-6667-4430-9
EBOOK ISBN: 978-1-6667-4431-6

OCTOBER 16, 2023 10:36 AM

This book is affectionately dedicated to:

Ivy
&
Liane

two beauties

Let the righteous man strike me—it is a kindness;
let him rebuke me—it is oil on my head.

—Ps 141:5 (NIV)

"The man who today forbids what God allows tomorrow will
allow what God forbids."

R.B. Kuiper

Contents

FOREWORD

LANCE STRATE

TECHNOLOGY IS NEVER NEUTRAL. EVERY tool, machine, and medium will offer certain advantages, but those advantages will always be accompanied by certain disadvantages as well. A hammer is biased towards the application of blunt force, hence the quip often attributed to Mark Twain, that when you have a hammer in your hand, everything looks like a nail. On the other hand, a hammer is not very helpful for many other kinds of activities, such as healing a disease, and in fact has the potential to cause significant damage and harm to the human body. An airplane is biased towards long distance travel, and would be downright disadvantageous if used in a city just to go around the block. The telegraph made it possible to transmit messages instantaneously, but its bias towards speed worked against slow reflection and delayed gratification, and its bias towards brief messages worked against long forms of written work. Whatever benefits any given innovation may bring, they will always come at a cost. And we often will not know what the cost will be until it is too late, in part because whatever we expect our inventions to do for us (and with us and to us), there will always be unexpected consequences and unforeseen effects. After all, when you introduce a change into a system made up of interdependent parts, such as a society or culture, or the human psyche for that matter, the effects of that change will have consequences that lead to other changes, and those effects will have still more effects, effects of effects and effects of effects of effects, and so on rippling throughout the entire system. In this sense, when new media or technologies are introduced, their effects are not additive, we are not left with the same old system that we had before, unchanged except for the addition of the innovation; instead, the effects are transformative, resulting in a qualitatively different sort of society, culture, and mindset.

Knowing this to be the case, you would think that we would proceed with great care and caution when it comes to adopting new media and technologies. But we rarely do. Criticize a new technology, or even question it, and you will be branded a neo-luddite (with no acknowledgement that the original luddites were acting quite rationally in defending their jobs and incomes). Admittedly, there tends to be a progression in thinking about technology, as the humorist Douglas Adams explained in an essay in *The Sunday Times* published August 29th, 1999:

1. everything that's already in the world when you're born is just normal;

2. anything that gets invented between then and before you turn thirty is incredibly exciting and creative and with any luck you can make a career out of it;

3. anything that gets invented after you're thirty is against the natural order of things and the beginning of the end of *civilization* as we know it until it's been around for about ten years when it gradually turns out to be alright really.

And it certainly seems to be the case that many who are technology boosters when they are young become more wary, less accepting, and more critical as they get older. But this is not simply a matter of becoming cranky or set in our ways as we age. Rather it has much to do with the fact that innovations seldom live up to their hype, and are typically oversold, so that their early promise to change everything and revolutionize our lives never comes to pass, while the potential harm they might cause is generally downplayed when they are introduced, and only becomes apparent later on. And the point here is not to reject everything that is new out of hand, or to condemn all technology as somehow evil or threatening. Rather, what is needed is sober assessment and thoughtful consideration. To that end, the great media ecology scholar Neil Postman suggested that we ask the following question regarding any new medium or technology: *To what problem is this a solution?* His point being that the entire *raison d'être* of technology is to solve human problems, and if the problem the new technology is supposed to solve is not really a problem, if it is a problem that has already been solved, or worse yet if no one can articulate what the problem actually is, then there is good reason to question the necessity of adopting the innovation. Additionally, Postman pointed out that we are always told what a new technology will *do*, but we also need to ask, what will it *undo*? Moreover, as another media ecology scholar, the computer scientist and artificial intelligence pioneer Joseph Weizenbaum, reminded us, just because we *can* do something does not mean that we *ought* to do it. What hangs in the balance, according to yet another media ecologist, the social critic and theologian Jacques Ellul, is nothing less than human freedom. Are we free to say no to technology? Can we say no to the pursuit of efficiency and convenience? Can we find a way to retain and reclaim our humanity in the face of constant technological innovation?

These are the kinds of questions that we need to ask, and these are the kinds of questions that Andrew Hemingway seeks to address in this volume. They echo the question posed within Psalm 137, "How shall we sing the Lord's song in a strange land?" In this instance, the strange land is not a conquering empire, but the electronic media environment, the product of technological innovation that has colonized every nation on our planet. And in doing so, it has brought us many gifts unavailable to the generations that came before us. Broadcast, cable, satellite, the internet, and on-line streaming services have made more information and entertainment available to us than ever before, delivered through a wide variety of devices, from our tablets, pads, smartphones, and other mobile devices; to our desktop and laptop computers; to our widescreen digital displays and home entertainment centers; not to mention the jumbo screens found in public venues. And yet, the questions posed by T. S. Eliot in 1934 remain with us: "Where is the wisdom we have lost in knowledge? Where is the knowledge we have lost in information?" To which we can also add, where is the wisdom and knowledge we have lost in entertainment? Also, where is the spirituality we have lost in the pursuit of efficiency? And, where is the humanity we have lost in our surrender to technology?

A century ago, the electronic media environment provided ways to maintain a sense of connection for those who, due to disease, disability, or distance, were unable to travel, to attend religious services or for other purposes. Microphones set up in houses of worship made it possible to broadcast worship via radio, and later, with the addition of cameras, via television. In the United States during the 1960s, Bell Tele-phone advertised its long distance service through the slogan, *it's the next best thing to being there*. What this slogan downplayed is the fact that it is a distant second at best, and a very poor substitute for actual human contact. In celebrating the technology, they obscured the tragic fact that technology has also shattered the extended family, so that grandparents often live far away from their children and grandchildren, and only visit on rare occasions. Bell followed in the 1970s with the slogan, *reach out and touch someone*, contradicting the obvious fact that true human contact involves something more than hearing a voice from afar. To be sure, a phone call is an im-provement over complete isolation, and the benefits of telephonic communication are myriad. But does the easy availability of electronically mediated communications also make it easier to avoid getting together in person? Does it absolve us of the re-sponsibility to look in on the isolated and the infirm? Such questions become ever more relevant with the addition of cell phones, social media, and innovations such as robotic companions.

When the COVID-19 pandemic necessitated a series of quarantines and lock-downs, many learned about video calling and conferencing services such as Skype, FaceTime, WebEx, Google Meet, Microsoft Teams, and of course Zoom for the first time, and became quite familiar with them. These and other types of electronic media allowed us to maintain connections with family and friends, and provided a means to continue participation in a variety of activities, such as office work, schooling, and worship. This served as a source of solace and relief in many instances, but also at times generated frustration and aggravation. We learned how very useful these services can be, but we are left with the question of what uses are appropriate for them, and what uses are not. For example, traveling long distances for a short meeting is wasteful in many ways, and Zoom and its ilk can provide an adequate substitute. Weighing the costs and benefits of working from home is a bit more complicated, and the answer will vary depending on the individuals involved and the nature of their employment. Schooling, on the other hand, clearly suffers, especially when it comes to primary education, less so for higher education. Religious experience is generally degraded as well. I would hasten to add that if circumstances dictate that we must be isolated from one another and use the electronic media as a substitute for face-to-face contact, then so be it. But to again invoke Psalm 137, we ought to echo the lament: "By the rivers of Babylon, there we sat down, yea, we wept, when we remembered Zion." Being forced to rely on video conferencing for religious services is not a cause for celebration. Neither is it a novelty that we should continue to employ once we can return to classrooms and houses of worship.

In an op-ed published on the Jewish Telegraphic Agency website on April 20, 2021, Rabbi Eli L. Garfinkel argues that Zoom worship is not sustainable, lacking as it is in a true sense of community and co-presence. As he puts it:

> Don't get me wrong, I understand that Zoom Judaism was necessary during the height of the pandemic and will continue to be so for some months. I recognize that Zoom has been a lifesaver for the physically challenged and that it has quickly brought about a revolution in Jewish adult education. My concern is that some Jewish leaders believe that the pandemic has given us license to reimagine a largely digital synagogue as a permanent replacement for real, physical Jewish community. This belief is predicated on the idea that Jews will continue to find Zoom Judaism compelling long after the novel coronavirus is finally vanquished.[1]

Rather than find it compelling, Garfinkel argues that:

> Life is an in-person affair, and Jewish life is all the more. Zoom Judaism under non-emergency conditions will promote the deification of what has been called the "sacred self," the notion that our own desires for convenience and comfort take precedence over God's command to be a kingdom of priests and a holy nation.

As for the possibility of hybrid services, he writes:

> It is so easy to log in and, relatively speaking, so hard to actually make one's way to a brick-and-mortar structure, that most Jews will take the path of least resistance if they take any path at all. This path, however, will merely lead us to an atomized hive of like-minded individuals, not a community. It will do to Judaism what Facebook and Instagram have done to friendship.

1 Garfinkel, "Sorry, but Zoom Judaism Just Isn't the Real Thing," https://www.jta.org/2021/04/20/ideas/sorry-but-zoom-judaism-just-isnt-the-real-thing.

Rabbi Garfinkel's arguments, like those of Andrew Hemingway, extend to all faith traditions, and beyond. To return, then, to Postman's question, *to what problem is this a solution?*, clearly the problem was the isolation imposed by the pandemic. And while COVID-19 is still with us, we have solved the problem of quarantines and lockdowns through a variety of mitigation measures, especially the vaccines that have been developed, and life has returned to relative normality. Having solved the problem, there is no longer a need to continue to apply the solution; to do so can be harmful, just as to continue to take the medicine that helped us overcome a disease can cause damage to the body. To Postman's question, *what will this technology undo?*, the answer is the very basis of our Abrahamic religions, based as they are on a sense of physical community, of gathering together to express gratitude, ask for blessing, and support each other through times of joy and grief. Traditional communities are made up of persons who are different from one another, and must find ways to live together, whereas online communities are echo-chambers of like-minded individuals who have no strong ties to each other, who can come and go as they please. What so much of our electronic media is also undoing is our almost four millennia of alphabetic literacy, and the kind of media environment that provided an important balance between the spoken and written word, that gave us the kind of abstract thinking required for monotheism, and that forms the basis of our moral and ethical codes. Followers of the Abrahamic religions are all *peoples of the book*, but when we replace our sacred texts with screens, that longstanding form of spirituality can come undone.

Marshall McLuhan, arguably our best known media ecology scholar, noted that environments tend to be invisible to us, not because they are transparent, but because they are ignored. Whatever is new or different comes into focus for us, but whatever is routine and expected no longer maintains a hold on our attention and thereby fades into the background. For this reason, the electronic media environment has become, for us, taken for granted, expected, and therefore all but imperceptible. A new medium like Zoom may stand out briefly when it is introduced, but quickly becomes part of the landscape that we overlook. This makes us essentially sleepwalkers, and to wake up and pay attention to our surroundings requires a reversal of the figure-ground relationships of everyday life, to turn our technological background into figures of conscious awareness. To do so, it is helpful, maybe even essential, to have at our disposal what McLuhan termed anti-environments or counter-environments, media environments whose biases are significantly different from those of the current one we live within. He pointed to art as an antienvironment, arguing that true artists have the sensitivity to pick up on the biases of the technological landscape and anticipate the changes that are occurring (he was fond of the Ezra Pound quip that *the artist is the antenna of the race*, to which I would also invoke Kurt Vonnegut's observation that the sensitivity of artists is comparable to *canaries in coal mines*); he also noted that art could serve as a means of training for the senses and education for perception. It is perhaps no accident then that this cogent critique of Zoom worship comes from a gifted artist such as Andrew Hemingway (of International reputation).

Similarly, Postman looked to schools as potential counter-environments, arguing that they need to provide a thermostatic function for society, and to serve as a counterbalance to the electronic media environment by conserving the structures and biases of the typographic media environment. And I know that McLuhan and Postman would agree that our traditional religious institutions also serve as important anti-environments, not the least because they are the product of literate cultures, shaped by alphabetic writing and the printing revolution; to this, Ellul would add that religious tradition also offers an alternative to the technological imperative that allows for only technical criteria to be applied to human activity, the criterion of efficiency above all. The Abrahamic faiths and forms of worship represent the kind of counter-environments that are desperately needed to provide some balance in the face of continual technological innovation, and the ubiquity of the electronic media environment. That balance can only be provided by the experience of actually *being there* (as Jerzy Kosiński put it), of separating from the profane space and time of everyday life, and communing with something greater than ourselves, and doing so communally.

The very meaning of words such as *sacred and holy*, going back to the Hebrew term *kadosh*, means to be separate, set apart, distinct. The electronic media, however, are notorious for blurring the boundaries between distinct sectors of society, areas of activity, social roles and identities, and situations and context (the concept of *context collapse* comes up repeatedly in popular discourse regarding social media). No longer sequestered in some form of sacred space, the distractions of home and other profane environments abound, undermining our ability to meditate or pray in peace. And it becomes all too easy to change the channel, click on another website, or read a text message or social media update, as our devices and apps frequently vie for our attention and interrupt our focus, leaving us distracted, perhaps even anxious, and not in a state of mind conducive to spiritual awakening.

The televisual image favors shots that are up close and personal, and screen worship often features intimate views of the faces of clergy and congregants. This may be endearing in some ways, but it is worth recalling that such views are unnatural, the close-up is an innovation made possible by the camera lens, introducing a sight that is impossible to achieve with the naked eye. The focus on the human visage is another form of distraction, substituting here for contemplation of the divine. Scripture tells us that human beings are made *imago dei*, but especially in the context of worship, screens can also be understood as violating the Second Commandment prohibition against graven images. Even if this is not seen as a form of idolatry, it is a far cry from the worship of a God whose medium of choice is the word and not the image, the God whose act of creation begins with a speech act, *let there be light!*, whose will was made known through the written word delivered to Moses at Sinai, who spoke to Elijah in a still small voice, whose emissary produces the writing on the wall that is interpreted by Daniel.

Whether you feel comfortable with our new media and technologies, or you instead experience the electronic media environment as a strange land, I would suggest that you ought to be aware of the arguments that Andrew Hemingway raises in this volume. Whether you feel that Zoom worship is "against the natural order of things and the beginning of the end of civilization as we know it," or that it will "turn out to be alright really" in the end, I believe it is important to ask the kinds of questions that have motivated him to write this important work. We need to think about the effects caused by our innovations, what they will do and what they will undo for us as individuals, for our institutions, and for our way of life. We need to ponder the consequences, weigh the costs and benefits, however imperfect our knowledge of them may be, and do our best to anticipate what we will gain and what we will lose. There is too much at stake to do otherwise, and not just the future of our faith traditions, but ultimately, for the very survival of our species, and our world.   .

Professor Lance Strate,
Professor of Communication and Media Studies,
Fordham University, New York

PREFACE

As I began to write on this subject I recalled the name of my namesake Ernest Hemingway, and considered his counsel: "Only write when you have something to say," and as the book in your hand confirms, I do have something "earnestly" to say.

But what of my qualification to write such a book? I am certainly not a historian, a psychologist, a scientist, a neuroscientist, a philosopher, a sociologist, nor a politician. Finally, I am not a theologian, but then neither was A.W. Tozer, John Bunyan, or even Charles Spurgeon. They all lacked the qualification of "Doctor of Divinity," but all have served as considerable warning voices to Christ's church. Where I lack expertise in the fields mentioned, I have called on those who, in some measure, make similar points to my own but with slightly different emphasis. My qualification is actually in the arts, and as a professional artist for almost fifty years, image-making has been my life's work, so I understand and have witnessed its extraordinary power. Since being converted to Christ at the age of nineteen I have studied the scriptures every day, and am still plumbing the depths of the word of God, serving Christ in my local church for over thirty-five years.

When the first UK lockdown, due to COVID, came into force in March 2020, it would only take a matter of days before "Zoom" worship was born. And whilst "Zoom" was certainly then flavor of the day, in 2020 New York schools took the decision to call an end to their use of "Zoom," because of the red flags which pointed to the insecurity of the platform (as reported by Kate O'Flaherty, cybersecurity journalist). Nonetheless the "powers that be" took action, regardless of its popularity, as they had a responsibility of care for those in their charge.

Not only was the world at large wooed by the new "tool" but so was the church, and whilst the church did not grasp that "the medium is the message" (Marshall McLuhan), the fact that the medium was the "massage" was quickly understood. In the summer of 2020, a church in the Cathedral City of Worcester, in the UK, gathered for "zoom prayer," and soon experienced the painful manipulation of that "massage;" their meeting was hijacked, invaded by troublemakers displaying homosexual pornography, punctuated with Nazi sentiments, profanities, and invoking Islamic religion. Unfortunately at this time the church was at its most vulnerable, COVID forcing the churches in one of two directions—close or break the law (a number of government officials, who had introduced the law failed to adhere to it themselves, the Prime Minister included). In light of the only two options open to the church (close or break the law), neither of which were satisfactory, consequently, almost immediately, huge numbers found a "third" way to worship "together" through a medium . . . "Zoom" worship was given birth.

In writing this book I have kept the image of an onion before me at all times, trying to peel back one skin after another, revealing the endless layers of what makes up the whole. I liken it to the onion skins being peeled back, and I have found one layer of "idolatry," another of "control" and still others revealing our predilections for "calibrated church weighing scales," the "business model," failure of "patience," and the "failing conscience," to name just a few of the many layers highlighted. These I believe confirm J. I. Packer's perceptive remarks about "deep level worldliness" in the church from which we have easily, naturally lowered our worship to a place where participants bow to the neon god.

I have often been asked, "What is the point of God?" From a human perspective my answer is always the same: "Our limitations." The need of Christ as Savior confirms this. Archbishop Trench has a wonderful way of putting this: "It is even so with the heart and affections of man; if they do not twine around God, they must twine around some meaner thing." Limitation, when acknowledged, tends to extol the virtue of humbleness but the danger for the church in this seminal moment is that it will reach out, even more besotted, drugged by a culture which promises limitless power leading to a limitless future. Nietzsche will have been proved to be right!

This book has been written to question these actions, and it is hoped there are still those in the church, who like the Bereans, have an enquiring, "open mind" (Acts 17:11, NET).

ANDREW HEMINGWAY
June 2021

ACKNOWLEDGMENTS

HABITS WE ALL APPRECIATE ARE easily formed but hard to break. Nevertheless, they possess a positive as well as a negative side. The positive habit of loving one another, if deeply forged with God at the center, can deliver some of the best things in life . . . a threefold cord is not easily broken. In order to write this book it has been necessary to have those around me who, above all else, believed and put into practice the words of the apostle Peter: "Love one another deeply from the heart" (1 Pet 1:22, 4:8). Those who must be acknowledged here have certainly excelled in this, no doubt finding additional help from the apostle Paul, who confirms the power of love which can bear all things. Certainly, those who have helped me have had to bear with me!

From the outset I must thank Jane James who initially alerted me to the practice of "screen" worship, hers was a genuine concern to honor God along with her husband Richard. It raised too many questions for which they found few, satisfactory answers. Together, on a snowy December day, they walked and talked with me, encouraging me to write and offered support in lots of ways. During the writing of the book, they have not faltered in that support.

My son, Joshua, has been my constant sounding board; he possesses an adept capacity for abstract thought. Calmly and objectively from the outset, when the experiment was first launched, ill at ease, he possessed a deep lack of confidence in himself to just "get on board" and rush into things. It provided time for both of us to ruminate on endless questions . . . no doubt we will continue to "chew the cud" together! I will always be grateful to him for his clear and incisive perception, he urged me on believing this needed to be written.

Ann Taylor, a friend in the church, had no idea of what I was writing, but after six months she and her supportive husband Rick kindly loaned me the most valuable of assets—time. Ann, by her own admission, had been "sitting on the fence" as touching the new worship, neither for nor against, and certainly I did nothing to put pressure on her to "come on board". She has worked tirelessly proofreading and editing to bring this to fruition. Her honest analysis and criticism, coupled with good humor (much needed during long sessions) have been a God given provision which I could not have anticipated.

Jane Beaumont possesses the old stoic mentality, quietly patient and willing to do anything. She has given hours of time to work through the quotes and footnotes, laboring against all odds, as I failed to note so many in my original hand-written manuscript . . . love bears all things.

Edward Schofield has provided much technical assistance. After long days at work he has always been willing and ready to humor and sympathize with my slowness to grasp the "techno-babel," as I call it. His patience is noted and appreciated.

Last but not least, Carol Singleton, who agreed, perhaps too readily, to assist me in my research, her skill at translating my handwritten scrawl into legibility is no mean feat! She could not have known at the beginning of 2021 what lay ahead. She has typed, typed, and re-typed the manuscript, never once complaining . . . not to me at least! The book has her labor written all over it and without her selfless dedication, it could not have been realized . . . love indeed bears all things.

I am thankful to God for these wonderful acts of selfless kindness, which I know have been offered first of all to the God and Father of the Lord Jesus Christ, and only after that offered to me.

Thanks must also go to the publishers, who from the outset of this project, have given above and beyond what might ordinarily have been asked to make this publication possible.

When these acknowledgements were first written, our beautiful daughter-in-law, Liane (Joshua's wife), was still with us. She always encouraged me to finish what I had started. In the late summer of 2022 she died of cancer, which she had fought so courageously. Her living by faith was the brightest of lights, as bright as any we have ever seen. This faith will forever be spoken of by those who knew her, because to know her was to love her. "Blessed are the dead who die in the Lord" (Rev 14:13).

INTRODUCTION

Something is Wrong

WHEN A.W. TOZER HIGHLIGHTED THE "missing jewel" in the life of Christ's church, in his own inimitable way he put his finger on the sad demise of worship as he observed the spiritual climate in his day. More than seventy years on from his searching perspicacity we need his contribution still, as a clarion call. Climate change is upon us. To add to his unique rich tapestry of thought, Dr. Robert Reymond, writing more than half a century later, expresses these sentiments on the subject of worship saying, "The Reformed worship tradition should remind every generation of Christians that the worship of God is the most important of all Christian tasks. That is the primary reason why the Christian should go to church: to worship God . . . not to evangelize, not to provide a comfortable consumer-friendly setting for the unchurched, not even primarily for the benefit which fellowship with other Christians provides, and definitely not just for lectures and devotionals, but in order to worship God."[1]

Further to this, Reymond writes, "Anyone who will take the time to study the matter will have to conclude that worship in evangelical churches in this generation is, speaking generally, approaching bankruptcy."[2] Reymond may or may not be right in designating worship as a task, this is open to debate. But . . . if Reymond thought that worship was approaching bankruptcy more than twenty years ago, then new failures have been added since, and some, of a most alarming kind are now emerging out of the spiritual landscape, these are evolving at break-neck speed as a result of COVID-19. For this reason I have followed Reymond's advice to "take the time and study." What follows is a result of both.

It would be a mistake for us to think of God as mercenary in any way, when he insisted that his people should be removed from Egypt so as to render him worship. Rather it must be supposed that the Divine Consciousness of God as God must be something (if I can put it like this) perfectly inescapable within himself. God must/needs to be worshipped as much as he must/needs to be true, this by itself alone makes the demand on his creatures, indeed on all creation. In the light of this, there can

---

1. Reymond, *New Systematic Theology*, 872.
2. Reymond, *New Systematic Theology*, 873.

never be anything more upright about our actions than to offer to God what he is worthy of. Without this we are in effect a living contradiction of the created order. Of an absolute necessity therefore, worship must be acceptable to him, ultimately this is the only criteria which matters. If this could be ingrained within us, we would save ourselves a huge amount of pain and distress.

Unfortunately, worship has all the *Ps*, both *past* and *present* it has *proved* to be a huge issue which *perpetually places* us in *problematic* territory, which raises contention of overwhelming *proportions*. It, like nothing else, has managed to divide *people*. The woman at the well needed straightening out regarding worship. At some point we all do. From Aaron at the foot of the Mount who lost *sight* (of Moses), to the apostle John who was blown away and overwhelmed by *sight* (of the angel), to the apostle Peter who did relatively poorly, when in full view of his Lord and Savior. With *sight* he wielded the sword and flirted with and succumbed to doubt and denial. Clearly, he did much better when he was locked up only to faith with the power of the Holy Spirit.

Though we may not want this pointing out to us, seeing is our Achilles' heel. Worship is a *life* of faith, never of *sight*. If faith without works is dead, then faith with *sight* is most certainly dead. Faith will not share a platform with anything, least of all *sight*. Faith, let it never be forgotten, is substantial as the thing hoped for (Heb 11:1).

On the face of it such an offering of worship looks uncomplicated as in fact it should be; and it would be, except for the fly in the ointment, *we* must bring it. If only we knew, the jewel in the crown of the church is worship, the pity is it has often lost its luster and dazzling beauty. Tozer was addressing what many of us have observed, creative invasions tend to leave the jewel scarred and disfigured, recut and polished amateurishly without care. As a consequence, the jewel ceases to reflect the glory of the light which strikes it (light is everything to a precious gem). Instead of it returning in scintillating strobes, the light is absorbed in the dull new polished surface to nil effect. The result, the gem now has the appearance of any common stone.

We should also never forget that it is innate within us all to steal from God, especially his glory. Adam and Eve perfected this, and they have proved to be mentors to the church down through the ages. Whether we like it or not, it is in us to be exalted, to our shame the creature must always in some measure be above the Creator. If we can, we will absorb the glory to ourselves. Sadly it looks as though many churches have begun a new journey of discovery which will lead to further self-absorption, by now quite the norm and acceptable in our narcissistic culture. In these recent times the jewel of worship has been assaulted yet again, and made subject to a new polishing and cutting. With my trained eye (in the arts) this has rendered it merely a lump of coal. The priceless diamond is returned to its base material, carbon!

For a century or more it can be easily observed how the church has given itself to the pursuit of mining, sadly it was not prepared to go deep, very deep, where it would have found priceless gems. Instead of a determined and costly search for the most precious and priceless stones, it has settled for the stuff up near the surface, easy to get at, which everyone is after, even if it means digging in the dirt. In coal mining parlance it goes under the title of "open cast" that which is easy to see, easy to extract and easy to manipulate.

It is expected on reading this that many will immediately point an accusing finger in the direction of charismatic practices. This though only addresses one side of the demise, in fact unlike the mining, the abdication is much broader and deeper. Very recently and currently, the drift has been at lightning pace, churches have morphed and shaped themselves to a market mentality. This has surfaced in the desperate rush for instrumentality. When COVID-19 struck it was this, though not exclusively, that gained the ascendancy and forced the pace, driving the church into a means/end rationalism, which can always be justified if a crop is being grown for eternal life. It seems the Great Commission will endorse almost anything if the market model accelerates instrumentality.

Whether we realize it or not, the predilections of twenty-first century worship have their forerunners to remind us of journeys and forays already made. Our not too distant ancestors, with prominent names, recall for us that they also walked this way only recently.

What is being practiced today would not be out of place with a Charles Finney or a Billy Graham. Nor would these have baulked and complained if described as rationalists and pragmatists. Finney's "New Measures for Revival 1830" would presumably have made the most of "Zoom worship" had it been available. He would no doubt have endorsed the lens in worship, the camera and crew, and riggers and sound recorders, and computer monitors and the rest. All this would have been seized on as the "one best way," manipulating the paraphernalia towards a means/end worship—coal was, and still is in abundance, why not use it?

To bring this analogy home with gentle force, coal very effectively serves this purpose. It has taken an awful long time for the world's economies to wage war on "King Coal," now like plastic it looks as though it may become public enemy number one. Once universally loved and believed in, and depended upon, the doyen of all our needs is now the industrial pariah. Now after all the damage is done we seem to have come to our senses and generally there is a worldwide recognition of the harmful properties of both these dependancies. Coal, with its soot, has marked forever the great towns and cityscapes of the old industrial North of England. The stonework is ingrained, the buildings are scarred forever and they remain a constant reminder of our love affair with carbon. Naturally cleaning up is hard to do. Regardless, the pressure of US Secretary of State John Kerry appears still to be needed to persuade the likes of India and China and emerging economies to change their habits. This will almost certainly prove difficult since at the heart of everything must be coin, a root of all evil.

In the same way the church has the habit of developing dependancies, ones which equally stain and scar us forever. Painfully it must be admitted the genie is now out of the bottle. The screen is the neon god, which Simon and Garfunkel alerted us to in their sixties songwriting, "The Sound of Silence." It is now in the church, and with its feet well and truly under the table it will not now go quietly into the night. With its acquisitive powers, it has moved smoothly, seamlessly and egregiously as a medium into the act of Christian worship with not a shot fired in anger, nor a question raised to test it (1 Thess 5:21), to halt its progress. This invokes the words of the scholar Neil Postman: "Technopoly and whose key symbol is now the computer, toward which there must be neither irreverence nor blasphemy."[3]

In all this the church is not mining gold, silver and precious stones, but wood, hay and straw. I expect now a generation will have to decipher what is, (as Daniel J Boorstin puts it) "really real." He says: "More and more of our experience thus becomes invention rather than discovery."[4] Sadly the young will have been introduced even by the church, to that deeper screen world of invention which is merely an extension of the god in their pockets. Consequently, the discovery of the divine will be just another element of their accumulated image-based experience, another pseudo-event, an illusion. Will they ever be able to distinguish the one true God who they must discover by the pursuit of faith alone and not by sight, from that of the pseudo-image created of him through the medium of the screen, in so-called "Zoom" worship?

My generation will soon be no more, my heartfelt wish is to provide something so that in the future when the neon god is even more in the ascendancy, there might be another voice with which to compare and contrast that of the impetuous screen experiment; it is the least I can do. Tozer, though he is dead, thankfully still speaks. He was trying to observe the climate change in his day, humbly, even if not quite so effectively. I am attempting to do the same thing.

The psalmist says, "Walk around Zion! Encircle it! Count its towers! Consider its defenses! Walk through its fortresses so you can tell the next generation about it" (Ps 48:12, 13, NET).

What is written here is with future generations in mind, but it is also for those who might like to take Reymond's advice now and "give time to study" because the spiritual education of today is the spiritual economy of tomorrow. Someone once remarked how C.T. Studd's sayings seem to stick like burrs, I can only hope mine will achieve the same without too much pain or bloodletting.

I wonder . . . was there ever a time when Christians could find a comfortable posture to write about those things which are wrong? Comfortable or not, we can be sure there will never be a time when this becomes an unnecessary task. The apostle Paul seems to allude to experiencing some pain when he wrote to the Corinthians in what he calls a "severe letter" (2 Cor 7:8, NLT). Something was wrong. But no matter, he was glad that the pain which the letter caused brought about a change in their ways (verse 9). We can be sure that Paul got no pleasure from writing what he did as he

3. Postman, *Technopoly*, 179.
4. Boorstin, *Image*, 257.

4

was keen on "building people up" not "knocking them down." What is clear from the passage is that his approach resulted in a very positive outcome and his actions were evidently used of God to the good of the Corinthian Christians.

Since Paul wrote those words, treatises have flowed along with books and pamphlets, and today with emails, confirming that actions are still wrong in Christ's church, things which it is perceived are in need of correction. This need I am persuaded will never go away. Along with this desire for practices that are wrong to be put right, there must always be the absence of a censorious spirit. To inveigh is to be hostile, and there has been quite enough heated hostility expressed in Christian print. Having said this, it must always be difficult to be "on a case" highlighting error and to do it dispassionately. Personally, I think it's impossible, nor for that matter should it be attempted. If something is wrong, the very act of taking up a pen to write about it must arise out of some passion. The hope must always be that objectivity will also play an important role to avoid raised temperatures. Neil Postman in his book (a critique of our cultural acceptance of technological sovereignty) gives good advice to the "resistance fighter." "You must try to be a loving resistance fighter."[5]

It is part of the law of life that when it goes wrong we want to see it straightened out and it is obvious to me (though I am no anthropologist or social scientist) that as a civilization we could not have got to where we are without this. Is it possible to speak of the kingdom of God as a civilization?[6] I like to think so, and the most perfect, complete remarkable civilization we will ever know. What a thought, a divine civilization!

The reality is that civilizations are always under threat from without and from within. The Americans are fond of speaking of "the American way of life" and the need to defend it and maintain it. Be that as it may, the threat to a way of life or a civilization should never be underestimated. This equally applies to the church. I am reasonably confident the church knows of the threat from without, namely the prince of the power of the air, but perhaps not so sure of the threat from within. This book is highlighting something which I believe is wrong which threatens our spiritual civilization.

That "wrong" is ubiquitous can surely have no detractors. However the things which are wrong and why they are so, present a deeper question altogether which leads into the world of ethics, theology, and philosophy. Wrong, whether we have ever thought about it or not, applies to all of us. It is one of those universals which unites us as human beings; in this we are all related. From the Christian perspective, if wrong is no longer a part of our lives, we are already in heaven, in the Land of Beulah where

---

5. Postman, *Technopoly*, 182.

6. The author's use of the term "kingdom of God" is employed so as to be the carrier of concepts. It does not imply that the meaning employed here is definitive; rather he acknowledges and appreciates the broad spectrum of views held by Christ's church on the subject. Revelation 5:10 (NET) offers the very best reason for his application throughout the book: "You have appointed *them* as a *kingdom*" (emphasis mine).

tears are wiped away. It is quite a thought that one day all will be right and nothing will be wrong, little wonder Abraham fixed his eyes on that place.

While we are here, we must admit that wrong is done by us, thought by us. Wrong is in us so completely, we have no difficulty or embarrassment in speaking of total depravity from a biblical perspective. Nevertheless, how very difficult this word is to use. Is it because it seems to convey only negative connotations, and none of us want to carry round the stigma of being one who lacks a positive constructive outlook? To overlook wrong is to bury our heads in the sand but the whole of life is one huge commentary of our reality, whether we wish to acknowledge it or not, atrophy is here to stay. The entire medical profession and practice exists because life breaks down, it goes wrong. Panorama's BBC Investigation Journalists investigated the COVID-19 Pandemic in the autumn of 2020, their discovery interestingly, revealed a number of senior scientists who acknowledged that they had not only been wrong about it, but also alarmingly suggested that this was viewed in their profession as a dangerous thing to do. Admitting being wrong was dangerous! Every funeral procession and cemetery speaks of something having gone wrong. Politics go wrong, democracy also. Relationships in marriage have the same habit and the church of Jesus Christ, whether we care to admit it or not, is subject to the same laws.

Not surprisingly, we all find it a difficult word and uncomfortable to apply to ourselves, though interestingly we find it quite easy to use about others. In this C.S. Lewis was right when he pointed up pride as "the great sin" from which all else flowed.[7] One of the glories (and there are many) in the doctrine of Christian salvation is the power of the Holy Spirit to convince us that we are wrong. Wrong about ourselves, wrong about our neighbor, wrong above all else about God. I take it for granted that all those who uphold the evangelical faith do so from the standpoint that all humankind is wrong in its relationship to God. At the center of our transformation from darkness to light is this putting us right with God, namely one almighty act of justification.

The Unspoken Word

Strange as it may seem, this word, though pivotal in its meaning to every Christian, is not so readily used, as if it had no ongoing purpose. How often do we hear Christians openly acknowledge that they are wrong, or have been wrong? It looks as though this word only served us at the inception of our faith but then sprouted wings and presumably flew away. Have Christians deemed the word "wrong" to be superfluous, thereby saving us from confessing openly the painful truth? How often do we hear of churches that got things wrong? Practically never. Even when the most appalling crimes have been committed, churches come reluctantly kicking and screaming to say they were wrong, and that only when public gaze had been focused on them. The evangelical

---

7. Lewis, *Mere Christianity*, 121.

churches have easily gloried in their triumphs, but with squeamishness remain silent about things which have gone wrong. Naturally all churches want to present their good looks. Perhaps in this regard the church has followed the model of the business world and politics, which rarely, if ever (unless forced to) acknowledges that they are wrong; presumably because this would be a PR disaster.

None of this can exclude the fact that we must always be ready to recognize the appreciable merits of Christ's imperfect church, and while we may have played some small part in these merits, the credit must ultimately go to the person of the Holy Spirit for his sanctifying work. Sadly, some churches seem to proclaim their achievements and soaring numbers and innovations perhaps rather too often for comfort. One wonders what a church spokesperson might say if asked the question "What's gone wrong with your church this year?" Yet the NT is not at all squeamish about revealing the reality, the church was often wrong. The letters to the Corinthians, the Galatians and Hebrews burn like a bright light to warn of problems which might emerge, bringing on the demise of the church. Five of the seven churches highlighted in Revelation need to repent. Jude's words and the need to earnestly "contend for the faith once delivered unto the saints" (Jude 3, KJV) are as needful today as ever. We are as likely to go wrong as our forefathers before us did.

The Long Struggle

The struggle with wrong began with our first parents, they were first to discover this and the seed is sown into every one of us. Most of us can tell the story of how our parents and siblings made some endeavor to point out the reality which Adam and Eve painfully found the knowledge of. In truth there is everything wrong about us, the Bible perfectly describes its extent, from the sole of our feet to the top of our heads (Isa 1:6, NIV). The endeavors of parents and siblings were further confirmed in our schooling. Which one of us has not blushed in class when we got something wrong? None of us enjoyed our errors being exposed, and so we have all learned to keep the thought of being wrong at arms length, indeed doing so has been an act of survival. Wrong is an established law, unless we subscribe to some form of nihilism. However, the law of wrong is imperative to our survival, after all it is going to be with every one of us into the future, just as it accompanied all those from the past. We get a real and honest appraisal of the consequences of this when the Bible tells us, in no uncertain terms, it will bring the world down. From the Christian perspective being wrong regarding the person of Jesus Christ will have the most dire eternal consequences for mankind. This is a word which carries such an eternal weight and we fail to pay it proper respect at our peril.

It is true that in many areas of life, being wrong does not result in the death sentence. After all we are constantly involved in a myriad of undertakings which we get wrong and we are able happily to extricate ourselves, although sometimes we are left wondering how!

Even so, in other matters the stakes are much higher, and there can be no risk-taking, no gambling. Some of the great projects which have been undertaken in history would not have been countenanced unless they were watertight. You could not be wrong when engineering the Empire State building, which stands proudly to this day. A groundbreaking piece of engineering architecture like Brunelleschi's Duomo, which was built without a centering for the dome (something never attempted before the Master of the Renaissance showed the world how to do it), could not remain standing unless constructed eliminating all errors. This tells us just how much rests on us getting things right.

In this we see the profound value of analyzing life, we try not to rush, we submit our thoughts to our peers and others. There is a well-known account of the trepidation and uncertainty which the great Robert Stevenson felt when preparing to erect one of his bridges. It is documented that he favored a different working method from that of his rival the celebrated Victorian engineer Isambard Kingdom Brunel. We do not all do everything in the same way, regardless of this, Stevenson humbly sought the view of Brunel, who apparently administered the much needed reassurance that all would go well. The bridge was successfully erected and still stands today. Stevenson needed confirmation that he had his bearings just right. Presumably Brunel, if after assessing the situation, had thought the scheme to be questionable would have said so, and no doubt Stevenson would have halted proceedings and returned to the drawing board. Undoubtedly there must be tokens of this kind of humility demonstrated in countless fields of expertise.

However, the church of Jesus Christ operates in a field of expertise where no other institution on earth can offer it a helping hand, it must humble itself under the mighty hand of God. Thankfully, over two thousand years as it followed the New Testament blueprint, it got more right than wrong. However, at this unique moment in our history we have entered upon an entirely new path, a path which has never been trod before, where the church has turned to the world for help to alleviate its trouble. We are now teaching people to walk in an entirely different way, one which the vast majority in the UK have never tried before. This book sets out why I consider this way of walking to be wholly wrong.

It may well be said (and with good reason) that we all walk differently, we all have a unique particular gait, a different way of simply putting one foot in front of another, whilst still arriving at the same destination, and that is what matters. In addition we need "to bear with one another in love" (Eph 4:2, NIV). While there is something here which we always need to appreciate, the need also presents itself "to speak the truth in love" (Eph 4:15, NIV); and to inform people that adopting such a gait may well bring on serious injury and life-altering conditions may be the result. Love, being the motive and directive, forces me to write in this manner, since I think a new way of 'walking' has been introduced, which will seriously debilitate us and teach others in the future to follow in our footsteps.

Since the end of World War II the church has never faced an upheaval of the kind forced upon it by COVID-19. This found the church ill-equipped, especially of faith, to cope with the new challenge which came its way. As a consequence a door was opened for the church to weave together the wishes and the desire of an egocentric age which required its needs to be met "immediately." Not forgetting that this is the age of "instant delivery," "infinite choice" of the "just in time" mentality. This outlook is now endemic, nor can its residence be viewed as a mere squatter, but a "mindset," here to stay. To be sure this is now reflected in society at large, and it is therefore not at all surprising that it is in the church.

I suspect not many who read this book will be familiar with the world of art museums as I am, but something has literally been reshaping them. The message which has developed is that of the buildings themselves and not the collections contained within. In 2021 Michael Prodger, art critic of the New Statesman, reviewed for *Apollo* Charles Saumarez Smith's "The Art Museum in Modern Times." In it the author charts a significant shift as he sees it. Under his title "The Notional Gallery," Smith points up the observations of a real sea change in thinking and in the perception of our national art institutions. Evolution is not underway, a new species has appeared. He notes, "The universal decline in belief in a master narrative made manifest through the display of a museum's permanent collection. In its place is a growing interest in the idea of exploration and the validity of individual response." He adds, "It is the shape of a museum that in turn shapes the visitor experience. What visitors often want are "social experiences as much as intellectual ones."[8] These comments are just way too close for comfort as they seamlessly cross all divides, even those of the church. The "master narrative" is in steep decline and in many places is already lost. The churches recent foray into experimenting with "screen" worship will only succeed in confirming that social experiences are to be pursued at all costs. The evolution of museums in the twentieth and twenty-first centuries means our eye may be drawn away to the external, we will have taken our eye off the ball. It seems that by and large we are more and more willing to be drawn away from what is internal to the external. Naturally the museums are designed by superstars (which the church is not short of) as fitting the age we live in, the receptacle then comes first and inevitably the treasures within comes later, much, much later.

The discipline of the church has been lost in our times, meaning the treasures of God *himself* now play second fiddle to the church *itself*, the receptacle must come first, with all that it can offer. The museums have their paraphernalia of shops, cafes and lectures (not unlike churches). Lecture theaters become as enthralling to the visitor as the real star of the show, namely Rembrandt, DaVinci, Picasso and the rest. The

8. Smith, "Art Museum in Modern Times," *Apollo*, 78.

art collection is peripheral to the "real" star. Author Tony Reinke, in his helpful book, lends a hand to articulate this when he quotes Oliver O'Donovan:

"Cherishing wisdom is a discipline of literacy. What literacy used to mean was a capacity to interrogate an appearance . . . Without wisdom, we foolishly get lost in the aimless now, in the explosion of novelty. Without wisdom, we foolishly get unhitched from our *past* and from our *future*."[9]

It is the novelty of "screen" worship which is in danger of becoming the master narrative of our times as we become unhitched from tradition in the best sense of that word, and get blown away by the powerful explosion. We must be prepared to "interrogate appearance" so as to do due diligence. It is this kind of interrogation, which the church in the past once excelled in but also failed in, and which we stand on the threshold of failing in once more. This is where a cursory glance at church history serves this book. Without a knowledge of church history "wrongs," i.e., where we have come from, we foolishly get unhitched from the past, we get lost in the aimless now, and novelty works its deep magic. Adam and Eve were beguiled and lost themselves in the "aimless now." Aaron at the foot of the Mount and King David with Bathsheba got lost in the "aimless now." Judas was lost to the same, unable to interrogate the duplicity of those who courted his favors.

An entire book could be written devoted only to the wrongs which the church has committed down through history, much of it very well documented, it is not possible to consider these issues without concluding that the church has forever managed to pierce itself through with many griefs, in other words it goes on stabbing itself to death (NET Bible). It perpetually gets things wrong. Even if we wanted to be charitable to church history we would be quite unrealistic if we failed to see the death wish that it has often exacted upon itself. Above all else in the multitude of wrongs committed by the church, there must be one ultimate cause to which all issues can be traced, namely the church, the individual Christian "loses connection with the head" (Col 2:18, 19). This is Paul's way of explaining what has gone wrong when the Christian gives way to falsehood. F.F. Bruce puts this down to "self inflation." He says: "Each part of the body [of Christ] functions properly so long as it is under the control of the head: If it escapes from this control and begins to act independently, the consequences can be very distressing."[10] With sadness we must say the church has been distressed through its history. Self inflation will probably have been responsible for desecrating most houses of worship and the wrong will have been elevated above what was right. Loss of connection with the head, or "not holding fast the head" (KJV) has been able to produce a vast array of doctrines and practices down the centuries. Asceticism and the worship of angels (Col 2:18,19) were only the beginnings of human inventions due to self inflation. From the "puffed up" Christians in Corinth who Paul describes sarcastically as

9. Reinke, *12 Ways Your Phone is Changing You*, 150.
10. Bruce, *Epistles to the Colossians*, 123.

"reigning like kings" (1 Cor 4:8) to the vaunted television personalities of our times and churches which operate more like businesses than humble houses of worship, the head is not just obscured, but actually cut off. The church as a local expression, is often tragically headless and if this is true, its divine nature no longer exists.

Overload

It is impossible not to notice the church like the world looks overloaded with stuff, stuff of its own creating. James Wallman in his book *Stuffocation* has a chapter on the clutter crisis, he speaks of clutter being a hinder.[11] Might not the church, following the world, be weighing itself down with not just unnecessary clutter but unbiblical clutter, hindering its spiritual life? Modern life is exerting an untold pressure upon people, much of it self-imposed, chief amongst these must be the young, which is where Reinke's book is a "must read" for every Christian family which cares about the pressures being placed on children. COVID-19's arrival gave all of us a chance to declutter and assess what we were doing with our lives. However, the overload just goes on and on and like lemmings, church people seem to gladly follow the world over the cliff edge. Going back to structures and engineering once more, the famous leaning tower of Pisa has undergone years of careful engineering analysis, no expense has been spared to secure its survival. In its recent history, at times, it has reached critical moments when its degree of lean has defied all the modeling which suggested its collapse. For those who do not know, the overload is on one side, so much so the bells may not be rung for fear of their weight of momentum causing a collapse. The bells are rung delicately now with a digital mechanism. It is believed that the magnificent white marble tower began to lean almost from its inception, the ground which it is built on is the problem itself, being silt and clay. Those who love the structure have worked tirelessly to discover what is going wrong so as to save it for posterity. To preserve it is a work which will always be a labor of love, so equally, churches must match this labor for the sake of Christ's church in order to recognize any degree of lean where there is one and carefully correct it.

Scars

All this easily suggests corollaries with the church. Although "Christ laid a foundation which none other could lay and the Apostles built upon it,"(1 Cor 3:11) it seems in no time at all, the apostle Paul speaks of his "laying a foundation as a wise builder and someone else is building on it. But each one should build with care" (1 Cor 3:20). This book suggests the church is being overloaded, but I fear not "with gold, silver and precious stones, but with wood, hay and straw" (1 Cor 3:12). My concern is that in

---

11. Wallman, *Stuffocation*, 37.

our present predicament we are scarring ourselves profoundly and deeply. Those of us who have physical scars can testify that they have the habit of remaining, they are always on display and they are unfortunately often noticed. They cannot be erased and sadly, time does not hide them nor change them. Some scars are small and relatively insignificant but others are life-changing and, in the case of the church, epoch making. We may have forgotten, the willingness of the church to embrace Schleiermacher, the German theologian (Friedrich Schleiermacher, 1768–1834) whose views have been life-changing. Even though Karl Barth writes in somewhat glowing terms of him and notes his many admirable and remarkable qualities, it remains the truth his negative impact on the history of the church has still not diminished. Seminaries and churches and individual Christians have been overloaded for two hundred years by his wood, hay, and straw. No one, I think, believes that the absolute genesis of liberal theology and higher criticism was the brain child of Schleiermacher. We need to look to the Enlightenment and the earlier Renaissance for that, but, as Iain Murray points out, "Schleiermacher is correctly viewed as the chief source of the massive change which has occurred in the historic Protestant denominations during the last two hundred years."[12] It would not be in the least bit surprising if many Christians confessed to knowing nothing of the German theologian and his impact and yet the same Christians may be very much aware of, and suffer from, the scars of "easy believism" which remain to this day very unsightly. This is in turn linked, though not exclusively, with the introduction of the invitation system much popularized by Billy Graham. Is it suggesting too much to connect all this with the emergence of the Charismatic Movement, big as it is on experience, thin on orthodox theology? Iain Murray says Schleiermacher was committed to "the supposition that true religion belongs essentially to the realm of experience—religion is a matter of a well-disposed heart and devout feelings."[13] It would be a brave Christian who could survey the last one hundred years of the Evangelical church and say we are not profoundly scarred by these events . . . by the "progressive" movement of thought and actions; even if we have not the least idea of the main players and their thinking.

But statistics and dates and names mean nothing if we lose sight of the lives of people which have been scarred forever. Of course there is always the argument that while many ideas did not carry scriptural warrant for their practice, regardless of this, the gains are so much more important than the losses. In this, the argument goes, the scriptural objective is fulfilled and this is what counts. Here we see the root logic, namely that of rationalism/pragmatism. So many of our deep scars are the result of this Enlightenment thinking and it has come to rule in the churches and an unspoken rule in the lives of individual professing Christians. In contrast risk is almost a dirty word. Gary Gilley points out that Christians today believe, for various reasons, "faith is true, 'because it works' (pragmatism), furthermore it is confirmed by

12. Murray, *Evangelicalism Divided*, 11.
13. Murray, *Evangelicalism Divided*, 7.

subjectivism."[14] He goes on, "the Christian faith is not true because it works; it works because it is true. It is not true because we experience it; we experience it—deeply and gloriously—because it is true."[15] Pragmatism's hold is so entrenched it seems the church cannot bear to operate without it (chapter 8 seeks to deal with this more fully). The Christian life in the late twentieth and early twenty-first centuries professing to follow the NT model in fact looks as if faith in practice is too big a gamble, too big a risk, faith alone will not suffice. Quite unlike that faith which Paul gave thanks for in the lives of the Thessalonian Christians, "I thank God . . . because your faith flourishes more and more" (2 Thess 1:3, NET). We must wonder what the George Mullers and Hudson Taylors of this world would make of our pragmatism.

All of this forms a back drop to what is written here. The church is scarred by its catalogue of wrongs, by those errors which have been committed in the past, but the trouble is that the church is not always a keen student of history. I am persuaded that at this moment, churches everywhere are on the brink of committing to something which will scar themselves and other generations for years to come when "my generation is remembered no more" (Eccl 1:11). Here is a malevolent force ranged against God's kingdom. This book is the appraisal of the practice of "screen worship." To some it will be thought to be a thing of no great significance, like Finney's introduction of the anxious seat, Billy Graham's invitation system, or the early pronouncements of Schleiermacher. These new practices at the time must have passed under the radar of all denominations. In many places the church willfully closed its eyes to the errors and it is difficult not to pin this on the craven spirit which seems to have grown common amongst Christians. I happen to believe that contending is still the demand of scripture however uncomfortable we find it.

The Astronaut

The word "unprecedented" is the flavor of the moment since COVID-19 pinned the nations to the ground with a move of such stealth.[16] Unprecedented means without previous instances or unparalleled. Also with COVID-19 came unprecedented practices in the churches and, just as we need to act to combat COVID-19 before it sinks us, so we need to act for the sake of the church, unless seeds are sown which will flower into the most dreadful weeds of the future: and while acknowledging weeds may have their own beauty and attraction, but in time tend to choke the life out of the more delicate and refined flowers of the garden. Six months after entering into the fray on the subject of "screen worship" a dear friend gave me a copy of Tony Reinke's book

14. Gilley, *This Little Church Omnibus*, 218.

15. Gilley, *This Little Church Omnibus*, 218.

16. At the time of writing two million people are now confirmed as dead worldwide, one hundred thousand in the UK and four hundred thousand in the USA. Up to date figures for USA now stand at almost one million.

"12 Ways your phone is changing you," it was a Christmas gift, which I read the day I received it (Christmas 2020). The friend who gave it to me did so because she had read my first paper to our church in which I wrote a modest critique of "screen" worship. She thought, on reflection, that in many ways the content of my paper and the book corresponded. I think they do. Without crossing every "t" and dotting every "i," I concur with almost all he has written, and thank God for it. Not least when he says:

> Self-criticism in the digital age is a necessary discipline—an act of courage. It is by being able to criticize that we show our freedom. This is the only freedom that we still have, if we have at least the courage to grasp it. Our personal freedom from the misuse of technology is measured by our ability to thoughtfully criticize it and to limit what we expect it to do in our lives. Our bondage to technology is measured by our inability to thoughtfully criticize ourselves.[17]

He goes on to say, "Are we courageous enough to ask?"[18]

The problem with the digital age and the near slavery to technology, is that there is virtually not a single outsider to be consulted on what they see. In many respects it should not feel so very strange to attribute merit to the "outsider" since every true Christian is just this in their relationship to the world. We are all outsiders, we are alive to Christ, dead to the world, so how very needful it is for us to stress our spiritual location since we live in this world with our feet far too often comfortably fixed. Who can forget too easily the truth, "we are seated in the heavenlies with Christ" (Eph 2:6). Tony Reinke quotes the historian Bruce Hindmarsh who suggests,

> "The church needs a few young Christians who are willing to live off the digital grid so that believers who are enmeshed inside the digital world can find a contrast and comparison for personal reflections . . . those off the grid function something like an astronaut living in outer space, who can return and report on what life is like in a different environment."[19]

Being seated in heavenly realms should in fact make this possible for every Christian, the reason why it is not can be left until later. Anyone who is a critic of an astronaut like myself might be tempted to accuse me of obfuscation in all this. But might it not actually be the case that today's Christian has become muddled in a morass of digital devotion and chicanery from which they are unable to extricate themselves?

Albeit I am not young, I am that astronaut, I like to think I am unmuddled and uniquely able to see into our world from my vantage point. I confess I have never used a smartphone, nor have I ever used the internet, or sent an email or text message. I do not really know what Twitter is, except the former president of the USA (DJT) had

17. Reinke, *12 Ways Your Phone is Changing You*, 194.

18. Reinke, *12 Ways Your Phone is Changing You*, 194.

19. Reinke, *12 Ways Your Phone is Changing You*, 196.

it for breakfast, lunch, and supper! I do not know about Facebook, Reinke mentions Reddit, what is that? Then there is Snapchat and TikTok and Instagram and I suspect lots of other "platforms!" I have been introduced to the images which I mistook for childish lego figures, these turn out to be emojis! As you can see I am a qualified astronaut! Some say over-qualified!

I think it is time that the world, where the church lives, needs a friendly outsider to peer into it. What could be the harm in that, or are outsiders unwelcome? The purpose is not to condemn since that would be alien to the Savior, whose manners we seek to emulate, but at least to send out a timely warning, and to tell what it is that I see.

It should also be remembered that the astronaut is at heart an explorer, and as such is not afraid to venture into other worlds. I have no phobia or fear of technology, (as some might wish to paint me) in fact I marvel at it and believe man's inventiveness points up the glory of the God who wired us with his genius, albeit we are fallen. It is this state of being fallen which necessarily colors everything we touch, and because we are in a moribund condition, however lively our innovations and creations, they are inevitably tinged with corruption. We fail in this at our peril. Put bluntly, technology has its uses and its abuses, it is not neutral, nor remotely benign. This is Reinke's strong point, he is not an outsider (he cannot cope with my atmosphere) but a very humble and honest self-confessed insider. Like my own, his concern is the church of Jesus Christ. I do think though, the title of his book, four years on from first printing should, may I suggest, be retitled "12 Ways Your Phone *Has* Changed You." He has dared to press the alarm bell but sadly I fear the alarm has not remotely awakened the church; the house is burning down as people quietly, peacefully sleep on. "What fire?" seems to be the snarled response in parts of the kingdom of God.

To be sure the church of Jesus Christ down through time has undergone countless changes, but none quite like the digital change. "Beyond the all-pervasiveness of digital technologies compared to inventions from previous eras, another difference is the shift from technology as a means to its being an end in and of itself . . . digital technology has the potential to become the end rather than the means: a lifestyle all of its own . . . becoming a world unto itself."[20] It is altering minds forever, these minds, we must be reminded, are the very minds which the apostle Paul speaks of as those "not conforming to the pattern of this world, but be transformed by the renewing of your mind." (Rom 12:2). Dr. Susan Greenfield says in her book (a must read for every Christian) "if it is the hallmark of our species to thrive wherever we find ourselves, then the digital technologies could be in danger of bringing out the worst in "human nature," not be rendered harmless by it."[21] It is hard to hear paltry comparisons made with Gutenberg's press and Apple, and not think that, even in this rationale, Christians are clutching at straws. Christians *have* been transformed by the technology

20. Greenfield, *Mind Change*, 17.
21. Greenfield, *Mind Change*, 3.

which they have bowed to and yielded to, like those in the world they seem quite powerless to resist, they appear to be mastered. The apostle Paul by contrast refused to be mastered by anything (1 Cor 6:12). In every way it looks like an addiction, like that of an opioid, and if this is true, what could be more wrong?

My hope therefore, is that the reader might dare to read on unafraid, of a difficult encounter with an astronaut and resistance fighter. I readily confess I have been both helped and encouraged by others of a like mind, I thank God for them. Neil Postman one of the best helpers, says:

> Those who resist the American Technopoly are people (amongst other things, emphasis mine) . . . who take seriously the meaning of family loyalty and honor, and who, when they "reach out and touch someone," expect that person to be in the same room; who know the difference between the sacred and the profane, and who do not wink at tradition for modernities sake; who admire technological ingenuity but do not think it represents the highest possible form of human achievement. A resistance fighter understands that technology must never be accepted as part of the natural order of things, that every technology—from an IQ test to an automobile to a television set to a computer—is a product of a particular economic and political context and carries with it a program, an agenda, and a philosophy that may or may not be life-enhancing and that therefore requires scrutiny, criticism, and control. In short a technological resistance fighter maintains an epistemological and psychic distance from any technology, so that it always appears somewhat strange, never inevitable, never natural.[22]

In Ephesus (Acts 19) Paul's message put the finger on the goddess Artemis and the result was an uproar. This not withstanding, the truth had to be made known, uproar or not, the goddess who stood in the way of God's kingdom had distorted the Ephesians's thinking, their lens on life was warped, it was wrong and had to be corrected.

The technology of our day is a god, it needs its detractors, who for a time float above the earth looking down on us telling us what they see.

22. Postman, *Technopoly*, 183–85.

CHAPTER 1

CRUMBLING CIVILIZATION

People like ourselves who are in the process of converting their culture from word-centerd to image-centerd.[1]

NEIL POSTMAN

Now faith is being sure of what we hope for, being convinced of what we do not see.

HEBREWS 11:1 (NET)

A Divine Civilization

I THINK ALMOST EVERYONE IS familiar with the concept of civilization, if it does not seem too forced, I would like the latitude, the freedom to describe the kingdom of God in this way. I prefer to think of it as a divine *civilization* and, by virtue of it being God's, it clearly has his name stamped upon it, and as such it can be distinguished from all others. It is the most advanced and complete in human history. Being that God's ownership is visible, it tends to attract a lot of bad press, but then the king of that place previously said this was to be expected, "If the world hates you, keep in mind that it hated me first" (John 15:18, NIV). It must be admitted, this bad press at times is brought on by the members themselves. Despite this, throughout its remarkable history, it has possessed a unique power to always recover, to coin a modern buzzword expression from the dictionary, it has shown "bouncebackability!" Each member of this *civilization* shares something in common, namely a deep and profound spiritual culture (whether individual Christians are either cultured or civilized is open to question!). Like no other, this one is unconfined, instead it is established throughout the world, meaning that beautiful, individual expressions of it are on display everywhere.

---

1. Postman, *Amusing Ourselves to Death*, 10.

They can, and do vary which only enhances its attractiveness; in fact the spectrum of color is other worldly. Naturally the people, the citizens, come and go freely, and while no one was ever born in it, (they all had to travel some distance to belong) yet it is their undisputed home and family. Just as in natural civilizations the numbers fluctuate, so that at times it can seem sparsely populated, but this is entirely regulated by its king, who is in fact the King of Kings and Lord of Lords. He alone gives admission into his *civilization*. What is more the nature of this *civilization* is wholly spiritual, so much so its people need always to remember that their real citizenship is in another place beyond this world, "Our citizenship is in heaven . . ." (Phil 3:20, NIV).

Evidently civilizations always come under threat, they may be assaulted from without and from within, and consequently suffer loss. At times inexplicably, the people of this *civilization* regress and hurt themselves, and history records that they have always done so. The reason is almost certainly that this *civilization* has a king and its livelihood and health are entirely dependent upon connection with him (Col 2:19). Very tragically this connection is sometimes lost, and because it is not immune to disease, it is apt to fall sick, and the sicknesses in its history have often lasted a very long time. Regrettably, the people of this glorious *civilization*, manifesting the traits of children, often get burned and are consequently scarred for life, but at other times there are even fatalities. The King has given warnings of the possibilities of this demise in his writings (Rev 1:19–3), and long history confirms that suffering has taken place. Although he, as the Son of Righteousness, continues to shed his light divine upon this *civilization*, the benighted leanings of its members renders it susceptible, so that growth and expansion are often interrupted, even curtailed.

This *civilization* behaves like all civilizations. It is a trading one. (I realize this makes it sound like a business, which I will later explain is what it should never be). It may well be true that it was trade above all others which established any civilization. But in this particular one not only do the subjects live to serve the king, but also to spread his name abroad, to expand his borders. They do this by trading in his goods, which are love, grace, mercy, kindness, pardon, forgiveness, righteousness, and peace with God, and ultimately the hope of heaven. These essentials of trade never alter, they remain a constant, and in return broken items are welcomed. In fact the king only deals in broken earthenware, and anything which appears already intact has no need of his handiwork (Mark 2:17, NIV). These are then totally restored, not just as good as new, but better because he puts his stamp upon them and like pieces of Royal Doulton pottery his unique hallmark is indelibly stamped upon them. He specializes in mending broken things and his workshop has never rejected anything nor failed in rebuilding the broken hearted who are always completely restored (Ps 147:3).

It is suggested that often at the heart of civilization writing has been the fulcrum. Andrew Robinson in his book says "without writing there would be no history . . . writing is among the greatest inventions in human history."[2] To understand God's

2. Robinson, *Story of Writing*, 7.

civilization is to recognize the monarch at its center, with his voice uniquely heard via his written word. This written word is of an unparalleled kind, and growth and prosperity by God's Spirit is entirely reliant upon it. The writing being gifted to this *civilization* is everything. It must rely upon word and word alone, there is no room for artifice, either ancient or modern. However, perhaps in a myriad of different ways the King's rule (his word) is always under threat. It is constantly questioned. It is attacked, sometimes brutally and not surprisingly at other times, the attacks are very subtle. Indeed these are the most dangerous attacks of all because they are not easily recognized. Neil Postman, who makes no claim to be a Christian, says in his excellent book: "People . . . are in the process of converting their culture from word-centerd to image-centerd."[3] He wrote those words in 1985, thirty-six years ago. Since then the *civilization* of God's kingdom appears, even in the blink of an eye, to have rolled over like the proverbial lap dog to have its tummy tickled by the new, image-based technology. The culture has been altered—word no longer rules! As I write, it is sad to say, it looks fully committed already, so much so it could not retreat even if it wanted to.

As with all technology the digital imagery which has invaded the church will demand more and more, and what was the centrality of word will become picture. Picture, images will fulfill the need of experiences. In his book, James Wallman tells us that social scientists and psychologists looking at our times reveal new findings which point away from happiness being found in earning more and buying more. Instead people are (shifting) "their loyalty from possessions to experiences."[4] We must wonder if the so-called worship via Zoom, which has taken off in many churches, will be more about the "experience" of appearing on a screen than that of possession of spiritual reality, (see experiences, chapter 12). The demise in civilizations is like that of so much in life, it is made clear by the passage of time and the invaluable tool of hindsight. The water dried up, the trade ceased, the King was usurped, the writing was no longer consulted, the culture was no longer valued as it always had been, and now the new was so much more preferred to the old. The focus had shifted and the climate change was unstoppable. People starved and died and the civilization was threatened. My proposition is that our *civilization* is seriously threatened by something from which it will never recover.

David Wengrow says "Civilizations are dynamic; they rise and fall; they divide and merge . . . and are buried in the sands of time."[5] What a warning is this to the *civilization* of God's kingdom! Have we forgotten so soon how priestcraft, the power of the medium, nearly buried the *civilization* of God's kingdom for a thousand years or more, until the Reformation? Those great civilizations, buried in the sands of time, could probably not see the writing on the wall, perhaps they said: "Everything will go on as it always has" (2 Pet 3:4). Many Christians will dismiss what is said here by comforting

3. Postman, *Amusing Ourselves to Death*, 9.

4. Wallman, *Stuffocation*, 21.

5. Wengrow, *What Makes Civilization*, 8.

themselves with the scripture which tells us that "although the Gates of Hell may seek to prevail, they will not" (Matt 16:18, KJV). True, but the gates can be seriously broken down and burned so that security inside may be greatly compromised. Civilizations divide and merge, so it is to be wondered whether Christians have not seen the great merger between the world's way of doing things and that of the kingdom of God. We are on the verge of being buried (if we are not already) by the digital age. We should be in no doubt this incredibly "useful tool" will demand its pound of flesh, it is the Trojan Horse of our day which in time will capture and overrun the *civilization* which is God's kingdom. It is not that we are "converting to image from word" as Postman prophesied, rather we have already gone over to the other side, and word is no match for picture when applied as a fleshly tool.

In my profession I may be considered an expert on pictures. It is possible that I know as much about European art as anyone in the evangelical church today. My entire working life, almost fifty years, has been that of pictures. I like to think that I know a little bit about art! Pictures, images have a power of which most people have not the slightest grasp. What I call the digital experiment is being carried out by those who appear to be ignorant of the fire with which they are playing. These are the same people who regard process as everything, and make utility a god. Tradition can "go hang!"

Lack of Perspective

It occurs to me that a lack of depth and perception may be at the heart of our trouble, we may be so locked in that we cannot now gain a correct perspective, as confirmed in Tony Reinke's excellent book. When I was a child I vividly remember the huge map of the world in our junior school hall. Britain was at the center of it, of course, and it was shockingly pink, confirming the extent of the British Empire and her exploits. Today those exploits regarding the treatment of indigenous peoples do not merely look suspect, they look downright pernicious. Much of what was done was no doubt supported by so-called Christian people and the churches. Slavery, much in the news today, was naturally and tragically a part of a civilized empire's exploitation. We look back on that so-called civilization, and rightly ask who were the "really" civilized people at that time? The perspective was clearly crooked, it is obvious to us now, as plain as day! We need little persuading, but we may ask how could they not see it? How is it that they were so blind to what they were doing? Often people failed to ask the question—just because we can do this does it mean we should do it? Exploitation looks, I hope, not just like a dirty word but a dirty thing, which is still tragically happening in our world today! Past civilizations made it into an art form, "the bottom line" was that it paid off. So here we are in the church in 2021, we can exploit the digital revolution to our advantage; it is just another "tool," as some have said in a rather silly way, like Gutenberg's Press (I will come to this later). I am convinced exploitation in this regard will come back to bite us, but it will be too late. If we did not know it already there are numerous "tools" which might destroy the foundations, and one of them is putting "God in a Box."

Faith Gone AWOL

Unless we had forgotten, the foundation of the Christian faith is faith itself. Quite rightly in the evangelical church we speak of that saving faith which is in Christ alone. We explain it as a faith which secures our justification (Rom 5:1). This alone can confirm that we have a God righteousness which in turn brings peace with God. In this we are spiritual relatives with Abraham (Gal 3:9). If we asked the apostle Paul who our close relatives are, he would start by pointing us back to Abraham . . . not a bad relative to have in your spiritual family tree! Abraham was justified by faith as we are. It may surprise us though that he provides an insight into our own faith fragility today. Like ourselves, he found that the *life* of faith, as love, does not run smoothly, and in this none of us should be surprised. Life throws up challenges for the Christian which have to be met by faith. We need to be constantly reminded that the aroma of the church must be that of faith. When I enter a coffee shop that beautiful aroma confirms to me that I am in the right place! If I cannot smell it, I take my business elsewhere. What deeply concerns me is that rationalism may have run faith out of the church, where its aroma is fading and in some places has gone altogether. We must remember Paul says, "we *live* (emphasis mine) by faith not by sight" (2 Cor 5:7, NIV). This *living* is daily life, the rumble and tumble of it. Faith is not only securing a justified status with God by his Grace, but proving him in the hustle and bustle of life, in sickness and in health, not only when life works out for us, but when it inevitably goes wrong. This is where we often struggle and where our ancient close relative Abraham also struggled. When this problem is highlighted and applied, it seems to raise evangelical hackles, nothing else except the question of latent atheism seems to generate acrimony like it; and we must wonder why it is a sore spot which we all feel. This is the question: are we in fact *living* by faith or are we being schooled, trained by our churches in twenty-twenty vision because our faith is so low?

Abram: A Bad Example

The account of Abram in Gen 12:1 is familiar to most Christians. God in a most uncomplicated way tells him to up and leave his native country. This specificity and clarity would only have helped Abram on his way, it is just what we would have felt most comfortable with. God said to him, "Go out from your country, your relatives and your father's household" (Gen 12:1, NIV). Three clear and simple requirements: country, relatives, his father's household—no room here for doubt and uncertainty. But then came the snag, where was he to go? This was not at all specific, all he had was

God's word, but surely faith in that word would be sufficient to carry him through, and God would make it plain. When he eventually finds himself in the place where God wanted him to be, he has it confirmed, God says to him "I will give your descendants *this* land," the very place he was standing (Gen 12:7). What could be clearer? He could be in no doubt that he was in the right place. Just then there appears a potential setback, a famine sets in. As I write this, the coronavirus is the fly in the ointment in our day, and has no doubt challenged the *"living by faith"* aspect of many professing Christians. It is undoubtedly lack of faith which brings on panic.

It must be acknowledged, since World War II, the church has not undergone any significant test to so profoundly test its faith. Abram was tested by the famine, and extraordinarily leaves the country where he knows God wants him to be, and he exchanges it for Egypt, a place he has not been directed to. He has received no leading whatsoever by the divine hand. He is now driven, not by faith or the God of promise, but by sense, by sight, by circumstance. He is the driver now, he is in control and, no doubt for a moment perhaps he felt secure. How is it at times we feel more secure in our own hands than those of God? A.W. Pink comments on this verse with his usual perspicacity (even if it comes from his early less mature theological pen). He says, "This is the first mention in Scripture of Egypt, and like all its subsequent references, so here, it stands for that which is a constant *menace* to the people of God symbolizing, as it does, alliance with the world and reliance upon the arm of flesh—*"Woe to them that go down to Egypt for help* and stay on horses, and trust in chariots, because they are many; and in horsemen, because they are very strong; but *they look not unto the Holy One of Israel*, neither seek the Lord!" (Isa 31:1, KJV).[6] What is clear is their faith was in themselves and what they could perform. "Far too often the church exhibits a bipolar disorder. (It) professes Christ but follows secular scriptures, accord(ing) authority to the biblical canon but abid(ing) by social codes."[7]

Identical Twins

The famine which Abram faced, was a significant trial and test to faith which few of us can begin to comprehend. The question must be, would we have passed it? What were the fears which assaulted Abram because of it, the same question might be asked in our unique moment in modern history. Without being overly critical, for the purposes of this book, we must say that the man justified by faith found it difficult to *live* by it. Pink goes on: "God would see whether he had such confidence in his goodness that even famine could not shake it. Alas, Abram did as we are all prone to do, he sought relief from all his difficulties, rather than profit by the trial."[8] Abram was driven by the flesh, he probably panicked in the moment, like Aaron at the foot of the Mount,

6. Pink, *Gleanings in Genesis*, 144–45.

7. Vanhoozer, *Pictures at a Theological Exhibition*, 177.

8. Pink, *Gleanings in Genesis*, 145.

and yet he had every reason to rest and relax in the God who had promised him. Pink's final word on this is what we should all listen to: "Sad that it should be so, but how like us today." I would say never a truer word spoken—"Like us today."[9]

The Three R's, Rationalism, Reason and (W)rong!

Many Christians may at this point argue with A.W. Pink, they may struggle with his assessment, and probably suggest that Abram did nothing wrong, he did the "logical thing," i.e., the "rational thing." He worked himself out of the situation, he resolved the problem himself, he was proactive and overcame his predicament, he did not just "let go and let God," but resolved matters which he could resolve. But observe his actions and where they lead him. When Abram's mixture of rational fear, self preservation and the rest kicked in, it did not merely open a door to leaving the place where God intended him to be, where he should be, but like Jonah, it thrust him into the depths, and a domino effect was set in motion. In Egypt he is forced to compromise his wife's safety by lying about her relationship to him. Abram is now in the wrong place, with the wrong people and is even mendacious. What a mess! Faith is far better than sight and this confirms, if we did not know it, that situations providentially arise to test faith, to see if in fact we can *live* by faith or only talk about it. What might we learn from the Puritans with their elevated view of the spiritual life? *The Valley of Vision*, a collection of Puritan prayers and devotions, provides something of their typically deep insight. One of those prayers reads:

> O Lord,
> The world is artful to entrap,
> approaches in fascinating guise,
> extends many a gilded bait,
> presents many a charming face.
> Let my faith scan every painted bauble,
> and escape every bewitching snare
> in a victory that overcomes all things.[10]

Abram was charmed and buoyed by the hope and help which Egypt could provide.

Charmed, I'm sure

In the history of the world, the screen has presented to us the most charming face ever, especially since now we can see ourselves in it, and our easily agitated narcissism is satisfied. My estimation is that the screen is a god like no other, and has succeeded

9. Pink, *Gleanings in Genesis*, 145.
10. *Valley of Vision*, 196.

in bewitching both Christian and non-Christian alike. Of course when you are be-witched you cannot *see* it, i.e. to have one's eyes spoiled! Galatians 3:1 "One of the goals of the ancient orator was to deliver his speech so vividly and impressively that his listeners imagined the matter to have happened right before their eyes. All kinds of techniques were recommended to achieve this effect, including impersonations and even holding painted pictures." Hans Dieter Betz, Commentary on Galatians. The church which has for so long beaten out the mantra of not "aping the world," is now subject to the "fascinating guise," the "gilded bait" of the "god in the pocket." It is true, Christians like all others were hooked long before COVID-19, but in February–March 2020 the charming face suggested something new, the screen could be used for the act of so-called Christian worship. It did not matter that God was joined to this device, which carries inextricably its own associations, associations which cannot be erased. In fact, if these were erased it would cease to be the medium which we recognize, and in our minds it would not be the "tool" we all know it to be. We forget at our cost it is overwhelmingly a medium of entertainment. It is in our culture as a carrier, not of musing but a-musing, and principally by revealing image (*NB*: it should be noted here that I am not against screen, television, cinema, or computer screens, I am indifferent to them). Our English word "image" has its roots in the Latin "*imago*," and in turn is related to the Latin word "*imitari*," which means to imitate. Boorstin comments on this and tells us,

> According to common American dictionary definitions, an image is an artifi-cial imitation or representation of the external form of any object, especially of a person. Images now displace ideals. But an ideal is much more difficult to define. It is, I suppose we would say now, an old-fashioned word and an old-fashioned notion. "Ideal" is related somehow to "idea." Our dictionaries define it as a conception of something in its most excellent or perfect form— something that exists only in the mind.[11]

Surely Christians understand that this is where God exists, in the mind (the heart). "The mind, controlled by the Spirit is life and peace" (Rom 8:6, NIV). Further to this Paul says "we have the mind of Christ" (1 Cor 2:16, KJV). We may legitimately call it the "mind's eye," but never, ever the "eye." The screen's association is all to do with "eye." It may be the "adulterous eye," the "acquisitive eye," the "murdering eye," the possibilities are endless, even the "religious eye."

Caution: Slow Down!

Extraordinarily, none of this concerned Christians in the rush for instrumentality be-cause what *mattered* was that the "tool," which ironically does not deal in *matter*, i.e.,

---

11. Boorstin, *Image*, 201.

things corporeal, could serve the church's purpose. What is obvious is that in the mad rush, long term results were never considered. Lance Strate says:

> The effects of a change introduced into a complex system will always be somewhat unpredictable, which suggests a need for caution in the face of technological progress, something we rarely exercise. One of the reasons why the results of change can be so unpredictable is that, once an innovation is adopted, it will result in direct effects, but these in turn will give rise to indirect effects, and these secondary effects will lead to tertiary effects, and so on, in ecological fashion. The indirect effects are often unanticipated, and all too often undesirable. It follows that it is absurd to think that the consequences of changes that we put into motion are entirely under our control.[12]

What was needed was the advice of the Puritan writer, to stand back and "let my faith scan every painted bauble." If he was with us today he might ask, "What faith?" The picture (not a pun) staring back at him would be of a church everywhere given to the worship of God using pictures . . . pictures of ourselves.

Going Round in Circles

To return to Abram for a moment. Regrettably, the NLT, which I am fond of and think is very helpful, is actually unhelpful at Gen 12:10 since it reads: "At that time a severe famine struck the Land of Canaan forcing Abram to go down to Egypt." But Abram was not *forced* to do anything. This rendering, unlike other versions, suggests the matter was out of his hands. Nothing could be further from the truth and, like Jonah who put himself in the bowels of the sea, Abram went to Egypt entirely of his own volition. Significantly when we find Abram in Chapter 13 of Genesis, he is back exactly where he started, in the place where he erected his tent, the place he should never have left. We might say a long journey for nothing, a waste of time and risking everything. Would it be reading too much into the passage to suggest that Abram possessed some knowledge, some intelligence of Egypt and the security and comfort which might have been afforded him in that place? It was, after all, a kingdom with a Pharaoh, with a palace, with the power to dispense gifts, a place where he could get help. "Woe to them that go down to Egypt for help" (Isa 31:1, KJV). Surely God would have given him all the help he needed if he had stayed where he was? It is impossible not to see the contrast between Abram in Egypt and Moses, "who thought it better to suffer than to own the treasures of Egypt." This is part of the great hall of fame of those who did not talk a good talk about faith, but did it, lived it, and gloriously recommended it to us (Heb 11:26, NLT).

---

12. Strate, *Amazing Ourselves to Death*, 56.

COVID-19

In 2020, the faith of God's elect was severely tested, but such testing cannot be put in the category of those who suffered in the 1916 Spanish flu, nor for that matter, the World Wars; Christians also endured these trials, and with far fewer comforts than we enjoy today, such as health care and the rest. Comforts aside, the Scripture points up the benefit of testing. "The testing of your faith gives endurance, a chance to grow" (Jas 1:3, NLT). Christians should always be careful in a time of testing not to panic, not to run for their lives. James also says, "God blesses those who patiently endure testing" (Jas 1:21, NLT). We might think it is a well worn expression, but there is real truth in the words "faith untested is no faith at all." A faith which can only work within the safe confines of a Western democracy with all the trimmings, is a faith which looks suspect and which one day will probably suffer loss. COVID-19, like nothing else for seventy years, has tested the faith of the churches. To the church's great detriment it looks like many of them ran off to Egypt!

In the Blink of An Eye!

Testing in the industrial commercial world is in place to find out if a given product is up to the task . The testing often, and not infrequently, reveals that which is faulty, the things which at one time secured certification, prove under test to be a failure (see Chapter 11). None of this is to disparage small faith, but rather to stir us up to ask if we have in fact in fear, in panic, set out on a course of action from which there will be no return. Dr. Lloyd-Jones' book *From Fear to Faith* would not go amiss in our times. Churches at the outset of the lockdown needed to be calm and collected, composed even. Instead like Uzzah, they reacted to the loss of church life by trying to solve problems their own way. This has led to congregations seeking to worship God through screens; to hold prayer meetings bowed before computer monitors; preaching conducted into a camera lens. Sadly it has been the same practice as that of Islam, the Jehovah's Witnesses, the Anglicans in Britain and the Roman Catholics, and all of these with little or no evangelical faith. In the blink of an eye, in panic, the Glorious Body of Christ fell for the "gilded bait," bewitched by the "painted bauble;" its faith tested and found out.

Faith Number One

Civilizations in the past probably thought they would never suffer loss, perhaps there was even a feeling of invincibility about them. They naturally looked to their rationale, their own prowess, to their own strength, their own inventiveness. "Natural" is the word and so "naturally," the good times just go on and on. But Christians breathe the air of a supernatural kingdom, not of this world, and that vital breath must be the oxygen of faith. God's kingdom can only live by constantly breathing it. Certainly without faith, whatever else it does, it cannot please God. Whatever else it pursues, it must pursue faith. The muscles in the eyes of every believer need a good rest, but on the other hand our hearts, our renewed hearts, require a much-needed workout. It looks like the church is totally out of shape.

Go and Do Likewise

Near the end of 2020 my wife and I welcomed a young Romanian woman into our home. She travels a sixty miles round trip to our small village every Saturday to sell a well-known British magazine, *The Big Issue*. (This is a street newspaper founded in September 1991, and offers homeless people or those at risk of homelessness, the opportunity to earn a legitimate income). She travels to this village because people are willing to buy her magazine, this way she can help to support her children. As a church we have had a longstanding contact and friendship with her. On a snowy December Saturday before Christmas, she turned up at our home needing to use a toilet. She was cold and hungry. We welcomed her in and gave her a hot cup of tea, a sandwich, some money, and tried to communicate a little with her about our concern for her and her family. We wanted to help her any way we could. None of this looks remarkable, nor should it, except it came during one of our serious, COVID-19 lockdowns. She did not come with a mask, nor to our knowledge with any other precautions. The Government policy at the time was clear, we were not to allow her in, and no doubt many people, Christians included, would have called our actions reckless and defiant of God's ordained government. The simple fact was she needed the toilet, warmth, food, and a measure of love and care. Surely in that situation the words of the Lord Jesus Christ take precedence over everything. His rule is clear, all we need to do, in faith, is to follow it. We have to ask in the light of the teaching on the Good Samaritan (Luke 10:30-37) what should we do? The parable points up the obvious, not least the risk. This risk, I am persuaded, is now neatly airbrushed out of the practice of much that presents itself as Christian.

What shall we say of the passage in Matthew 25:42–46? Here Jesus in effect corners every one of his people by his kingdom demands, his highly civilized commands. Not one of us who profess to follow him can wriggle out of what he is teaching . . . "for I was hungry and you didn't feed me. I was thirsty and you didn't give me a drink. I was a stranger, and you didn't invite me into your home, I was naked and you didn't give me clothing. I was sick and in prison and you didn't visit me! Then they will reply, Lord when did we ever see you hungry or thirsty or a stranger or naked or sick or in prison and not help you? And he will answer, "I tell you the truth, when you refused to help the least of these my brothers and sisters you were refusing to help me." Dr. Hendrikson captures the sense of Christ's meaning when he says: "Throughout his ministry, by means of precept (i.e.: rule of action or conduct, emphasis mine) and example, Jesus had stressed the necessity of feelings and works of love, mercy, and generosity . . . So it is altogether natural that this is what he expects of his followers."[13] Christians make the bold claim to be his followers, and if anything reflects this truth, it is our faith and certainly not rationalism.

Without faith like this the church faces trouble ahead. I repeat, it is risk taking and not careful business management which will ensure the longevity of this *civilization*. To have turned away our Romanian friend, cold and hungry, without help would have been "wrong," and we could never hold our heads up as those who profess the Christian faith.

The Rabbit Hole

This story serves my purpose because it highlights the struggle which I believe the church of Jesus Christ is suffering at this time. COVID-19 has shown me something which must be highlighted. We face a real and pressing problem with the issue of rationalism. To be sure our actions with our Romanian friend will be judged as recklessly foolish and putting the Lord "to the test." It points up the dichotomy between the intellect and the heart, between logic and faith. Rationalism is undoubtedly winning and with its conjoined twin pragmatism, has come to rule. My estimation is that the church in this is in very serious trouble indeed. Of course logic is a wonderful thing and the apostle must have been alluding to this when he said "keep your head in all situations" (2 Tim 4:5, NIV). In fact this "keeping of one's head" might have saved many churches and individuals from descending the rabbit hole of attempted "screen" worship. Sadly, pragmatism's voice is louder than any, and this is what is directing actions regarding church worship at this present time. Nadab and Abihu (Lev 10:1,2), might have been the first in worship to enact their pragmatism, but to fatal consequences from which we appear not to have learned the lessons.

The motto of the philosophy of the enlightenment was as Colin Brown tells us "Dare to use your own understanding."[14] "As a technical, philosophical term, the word [pragmatism] was coined by Charles Sanders Peirce [1831–1914] . . . [It] derives from the Greek *pragmata* which means 'acts,' 'affairs,' and 'business.' It has come to be associated with such slogans as 'Truth is what works.'"[15] Brown says: "This leads to the notion that the sole test of truth is its practical consequences. Truth is, therefore, relative."[16] This was the undoing of Nadab and Abihu. The church has to face up to the reality, by and large faith as a *life* is probably unknown to many Christians. Instead subscribing to a creed, going to church meetings, going through the motions, all usually attributed to mere nominal Christians, may in fact be the life of much evangelical

13. Hendrikson, *NT Commentary Matthew*, 888.

14. Brown, *Philosophy and the Christian Faith*, 91.

15. Brown, *Philosophy and the Christian Faith*, 145.

16. Brown, *Philosophy and the Christian Faith*, 145–46.

profession. The Scripture warns us "Let a man examine himself to see if he is in the *faith*" (2 Cor 13:5, NIV). If this examination has not been undertaken very often, we can see why many Christians would have sent our Romanian friend packing. The words of Jesus would carry little weight.

How Did We Get Here?

My estimation as to the reason we have arrived at this juncture, is that for so long we have neatly packaged our lives. We have almost everything sorted, in truth in many things God is not needed, life works like clockwork but in fact this is more like deism. Kevin J. Vanhoozer takes no prisoners and expresses the same, as he looks through an American lens:

> The good life, according to the American Standard Version (the authorized version of the American dream) includes 2.2 children, a single family home, an SUV, a 401K retirement plan and dinner out once a week (at least). There's room for God too. God is the giver of the good life, guarantor of the status quo, bestower of rewards for overtime. At least this is the caricature of God in which America's teenagers apparently believe: the god of Moralistic Therapeutic Deism, the God who wants you to be nice to others and feel good in the process. This is the picture of God that currently has a lock on the popular American imagination.[17]

What Vanhoozer writes here is in fact no mere American phenomenon. Craig M Gay substantially makes a similar point, he says:

> The subtle secularity that science and technology have *already* instilled in the popular imagination . . . science and technology have substantially reinforced the *plausibility* of practical atheism in modern society and culture. They have made it easier for us to go about our daily business and even to live out our entire lives without giving God much thought.[18]

With everything in place we can mitigate against loss. I use the word "loss" because most people fear this the most. We have as twenty-first century Christians so much to lose. Private health care, pensions, insurances and any number of other provisions to cover us, providing us, as the world would say with, "peace of mind." This is not to suggest that these things are wrong per se, nevertheless the shift, particularly in the last fifty years, is one which undoubtedly satisfies the world, but sadly also the church.

17. Vanhoozer, *Pictures at a Theological Exhibition*, 178.
18. Gay, *Way of the (Modern) World*, 82.

A Comfort Blanket

A church of more than fifty years ago, dealing with our current difficulties, might have heard its people exult in the truth, "Underneath are the everlasting arms" (Deut 33:27, NIV). However, it is more likely that, not only is this text unknown, but the above mentioned securities are the arms in which people feel more secure. Here is our modern dependence, it was fashioned by ourselves in the civilization which is this world, but not in the kingdom of God. When Habakkuk says "The just shall live by faith" (Hab 2:4, NKJV) he surely implies that this living puts faith on *view*. This faith touches the stuff of life.

Allow me to digress for a moment and explain how this has ramifications for the gospel. It is to be wondered if Christians have ever realized that the faith which they want to make known to their children, neighbors and congregations, is that knowledge of Christ which brings a justifying faith; yet to a child or unbeliever this faith is an abstraction, an unknown, a strange thing. A child needs time to make sense of the nature of faith which becomes the means of salvation through faith in Christ, but never to be mistaken for faith in faith. This faith as a concept is always at arms length, it is elusive to the unbeliever, hard to reach, hard to comprehend and "without God's grace impossible" (Eph 2:8, NIV), admittedly often confusing to children as they hear about it in church during the preaching and conversations. But here is the rub, they have nothing to *see*. This faith which is talked about and preached in Evangelical churches is often really only about risk aversion, with all the bases covered so as to have the world's "peace of mind." As a consequence of this, the church, the believer, is missing a vital component which is meant to be one's *life* of faith, the children have nothing tangible to look at. This is where "seeing" should have its place. The unbelieving, perishing world needs to see something, the faith of God's people. "You are the light of the world, let your light shine before men," (Matt 5:14-16, NIV) is clearly about sight. This is not in the first instance by tract, pamphlet, evangelistic campaign, knocking on doors or church evangelistic work, but a real, visible faith which shines with a bright light. If the light within us is rationalism, how great is that darkness! It should in fact be the case that children look at what adult believers have, and as a result what they see recommends itself to them so they can in turn say "I want that faith, faith that makes a difference," the faith of the Good Samaritan, not in words only. Children may be pointed to God's word and much prayer offered up to God on their behalf, but without this faith on display the vital ingredient is missing. Faith, if we did not know it, needs to be worn on the sleeve so that all can see it. Life is either based on faith (not just the word) or it is not. Faith must be the controlling power by God's Spirit. Sadly it appears the controlling principle in the churches and in individual lives is pragmatism, calculation, worldly wisdom, a "shrewd and balanced view" based on all the facts, figures and human knowledge. Alarmingly, the church has done much to mirror big business, and many would argue, "Well why not?" In the meantime faith has departed, we are left high and dry, and Christ's church has nothing to run on except its own understanding. Tozer's "The Dangers of a Shallow Faith" would be a good read for all.

Reckless Faith

I may be wrong, but I think late twentieth and twenty-first century Christianity, might be more akin to business management and could be inadvertently responsible for the emergence of the Charismatic Movement, which yearns to have some sight of the supernatural. The church could not have gone far wrong if it had applied the extraordinary example of faith from Ezra 8, where the passage reveals faith over sense. It records the exiles return to Jerusalem from captivity in Babylon. Here we *see* true faith, and it is very pronounced, casting its shadow over shame, over unbelief, over worldly wisdom, sense, sight and pragmatism. Here we *see* the triumph of real faith. To be sure this is what many genuine Charismatics really wanted, what they were looking for. A vital faith that can move mountains which does not just say it trusts God, but actually trusts Him. Whilst they can trace out the sterility in the church, desiring a living alternative, they become sidetracked looking in the wrong places to touch the spiritual. The passage in Ezra to make any sense to us must be applied, it demands that we ask ourselves if we might have done the same with our faith? I think I can hear the overwhelming sound of Christians crying out "these actions were reckless." The passage makes plain that much was at stake, children were involved. The road obviously was known to be frequented by pirates/bandits. They were carrying all their possessions, the risk level was enormous, about as high as it could be. This is where we should take careful note, they obviously saw that a lack of faith in this situation would confirm a lack of faith in their God. They were confident though that the gracious hand of their God was upon them, and their faith in him at that moment was being tested. They desperately did not want to fail the test. They proved the words of the poem by Minnie Louise Haskins used by King George VI in his Christmas broadcast 1939:

> I said to the man who stood at the gate of the year,
> "Give me a light that I may tread safely into the unknown."
> And he replied "Go out into the darkness and put your hand into the hand of
> God. That shall be to you better than light
> and safer than a known way!" So I went forth and finding the
> hand of God, trod gladly into the night. And he led me towards the hills and
> the breaking of day in the lone East.
> So heart be still: What need our little life our human life to know,
> if God hath comprehension!
> In all the dizzy strife of things both high and low,
> God hideth His intention God knows, His will is best.

The stretch of years which wind ahead, so dim to our imperfect vision, are
clear to God,
our fears are premature: In Him all time hath full provision,
Then rest: Until God moves to lift the veil from our impatient eyes, when as
the sweeter features of lifes stern face we hail, fair beyond all surmise
Gods thoughts around His creatures our mind shall fill.

The trouble which lies ahead is that rationalism is not just giving faith a run for
its money, it is winning hands down.

Some years ago news of a new church plant was brought to my attention, the
people involved launched their effort of course, via the internet. Churches were made
aware of what was needed for this "work of God" to be established. In many ways I
recall thinking it was in effect a huge begging letter. The requirements to make this
church plant work still strike me as breathtaking. The sums of money needed were
greater than we in our own church had spent in twenty years. The list of needs ran
from pension plans, to computers, to salaries and so on, a list as long as your arm.
Faith looked conspicuous by its absence, business was in the ascendancy. All this
could easily be accomplished without God by employing a good accountant, and having a business plan. By contrast, the faith of the exiles (Ezra 8) appears both remarkable and quite astonishing, and what is more, desirable. This kind of faith like that of
George Muller will always be talked about while ever God's *civilization* exists. Equally
astonishing in the light of this, is the way evangelicals are ready to look back at church
history, extolling the virtues and values of those who exhibited this same astonishing
faith, but just as astonishing is how far short of all this ours, by comparison appears to
be. If the saints of the past were to visit us, one wonders whether they would be able to
describe our *faith* as "that (which) was once delivered unto the saints" (Jude v3, KJV).

The author Vishal Mangalwadi touches on the development of rationality in his
book. In many respects he tells us what we have known for a long time, that Protestantism based its faith in Christ alone, the fountain of all *knowledge*. Naturally this
knowledge delivered rationality to the nations which embraced the Bible as authoritative. He concludes his observation on this subject by pointing to something highly
relevant to the point I am making. He says: "biblical rationality was the key to the
development of the West's freedom and prosperity . . . one of its fruits—technology."[19]
Regrettably, he fails to point up the dangers of rationalism.

Our "isms"

It is difficult not to be left wondering if the more we have grown in prosperity and
freedom (what Francis Schaeffer describes as personal peace and affluence) the more
reliance we have shown in technology, in our own ingenuity and power. The end

19. Mangalwadi, *Book That Made Your World*, 91.

result—there has been less faith in God. Zerubbabel's words might have helped, if we had been familiar with them: "Not by might nor by power, but by my Spirit says the Lord Almighty," (Zech 4:6, NIV). Rationalism, like so many other "isms" has turned into a curse. Perhaps this has blinded us and may even have begun to poison us. Lewis Mumford, in *Technics and Civilization*, shows us the connection with the machine age (i.e. technology and capitalism) when he says: "The style of the machine has up to the present been powerfully influenced by capitalism: the emphasis upon bigness, for example, is a commercial trait."[20] Not surprisingly it took relatively little time for churches using "Zoom" to extol its benefits, especially the new increased numbers tuning in to "worship." Mumford adds this:

> "Capitalism utilized the machine, not to further social welfare, but to increase private profit . . . It was because of capitalism that the handicraft industries in both Europe and other parts of the world were recklessly destroyed by machine products, even when the latter were inferior to the thing they replaced: for the prestige of improvement and success and power was with the machine, even when it improved nothing, even when technically speaking it was a failure."[21]

Nevertheless rationalism drives "progress" forward even at an exponential rate. Colin Brown compares the Reformers of the sixteenth century with the rationalists of the seventeenth: "The rationalists of the seventeenth century were absorbed not so much by God but by the world."[22]

Where a "life" of faith failed, being little exercised, technology made sure it did not matter, the world could put faith in its place! Prestige, improvement, success, power and sadly to say, money amply supplied what was needed—the "Power was with the machine." In the past it was easy to reprove the Church of Rome for just such a mentality, but a good look in the mirror for the Protestant denominations would certainly not go amiss. We have drifted from vital faith to a love affair, which continues to deepen, bewitching us as we kneel at a technical altar, and with panache we were able to pin on our screens the message, however false, "Business as usual." Mumford says: "the emphasis upon bigness, for example, is a commercial trait." "Zoom," lest we forget, was built for business, it naturally suggests itself to our instincts, but the question is: Are those instincts wholly spiritual?

Size Matters

It is hard to both ignore and understand the mindset of the one who is given over to the thinking of the cults, very often these people are overwhelmingly impressed by size, by numbers, by success. These powerful organizations display the ambitions of the

20. Mumford, *Technics and Civilization*, 28.

21. Mumford, *Technics and Civilization*, 27.

22. Brown, *Philosophy and the Christian Faith*, 49.

market where size is everything. There was once talk in the 1970s of the Watchtower having the largest printing press in the world for churning out its dark propaganda. It needs little imagination to think the churches surveyed this with an envious eye, bigness coupled with prosperity is almost irresistible. As a result Christian thinking might develop in such a way as to have little or no room for Zechariah's words: "Do not despise the day of small things" (Zech 4:10). This might be swept away by the impressive impact which size makes on us. For Billy Graham size clearly mattered, number crunching was evidently a factor in his operation. His acknowledgement of the use of television to reach the millions gave voice to this.

Mumford again observes: "It was because of the possibilities of profit that the place of the machine was overemphasized."[23] This means a dependency was developed and inevitably the dependency might force other things into subordination. Mumford has no wish to frighten us but states the obvious: "In so far as the phonograph and the radio do away with the impulse to sing, in so far as the camera does away with the impulse to see, in so far as the automobile does away with the impulse to walk, the machine leads to a lapse of function, which is but one step away from paralysis."[24]

Surely we understand the machine has the power to take over, it becomes bigger than everything else. The possibilities which "Zoom" presented to the church, and will yet suggest, hits the dopamine button in us, and in this is likely to drive home deeper the dangerous mechanical disposition of worship, which also exists in the Christian churches as it does in comparative religions.

We may see in Mumford's remarks how people have always been bewitched by the power of technology. Money, power, influence, size, all apply pressure, even if less quality is produced. Often in our modern world the mantra is "quantity and not quality." Mumford does not hold back, he does not mince his words regarding the preoccupations and blandishments, i.e., flattery and enticements which all of this supplies. He rounds on it by describing it as: "these vices (which) have in fact grown more enormous, and the dangers to society as a whole have likewise grown proportionately."[25] With a heavy heart it is noted they have also grown in Christ's church.

Red Flags

The willingness to appraise these matters makes it possible to chart the age of the screen as part of the tech world, which has made its way slowly but surely into the churches. Equally easy is the observation that when the church is running low on faith, it looks not to the Holy Spirit for help but to rationalism, and in turn to pragmatism, i.e., to that which works. Perhaps nothing works better for the flesh than tech, leaving people starry-eyed. The emergence of the screen permeating more and more

23. Mumford, *Technics and Civilization*, 27.

24. Mumford, *Technics and Civilization*, 343–44.

25. Mumford, *Technics and Civilization*, 27.

evangelical churches is, in my view, natural. Why so? The reason being the "product" is all important, the *conquest* is the focus, meaning that the tradition, if necessary, can be crushed underfoot. Despite the blandishments which come with the "God Channels," and the pragmatic prayer meetings on "Zoom" (television cameras dictating the duration of the preaching so as to fit in with the broadcasting schedules etc), all that matters is the outcome! Who cares for the leading of the Holy Spirit when we can lead ourselves? It is tempting to wish for a voice like that of A.W. Tozer to speak to this threat to our spiritual *civilization*. He recognized the Hollywood Christianity of his day for what it was, and flagged it up regardless of the ructions it caused. Remarkably he was speaking seventy years ago about a "shallow faith." It is to be wondered what that unique voice would pronounce on today's shallow faith. Nor should we miss the fact that such shallow faith is always on the look out for the next good idea. These good ideas are rarely tested, rarely subjected to Paul's blueprint for the church i.e.: "Test everything" (1 Thess 5:21, NIV). Pragmatism trumps Paul every time.

Francis Schaeffer, albeit making a wider point, explains the concept of ideas: · "Ideas are never neutral and abstract, ideas have consequences in the way we live and act, both in our personal lives and in the culture as a whole."[26] This means you cannot introduce the Spinning Jenny into a culture without an earthquake. It is not neutral, it is an idea which reshapes the social and economic landscape. This is what the introduction of the "screen" will do in our churches. It will alter an entire culture. There may be trouble ahead! No, there is trouble ahead!

When Will We Ever Learn?

To illustrate this with force allow a little history to instruct the conclusion of this chapter. The story of the cotton gin is more germane to this entire subject than any other. Paul Johnson in his book makes searching and compelling connections, when he says:

> Religion would have swept away slavery in America without difficulty early in the nineteenth century but for one thing: cotton. It was this little, two-syllable word which turned American slave-holding into a mighty political force and so made the Civil War inevitable. And cotton, in terms of humanity and its needs, was an unmitigated good. Thus do the workings of mysterious providence balance good with evil. Until the end of the eighteenth century, the human race had always been unsuitably clothed in garments which were difficult to wash and therefore filthy. Cotton offered an escape from this misery.[27]

The result was extraordinary, cotton changed the world, but with the demand for it came the need to process vast quantities of it quickly. The Southern States of the U.S. sent their first bale of cotton to Liverpool in 1784. The story breathes the all "American dream" when we learn of a life-long bachelor driven by his Calvinistic

26. Schaeffer, *Great Evangelical Disaster*, 30.
27. Johnson, *History of the American People*, 255.

work ethic, toiling away in some crude workshop developing the cotton gin. Eli Whitney presented his invention in 1794, a slave using it on a plantation could process fifty pounds of cotton a day instead of one. Johnson gives us the breath-taking power of this technology. He says: "Whitney's cotton gin enabled the slave-system to survive and thrive . . . It also created "the South" as a special phenomenon, a culture, a cast of mind."[28]

It would be hard to argue that the effects of that little piece of machinery are not still finding a voice in the USA today as the conflict between black and white continues. Ideas are never neutral, Schaeffer was absolutely right. COVID-19 has forced the church into panic, to experiment. The experiment which is underway is to join God to the screen, to make him accessible "*together,*" this means wherever you are you can join in, you can pretend to fulfill the apostle Paul's words which he writes to the Corinthians: "When you come together" (1 Corinthians 14:26, NIV), but this introduction of a medium which supplies pictures of the worshippers themselves, and which in fact and in truth cannot ever do "*together,*" will affect us long into the future. As a result, the concept of God in the minds of many will be shaped and reshaped by this medium of the screen, which has become in itself a "god in our pockets." The screen has been let loose and, like the genie out of the bottle it will not go back in. Just like the Spinning Jenny, once unpacked, it refused ever to go back into its box. The screen is like a cancer in countless lives and there is no cure. The problem is the host does not realize it is there, and consequently seeks no cure.

R.W. Mecklenburg in his book does all the work we need to convince us. He says: "Where the cancerous cell grows beyond its bounds to destroy its host, it similarly destroys its institutions, too."[29] Being as I have suffered the effects of cancer, I am in a position to confirm the truth of this. The good institutions of the church confirm the *civilization,* which we call the kingdom of God. God's church for whom Christ died, is under the most subtle forms of attack, Satan's schemes are varied. While we are closely on the look out for another Schleiermacher, or searching the horizons for more sad firework displays coming up out of the Charismatic Movement's thirst for novelties, we will probably miss our own cardinal errors. The fear I have, is that the splinter in our own eyes has already blinded us.

---

28. Johnson, *History of the American People,* 257.
29. Mecklenburg, *Philosophy of Size and the Essence of Enough.*

CHAPTER 2

Suspect Foundations

"The die is cast"

Julius Caesar (At the crossing of the Rubicon)

*"When the foundations are destroyed,
what can the righteous do?"*

Psalm 11:3 (NIV)

Foundations are wonderful, even if not particularly attractive, but perhaps this does not matter since most of them cannot be seen, but nonetheless they are absolutely vital, and we cannot build without them. No doubt, like me many of us will have marveled at the pictures which come up on our television screens revealing the aftermath of a tornado. Homes have been reduced to sticks, wreckage is strewn far and wide, it is a scene of devastation. Whenever I see these pictures I find myself remarking on what looks like poor construction, but more than anything on the fact that clearly, the foundations are left intact, preserved and for the most part, untouched. Even the unstoppable inferno which swept through paradise in Northern California in 2019, while consuming everything, the foundations of the buildings were untouched, they withstood the ferocity of all that nature threw at them. Foundations will always be needed. For Christians, the words of the hymn-writer capture the essential foundation, which is Christ: "On Christ the solid rock I stand, all other ground is sinking sand."

The house which I live in is unusual, most people who visit us comment on its unconventional character, mistaking it for an old English church but in fact it is an old English village school, circa 1860. It has three impressive gables and the entire build is of natural stone, hand cut in what is called "parallel-punched" stone, every piece handcrafted. It is a beautiful and unique house. Set into the roof are ingenious vent finials designed to bring in and circulate fresh air, no doubt very bracing in the winter months so as to keep Victorian children on their toes! Gothic windows and door frames all in stone, add to its charm and beauty. The building is a bit of a masterpiece and we love it, feeling that we always need to tend and look after it as custodians for its future. If it was left uncared for then decay would set in quickly and the loss would be very, very profound. My wife and I might now be described as "old bones," but we very much hope that "young bones" will continue what we started at the Old School Skelmanthorpe, in the name of him who is our Savior. This building always reminds us of Christ's church, old but beautiful, well-built, intricate, magnificent in splendor, admired for its uniqueness, "beautiful for situation" like Christ's church, though cold at times, being vulnerable to deterioration and even demise. Christ's church needs people who deeply love, care, and expend themselves for it, so that when "old bones" are finished new ones know how to care for it into the future. It is this care for the church moving on into the future which necessitates this book.

The Old School holds a secret, not at all immediately apparent unless you were looking for it. That is, in the County of Yorkshire where I live in the North of England, the geology has fixed great stone shelves in place which sometimes even protrude up out of the earth, and these have often been used to great constructional advantage. It is not unusual here to see houses built directly off bedrock. The builders of the Old School did not use concrete, but made the solid rock the foundations themselves. We are the living illustration of the "wise man who built his house upon the rock," (Matt 7:24-27, NET). Another powerful visual example of this is the feat of architectural genius which is Frank Lloyd Wright's building constructed in 1935 in Pennsylvania called "Falling Water," a sight truly to behold.

At the Old School some years ago, very unusual for us, we suffered a minor earthquake which we felt through the fabric of the building, thankfully the foundations stood firm and our home with it.

The leaning Tower of Pisa is a wonderful visual illustration, if ever we needed one, to respect foundations. The superstructure can have all the finery we like, all the glitz, all the show, but if the base is faulty then ultimately the building's future is certain, "great was the fall of it" (Matt 7:27, NET).

I recall years ago whilst living in London I discovered a term I had never heard before: "underpinning." London is well known for its soft clay soils, and friends of mine had a house where tree roots had ingressed the foundations and cracks began to appear in the walls of the property. At huge cost and lots of concrete, the house was saved and prevented from falling down. Underpinning was the answer. This was testimony enough that foundations can be seriously threatened. The family who lived in the house were unhappily disrupted and had to move out. When foundations are so badly assaulted as the psalmist describes in Psalm 11, the superstructure above may be beyond saving. Equally when church foundations have been attacked history teaches us that the consequences are devastating.

In Britain, over the years, the spiritual foundations of countless churches have been destroyed, (we will come to some of the reasons for this later). The figures are both frightening and heartbreaking. The Church of England with its great Reformation history and extraordinary thirty-nine articles of faith and prayer book, is a shadow of what it was. In 1980 that church across the country attracted one million three hundred and seventy thousand people, by 2015 it was down to six hundred and sixty-six thousand, a drop of fifty percent. The Methodists, famous for John and Charles Wesley, were down from six hundred and six thousand to two hundred thousand. Only the Pentecostal Church seems to have bucked the trend. Baptists (my own church) and Presbyterians do not come out of the survey very well either. The truth is, wherever we look, the foundations are being ingressed or even destroyed. For the time being I want to focus on those which are being compromised and placed under threat by what I see as a new and insidious assault upon them. While there is no evidence right now of outright collapse the "prophet" in me points to the future, and this is my concern for generations to come. This makes my work in this book a job of underpinning and there is not a moment to lose.

How Firm a Foundation?

How should we secure a Christian response to the fundamental place of foundation? The very best way is to reveal God's view of foundation. What does he think? When God wished to expose Job's frailties he pointed to his own foundations of the earth. God asks the remarkable Job, "Where were you when I laid the foundations of the earth?" (Job 38:4, NET). When God makes his claim as the Creator he points to foundations (Ps 102:25, NIV), "In the beginning you laid the foundations of the earth." It is surely the temple and its construction which convinces us and forces any reader of the OT to sit up and take notice of the supreme role of that place, given the emphasis on its foundations (2 Chron 3:3; Ezra 3:11-12, NLT). "With praise and thanks, they sang this song to the Lord: "He is so good! His faithful love for Israel endures forever!" Then all the people gave a great shout, praising the Lord because the foundation of the Lord's Temple had been laid. But many of the older priests, the Levites, and other leaders who had seen the first temple wept aloud when they saw the new Temple's foundation. The others, however, were shouting for joy." At the very least the people who constructed it were to understand that it was meant to last, even if the religion practiced in it was meant to fade in the light of newer, better abiding foundations, (Heb 11:10, NET; Rev 21:19, NIV). God's work of building, whether temples or his eternal kingdom, is based on foundations. The very best insight we have of God's commitment to foundations is beyond dispute, namely the kingdom of his own dear Son which is established upon his unshakeable love and grace, which even the gates of hell shall not be able to overthrow. We must remember, that which God builds in Christ is not designed to be transient, but built to last, to go on and on, his foundations are not flimsy, they have no built-in obsolescence. Therefore Christians must care deeply about the foundations and constantly run a check to see whether they are under threat in any way; remembering it is the foundation of unique apostles and prophets, which means it is already laid, nothing else must be attempted to be added. This must make us extremely vigilant to care for the foundation which has come to us in the word of God.

Is Breaking Up Really Hard to Do?

If a manual existed explaining how to successfully break up foundations one suspects it might be a very short read. The human will, coupled with the essential tools of explosives and pneumatic hammers are really all that is needed. This is after all in part what Guy Fawkes possessed. The approach to breaking up God's foundation is somewhat more complex and the "how to do" manual, would probably run to several hundred pages. History cannot record every destructive act, but it certainly points up the major attempts at the acts of demolition. As to all the particulars of the destruction and how this has been achieved is for another subject altogether. The word "achieved" implies that some of the historic assault has been purposeful and deliberate, which it clearly has. Undoubtedly the destruction has demonstrated design and stealth coupled with craft. Others have been able to wreak destruction by default as they stumbled upon their explosives, not realizing what they were handling.

Nor have the demolition crews been focused in one place. The disenfranchised Charles Taze Russell set about his work in the USA, where the perfect social environment provided him with all the fuel he needed to assault God's civilization. It might be argued that Rome used the most destructive tools of all to rip the foundations to pieces, and then laid its own wood, hay and straw.

At other times great minds have employed their acumen to destructive purpose. Schleiermacher has already been mentioned, but there are others who have worked from within the hallowed walls of Protestantism like Arminius, Strauss, Ritschl and Von Harnack, these were undoubtedly some of the most successful men ever to attack the church.[1]

In the last one hundred years or so the skill of destructiveness has not diminished, in fact it has managed to carry on a pace, so that today hearing some Christians speak, one might be left wondering if they have a foundation or even know of one. Furthermore across the evangelical church, foundations have been broken up by a "could not care less" attitude, people just couldn't be bothered by the issues. Deliberation over matters of a theological nature can be extremely bothersome, and in our day we easily prefer the least line of resistance. If Christians do not know about the foundations why would they care about them? It appears that many Christians in the

1. Many became "embalmed" (to use Brown's turn of phrase) in Albert Schweitzer's famous survey of the quest of the historical Jesus (1906).

past cared only in a theoretical way, but rarely caring from the heart, that was seen as the job, the preserve of the minister and elders. Instead a spirit of reverie, a dream-like mindset, seems to easily prevail over the sheep themselves, no matter the date in history. The foundations are dismantled without anyone particularly noticing their disappearance.

Intellect and ignorance, power and stealth have all been instruments to undermine this civilization. While we admit the tools of such destructiveness have been extremely varied, some more than others attract our attention and naturally receive our well deserved ire. But why should this be? It has been noticeable that we appear to have been much more animated when attempts to break the foundations are exercised through false *doctrine* than we are by false *practice*. Over the last fifty years, mainstream evangelicalism seems to have been more than willing to criticize both doctrine and practice of the Charismatic churches, which it found fault with. Remarkably this perceived error was seen with a "crystal clear" eye, at all costs the foundations *had* to be preserved. The evangelical church to its immense credit (for which we must all be deeply grateful) has often put up a "bulwark of defense" against assaults made on the truth.

Perhaps in Britain today, few remain who are able to recall the difficulties which evangelicalism visited upon itself in the mid 1950s and 1960s. It is not too unkind to describe the ructions which arose as being the result of flirtations. These were particularly exemplified as new ground breaking methods, approaches to reach out to the world, were being explored. Dr. Billy Graham and his campaigns presented new challenges, not least questions of ecumenism, but also those of techniques. Churches throughout the UK were widely influenced, and the effect is still felt, those early flirtations developed into a love affair which continue to produce offspring. The author, Ian Murray, reliably informs us there was at least one lone voice who questioned the enterprise: "There was only one senior evangelical voice raised in Britain on the danger facing evangelicals. It was that of Martyn Lloyd-Jones."[2] One author read of the cause of Lloyd-Jones's concern when he wrote, "In retrospect it looks as if the Conservative Evangelical Movement in Britain crossed the ecumenical watershed at Dr. Billy Graham's Crusade at Harringay in 1954."[3] Lloyd-Jones albeit in a wider context after an address was reported in a church newspaper as "nothing short of hare-brained."[4]

Obviously the "Dr." had touched a raw nerve, he was acutely aware that distinctives might be lost and that they would be hard to recall. It is impossible looking at that situation without overlaying the one submitted here, except so many of those who now reflect on this error of the 1950s and 1960s, are now participants in a new and very acceptable experiment. Hypocrisy comes to mind! It was inevitable that

2. Murray, *Evangelicalism Divided*, 44.

3. Murray, *Evangelicalism Divided*, 43, quoting Lawrence, *Hard Facts of Unity*, 68

4. Murray, Evangelicalism Divided, 48, quoting "Church of England Newspaper," 28 October 1966

Lloyd-Jones would to some extent be tarnished by the miasma of scandal, after all he was opposing the majority, the status quo.

In my own estimation the cult of bigness was certainly a key player. The author, R.W. Mecklenburg expertly grapples with these questions in his book, *The Philosophy of Size and the Essence of Enough*. This philosophy is in both the world and the church, and where relativism is now the "norm," the "big new thing" can steamroller tradition without any other voice being heard. Was Lloyd-Jones the pessimist or the optimist? I think neither, dealing with the revealed truth of God's word he was the realist, for which Mecklenburg supplies a simple illustration:

> The optimist rearranges furniture as his house is burning, while the pessimist calls the fire department when he burns his toast. The realist is perhaps wisest, for he has aligned his perception with the reality. And is that not the definition of truth?[5]

"Screen" worshippers were pessimists who saw their faith and the church in danger of burning down. The realist is able to stand back and assess the current circumstances, take a deep breath and decline the invitation which "Zoom" worship or any other suggests. "Whenever something is wrong, something is too big"[6] is how Mecklenburg sees it as he opens his book quoting Leopold Kohr. The Graham Campaigns were "big," "Zoom" is "big," something was and is wrong when the church bows the knee to new tech-driven relativistic proposals in its attempt to offer worship.

Vulnerable Sheep

In fact Lloyd-Jones was not the only prominent figure to voice his concern, Francis Schaeffer, to his great credit also raised the alarm bells. But to many in the churches these men were out of step with the then current thinking. From a distance, with hindsight, those who were "out of step" were not willing to be railroaded and put under pressure to bend to the wishes of the majority. They appear to take time to think and weigh everything up, clearly their consciences could not endorse the mass approval which the church was unthinkingly acceding to. Looking back, it is important to be generous to those who supported the Graham campaigns who, in many ways, must have entered into, or stumbled into that new "experimental" world, unthinkingly following the lead of those they trusted.

We must wonder what in fact did the average church member in the 1950s and 1960s actually know about the American evangelist and his methods. We can be sure the very least that they knew was that his approach produced the goods, his methods were successful and a sale can always be made on this pitch. My point is, church members though not all, without any thorough investigation simply tagged along, if

5. Mecklenburg, *Philosophy of Size and the Essence of Enough*, 111.
6. Mecklenburg, *Philosophy of Size and the Essence of Enough*, X111, quoting Leopold Kohr.

all the other churches were involved, it must have been right. Understandably many Christians at that time had never encountered the mass decisionism which Billy Graham employed, so what were they to make of it? All of this dovetails neatly into our current situation, and throws a much-needed light on the new direction in which the church is heading.

I expect some who read this will be inclined to dismiss this as "hare-brained" and the connections with the past as an irrelevance, pointing out that what the American evangelist did by his inventiveness actually reshaped the foundations. But what can be more foundational to the church than its worship of Almighty God. Graham significantly colored forever the offer of the Gospel. We are re-coloring by our inventiveness the "fundamental act of worship." The "tools" of demolition in the 1950s and 1960s were, in some respects, "big" and new for that time, the ones which are being called on now are equally "big" and new. Graham and others presented a case for newness, and newness was equated with success, i.e., that which worked. This mindset is now so entrenched in the church, and though perhaps not realizing it, we have followed him. Newness is naturally harmless and good for us, who can argue with it? Quoting Henry David Thoreau: "Every generation laughs at the "old fashions" but follows religiously the new." He is right!

Added to this there is the "everybody is on board" argument which has already been presented for a justification of "screen" worship, so why would one not support it when the new is so moderate? It is just for these kinds of reasons church members blindly get on board with the new; it is the "herd" mentality, and unfortunately, the spirit of the Bereans looks to have "gone absent without leave." It has been observable over the years how many have been drawn into the cults, showing scant regard for precaution, they join with little thought. Uncomfortable as it is, this state of mind is so often found in Christ's church, for this reason it is never able to sing along with Edith Piaf: "*Non, Je ne regrette rien!*" . . . destruction always comes with consequences.

Little do we realize that with the onset of "screen" worship we have been introduced to something at least if not more destructive and influential than Grahams, but comparable to it. Today his ethos, like that of Schleiermacher, is in the churches without many even having heard their names, never mind knowing that for which they stood.

With the emergence of "screen" worship we encounter something far more powerful and potentially far-reaching. Billy Graham's influence brought about a theological shift, in particular, regarding the offer of the Gospel. The new experiment confronting us will develop a shift in our understanding of the most fundamental aspect of our corporate life, namely Worship. The *view* of God via the screen, in which people also play a part (a form of theatre) will lay down markers for worship far-reaching into the future, the screen is here to stay. Whether we like it or not, it will outrageously color the character of God. With this "tool" let loose on the foundation, "breaking up will prove not at all hard to do!" What you permit you promote.

The Power of Ideas—Our Unfortunate Connections

If explosives being used to demolish foundations look overly dramatic, then we have not really considered the deep and profound place which ideas have had on the church. The devil's demolition crew have been at work for hundreds of years using ideas for high explosives.

When casting his eye over the nineteenth century, Colin Brown gives us a picture of its considerable influence upon the twentieth and necessarily the twenty-first . . . ideas have longevity. During this period Christianity was being fundamentally rethought. Brown remarks on how "the history of philosophy in the twentieth century shows painfully in what way the Christian church has inherited the legacy of the nineteenth century."[7] Emerging out of that century of extraordinary flux (though nothing like that of the twentieth and twenty-first centuries) Schleiermacher's influence began to make its mark. His thinking, his ideas, would change the religious and spiritual landscape forever. The early twentieth-century church was remodeled by his considerable mind. Karl Barth quoting an impressed student tells of a letter written to "the great man;" "There is no one who can make me waver in my belief that your dogmatics herald a new era, not only in this one discipline, but in the whole study of theology in general."[8] Since that devoted student bowed in genuflexion many others have followed. His emphasis on religious experience is surely impossible to separate from the expressions of so-called "faith explored" within charismatic circles, the emphasis in both being that of experience. It is not insignificant that Schleiermacher was, in his day, one of the leading intellectuals, he was an authority on Plato and much more. His significance cannot be underestimated, he helped to found the University of Berlin. Karl Barth attributes to him extraordinary influence, when he says: "He did not found a school but an era."[9] Barth also adds (ominously) that the nineteenth century "was his century" (and) "His influence did not decrease, it increased as time went on, and his views established themselves more and more. He was studied, honored and made fruitful much more in 1910 than in 1830."[10] He was a giant especially in thought and ideas. Francis Schaeffer says: "It is interesting to note that there was a span of approximately eighty years from the time when the higher critical methods originated (i.e. Schleiermacher) and became widely accepted in Germany to the disintegration of German culture and the rise of totalitarianism under Hitler."[11] Schaeffer goes on to ask if his readers understand what the battle is about in the area of culture and ideas. The problems which many churches face today, (whether they realize it or not), are

7. Brown, *Philosophy and the Christian Faith*, 166.
8. Barth, *Protestant Theology in the Nineteenth Century*, 425.
9. Brown, *Philosophy and the Christian Faith*, 108.
10. Barth, *Protestant Theology*, 425-426.
11. Schaeffer, *Great Evangelical Disaster*, 35.

connected with the deep errors of the past. Only those with an almost zero grasp of history, who cannot make connections or do not want to, fail in this.

Schleiermacher and others worked a deep magic which Christians were unable to resist. Its new charm re-drew the map of our spiritual civilization and our borders, consequently our trading powers have never been the same, they have never recovered and, humanly speaking, they never will. The question is obvious: can we recover from our own creative cartography?

Connections—Our Unfortunate Family Tree

In 2015 I was diagnosed with prostate cancer. Like most men in my predicament I knew nothing about it. I was quite ignorant of the condition. By now the reader will understand that I did not consult the internet for help! Instead I chose to look into it by consulting four different opinions. In doing so I was suddenly awash with material on a subject which I had to calmly get my head around. To make matters more difficult, the diagnosis opened a door, to not just one treatment, but various treatments, which in my case was left for me to decide. What a quandary! The strangest thing about this time was that just as I received my diagnosis, a dear friend of mine, not a Christian, was also informed by his doctor that he also had prostate cancer. When he told me this I immediately offered to share with him everything which I had gleaned from the consultants who had seen me. To my astonishment he was not interested to know anything, he refused to answer my telephone calls, he did not care to talk. My dear friend was happier to be oblivious of all that was going on. The foundations of his life were crumbling, but he did not want to face it. I cannot begin to judge or criticize him because none of us know how we will deal with this kind of trial in our lives. This illustrates just what I see in the history of the church, most people at any given time are quite ignorant about the disease which is developing under their noses, destroying the very foundation of their spiritual lives and of our heritage.

Millions of innocent church people would have never heard of Schleiermacher in his day or known of his questionable doctrine, they simply followed the lead of others, their pastors and teachers. When the disease came to light, millions would not have known what to make of it. Others who were aware of what was going on, understandably did not want to talk about it because of the pain, the possibility of division and so on. The numbers who were willing to engage and ask the questions so as to get to grips with the new teaching must have been, in truth, few and far between. This we have to assume, because countless churches, like my friend, died. The disease infecting the church rolls on and becomes unstoppable, ignorance, fear and cowardice, must all play their part. (Francis Schaeffer says, speaking of the situation in the USA, "By 1936 the liberals were so in control of the Northern Presbyterian Church that they were able to defrock Dr. J Gresham Machen . . . (who) had been a brilliant defender of

Bible-believing Christianity").[12] Princeton fell, necessitating the birth of Westminster Theological Seminary.

Eureka—Maybe not!

It should be obvious, my personal story illustrates it can be fatal to overlook matters we do not understand. This does not mean we should be neurotic about our churches, nor that we should be "nitpicking." However, there is no cancer which should go un-investigated. and anyone who says so, does not have health welfare in view, so must it be with the church. The spiritual welfare of the churches who took Schleiermacher to heart became disease ridden. Let us not lose sight of the innocent souls who would not have had the slightest idea of the cancer which was developing in the form of noxious ideas. Allow me a warning in the present situation which is changing as fast as I write. Permit me to show what happens when we are connected with ideas, with philosophies, which at first appear benign.

Exactly what the order of our thought processes are we may never know, but it must be obvious that thoughts lead to ideas. In this we have to ask where is the source of our thinking which then leads on to ideas. To whom are we connected? Who is influencing us? (Chapter 8 is dedicated to this question). I think on examination, we may be surprised what we find. Is it too outrageous to suggest that Steve Jobs's ideas have influenced the world? Just what were the thoughts of the one who invented the wheel? We can imagine the response was like that of Archimedes's euphoric cry . . . Eureka! Perhaps Jobs responded in the same way with the iPhone. But what of the processing of our ideas? Our world is changed by them and all too often, so is the church, with dire consequences.

Who Says It Is a Good Idea?

Many Christians have taken to describing "Zoom" worship as "God's provision." If it is to be attributed to God, then of necessity it must be a good idea, though God is now remarkably the author of "technoference!" Ideas change our world and we have good reason, under God's providence to be thankful for many of them. It is impossible to measure the influence which the wheel has had on our lives, but if we suppose it has only brought about unbounded good, then we are clearly mistaken. The moment we hear the story of a pedestrian being knocked down and run over by a car, crushed by the wheels, we think about wheels in an entirely different way (one of my cousins lost a leg as a child from such an accident). In the nineteenth century the wheel was central to the huge industrial complexes which worked the machinery, producing countless vital components which changed the lives of people around the world, creating wealth

12. Schaeffer, *Great Evangelical Disaster*, 34.

by the Industrial Revolution. This was a good idea if ever there was one, however to the family who lost a child (and there were many of them) mangled in the wheels and mechanisms of textile mills, the great invention took on an entirely different meaning and significance. To them the wheel would always spell death. One of our problems is that we hardly ever want to acknowledge the downside of our ingenuity, and pragmatism/utilitarianism shuts out the voice which might helpfully give us another perspective. Our climate crisis surely convinces us of this. When plastic was invented in 1904, no one could see its downside and if they could, we have never heard from them. The plastic bag was invented in 1965 and now in Europe at least, it is seen as "public enemy number one." We are in a plastics crisis as it poisons our oceans, with twelve million tons (UN figures) being dumped into them every year. Good ideas over time may well turn out to be poisonous, even deadly.

Clocks

Consider how we marvel at clocks, both antique and modern. Lewis Mumford in his book explains how clocks emerged out of the monastic world: "At one time there were 40,000 monasteries under the Benedictine rule."[13] "The bells of the clock tower almost defined urban existence. Time-keeping passed into time-serving and time-accounting and time-rationing. As this took place, Eternity ceased gradually to serve as the measure and focus of human actions."[14] Most profound of all Mumford observes: "The clock is not merely a means of keeping track of the hours, but of synchronizing the actions of men."[15] He concludes: "No other machine is so ubiquitous."[16] I suppose this last observation may have to be revised, the screen probably now takes number one slot. Can anything compete with it? In this we see how thought in the monasteries gave way to ideas, and ideas to machines, and machines to a way of life which has in turn altered our world. Our inventiveness in the church in our practices is naively viewed by some as being insignificant, even temporary, but this is historical naivety and a failure to look beyond the moment. This failure is common to ideas, especially where any kind of commerce is attached preventing discernment beyond anything advantageous. Mumford helps us in this, he asks regarding the clock: "Was it by reason of the collective Christian desire to provide for the welfare of souls in eternity by regular prayers and devotions that time-keeping and the habits of temporal order took hold of men's minds: habits that capitalist civilization presently turned to good account?"[17] This meant the clock in the bell tower was not subject to the clouds that paralyzed the sundial. The freezing water which could halt the simple water clock on a

13. Mumford, *Technics and Civilization*, 13.

14. Mumford, *Technics and Civilization*, 14.

15. Mumford, *Technics and Civilization*, 14.

16. Mumford, *Technics and Civilization*, 14.

17. Mumford, *Technics and Civilization*, 14.

winter's day or night was no longer an obstacle. It was now possible for time-keeping to be measured by the "clank of the clock," the bells brought a new routine into the life of a workman. The clock, what a thought, what an idea, what a machine, what an affect on us all! Surely no one could lose by such a technical advancement, not forgetting "the clock is not merely a means of keeping track of the hours, but of synchronizing the actions of men."

One thing leads to another. "Ideas are never neutral and abstract."[18] says Francis Schaeffer and Mumford agrees: "The clock, moreover, is a piece of power-machinery." This is certainly how the textile mill workers who I observed in my childhood would have thought of it. Their lives were dominated by "clocking-on" and "clocking-off." Their wages, or lack of them, could not be separated from the "power machinery." It would be the philosopher, Benjamin Franklin, who coined the phrase, "Time is money." To become "as regular as clock-work (Mumford says), was the bourgeois ideal."[19] The point is, powerful thoughts give way to powerful ideas and in turn powerful machines, which shape our lives altering them forever and the world we live in. History confirms that powerful ideas work the same unalterable change in the church also.

Marco Polo connected with the ideas of China and influenced us all and thankfully brought ice cream, amongst other benefits, back to Europe. On the other hand, Sir Walter Raleigh, connected with life in the Americas and introduced the leaf laden with nicotine and other toxins to our shores. We have been addicted to it ever since, but millions of lives have been lost to it. Ideas are not always good! Sixty years after the plastic bag, many of us are saying, in a kind of self righteous way: what a dreadful idea, what a devastating experiment, yet one we have been part of. We did it! We might even, in our honest and sober moments, be ready to admit that we are fools, (Rom 1:22, NIV): "Although they claimed to be wise, they became fools." The problem, the damage is done; it cannot be undone. In years to come will another generation of Christians look back at the church and question its inventiveness and haste in the introduction of cameras, television units and computer screens, to our "so-called times of worship"? I predict they will. What seems astonishing is the way evangelicals are robust and resolute when considering doctrine: "Let no one dare to touch the doctrine of Christ's substitutionary atonement, or justification or election, or Christ's divinity" (quite right too). But the *means*, the tools of dissemination of such truths when handling these, it seems as though we do not care, it looks as though we are going backwards, and the circumstances globally regarding COVID-19 have convinced us (to quote the well-known line of a popular song) to "do it our way." The church is looking primitive, returning to pictures—albeit digital which strangely and astonishingly seems to possess the ability to sanctify them!

18. Schaeffer, *Great Evangelical Disaster*, 30.
19. Mumford, *Technics & Civilization*, 16.

New Popes

It has already been established that we are linked to the past, more so than we realize. We are connected philosophically whether we are conscious of it or not, to a thinking which might be described as the "High Fruit of Philosophy." Of course people will dismiss this as irrelevant, but it would be like trying to dismiss Schleiermacher from his ultimate influence over Christianity in the last hundred years.

It has been necessary in a later chapter to ask the question about influences, influences which down through time have come to bear upon the church. Who delivered them and how significant are they? Are Christians the offspring entirely of God's word or the philosophies of this world? When we look at our shape perhaps we have overlooked what we have been consuming to produce the figure we have. That we have been configured by the thinkers of the past is surely not out of place to propose, nor difficult to prove. And if we have been squeezed by the ideas of bygone generations then why not our own? Vainglorious concepts may be rehashed, revealing "there is nothing new under the sun."

Ideas/philosophies may create euphoria, but the euphoric in time gives way to the new normal. The initial rush is lost and the idea becomes the "norm" and a way of life. Mecklenburg proposes what should be evident to us all: "Philosophy is truly the root of all things. Philosophy, one's guiding principle, will exist whether the means to manifest it exist or not."[20] But watch what happens when the means are available. However, as Postman illustrates: "To a man with a hammer everything looks like a nail."[21] Homer Simpson is pictured happily becoming a signed-up member of the NRA upon which when he acquires his rifle he turns it to a multitude of uses; he turns out the light, closes the doors and switches off the oven by shooting them! In the same way the philosophy of tech suggests itself to everything, including worship. The philosophy of the Enlightenment squeezed the church, producing a new "High Fruit" which provided food for thought for Schleiermacher and others. The thinkers who picked the "High Fruit" are names which trip off the tongue. Of Kant, Colin Brown says: "His skepticism cast a long shadow over the nineteenth century."[22] That shadow could hardly fail one way or another to encroach on Schleiermacher's "light," who in turn "illuminated" the churches, where an emphasis on experience came to the fore. According to Colin Brown: "Thomas Aquinas is more influential now through his writings and his impact upon Catholicism generally than he was in his lifetime."[23]

"Screen" worship springs from a philosophy of relativistic thinking which courses through the whole of life, even church life. We have forgotten that, "the Law of the Lord is perfect," (Ps 19:7) meaning God's word is not subject to relativism which

---

20. Mecklenburg, *Philosophy of Size and the Essence of Enough*, 96.

21. Gay, *Way of the (Modern) World*, 87, quoting Postman, *Technopoly*, 14.

22. Brown, *Philosophy and the Christian Faith*, 91.

23. Brown, *Philosophy and the Christian Faith*, 12.

denies universal laws. The church is not free to experiment with tech worship any more than it is free to introduce other relativistic experimental models to its supreme responsibility. Naturally like one who comfort eats, the Christian may be vulnerable to giving a self-congratulatory slap on the back, confirming that nothing of this world's philosophy is at work in their life or in their church. Time for a reality check! Evangelicals fail to grasp that what is said and done now may well look small and insignificant, history teaches us that this shortsighted view allows seeds to grow, even to monstrous proportions: "Sow the wind and reap the whirlwind" (Hosea 8:7, NIV).

Is Kant too distant now that he is unable to influence us? Or is he in our thinking without us even realizing it? Is he unbeknown to us the "Uninvited Guest?" Is Schleiermacher, in the churches, in sermons and in the minds of young preachers being trained for the ministry today? Is the sermon in turn in the minds of people who have never even heard of him? Brown tells us: "Kant asked himself the question: *What is enlightenment?* The answer . . . (produced the motto) Dare to use your own understanding."[24] This I suggest, we have in the church in abundance and even though God counsels us "not to lean or rely on our own understanding," (Prov 3:5, NET) we still do. One can safely take Kant's advice, because at one level this is healthy, but after daring to use it we need to check in with a much higher understanding, and lean on the divine comprehension. Adam dared to use and lean on his own understanding, and we must admit we have been following his lead ever since. Kant went further and applied his thinking to religion, he said: "No generation should be bound by creeds and dogmas of bygone generations."[25] So here we are. It does not need a particularly fertile imagination to recognize the influence this has had not only on the church, but on the world at large.

Many Christians will know that Nietzsche influenced Hitler and the Nazis, Hegel influenced Karl Marx. We must wonder who influenced the forty-fifth President of the USA, we know for a fact that he recently influenced seventy-million people, and the effects of this will potentially be far-reaching. Of course the author recognizes "Beauty is in the eye of the beholder," therefore it remains for the reader to decide whether such influence is for good or ill, but the illustration serves my purposes. The church is always under "the influence." Mecklenburg offers his own analysis:

> The medieval Christian was totally dependent on his collective and its leaders—the popes, cardinals, bishops, and priests—for salvation. The Enlightenment shattered this dependency, but I believe we have begun to reengineer it—this time, with new popes.[26]

The relativistic philosophy which has led the churches to obey tech's every "spring and lever" has opened the door to experiment with "screen" worship, countless

24. Brown, *Philosophy and the Christian Faith*, 91.
25. Brown, *Philosophy and the Christian Faith*, 91.
26. Mecklenburg, *Philosophy of Size and the Essence of Enough*, 143.

numbers of people have been re-engineered overnight! One evangelical church even proclaims in a loud boastful voice, how many devices are logged on to "screen" worship. It is reminiscent of the words of Billy Graham who said: "I can preach to more people in one night on TV than perhaps Christ did in his whole lifetime." When the popes in any dress speak, the sheep tend to listen. The world's philosophies are "alive and kicking" in our churches.

The Billy Graham campaigns were in many ways about numbers, "bigness," this is the "low fruit." "Low fruit" in this sense is easy; easy to get at; easy to access; easy to pick. Everything about the "low fruit" recommends itself to us; so how could anyone turn it down? The fruit in the upper branches on the other hand, require some "scratching of the head" to know how to reach it. It might even be dangerous to get, caution from outside will probably deter the would-be fruit gatherer from attempting such a dangerous and reckless enterprise. What is more, the "High Fruit" might only be accessible through the construction of an elaborate scaffold and ladder system. But this fruit having received the best of the sun will be delicious, sweet and worth the effort to pick.

This construction to reach the "High Fruit" will inevitably take time and deliberation. The "low fruit" takes no time at all and time is a vital factor because no one has any of it, everyone is in a rush making haste (this as much as anything has precipitated the experiment of "screen" worship). The thought processes needed more "scratching of the head." The tantalizing delicacy of the "High Fruit" is always on display, but one needs to stand back to see it, to appreciate it, and then dare to pick it. Only those brave enough to go up into the heights can taste the delights of what awaits, hence "hinds feet on high places" (Ps 18:33, KJV). Perhaps one thing above all others might deter the would-be fruit picker from ascending the heights: fear! We can only imagine how much "High Fruit," delicious sweet fruit, has never been picked and left to rot by those too afraid to attempt the feat.

Hans Rosling in his book, gives much "down to earth" advice, he offers this: "Beware of simple ideas and simple solutions. History is full of visionaries who used simple utopian visions to justify terrible actions. Welcome complexity."[27] If Steve Jobs is not a visionary I do not know who is, and while I have not a bad word necessarily for his remarkable innovation, he is not welcome in the church. His solutions and others which go under the banner of "simple solutions" should have been subjected to examination (1 Thess 5:21), it might have been more complex, but at least the "High Fruit" would have been worth straining for. It has come to something when the author appears to have more in common with Neil Postman (not a Christian) than he does with the church. Postman is able to reach up into the high branches and, if the reader is willing to listen to him, he can give a helping hand to reach up also. The fruit may not be so easy to obtain, but it is no bad thing to have to go through difficulties, complexities, to pick the best and the sweetest. The foundations will thank us for the effort.

27. Rosling, *Factfulness*, 203.

CHAPTER 3

OUR CREATIVE SIDE

"Nothing produced by technics is more final than the human needs and interests themselves that have created technics"[1]

LEWIS MUMFORD

"You shall not make for yourself . . ."

EXODUS 20:4 (NIV)

WE MAKE THINGS, AND THIS should be no surprise to any one of us, after all we are made in God's likeness, in his image. That we make things, and a lot of them, has recently been confirmed by a team at the Weizmann Institute of Sciences in Israel who have concluded that human-made objects outweigh living things: "For every person in the world, more than their body weight in stuff is now being produced each week." This confirms we are creatively prodigious. "We are showing perhaps at an alarming rate how our species is transforming the Earth," in truth we have always been transforming the earth, more often than not in a utilitarian way, but not exclusively so, artistic expression is never far removed from the myriad of objects which we make. On the face of it, our mechanical prowess may look as though it is sufficient to satisfy, but when inevitably the utilitarian meets the soulishness of man, the aesthetic in us demands succor. For example, somehow the old jobbing typewriters were only complete and up to the task when given the elegance of some floral decoration! Shotguns, sewing machines, radiators, steam engines, cash registers, even the Eiffel Tower, all seemed to need the help of some form of aesthetic embellishment. We were never made to be utilitarian, it is unnatural, we are unable, we cannot do it however hard we try.

---

1. Mumford, *Technics and Civilization*, 244.

The Bible records for us the emergence of art which comes up from the fingers of Jubal who appears to have invented musical instruments: "the first of all who play the harp and flute," (Gen 4:21, NLT). John Calvin (some might think remarkably) believed the passage speaks of "excellent gifts of the Holy Spirit." He believed God had given to Jubal artistic instruction and enriched him and also his posterity with rare endowments Abraham Kuyper observes in Calvin's comments: "that these inventive powers of art prove most evident testimonies of the Divine bounty." More emphatically still, he (Calvin) declares, in his commentaries on Exodus, that "all the arts come from God and are to be respected as Divine inventions."[2] Furthermore very interestingly, Calvin speaks of "these precious things of the natural life we owe originally to the Holy Ghost.[3] "The arts, says he, have been given us for our comfort, in this depressed estate of life. They react against the corruption of life and nature by the curse."[4] Calvin was even willing to defend this position against one of his colleagues at Geneva who needed correcting on this matter. I cannot help but think the church of our day could also do with some straightening out.

The Land of the Giants

Probably since the time of the Puritans, we have tended to drift in the opposite direction from Calvin's thinking, and consequently a general ignorance of such matters resides firmly established in the evangelical church, meaning a cultural voice is unable to sound any note of comfort. The Puritans are in us for good or ill. Consequently there is an undoubted and mistaken view held regarding man's creativity, the unpalatable truth is that this reflects the Philistine in us, not a pretty sight. Furthermore, it is one which shuts God out of our lives as Creator, that is if we believe in him as the Creator at all. It is not unusual to get the impression that the only notion Christians have of God as the Creator is confined to the first three chapters of Genesis. It is surely not unreasonable to suppose that Christians have journeyed deep, deep into Philistine country becoming settled there, so that no gracious effort can extricate or retrieve them. There may be many reasons for this, but chief amongst them must be that while in that land of giants they were made to bow, not only the knee, but heart and mind, so as to worship at the shrine of utility. As a result a Christian appreciation of art and design to God's glory may never have been countenanced. Might not the creation of a Ferrari be judged then, not only as aggrandizing sin but also as a waste of time? The same could apply to a great painting by Rembrandt or a Faberge egg. Slowly but surely the church has shut the door on the Holy Spirit comforting our "dreadful depressed estate of life" (Calvin), through the gift of art. We have tried to dodge art and shut it out, settling purely for a utilitarianism which we can justify. With such a

2. Kuyper, *Lectures on Calvinism*, 153.

3. Kuyper, *Lectures on Calvinism*, 153.

4. Kuyper, *Lectures on Calvinism*, 153.

mentality—everything has to be *for* something! On careful analysis though this ratio-nale will not stack up, why? Because we are made in God's image. Naturally then, we refuse to bow to a Puritan or any other view of life which excludes this creativity, in-deed we cannot, the creative cannot be transfused out of us. Nevertheless in a clumsy and sometimes brutal way the attempt is made, but this leaves us malnourished, with only the "bare bones" of utilitarian relativism. Houses are good but only certain ones, new kitchens are OK but they must not be ostentatious, cars need to be roadworthy but at all costs they must not be designer ones. In my time I have heard it all! There is a deep and unhealthy unspiritual bias, even a judgmental one. Undoubtedly the thinking of many Christians regarding creativity, reveals fear is at its heart. Remember the house we live in was designed along with the wallpaper and carpets under our feet. Our clothes, jewelry, hairstyles are all the result of our creativity; as are the wrought iron railings which fence off the boundary of the parks, much used and loved by the Victorians. The potter, the weaver, the blacksmith, the flautist, the painter, the sculp-tor, the actor, all contribute to the rich creative tapestry of life, which recalls God in a way that nothing else can. One does not have to be a keen observer to trace out major discrepancies of thought in Christ's church on this subject. Usually these have been built on prejudice over the years, and are often then passed on by an "authority" in the church, resulting in one generation leading another, as if their lives depended on it . . . deep, deep into Philistine country! Never to return and gain their freedom. Not forgetting of course, they "gouged out eyes" in that place as Samson painfully discovered (Judges 16:21, NIV).

In a film directed by George Clooney in which he also acts, he plays the part of one in charge of an elite team of experts sent into Europe during World War II. "The Monuments Men" explores the need to save for the world in the midst of the carnage of war as much art as might be feasible. Clooney (Lt. Frank Stokes) at one point argues that "We are fighting for our culture, our way of life. You can wipe out a generation of people, but if you destroy their achievements, their history, then its like they never existed." He captures the thought that we gloriously shape our world with our culture, we are unique, we are made wonderfully in God's image and reflect him in the works of our hands. Our world is richer for it. Michelangelo's Pieta in Bruges was as impor-tant as Bruges itself. When Notre Dame burned the people stood and wept, the loss is so profound.

All Hail the God of Utility

Set against this cultural backdrop is the view which some Christians seem to be most comfortable with, namely utilitarianism, just so long as it does not suggest anything of politics from the East! Science, no fault of its own, serves this perfectly and not only assists but justifies it, these in the end tend to look like soulmates. Typically Christians who have no issue with science, do have major problems with art. While one creates no discomfort at all, the other is an impossible "stone in the shoe" always needing to be pulled out and eliminated. This leaves our glorious civilization of God's kingdom, the body of Christ, looking lopsided, narrow and peculiar, but more than this, extremely vulnerable to a mindset, leading to particular manners and behavior which renders it weak (this is covered more thoroughly in Chapter 10). Those with little or no appreciation of the arts are more than likely to be those with an overly developed bent in a particular direction. Craig M. Gay cites Peter Berger:

> The technological society tends to foster a style of cognition that is at once highly pragmatic and deeply skeptical. The pragmatic cast of this style of mind owes to the matter-of-factness with which science and technology confront the world of objects. Its skeptical bent betrays the assumption that the scientific way of knowing the world is superior to all others.[5]

Lewis Mumford thinks: "Science and technics form two independent yet related worlds: sometimes converging, sometimes drawing apart."[6]

Bandages

If art in general was viewed by the evangelical with some skepticism, then art and the church was anathema. This was something which distinctly separated "nonconformity" from the wider expressions of faith. Interestingly even in nonconformity, concessions have abounded in the form of second rate stained glass windows, carved pulpits, pews, decoration and much more: albeit subdued, art found its way in. Art has always proved difficult to keep out of the church. It is as if we must have it, we cannot resist it in one form or another. The German scholar and philosopher Von Hartmann says: "Religion is still inclined to loose itself in the aesthetic form."[7] Speaking of the early periods (of church history: emphasis mine); he captures the danger of any marriage between art and religion . . .

> All the arts, he says, engage in the service of the cult, not merely music, painting, sculpture and architecture, but also the dance, mimicry and the drama. The more, on the other hand, Religion develops into spiritual maturity, the more it will extricate itself from art's bandages, because art always remains incapable of expressing the very essence of Religion . . . Religion, when fully matured, will rather entirely abstain from the stimulant by which aesthetic pseudo-emotion intoxicated it, in order to concentrate itself wholly and exclusively upon the quickening of those emotions which are *purely religious*.[8]

---

5. Gay, *Way of the (Modern) World*, 88, quoting Berger, Berger, Kellner, *Homeless Mind*, 1973.

6. Mumford, *Technics and Civilization*, 52.

7. Kuyper, *Lectures on Calvinism*, 148, quoting Hartmann, *Religion and Art*.

8. Kuyper, *Lectures on Calvinism*, 148.

Perhaps for evangelicals the great disconnect with art dates back to the darkness where the church was driven by pseudo-emotion, the stimulants which intoxicated it. No doubt this was the historical background which informed those who produced the great Westminster Confession and Baptist Confession of Faith, as they examined what was appropriate in worship. They would have been profoundly conscious of the dangers of ingenuity in the form of *anything* invading the worship of God which would compromise it. They knew their history. Pictures, images of any kind in any form, were outlawed, they were bandages. In the second and third centuries the question of images of any kind had been addressed by Tertullian and Clement of Alexandria. On the one hand, Clement viewed images as articles to be regarded as belonging to the demonic world of paganism, therefore completely prohibited. His observations, though flawed gives a little insight into our contemporary situation. Seals of different shapes and sizes were in vogue, and he recognizes the danger of their employment since these "a pagan might use." Nevertheless, trying to be accommodating he says: "These seals are neutral from a religious or moral point of view and either pagans or Christians could happily use them."[9] The bandages go way back!

Masters of Art

Rome makes no apology, and why should it, for its reliance on art. Art works. At one level we might assume that it deeply cares about Michelangelo's Sistine Chapel or the remarkable Pietas which he sculpted, we see a plethora of cheap carved plaster and painted virgins and saints, and exquisite carved altar pieces in many beautiful ornate baroque churches across Europe (some of these artistic achievements are overwhelming, they are breathtaking). These creations do exactly what they were meant to do, they transport you, but to where is another thing altogether. Who could not be impressed and moved by the windows in Canterbury Cathedral, who could not be in awe of the architecture of a Notre Dame or York Minster? Making art in the church works . . . It still works today.

There can be little doubt that one of the chief motivations which is attractive to those who seek out Roman Catholic worship is the spectacle of it all. It possesses a mystery in abundance, with its priestcraft and power to perform its own unique kind of magic in the Mass. These visual delights have always kept a rapt attention and the people enthralled. Speak to any Roman Catholic and they will almost certainly confirm that the "event" all by itself never leaves them, rather an indelible impression is imprinted. One friend, a former Roman Catholic, speaks of the Gospel's power to blunt it, but the consciousness of the visual is never fully extirpated. Even those who profess evangelical conversion speak of the long and lasting effect of these powerful dramas which remain a specter that can haunt people and torture them all their lives.

9. Chadwick, *Early Church*, 277.

None of this should be at all surprising, since the church has always needed stimulation of a visual external kind, it still needs it. Christians seem not to have grasped that "screen" worship is just this, it is pseudo, a pseudo-event, driven by pseudo-emotion. These are Von Hartmann's "bandages." The screen is art whether we like it or not, however this "bandage" is incapable of expressing the very essence of religion; rather, expressing the indomitable *itself* and *ourselves* it consoles and reassures, tenderly binding up our wounds, not forgetting to enthrall us in the process.

Our Strange Desire for Monarchy

In the south of Holland, in the beautiful old city of Maastricht, tucked away in a side street, is a Roman Catholic Church "The Basilica of our Lovely Lady." To enter into that place is a penetrating insight into the fact that "visual delights" work, just as much today, as they always have done. It is a profound statement on the spiritual and literal darkness of Rome, but also a living example to us all of the dangers of the "visual," visuals of any kind being employed in worship. The entrance to the church is ingenious, a portico leads you into the nave shrouded in deep darkness, it virtually sucks you in, cleverly, ingeniously leading and drawing you to your journey's end, delivering the worshipper into the darkness, but not before being confronted with a medieval screen behind which stands the alluring "Queen of Heaven." She beckons in her royal blue and gold (in truth just a plaster cast). Everyone stops, everyone lights a candle, everyone gazes, everyone is transfixed. Of those who pay their obeisance some appear to display a simple "matter of fact" attitude, others stop for prolonged periods. On the faces of some visitors, grief is etched coupled with pain, and it is not difficult to feel the deepest sympathy for those used and abused by the cult of Rome. Of course she, the "Queen of Heaven" as always remains silent, the only sound in fact is the sound of emotion and the clank of money being deposited for candles and whatnot. Well, business has to go on as usual, and whatever else, she is a "good business" woman.

As someone steeped in the visual, one who has made the visual his life's work, I always marvel at the ease with which visual delights can manipulate people, alter them, even control them. Watch a modern "pop group" (for want of a better word) leading a so-called time of worship in a church today, they so easily elicit emotion. Any choir is able to elicit the same. The psychology is altered from introspection to behavioral. The Art or whatever it is which is introduced into worship impacts behavior. The golden calf is made and human behavior changes. Exodus 32:5 (NLT): "Aaron saw how *excited* the people were." The new god of gold excited their emotions, raised their temperature and brought up new self expression, probably animistic. "The people got up the next morning to sacrifice burnt offerings and peace offerings. After this they celebrated with feasting and drinking and they indulged in pagan revelry" (Exod 32:6, NLT). Introduce a god, a statue, a manmade *thing* of any kind, place a camera in front of people and watch the behaviors which follow, they are as certain as night follows day.

I have observed carefully the behavior of the Japanese Buddhists who genuflect in front of the famous Golden Buddha in Nara, offering a continuous feast of perfectly good wholesome food which, not surprisingly, the oversized statue is unable to benefit from. Let us be in no doubt creativity alters our behavior in worship. Mumford observes the obvious: "one poses for the camera, or still more, one acts for the motion picture. The change is from an introspective to a behaviorist psychology . . ."[10] We "re-do" our hair and readjust our attire. The psychology which is altered by something external to us is easily observed, and surely not difficult to prove and very easy to document. Mumford captures something here so profound to this book when he writes: "Need I stress again that nothing produced by technics is more final than the human needs and interests themselves that have created technics?"[11] What we create has our interests at heart. In the church our technical innovations of every description will have our interests at heart . . . here is the overwhelming and obvious danger. Do we really need to be told that church interests must be those of God, and not of ourselves? The worship of almighty God by his people must have his interests at heart, and his alone: "that in everything he might have the supremacy" (Col 1:18, NIV); lest we fall into "will worship." The behavior of God's people before him can no more be assisted by a piece of modern technology in the form of a camera or a screen, any more than we can be helped by a fresco on a wall or a plaster cast of the Virgin (a subject which I will come to later, which we must grapple with since it exists to bring in pictures).

The Boasting Twins

The verse at the head of this chapter, Exodus 20:4: "You shall not make for *yourself*" confirms most pointedly what Mumford says: "What we create has our interests at heart." God said to the people "you shall not make for *yourself*." In life we spend ourselves making for ourselves. We center on self, we focus on self, selfishness is at the heart of our sin. We make homes for ourselves and in our education we are naturally focused on self. If it is betterment by university or a job, it is for self. Marriage is one of those wonderful provisions which potentially breaks the selfish hold upon us where we hopefully learn to practice the ultimate sharing. It is noteworthy that in the early church their conviction was that what they owned was not their own, therefore "they shared everything" (Acts 4:32, NIV).

Often though this breaks down because of the things which people still selfishly yearn for. When we see a young person, or indeed an older person, holding a phone stretched out with the intention of making a photograph it is always referred to as a "*selfie*." What else could it be?

10. Mumford, *Technics and Civilization*, 243.

11. Mumford, *Technics and Civilization*, 244.

The warning against making (Exodus 20) is in the first instance, to address not the thing to be made but the one who makes it. "You shall not make for *yourself*." God knows we are greedy for self. He knows our leanings. He knows that we put ourselves at the center. "Will worship" is just this, the imposition of *self* upon worship by any means. The church in history was always looking at what its hands had created, its natural strength and ingenuity, its designs, craft and pure art. All around the church one could point to "selfies!" It will be naturally protested against that the motives were good, and the motives are all that counts. Well, let us be generous and say the motives of these churches in history, and the citizens of them, were pure and noble. The cathedral's spires soared to heaven pointing everyone to God, (a great motive) whilst the Virgin's countenance proclaimed her pity, and the Cross pointed back to the ultimate sacrifice of Calvary. The fact is the worshipper saw these *things* and ultimately, the objects themselves, proclaimed in a visual voice "Look at what we have made." Eventually God was only a "bit part" player, no longer having a speaking part in the entire performance. God was nowhere to be seen. The *thing* could not be silenced, it was out there, but unlike the modern idol of today's tech (it had a certain sophistication) it did not need to make a noise to draw attention to itself. In his book Peter Korn quotes from Matthew Crawford's book which alerts us to our own predicament:

> The satisfaction of manifesting oneself concretely in the world through manual competence have been known to make a man quiet and easy. They seem to relieve him of the felt need to offer chattering *interpretations* of himself to vindicate his worth. He can simply point: the building stands, the car now runs, the lights are on. Boasting is what a boy does, who has no real effect in the world. But craftsmanship must reckon with the infallible judgement of reality, where one's failings or shortcomings cannot be interpreted away.[12]

Michelangelo's entire oeuvre speaks of his genius, from the Sistine Chapel to his immaculate Pietas. Brunel's engineering feats still obtain a voice, and many visitors still make the pilgrimage to Pennsylvania to view Frank Lloyd Wright's ingenious, acclaimed piece of architecture, "Fallingwater." These works still find a voice and as Matthew Crawford puts it: "this relieves them of the need to secure the chattering interpretations of themselves." The work of the above does the talking for them, they need not perpetually strain at the leash to be noticed, they have no need to boast. Later in this chapter Brunelleschi's Duomo in Florence is highlighted, which will forever recall the Florentine master. In his masterpiece, the Dome (erected without a centering) delivers Brunelleschi from the ugly manners which so many moderns now display, i.e. the need to draw attention to themselves. At the hands of these creative giants their achievements have altered our world forever, and for the better. We may add with some certainty no "Renaissance," no "David", no "Ferrari," no "Eiffel Tower." In every case the "Cathedral," the "Dome" the "bridge," the "tower," the "David," all

---

12. Korn, *Why We Make Things*, 56, quoting Crawford, *Shop Class as Soulcraft*

secure boasting for their creators. And while they themselves are able to comfortably stand back, the plaudits inevitably ring out, but what does it matter, the "thing" which brought them the deepest satisfaction beyond all the talk, stands. Michelangelo's "David" vindicates him forever.

What a stark contrast with our age of "chattering interpretations of ourselves" and our "need" of it all. Living as we do in a "service" orientated world we seem to care very little for making, interestingly, art in the school curriculum is all but marginalized as unnecessary. Having made nothing, or very little, we have nothing to boast for us, leaving only ourselves to boast about ourselves! What is more we have precious little in our technological school in the way of manual to excite our gratification, and scarce soul satisfaction, if any at all. After a day of "hard" work at the tech bench people understandably appear to be soul drained. The only manual demand levied is to press the "on/off" button. All is not well with us. Up out of this emerges the vacuum and we of necessity, being soulish, need to "get creative," in truth that is what gods are all about, surely it cannot be lost on us how filters aid our creativity. Hamstrung by the "new" "Brave New World" we are desperate, hungry to be filled with something, anything, this is why over the last fifty years the church has become so "creative" in worship. The result, the church in complacency turned to the new god, the tech which was able to sculpt us, kindly invited us to share its stage.

In the past the fresco of the saint was an extension of oneself, a greater more profound and perfect self. It is therefore not at all surprising that the Psalmist concludes those who make idols become like them (Ps 115:8). The tech being the new idol makes us in its own image, we just cannot see it. In the lockdown church complacency prevented it from grasping the fact that at heart *it* needed to be "seen," that is put in a performance of kinds, and entirely unembarrassed, as so many boasters are, it turned to that which could naturally achieve this end. But what a legacy Michelangelo has his "David" and Brunel his "Great Western Railway," Brunelleschi his "Dome," while the modern church in this unprecedented moment . . . creates "Zoom" worship. Nor should we try to find cold comfort, deluded in our desperation for satisfaction, to create something. Whilst the church obviously has no interest in carving idols out of lumps of stone or even raising impressive edifices reaching into the heavens (these take too long to construct nowadays!), nevertheless it remains we are made in God's image with a deep incurable desire to be creative. This like nothing else is able to bring up soul satisfaction, and we know it. The tragic form in which "Zoom" worship has developed will do nothing, to quote Crawford, to make us "quiet and easy." The screen, as employed by tech trades in other goods, and easily succeeds in making people anxious and agitated. What a dreadful contribution the church has made in our times, "Zoom" at every church level is an enemy to spiritual and vital cultural civilization.

Furthermore whenever we bring artifice into the worship of God, while it points inevitably to the maker, it also draws attention to itself, this is the "boasting boy!" Just like ancient idols it creates dependence, people cannot do without it. It quickly establishes itself as integral, becoming a fixture. It cannot be removed, it will not be removed, and if one tried to there would be such an almighty outcry. Idols often have either size or splendor in their favor which may be simple or embellished. In every case idols are there to steal away the hearts of the people. They are above all else to be *looked* at.

In Egypt the children of Israel would have seen remarkable feats, things sufficient to enable their own creativity to flourish when required. In that land of ingenuity they secured the necessary skills to cast the golden calf. Indeed, their tech to achieve what it did was not something which miraculously emerged out of the ether, as Aaron seems to suggest (Exodus 32:24, NIV). Instead it was a work of innovation, of art and craft, no less than a computer screen today. Both possess alluring, powerful attributes, like the Virgin, designed to draw us in and gain our devotion and admiration. It is impossible to visit York Minster or Notre Dame (before the tragic fire), or climb inside Brunelleschi's Duomo, without being inspired and moved, for myself I am affected and profoundly so, yet remarkably God is farthest from my thoughts. In fact the worship of God is not truly really engendered at all, crucially the medium stands in the way, one cannot help but be in awe of it. One is always overwhelmed, it is an imposition. If we did not know it, Brunelleschi is God in his dome, everyone quite naturally talks about *him* he never needed to be the "boasting boy" of today's worship via digital means. Brunelleschi's Masterpiece stays in one's mind, it is never erased, just like the mobile telephone or computer which has captured so many hearts today. These are undoubtedly monumental. The difference is one is outside the church the other is now inside. Since all these are substantially "larger than life," they cannot but help themselves by leaving their impression. They "steal the show" so to speak, larger than life, larger than God. Stonehenge achieves this, as does the Great Wall of China, the Pyramids and the carved heads on Easter Island. All these if we did not know it are mediums through which to travel, gaining access to another place. Stonehenge enables one to get from "here to there," the Pyramids of Giza exactly the same, the medium is the vital component. Furthermore it does not matter what the cost is to erect it. The screen in "worship" is a direct relative. Here are the masters of art, and we as creatures made in God's image are impressed with such powerful creativity. They possess the power to draw us away to themselves.

Augmenting Reality

The fact that we make art and have become masters at it testifies to our soul's need of it. Bearing all this in mind it seems rather strange that those who have invested a commitment in the technology, as a carrier of the divine message, are unable to see this for what it is. Perhaps the church has a very truncated, narrow appreciation of what it is experimenting with, since the technology is an art form, in my view a very low art form, but art nonetheless. Consider the movie, is this not an art form? What we look at on the screen are movies, they all move. "Zoom" is in the business of extending the movie, art as the screen demonstrates will not be confined, it does not stand still. We should be alert to the reality that people are intoxicated, not with a medium which is dead and frigid, but one which is suggestive and expansive (we have moved on from Stonehenge) to the present day's alluring technology as it appeals to our senses; why else do we think it is so successful? In June 2022 the BBC "Click" program (a viewer's guide to what is new in tech) reported on even newer methods of getting the message out (presumably this will also be seen as God's provision for the church). President Zelensky of Ukraine has made a case to the world's parliaments and forums for the need to support his people in their time of need, but for the most part he has been confined to his beleaguered country; that is until recently. He has appealed to the tech world to aid him in his efforts. Brent Hoberman, Executive Chairman Founders Forum, said "We need to go one step further beyond 2D and Zoom." The result … Zelensky appeared as a hologram. Hoberman explains the tech. "Transparent LED screen and volumetric capture are used, images are stitched together to create a 3D model of the President and this is viewable in augmented reality by anyone anywhere so long as they have a 'new enough' device, just by scanning a QR code." Is it too outrageous to imagine the church in the future inviting the pastor into their living rooms to watch him preaching at Sunday morning worship or at the prayer meeting and Bible study? After all if "Zoom" worship is God's provision, "hologram" worship we should expect will also wear the divine mantle! What is more, none of those who experimented with "Zoom" worship would have "a leg to stand on" if found criticising augmented reality.

An Apple a Day Keeps the Doctor Away

If the above is true, medics would have a much simpler life. How ironic the apple most people think of, is not the malus sylvestris (forest apple), but the one in our pocket! Many will have seen the queues in the High Street outside the Apple stores worldwide, which make news headlines as a new piece of kit is unveiled. There the adoring fans and "worshippers" gather to reach out to touch the re-configured neon god, the new up-to-date work of art. With it comes the absolutely necessary new magic which can outperform its predecessor, and the promise is that the ever more powerful drug can take the user to a new nirvana. Naturally the sinister side of all this no one wants to see, but Vaughan Roberts grasps the nettle in his book on transgender, he includes a Chapter titled "The I World," in which he tells us that Steve Jobs,

> had an acute understanding of the spirit of the age, which enabled him to create a brand that appealed to our culture's deepest longings. The names of his Apple products—the iMac, the iPod, the iPhone, and the iPad—are striking.

Jobs knew that we live in the iWorld, in which everything revolves around the individual.[13]

This is the inherent danger which the church seems unable to comprehend, but is inescapable, God is joined to the technology, the new art form. Gay quotes Martin Heidegger who observed so insightfully that "technology has become the metaphysic of the modern age,"[14] i.e., the first cause, the first principle. Do any of us need reminding there is only room in this civilization of God's kingdom for one "first cause?" Lest we forget, Brunelleschi and his Dome are the "first principle," God in truth is not even a "bit part" player, in the Santa Maria Del Fiore. To quote Heidegger, "Were contemporary man seriously to become aware of this character of his life and of his thinking, he might, with the modern physicist, well say: 'It seems as though man everywhere and always encounters only himself.'"[15] The profound danger of this comes out in a further quote from Helmut Thielicke:

An architect built many houses, cities and squares, but no one could learn his art or match his skill until several people persuaded him to teach them. When they had learned it they quarreled with him and set up as architects themselves at lower prices. Then the people stopped admiring the original architect and gave the commission to the apprentices. In the same way God has created you in his own image and likeness. But now that you, like him, have created marvelous things, it will be said: There is no God in the world apart from you."[16]

Re-Drawing the Map

Maps generally speaking, give us an accurate outline of the lie of the land, but while being ingenious they have also been inaccurate. It is remarkable that they have not been more so, given the instrumentation which early cartographers had at their disposal. Some older maps which may be consulted today are in fact extraordinarily reliable. However, with the aid of modern technology and particularly with GPS, the exact positioning of borders and countries is pinpoint accurate. Nevertheless, every year land masses of the earth alter, parts get swallowed up and others grow, Iceland being a case in point, its coastal form often being re-drawn by the violent volcanic activity.

So also in the church, during our lifetime we may encounter a re-drawing of the map, this has happened down through history. Naturally this has often been tectonic

13. Roberts, *Transgender*, 25.
14. Gay, *Way of the (Modern) World*, 81, quoting Heidegger, *Question Concerning Technology*, 3-35.
15. Gay, *Way of the (Modern) World*, 81, quoting Heidegger, *Question Concerning Technology*, 3-35.
16. Gay, *Way of the (Modern) World*, 79, quoting Thielicke, *Evangelical Faith*, 234.

and therefore not surprisingly the changes in shape and contour have been tumultuous. The Reformation was the greatest shift of all, but then there have been countless others which have revealed new shapes and structures, sometimes the lie of the land has looked extremely altered by a spiritual volcanic eruption. In geological changes it is possible for people living in a location to be unaware of significant alteration, and their lives proceed as normal. At other times the top of a mountain is blown off, as in the case of Mount St. Helens. Likewise in the story of the church there have been explosive changes, but also subtle ones which have re-configured the landscape of our civilization. However, many changes are so subtle the average church member never picks up on the fact that the landscape has changed around them forever, never to return to its former shape. Schleiermacher set about redrawing the map, which by now in many places is the new and accepted shape of things, few dare question it, even if they were conscious of it. History will probably show that the Charismatic Movement has re-drawn the map, but with less intellectual explosives, nevertheless it has been dynamite. If the church re-draws the map in significant ways it is more than likely people will become confused, only to add to an already confused world lost and trying to find its way. What hope is there for our civilization if the church is also lost?

We can be quite sure the idea of re-drawing a map is so that there might be greater accuracy in finding our way to our desired haven. However, the re-drawing of the spiritual map under Luther and Calvin and others, was so that "the way, the truth and the life" (John 14:6, NIV) might not be obscured. The hills and dark valleys of Rome needed to be re-configured so as to make a plain, to make a highway for the Lord (Isa 35:8, NIV). Yet even they struggled with *all* the re-drawing, not all the new lines were in quite the right place. The Puritans went on to chart what they thought were the most accurate ways (and some of us think they were the best map-makers ever). Nonetheless they made errors which have necessarily come down to us, these continue today to point in the wrong direction, but of course not intentionally. This only proves that "the best men are men at best," it seems ironic that one of the strong points of the Puritans was their keen eyesight to identify error, sorting out those things which were wrong. Sometimes the turn in the road was so altered by the church it did not so much look like a turn, but an entirely new road. At this juncture the map is being re-drawn. The lie of the spiritual landscape is going to look very different when COVID-19 releases us (as it must under God's providence), and our churches return once more to a *normal* way of life. A squatter though, something that reminds one of Orwell's "Animal Farm" characters will be well and truly ensconced and more importantly, unable to be ejected.

A Case of Mistaken Identity

If a picture of the "Queen of Heaven" had been reproduced in this book, certainly almost all Christians reading this would easily identify her as an idol, a god. This confirms we have fixed viewing points and perspectives already established. Let us imagine a Christian like myself who has collected over the years beautiful works of art, some of them artifacts, Roman Glass and the like. What if I had a Hindu sculpture on a shelf or a South American Aztec deity . . . . . . perhaps a visiting Christian friend might be uncomfortable and offended (this is always possible and great care must be taken, love being the guiding light). If a survey of evangelicals was conducted one might expect the uniform response to my collection of sculpture would be one of alarm, deeming them to be idols, little gods and certainly should be outlawed by the Christian, a value judgement would be placed on them, along with a spiritual one. It would confirm that we recognize in our mind's eye at least that which conforms to the description of an idol. Would a Christian be comfortable to walk around the British Museum or the Louvre, admiring and appreciating the great collection of objects which were carved and cast in cultures which used them to focus upon in their worship? I somehow doubt this. This experiment though is as yet untested, but my history and professional life tends to suggest this would be the answer.

What is it to "idolize?" We speak of a child, a wife, or a famous celebrity being idolized. To "idolize" is to regard with blind adoration. Adoration is to pay honor and to revere, if we revere something we respect it; we hold in awe, we venerate, we elevate it. The act of idolizing is surely one of love, devotion and need, when we "idolize," we are receiving something from the idolized object. The idol in time becomes established, and one upon which we demonstrate a dependence, it impacts us at the deepest level, so that as our minds change, so in turn our behavior also. The "Queen of Heaven" draws people back to her again and again, she becomes a fixture in lives. But the adults who found her to be a help and support, having called out to her for twenty years or so, probably introduce her benevolence to their children, and thereby encourages the same lifelong dependence. This is how idol worship becomes embedded in a culture, a civilization, and continues.

Because of our over-simplified and stylized view of the idol we are probably not able to recognize our idol dependence today. After all we have given up on carving stone gods and casting them, it has all been done before. Does this mean we have outgrown the idol and that our Christian sophistication renders us safe from the painted allure of a modern day "Queen of Heaven?" Hardly, she is now found in the pocket, on the wrist, and virtually in every home, magically trading in images at the touch of a button. She is dominant, everyone needs her and looks to her and has a growing dependence on her, (this by the way is not the TV). She is undoubtedly worshipped and holds sway over all the world. Dr. Susan Greenfield remarks:

> But we now know that TV was a technological molehill when compared to the heady scientific heights of this third millennium. The convincing and attractive cyber world has played havoc with our sense of space and time.

Traditional real relationships in real time are atrophied. And the family unit as it used to be, even in its most liberal form, slowly vanished . . .[17]

NB: How many Christians have been anti-TV yet are now pro-screen as it serves up its utilitarian wares?

Dr. Susan Greenfield expresses concern for us all:

digital technology has the potential to become the end rather than the means: a lifestyle all on its own. A car gets you from place to place; a fridge keeps your food fresh; a book can help you learn about the real world and the people in it. For the first time ever, life in front of a computer screen is threatening to out-compete real life.[18]

In view of this, what might the ramifications be for the church? Greenfield asks: "to what extent, screen technologies could be transformational."[19] The new idol is the computer screen with you in it. We are aided and abetted by the technology to exhibit ourselves, which is what everyone is practicing, and Christians are no exception. Today it is a sad fact, everyone wants to be noticed, a preoccupation with self. Who cares what the "Queen of Heaven" looks like when the world can see me! Here is the cheapest idolatry. The need to fabricate well-knownness, is as much as anything the idolatry, the church may have pursued a life where it tried to free itself of art, instead it has bought into the most ephemeral of experiences. Christopher Dawson has said,

We have entered on a new phase of culture—we may call it the Age of the Cinema—in which the most amazing perfection of scientific technique is being devoted to purely ephemeral objects, without any consideration of their ultimate justification. It seems as though the new society was arising which will acknowledge no hierarchy of values, no intellectual authority, and no social or religious tradition, but which will live for the moment in the chaos of pure sensation.[20]

Mumford tells us,

The most powerful prince of the seventeenth century created a vast hall of mirrors, and the mirror spread from one room to another in the bourgeois household. Self-consciousness, introspection, mirror conversation developed with the new object itself.

This is a terribly painful truth to set before the church. The truth, once embraced and legitimized, the real object of our worship is skewed, the chaos of pure sensation will live for the moment as the idol works its creative magic.

17. Greenfield, *Tomorrow's People*, 41.
18. Greenfield, *Mind Change*, 17.
19. Greenfield, *Mind Change*, 48.
20. Gay, *Way of the (Modern) World*, 181, quoting Dawson, *Progress and Religion*, 228.

Tony Reinke says: "The object of our worship is the object of our *imitation* . . . What we want to become, we worship."[21] Art is in the church this time not as a fresco, not as a statue, but in the form of technology, specifically the screen, and we are not just the compliant actors, but tragically, like the world auditioning for the lead role. This introduction of the computer screen is a momentous retrograde step because it is the number one idol in the world. The people in the "Zoom" worship must, by virtue of the medium, be to some extent performers, the screen demands it. If we did not know it, the mirror has had a most profound effect upon the development of our personalities. Mumford says: "it helped to alter the very concept of the self."[22] The mirror, the screen, focuses upon ourselves, with great insight Mumford says: "When one is completely whole and at one with the world one does not need the mirror: It is in the period of psychic disintegration that the individual personality turns to the lonely image to see what in fact is there and what he can hold on to."[23] This new idol in the church is perfect for an age of disintegration. In an age of sight over faith, an age of loneliness and uncertainty, it is perfect for this age where everyone, for a moment, can come to the fore, shine and be seen. To quote Andy Warhol "In the future, everyone will be world-famous for 15 minutes." The disintegration however, tragically provides for the most unhealthy introspection. In contrast the gospel points away from self to another, speaking peace, whereas the new technology only points up oneself and adds the deadly poison of stress and anxiety. Everywhere in our day we see the clear evidence, we are mentally in trouble. In truth it would be very interesting to know how many who come to a "Zoom" worship are terribly conscious of their appearance for the sake of the camera, introducing stress to the "worship." The camera alters behavior, just like the idol, the "Queen of Heaven" demanding a "different attitude and posture," a look, an approach, you cannot just be yourself. She may elicit the emotion of grief and sadness, when otherwise it might not have been forthcoming. This is false, yet this is what the idol produces in us, the camera, the medium of screen does the same, the technology has power on an entirely different level. This has the power to draw up out of us the most vacuous of responses, perhaps not unlike the marketable "virtue signaling," which is now "all the rage." Here is what the church has gladly and willingly submitted itself to; the young people especially will have received an open door to the "acceptable world in the church," which even twenty years ago the very thought, would have been dismissed and laughed out of the pulpit.

"Technological change is thus not simply addictive to or subtractive from a given culture; rather, it is *ecological*."[24] Craig Gay takes this a step further:

21. Reinke, *12 Ways*, 113.

22. Mumford, *Technics and Civilization*, 128.

23. Mumford, *Technics and Civilization*, 129.

24. Gay, *Way of the (Modern) World*, 87-88, quoting Postman, *Technopoly*, 18

It changes the culture altogether. Modern technology has altered the structure of our interests and the things we think about. It has altered the character of our symbols and the things we think with. And it has altered the nature of community and the arena in which our thoughts develop.[25]

The result, to continue his thoughts will be: "an overemphasis of human agency at God's expense."[26] Brunelleschi confirms this.

When the Catholic Church thought about the great idea of installing "The Queen of Heaven" in the "Basilica of our Lovely Lady" in Maastricht, they could not have known how long her service and influence would last, no doubt she has repaid its faith in her a million fold. Thankfully however, her influence there has been limited to that place albeit over the last several hundred years, whereas the screen entering our churches makes her look like a rank amateur. The intruder into our worship is an "image maker" par excellence, nothing before has ever come near to match its power and hold upon us through the guise of modern technology. Nothing to my mind is more dangerous to our civilization. "You shall not make for *yourself*" (Exod 20:4, NIV).

25. Gay, *Way of the (Modern) World*, 88, quoting Postman, *Technopoly*, 20.
26. Gay, *Way of the (Modern) World*, 88.

CHAPTER 4

THE MAGIC SHOW

"Any sufficiently advanced technology is indistinguishable from magic."
ARTHUR C CLARKE

"Large numbers of those who had practiced magic collected their books and burned them up in the presence of everyone. When the value of the books was added up, it was found to total fifty thousand silver coins. In this way the word of the Lord continued to grow in power and to prevail."
ACTS 19:19-20 (NET)

The Magic Show

MAGIC IS A MOST IMPRESSIVE spectacle, none of us have watched David Blaine perform without being astonished; although amazingly, magic in the modern world of reason still attracts us. Magic is very old, very old indeed and yet remains extremely tantalizing. In fact magic as a form of entertainment like so many amusements is an escape, it translates us to another place of possibilities. Could it be thought by the reader that I am an anti-modernist because of what is postulated in these pages, even an escapist? That would be understandable, but nothing could be further from the truth, I have always been interested in modernity, the contemporary (i.e. the now). In my field of expertise I am known as a contemporary artist, exploring contemporary themes and certainly not to be associated with the pastiche. Historically in creative expression art that made a difference was of its time. The greats of art may have stood on the shoulders of the giants of the past, but their feet were firmly planted in their present world. I am not a luddite but I do admire them, knowing their courage to question "modern magic" will always be needed. Let us not stone them too hastily! I truly believe there ought to be at least a percentage of luddite in us all, guaranteeing a certain balance as we confront our age.

When the Spinning Jenny was put through its paces, it is easy to imagine people were "blown away"—here was a new kind of magic. The cotton gin must have had the same effect as did the first electricity bulb, and even the airplane defying gravity. It is hard for us to enter that world and understand how people must have felt, maybe the way we feel when we now see a driverless car, with robots building them.

In the world of illusion there exists an extraordinary power to amaze, the sleight of hand is used by the magician, coupled with psychological skill to manipulate the paying customer. Success depends on all the parts or pieces coming together at just the right time, timing is everything. The goal of the magic act is to perform a successful trick, while attempting to astonish the one who observes and participates, thereby becoming an enthralled believer. The magic usually has to reveal something "out of this world," something beyond the ordinary—sawing someone in half is impressive, as is bringing a bird out of a hat. The point being when we see it, it is hard not to smile, it is hard not to join in, being almost obligatory to applaud with appreciation. We remain the uninitiated as to how the trick/illusion is done, yet it is successfully performed before our very eyes. How could anyone think of such a performance except in a positive light? We are willfully credulous in the hands of the magician. What is more, whoever witnessed anyone "sawn in half," or made to "disappear," which ever resulted in anything but a happy ending? We would probably think someone extremely dull and churlish who could not put their hands together after such an impressive magic performance.

Gamekeepers turned Poachers

I expect it is possible for an astronaut to be on a mission and encounter the unexpected, which might take them by surprise and scare the life out of them. On the 15th of February 2021, *The Social Dilemma*,[1] a documentary by Netflix, was brought to my attention. The program of one hour and thirty minutes, contains searching material, there are no "stars" to entertain only a collection of brains displaying qualifications to the highest degree, whose employment has been in the tech industries. These "brains" were in part responsible for building the systems which everyone is using, relying on today. One contributor, Jaron Lanier, was named one of the one hundred most influential people in the world by *Time*, one of the one hundred top public intellectuals by *Foreign* Policy, and one of the top fifty world thinkers by *Prospect*. In other words he knows his stuff! After listening to these experts, it is impossible not to think with compassion of how the world at large and Christ's church are self-harming. These experts make no claim to be Christians, but Christian or not, after listening to them one is left with the overwhelming impression, they care, they care deeply. For our sakes all these people risking much, seem to be running towards us at breakneck speed,

1. Harris, *Social Dilemma*, Netflix documentary.

waving their arms and flags to get our attention, whilst shouting at us at the top of their voices. They appear without exception to be impassioned about their message and the need for us all to listen up and to take them seriously. But as it is, they appear to be running past the church which is heading in the opposite direction, with fingers in its ears, unwilling to listen to these people who know the dangers which tech can exert, the technology which is ruling our lives, and in their estimation is at work in destroying us. Their message is that the "magic show" (an expression they use) which they produced, is not just pretending to "saw" people in half, metaphorically it is. This is not a performance, this is not entertainment, this is for real. They tell us, in a kind of revelatory way if we had not noticed: "There are only two industries that call their customers 'users:' illegal drugs and software."[2] Tristan Harris, who is the main spokesman in the documentary was former Design Ethicist at Google and Cofounder for the Centre for Humane Technology. He poses the question: What is wrong? "It feels like the world is going crazy. Is this normal or have we all fallen under some kind of *spell*?"[3] Here is the magic! Harris's keen analysis reminds us of a well-known film: "Who's going to know what life was like before the illusion? How do you wake up from the Matrix if you don't know you are in the Matrix?"[4] While he acknowledges that we cannot put the genie back in the bottle, nevertheless there is hope, it is Lanier who encourages all of us to evaluate matters, as he says: "the critics are the true optimists."[5]

Criticizing All Addictions

It may feel uncomfortable to be confronted with the proposition that the world at large is addicted to a stimulant which is neither drunk, smoked nor administered intravenously, but a drugged society is what we are nonetheless. One can go into any restaurant, coffee shop, hospital waiting room, walk down any street, and there we will find conclusive evidence, the opium of the people is now something other than that which Marx observed, rather a new opioid is ubiquitous, providing "highs" for the masses. Religion is alive and well!

Dr. Susan Greenfield presents her research which churches and individual Christians would be wise to consider. Her research leads her to think:

> When you are highly excited, aroused or feel rewarded, or indeed if you are taking drugs, this same single transmitter will somehow play a key part in delivering these different subjective experiences. In all these cases, dopamine plays a pivotal role by being released like a fountain . . .[6]

2. Harris, *Social Dilemma*, Netflix Documentary.
3. Harris, *Social Dilemma*, Netflix Documentary.
4. Harris, *Social Dilemma*, Netflix Documentary.
5. Lanier, *Social Dilemma*, Netflix Documentary.
6. Greenfield, *Mind Change*, 92.

Elsewhere speaking of dopamine's function she says: "the transmitter dopamine is linked to many different brain processes, such as arousal, addiction, reward and initiation of movement."[7] Let us suppose in this inquiry we are locked up to the means of observation alone, therefore we cannot but conclude we all, including Christians, belong to an age addicted to addiction. The dopamine rush which works on gamblers and gamers alike, is undoubtedly at work in those addicted to their tech. The screen is by now almost impossible to turn down. Hence, the immediate take up with "Zoom" was almost certainly, in part, the "hit" of a new but different "high" from that ordinarily experienced. Put quite simply, the church had no power to resist the new drug!

In Ephesus Paul was willing to be God's appointed critic, who enabled the people devoted to their magic, to recognize it for what it was and to abandon it. His gospel brought them to their senses but did not leave them in their former condition, rather it wrought conversion bringing a change of mind and heart. However, this "magic" of the digital age which the church has bought into and joined to the worship, is on another scale altogether. Although Messrs Harris and Lanier, the brave detractors, have helped us to see clearly, the drug, the magic, the spell, the illusion, which is by now so ingrained, mitigates. Overwhelmed by the dopamine rush we are unable to free ourselves, we have become what Paul said he would never be, "mastered by anything" (1 Cor 6:12, NIV). Paul said: "I subdue my body and make it my slave" (1 Cor 9:27, NET). Seneca, the Roman satirist and philosopher might have said "Be harsh with yourself at times."

Perhaps we might listen to Shakespeare, he saw this Ephesian world of magic as he sums up the reputation of that place, and voices it in his Comedy of Errors:

> They say this town is full of cozenage: (to cheat, to defraud, to
> persuade, to act deceitfully)
> As nimble jugglers that deceive the eye,
> Dark-working sorcerers that change the mind,
> Soul-killing witches that deform the body,
> Disguised cheaters, prating mountebanks,—(Swindlers, a charlatan,
> a clown, one who appeals to an audience from a platform, a quack)
> And many such-like liberties of sin:[8]

Shakespeare's words of four hundred and thirty years ago articulate the sentiments of the experts who today are so outspoken in this documentary. The "magic" of Ephesus was in the people root and branch, it was an industry, and as a consequence everyone had so much to lose. All the experts agree that the danger of the power of tech is that it cannot be overthrown because of monetization. In Ephesus the value of the scrolls (the books) was (NLT) "several million dollars"! Wonderfully the gospel, which is the "power of God," broke through. The question must be, will it break

7. Greenfield, *Mind Change*, 53.
8. Shakespeare, *Comedy of Errors*, Act 1, Scene 2, lines 97-102.

through with us today? Can we be liberated or are we in too deep, has the screen/tech the mastery over us?

Having journeyed down this rabbit hole, the church has subjected the worship of God to tech, creating for itself a kind of "social platform" (Chapter 11), thereby optimizing embroidered worship, with all its destructive consequences, to which naturally the church will adapt. "Zoom" has beguiled Christians to bow before their screens; screens which Harris believes tech has fashioned to keep us pre-occupied (page 109). The result, quasi-worship, into which Harris's world has surreptitiously lured the church, is able, as the New Testament warns, to potentially "make merchandise of us" (2 Pet 2:3, KJV). Returning to the documentary, is this so far removed from what one Harvard professor observes about our new digital masters? We become a resource like "pork bellies" or "human futures." Harris, ominously, proposes this could be "checkmate." The magician in us though, with "sleight of hand," might attempt to disconnect what is done on established social media platforms, from that now practiced by churches, as if these are entirely unrelated. In reality, tech knows no boundaries. If, as Dr. Lembke writes: "The smartphone is the modern-day hypodermic needle," it is hard to resist the thought that other expressions of tech's derivatives will forgo the opportunity to extend their own far-reaching, influential abuses, not least, excessive over-consumption ... recalling the cotton gin and Spinning Jenny! Nor will New Year's resolutions work their magic, a digital diet, in and out of the church, looks all but impossible. Harris observes, "The technology's ability to bring out the worst in society and the worst in society being the existential threat itself." (He expresses his concern about what has been created): "the loneliness, outrage, alienation, populism, distraction, inability to focus on real issues," resulting in society's inability to heal itself.

While "Zoom" may not enjoy a direct "blood-line" with the nefarious heads of the digital family, nevertheless, it has the capacity, over time, to lead an ecclesiastical race to the bottom. We should be in no doubt, tech will find a way, especially considering "what we have permitted we have promoted." What next? Will augmented-reality worship extend "Zoom's" pioneering work? Indeed society is incapable of healing itself, yet the church has become spellbound, joining hands with a world which, on average spends four hours each day on screens, glued to the "tinted message." Furthermore, what an embarrassment, churches historically persecuting, waging war even on TV, theatre, the ballet, Shakespeare, alcohol, cinema, the arts in general, yet now engaging with a medium used in worship, with the capacity to be an existential threat to our spiritual civilization!

Tristan Harris, the main spokesperson in the documentary, is an ethicist who cares. It is tempting to ask whether Christian ethics have anything to say to us, when the exalted God of Heaven is associated with such unshakeable and chilling darkness? Association conveys the ideas of connection of ideas or a common purpose. When Lance Armstrong, the American former professional road racing cyclist, was discovered to be a drug user enhancing his capabilities of winning, many of his sponsors dropped him like a stone, they could not afford to mention him in the same breath. The "Prince of the Cycle" was now the pauper. The "star" of the podium which had been, was now relegated, no matter his achievements, all was now sullied and tarnished. The game was up for this apparent elite cyclist, Armstrong was automatically banned, effectively ending his career. Similarly Kate Moss, the model was exposed for drug use in 2005 by a British tabloid newspaper. Even her "bad girl" image which might have served its purposes could not save her sponsorship deals with major companies. A low-grade association is not to the liking of big business, they know, like no one else, that "mud sticks."

Is God somehow paying into Zoom? Is God being harvested and mined? Is God making money for a major tech company? Is God a commodity like all the rest? More than anything, the speed of this move has been one of the most extraordinary sights (as discussed in Chapter 11). The irony is the church which stood for years against the world's form of worship by employing the "second rate" pop-group at the front, is now in front of cameras and computer screens. For years performers who were recognized as pandering to the flesh were kept out, but now all the church members can be performers in front of the screen, what is more, it can be justified. Magic indeed! Here is the sleight of hand, here is the trick, it is the screen in its most alluring form, in its provocative dress of beguilement, it is not the TV, it is the mirror, this is deep satisfaction, this is probably sacrilegious narcissism, this is Andy Warhol's "fifteen minutes of fame." A generation like none other who yearn to be noticed can now find that pseudo-fame in the church, what is more it is safely concealed under the guise of Christian worship. Of course the transition was easy as it was natural, the people dominated by the screen in their pockets would find a way to join this most "useful tool" to the service of our divine civilization! What prevented them from seeing this "useful tool" as the idol? Perhaps the answer lies in the tech to which people are addicted. Michael Harris in his book says: "We're led into deep intimacies with our gadgets precisely because our brains are imbued with a compulsion to socialize."[9] The deep and obvious danger to most Christians experimenting with "screen" worship is that it may be only an extension of all other screen social networking/contact. What do we think the Jehovah's Witnesses, Roman Catholics, Islam and others are doing on "Zoom," are they worshipping? No, a social need above all else is being met. Even when the church meets, when it actually "comes together" fulfilling Scripture (1 Cor 14:26, NIV) people always need to be reminded of the chief reason for gathering, i.e.: not for one another, but above all else, for God himself.

9. Harris, *End of Absence*, 54.

Queen Versus Screen

Hard as it must be for Christians to read these words, yet it should stand to reason that the tech and the screen, functioning no longer as a visitor, no mere "tool" but a fixture running through the bloodstream of our lives, like any drug it incapacitates us, rendering us out of our minds. The tech, as our experts tell us is a drug, also seconded by Dr. Greenfield.

The drug blurs our vision and can be demonstrated in the following instance: Ask a Christian to give their opinion and estimation of the Queen of Heaven in the Basilica in Maastricht. Ask if she is in fact an idol, and with little difficulty most of them will confirm this. Why? Obviously because she looks like one and equally obviously she is instantly perceived as being religious. Unfortunately this very simplistic and unsatisfactory answer is what might be expected from the majority within the church, as suggested earlier (in chapter 3) if we presented in this book a visual of a smartphone next to the Queen of Heaven, posing the question: "Which of the two is an idol?" . . . the outcome could be easily predicted. I am given to understand comparison websites are popular today. So why not compare these two, the screen and queen? Perhaps then we can arrive at a near definitive answer to the question, this way we will not suffer from any sleight of hand nor be hoodwinked.

Consider the facts: the Queen of Heaven has longevity, her origin goes all the way back to the Bible (Jer 44:17-25, NIV). Her history is a dark one powerfully influencing the lives of countless people, successfully blocking out the light of God. In Maastricht admittedly she is both peripheral and parochial, and for the most part unknown. Probably her devoted followers are no more than a few thousand each year. To be sure she has influence over coin, but in that parochial setting it must be limited. In terms of influence, power and prestige, she is really a non-starter.

Having revealed this much, we can be certain the Evangelical church above all the others can recognize her for what she is an out and out idol. How then does she compare with the screen as it is used to access modern technology? Although the screen is a "late comer" to the masses who seek something to worship, nevertheless since Logie Baird and Philo Farnsworth introduced it, the world has been taken by storm. The screen dominates and whilst Christians can be heard defending its commercial benefit, in truth we all know of its power which lies far beyond the commercial. Neil Postman was not familiar with screens as we are today, he confined his reference mainly to television, he is very observant when he says, "To put it plainly, television is the command center of the new epistemology. There is no audience so young that it is barred from television. There is no poverty so abject that it must forgo television."[10] We do not need a great deal of imagination to know what his take would be with our love affair with screens today. This of course is what most Christians find difficult to admit. In the world where people have no running water there we find the

10. Postman, *Amusing Ourselves to Death*, 79.

smartphone, the computer screen. In homes in the UK where nutrition is found wanting and heating is in short supply, nevertheless there is the smartphone, sometimes more than one. It seems no sacrifice is too great for people to ensure their "fix." The screen rules. In popularity stakes nothing can match it, its influence in our lives is absolute. We depend on it, we are devoted to it, we pay for it, we love it. Its popularity beats sport and music, and is the undisputed master of our age, calling all the shots. The concern must be that its master stroke, like the Queen of Heaven, has convinced us of its benignity, and of course being only a force for good. She holds up her hands so to speak in innocence, like the magician she has no cards up her sleeve. However, her sleight of hand is so deft her deep magic convinces us that she only has our best interests at heart. How could you not fall for her? Anything sinister is eliminated. Tristan Harris, though is not hoodwinked, giving evidence to congress in the USA, he describes the tech as Frankenstein's monster. With real humility he recognizes the danger this monster poses to us all, so he should, he was Dr. Frankenstein!

When is a "Tool" Not a "Tool?"

Tony Reinke very helpfully and honestly shares with us just what power the screen/tech has in his life. He says his phone even accompanies him to the bathroom. What honesty, but do we realize how Christians are under the same powerful drug which the world is injecting? People are blithely unaware that the tech is dominating them. There is hope for Reinke yet, because to his great credit, and confirming the thought of Francis Bacon, he goes on to say: "Self doubt is a hallmark of wise creatures. And self critical conversations about our personal behaviors require a big dose of humility."[11] "God resists the proud but gives grace to the humble" (Jas 4:6, NIV). In addition Reinke says he has a big question, which is in fact my own: What effect is the technology having on our spiritual lives? So far in our comparison website the screen is looking for all the world to be the equal of the Queen, there is not a hair's breadth between them. If we were to subject them to an identity parade for their fame, they would both easily be singled out from the rest. They are both idols.

When is a Bicycle Not a Bicycle?

John Piper, writing in the foreword to Tony Reinke's excellent book, appears to think otherwise, he attributes to tech the same capabilities of any *other* "tool." The magic has been administered. He sees no real distinction between that of papyrus, the codex, paper and the printing press the organ of mass distribution, and that of modern day tech, which the entire world is now dependent upon. In this he is not alone, both in the church and the world at large the sum of these thoughts are shared. But to speak

---

11. Reinke, *12 Ways*, 24.

kindly this is vastly over simplified and even naively misleading. It is not surprising therefore to hear the mantra "trotted out" that "modern tech is just another form of Gutenberg's press." In fact what Piper and others are indulging in is what McLuhan described in his 1967 book *The Medium Is the Massage: An Inventory of Effects*, actually it is what we all tend to indulge in. "We look at the present through a rear view mirror, we march backwards into the future."[12] The result of which is the comforting attachment to a framework from the past, which will provide justification for and explain our present actions.

Perhaps it would be helpful to point out that Gutenberg's press, paper and print in *themselves* never engendered idol worship: no one ever genuflected before these: no one ever lived their lives for them . . . Gutenberg excepted! The reason . . . they were just "tools!" This is the glaring weakness of our current appraisal of what we have created, we possess few powers to appreciate what the tech is and what it is not. As a god it flatly refuses to be used as a mere "tool" because it itself is always striving for first place, the algorithms demand it. Frances Haugen, whistle blower at Facebook, has made this perfectly clear. The screen is not like the Spinning Jenny, nor the cotton gin, they distinctly lack the power to entertain. Could they ever be described in the way Michael Harris describes tech as "manic digital distractions we've grown addicted to?"[13] If we did not know it tech comprises an ethic all of its own. The heart of the problem is when we try to compare like with like, but these are apples and oranges, they are not alike in any way. What is more, looking in the rear view mirror for too long will inevitably result in a crash, possibly a fatal one! Tristan Harris has the measure of all this when he takes up this proposition and he compares modern tech with a bicycle . . . as if they could ever be compared! He asks the question, "Did the bicycle help in the overthrow of any society? Was it ruining the world?"[14] He observes the bicycle was always waiting to be used but never crying out for your devotion.

Another spokesperson from the documentary describes the tech as a "religion." In his book Craig M. Gay addresses this and recognizes that,

> modern technology (the screen presents, emphasis mine) . . . the possibility of a certain kind of relation to the world. Such a relation may be loosely termed "religious" both because it is commonly expressed in religious terms and, more importantly, because it recognizes—often in nature the existence of an Intelligence and Will superior to and encompassing the human will . . . We have, in effect, become religiously tone-deaf.[15]

The reason why the screen is in the church and trying so kindly to "help us out" with our "worship," employing its magic, is because we are religiously tone deaf. The

---

12. McLuhan, *Medium is the Massage*, 75.

13. Harris, *End of Absence*, 133.

14. Harris, *Social Dilemma*, Netflix documentary.

15. Gay, *Way of the (Modern) World*, 94.

mechanical idol entering the sanctuary of God's stainless holiness is not recognized, and the corporation running "Zoom" (for profit at all costs) knows our attention can be mined. We are profitable when at prayer and when transfixed, mesmerized by the screen, when we use it for so-called worship. Harris in a lecture says,

> We are all looking out for the moment when technology would overwhelm human strength and intelligence. When is it going to cross the singularity, replace our jobs, and be smarter than humans? But there is this much earlier moment … when technology exceeds and overwhelms human weaknesses. This point being crossed is at the root of addiction, polarization, radicalization, out-ragification, vaniti-fication, the entire thing. This is overpowering human nature, and this is "checkmate" on humanity.[16]

Does tech look like an idol now? Does this look like any other tool? Is this really to be equated with papyrus and the printing press?

Those familiar with the film *Oceans 13* will recall Al Pacino almost faints in a moment of sheer ecstasy as he receives the gift of a special Samsung phone, which he strokes with near sensuous satisfaction. The film makers must have understood this to be a universal or else they would never have employed it. Worldwide, everyone would be able to make sense of Al Pacino's genuflection, everyone gets it, everyone it seems, except the church. It is very doubtful that anyone ever stroked a model of Gutenberg's press which they carried around with them, fawned over, and loved like life itself.

The Anthropocentric Spirit

It is inevitable that in the act of creating we necessarily draw attention both to the object which we make and to ourselves. God's creation does just this, it wonderfully draws us to itself, which in turn should open our eyes to the one who is the Creator, so that we can glorify him. The judgment: "Our thoughts became futile and our hearts senseless" (Rom 1:21-22, NET). The Creator is relegated. It is bewildering to read these words and think that we could be so blind, when faced with the obvious, yet it is just here that Christians are able to trace the power of sin, and specifically the power of sin in their own lives. It is senseless, yet we tend to love the "created" rather than the Creator, except when it comes to our own inventiveness, i.e. our own acts *ex nihilo*. This is how magic of any kind is able to keep us transfixed.

Unquestionably when we look at Brunelleschi's Duomo we are quite rightly mesmerized, after all it is a mighty act of creation. It has power like the Grand Canyon to draw us to itself, but equally to the great man himself. His masterpiece of art, architecture and engineering places him (and some would argue, "Why not?") at the center. Fleming is at the center when we think of penicillin and Gutenberg with his printing

---

16. Harris, *Social Dilemma*, Netflix documentary.

press, none of these are "shrinking violets." The thing created and the creator will not be separated, they both possess without actually speaking, a booming voice.

By virtue of his creation Brunelleschi is pointed up, he is focused on, he is talked about, in truth he will never be forgotten. Any visitor to Florence quickly finds out his work of "magic" always draws the crowds to the Santa Maria del Fiore, many only being satisfied when they climb to the pinnacle of the cathedral. The Duomo dominates the Florentine skyline, nothing can match it, nor compete with it, dwarfing all other would-be competitors, it is crying out to be seen, to be noticed. The Duomo towers above and presents itself as the number one attraction, in its wake, there appears to be no alternative.

One need only stand in front of the great Renaissance edifice and the lure to enter in and drink deeper of the "magic" is overwhelming, resistance is almost impossible. However, we need to go beyond the tourist visiting this magnificent place and observe the one who enters as a "worshipper." Once inside, Brunelleschi's medium is in total control. It motivates the content of any worship, after all it was designed to this end and that being so, it does it with aplomb. If that were not the case, it would be a failure. The medium which embraces the worshipper and which in turn is embraced, draws out the visceral response. The worshipper is now manipulated, the power of the medium is irresistible, its efficacious magic makes the supplicant putty in Brunelleschi's hands. This is the ultimate card trick. Here is a kind of "magic" by which the worshippers are now beguiled, as they gaze up into the great expanse (heavenwards of course). Any keen observer can note that the Duomo is not the servant but the undisputed master, no mere "tool" but an audacious brazen power house, magically dominant like the goddess Artemis in Ephesus. Naturally, Brunelleschi by virtue of his medium and his deep magic emerges as God, and by comparison the other God, the only true God is but a vague apparition. Here is the age old anthropocentric spirit aided and abetted by deep magic. Our human experience, our values like cream always rising to the top, we cannot help but lick our lips at the means which encourages and ultimately secures this anthropocentric goal. The tech works in us the same magic as does Brunelleschi's masterpiece though the difference is obvious, the Renaissance man is "one man and his dome," whilst now it is "everyone on their phone." Screen magic can place us at the center to which we willingly acquiesce and which "suits us down to the ground." Everyone wants to be Brunelleschi! Everyone can now perform their own magic act!

So deep and jealous is the "magic," it hides from view any other alternative to itself. When "screen" worshippers could see no other possibility to that of "Zoom," the tech was like the dome above the skyline in Florence, where everything else is dwarfed, nothing else in propositional terms can compete with it. Neil Postman makes this observation:

> Technopoly eliminates alternatives to itself in precisely the way Aldous Huxley outlined in *Brave New World*. It does not make them illegal. It does not make them immoral. It does not even make them unpopular. It makes them

invisible and therefore irrelevant. And it does so by redefining what we mean by religion, by art, by family, by politics, by history, by truth, by privacy, by intelligence, so that our definitions fit its new requirements. Technopoly, in other words, is totalitarian technocracy.[17]

The magic of tech has "pulled the wool over our eyes" hiding the fact that it is a totalitarian one. Now everyone *must* applaud, everyone *must* get the trick and appreciate it, everyone is obliged to become a believer, everyone should join in with "Zoom" worship. These are its obligations and this is why almost all Christians and churches had their definitions and practice of worship "shoehorned" into the new requirements. Totalitarian technocracy rules!

When Brunelleschi's Dome appeared it made all other landmarks invisible and understandably somewhat irrelevant. When the tech "proposed" worship appeared, the "traditional" was magically, at least in the mind, made to disappear through the magician's "puff of smoke," out of sight, out of mind.

However, what was very much in our sight was the mirror image. When the mirror first appeared it put us at the center, it was the ultimate anthropocentric tool. The mirror possesses the power to keep us transfixed with "yours truly," just like the unsettled wicked queen in "Snow White" who needed confirmation as to "Who is the fairest of them all?" This act of vanity which the mirror affords, is, as Mumford observes that which helps "to alter the very concept of the self . . . when one is completely whole and at one with the world, one does not need the mirror."[18] But "smoke and mirrors" are the foundation stones of illusion, they have always worked, and still do today. In the process of inviting us to become one with it, the tech idol has made it difficult for us to decide which should be loved more, worshipped and venerated, the object itself used in the performance, or the one who "stars" in it; the rabbit which emerges from the hat or the one who draws it out.

Screen or Queen, the answer is clear to any unbiased eye. The Queen of Heaven and her "relatives" around the world are renowned for their occasional displays of extraordinary magic, capturing hearts and minds; a crying Virgin still possesses credence and devotees. Thankfully the majority of people can see through these baseless claims. The apostle Paul knew where these nefarious tricks had their origin, he knew where the one who walked in the shadows was able to be "transformed into an angel of light" (2 Cor 11:14, KJV). However, in a much more powerful way the new world idol is able to advertise its astonishing wares which emerge just as breathtaking, and that not occasionally, but every minute of every day. The Queen might only attract a visit once a week, confirming her powers are quite insignificant next to the "screen" god. Consequently people drink deeper and deeper at the well of its trickery, ensuring that partakers remain not just admirers, but worryingly, they become dependents. The least which should be expected of all Christians is to look at themselves in the light of

17. Postman, *Technopoly*, 48.
18. Mumford, *Technics & Civilization*, 128-129.

these things, i.e.: in the mirror of God's word and ask, "Is this happening to us?" and if so, "How could we have allowed it? How can we allow this to go unchallenged?" While ever some Christians are free of the "spell," unimpressed by the magic show (though by nature no less credulous) it behoves these Christians to speak out in the hope that some might see the need to dispose of their magic books for worship, no matter the cost, recalling the combustibles at Ephesus, several million dollars in today's money.

Rubicon

When Julius Caesar made history in his military campaign of 49 BC he did more than just cross the Rubicon River to start a war with Pompey, he left forever this idea of a boundary once crossed being an irreversible commitment to something. There was no turning back. History must be littered with many such decisions, some inconsequential, while others have been life changing, even epoch making. Hitler's decision to take back the Sudetenland was just such a Rubicon, it was his first step to change the world, there is always a first step. Tragically World War II followed, ushering in five years of unspeakable misery, heartache and death. Europe was devastated and Hitler's disease was exported around the world, where his influence still lives on. Many on the German side of that conflict spent all their lives with the deepest regret and sadness. Eastern Germany emerged as a result and the painful annexation of Berlin resulted, lasting for nearly thirty years subjecting the people to the most tyrannical Soviet rule. To see the wall exhibition in Berlin takes a day, but what a lesson in life! Crossing established borders as Strate also observes, has to be profoundly considered with a thoughtful estimation of the consequences weighing heavily upon us, bearing in mind just because we can do something does not necessarily mean we should.

Inevitably culture has the habit of colliding with nature. Provide a violin or piano for a child, and certainly in the early days before meagre proficiency is found, ears suffer. Paper is invented, it collides with nature, the printing press likewise, the tech/screen no less so. The problem is that nature, when once removed, means we inevitably lose something forever. The car when first invented exposed the driver to the elements, eventually this must have been a great inconvenience. Therefore the "enclosed" model emerged, but then on a beautiful spring day the experience of the wind in one's face and hair, was lost, the power and experience of nature was gone. Something was gained, something was lost. The same must be said of technology and especially its infringement upon the worship of God. In "Zoom" worship everyone is seen by everyone but the "worship" is processed like any product, it is "machine made," the alien medium imposing itself. People inevitably have to pray and sing toward the object which is making the connections, and if it is argued that they are not, then we might ask what is the screen doing? The disconnect here, for many people, is they dangerously see this tech in the church worship as merely a "tool." Tristan Harris provides the answer:

If something is a "tool" it normally, genuinely is just sitting there, waiting patiently to be used. If something is not a "tool", it is demanding things from you. It's seducing you. It's manipulating you. It wants things from you. And we've moved away from having a "tools-based" technology environment to an addiction—and manipulation—based technology environment. That's what's changed.[19]

Something fundamental has changed us, all of us. Harris says "Social media isn't a tool just waiting to be used, it has its own goals and it has its own means of pursuing them by using your psychology against you."[20] Could it be that our conversation with nature, i.e., with God himself, may be broken forever or interfered with, skewing our lifelong perspective? Not only this, if I am not mistaken I think Harris and his colleagues would say to the "Zoom worshipper" in our churches: "if you are not paying for the product, (it is because) you are the product." By virtue of the use of this "tool" it looks like worship has become a product.

Have we lost our godly jealousy? Have we crossed the line? Our *natural* conversation with God in every way must never be broken, because how will it be reopened? Weld a roof on an open-top car, now the wind in your face is gone for all time. Craig M. Gay in his book suggests "the conversation might be cut off," the line having been crossed. This is just what we say when reprimanding an unruly child, "you have crossed the line," the boundaries have been breached. In this we convey the deep seriousness of what has taken place by this experiment.

In "Letters from Lake Como," Romano Guardini paints a compelling picture to help us . . .

> Go even further (from nature) and the sailing vessel becomes a steamer, a great ocean liner—culture indeed, a brilliant technological achievement! And yet a colossus of this type presses on through the sea regardless of wind and waves. It is so large that nature no longer has power over it; we can no longer see nature on it. People on board eat and drink and sleep and dance. They live as if in houses and on city streets. Mark you, something has been lost here. Not only has there been step-by-step development, improvement, and increase in size; a fluid line has been crossed that we cannot fix precisely but can only detect when we have long since passed over it—a line on the far side of which living closeness to nature has been lost.[21]

---

19. Harris, *Social Dilemma*, Netflix documentary.

20. Harris, *Social Dilemma*, Netflix documentary.

21. Gay, *Way of the (Modern) World*, 96, quoting Guardini, *Letters from Lake Como*, 5.

Virtuality—the New "Reality"

Guardini sees a line, a fluid line has been crossed, we can only detect it when we have crossed over. Closeness to nature as a consequence is lost. Nature he sees as no longer being *on* it. Nature's influence is no longer present, no longer experienced, no longer a living actual encounter. If anyone has been on a beautiful sailboat they recognize this. Could it be that life for the majority today is a life lived through the screen? Tristan Harris says, "The Major Tech is designed as a business model to keep people engaged with the screen."[22] It has worked, even worked in the church. In his book Tony Reinke seems to question whether we have lost touch with reality, he challenges his readers saying, "Church is a place for real encounters with others."[23] He then quotes Oliver O'Donovan: "cherish corporate worship, that most counter-cultural of practices, for which no virtual substitute can be found."[24] O'Donovan cannot be the only one along with myself who believes *no* virtual substitute can be found. Only if the magic trick has worked such a profound influence upon us could this possibly be defended. Nor should we think it impossible that such a colossus will move aside in a gentlemanly manner for nature to return as before. God in his nature is real, genuine, true and everything about communion with him must always reflect this first hand, this is no mere illusion. Christian worship must breathe reality, never falsehood whether by doctrine or practice. The screen deals in illusion, it is a false impression of reality. When a screen is joined to the worship of God this is a contradiction. Why? Because it is inevitably misleading. Yet reality has always been, and must always be the currency of the church, lest we appear to peddle something which proves to be counterfeit. All magic is counterfeit!

Neil Postman says, "Pictures have little difficulty in overwhelming words, and short-circuiting introspection."[25] But here is exactly where the line is crossed, the screen exists above all else to tease us with pictures, in the case of "Zoom" tragically these are pictures of ourselves. Pictures are most likely to make us self conscious, "Oh do I really look like that? Must check my hair and make sure my appearance is what I want it to be." Therefore, this forces a focus on the external and not the internal, the exact opposite of what God has a special interest in (1 Sam 16:7). The introspection of the Christian is to examine the heart before prayer, before worship, yet here the pictures dealing with illusion take the Christian not into the spiritual, but into that which is fleshly. But as we know on authority, the flesh counts for nothing (John 6:63, NIV).

22. Harris, *Social Dilemma*, Netflix Documentary.

23. Reinke, *12 Ways*, 73.

24. Reinke, *12 Ways*, 73, quoting O'Donovan.

25. Postman, *Amusing Ourselves to Death*, 105.

Gentile and Jew in Agreement (Tozer and Postman)

Gavriel Salomon, as quoted by Neil Postman, has written "Pictures, need to be recognized, words need to be understood."[26] And while the screen is able also to supply words which need to be understood, these are pitched against the colossus which is the image . . . and the winner is? Not the words! Most people who love taking pictures/photographs will be unfamiliar with the name Louis Daguerre. The "daguerreotype" was the original of our modern day photograph. When Daguerre was seeking investors in his new invention he said: "The daguerrotype is not merely an instrument which serves to draw nature . . . (it) gives her the power to reproduce herself."[27] Today almost two hundred years on from those words, people are looking into the screen and seeing themselves reproduced. The line has been crossed, nature has been altered. The picture, the image seen, which we have made, has forced one almighty collision in the act of worship. This is perhaps the most dangerous of all collisions, like a fatal car crash in the church, resulting in our mental faculties being altered (something not at all lost on Dr. Greenfield). In these days of growing mental ill-health our mental disposition must be guarded and protected with jealousy. Our care for the young and vulnerable should be of particular concern to Christ's church, and it is therefore imperative that Christians remember God's means of communicating with his civilization is by word alone.

Postman looks back to the time where word ruled in the form of typography, he says:

> For two centuries, America declared its intentions, expressed its ideology, designed its laws, sold its products, created its literature and addressed its deities with black squiggles on white paper. It did its talking in typography, and with that as the main feature of its symbolic environment rose to prominence in world civilization.[28]

Postman calls this the "Age of Exposition," something which once reigned supreme in Christ's true church:

> Exposition is a mode of thought, a method of learning, and a means of expression. Almost all of the characteristics we associate with mature discourse were amplified by typography, which has the strongest possible bias toward exposition: a sophisticated ability to think conceptually, deductively and sequentially; a high valuation of reason and order; an abhorrence of contradiction; a large capacity for detachment and objectivity; and a tolerance for delayed response. Toward the end of the nineteenth century, for reasons I am most anxious to explain, the Age of Exposition began to pass, and the early signs of

---

26. Postman, *Amusing Ourselves to Death*, 73.

27. Postman, *Amusing Ourselves to Death*, 72, quoting Daguerre, *Sontag*, 165.

28. Postman, *Amusing Ourselves to Death*, 64.

its replacement could be discerned. Its replacement was to be the Age of Show Business.[29]

Postman sounds very much like the critic A.W. Tozer who observed the tragic decline of the church into the same world of the silver screen. He wrote: "The American genius for getting things done quickly and easily with little concern for quality and permanence has bred a virus ..."[30] These two remarkable bedfellows project light into our present-day darkness, but will we listen?

The Forerunners

In 1961 the BBC first broadcast "Songs of Praise," whilst not surprisingly it eventually became "Stars on Sunday." The age of spiritual show business had arrived in the UK, more than twenty years after America's spiritual creativity found expression, and as we all know "If America sneezes the world catches a cold." These were the first televised services of worship which could be viewed by the public in the UK. By 1998 its average viewership was between five and six million. In 2009 the figures were calculated to have fallen to 3.4 million. The current figures seem to vary between two to three million. Regardless of the drop in numbers, this approach to Christian worship has certainly stood the test of time.

Predating the TV, radio provided a religious service as early as 1928. It has been running for eighty years continuously throughout the world (radio in the US seems to have given way to the TV around 1949). This confirms there has been a long established harnessing of media in an attempt to transmit religion. If a case can be made for legitimizing radio broadcasting of things spiritual, we might at least acknowledge that the receiver of the broadcast is in the safe hands of word only, but whether this ever connected the worshipper through the bakelite (the radio) in an act of "worship," is open to question.

Were the people in the outback of Australia or out in the sticks of the USA, when listening to the religious program (preaching included) "actually" engaged in worship? Are the people tuning into "Songs of Praise," or "Stars on Sunday" actually worshipping God? Are they worshipping in Spirit and in truth? If not, in the light of this question, we must ask what are the people "actually" doing? This would certainly be a pertinent question to present to British evangelicals in particular, who until the experiment with "Zoom worship," could have given a crystal clear answer.

29. Postman, *Amusing Ourselves to Death*, 64.
30. Tozer, *Incredible Christian*, 23.

Watching the Birds!

Prior to 2020, let us imagine a family regularly in attendance at a good church, a gospel church, living life under the authority of Scripture, now planning to make a major change to their traditional Sunday worship. This Christian and his family will no longer be in physical attendance as usual, but instead will be joining with worshippers on television. They are going to be part of "Songs of Praise." The minister of that church, counseling this family, might do so in this way. "Songs of Praise is "screen" worship and regardless of the fact that the content may be questionable, in fact you will be "watching" worship. You will not be meeting with anyone, you will not be gathered, you will not be corporally present, you will at all times remain a viewer and that is all. Worship like this together is purely an illusion." I think he would have done his best to gently point them to this reality—unreality and God can never be joined. Screen worship in "Songs of Praise" would in truth never have been endorsed by evangelicals, and would have been criticized to boot. But now, not to put it too finely, the "boot" is on the other foot, and a one hundred and eighty degree turn has been quickly made. Suddenly the evangelical churches are not so squeamish about the screen, quite the opposite. Some are now investing in even better kit to make "Zoom" time more professional hoping to reach more church members. Fear of COVID-19 as they see it, has made this even more necessary, no need to drive people past their fear and on to faith, the tech will take care of all this.

Suffering under the influence of the magician we have failed to grasp the reality that "watching" worship is the same as "watching" birds, or "watching" films or "watching" whatever. It is surely not difficult to picture someone in COVID-19 isolation in their home, with a meal on their laps, "watching" the worship and needing to break for a moment to let the cat out, or make a fresh cup of tea or even press the pause button and fast forward to the part they prefer. In a shockingly judgmental way we could well imagine this being the criticism of the "Songs of Praise" worshipper as they "worship" from the comfort of the living room couch, yet the committed evangelical "Zoom" worshipper is really no different from the trailblazers who pioneered the art of "watching worship."

One final observation, BBC so-called "worship" is in appearance at least top quality, meaning the pictures are the best, the lighting, the camera work, the presentation, the sound, everything is professional. Contrast this with the "Zoom" worshipper who relies on a questionable quality of transmission, possible glitches must play their part, and internet "drop off," poor signal, poor sound and the rest. One only needs to see the news studio conducting an interview using Zoom to observe what its impoverished limitations are for the worship of God. In every way, we cannot fail to notice this has the marks of Nadab and Abihu on it (Lev 10:1, 2). Is it not strange that the many expressions of evangelical faith have always been able to see the "strange fire" burned by others, yet now evangelical fingers are being burnt also? Tragically the practice of "screen" worship has placed Christ's church in the company of the Church of England and Rome, the cults and Islam also. Our hard fought distinctives lost in the click of a button. Remember: what is seen first will be remembered first. Word is no match for picture.

Magic operates in a world of illusion, this is what the screen successfully serves up, it is its DNA. Postman says: "We rarely talk about television, only about what is *on* television."[31] The screen serving up a constant performance is always calling out to us, enticing us by the magic which it projects. Inevitably we are drawn in. The magic show of which religion may just as much be a part as anything else, is a powerful, attention grabbing performance. This is why Billy Graham wrote,

> Television is the most powerful tool of communication ever devised by man. Each of my prime-time "specials" is now carried by nearly three hundred stations across the US and Canada, so that in a single telecast I preach to millions more than Christ did in his lifetime.[32]

All the "Zoom" worshipping churches have equally appreciated the truth of Graham's statement, but at the same time they failed to grasp as Graham did that which Neil Postman also observed: "It is in the nature of the medium that it must suppress the content of ideas in order to accommodate the requirements of visual interest."[33] For magic to work successfully and gain admirers it needs to get the angle of the trick just right. It requires concentration on the visuals of the trick itself so as to avert attention from the truth. The screen is both the magic and the transmitter of the magic show, and while we engage our ears during the performance, it is what we see above all else that keeps our focus on the show, and more importantly ensures we remain mesmerized.

Recently this was easily observed by televisions way of dealing with lockdown of our national game of football. Due to COVID-19 it was not possible to attend a football/soccer match in Britain, rather like the church, people were not allowed to gather. This for football presented a major challenge because the "beautiful game" as it is known, is our national sport, having millions of worshippers, devotees. People attend football matches as a spectacle, like an act of worship. However, in these unprecedented times the game had to go on, the schedule continued as normal but something was missing . . . the vital atmosphere produced by the fans. The sense of theatre was gone, the stadium appeared dead, the magic was lost. Anyone who is a student of the "beautiful game" knows the atmosphere is highly relevant to the players, because they are profoundly affected by the crowd, which is often called the twelfth man (only eleven players in each team of football). This twelfth man was "actually" in fact absent, there was no noise, no presence of their influence, no singing or shouting, no roar

---

31. Postman, *Amusing Ourselves to Death*, 80.
32. Postman, *Amusing Ourselves to Death*, 120, quoting Billy Graham.
33. Postman, *Amusing Ourselves to Death*, 94.

of approval. The stadium was "actually" empty. Ingeniously this was no problem for those selling the game to the audience, they got creative and filled the stadium with photographs, images of tens of thousands of fans. Pictures did the trick! In addition they added the sound of the fans, which gave the needy "worshipper," via the screen, his/her fix. Of course it was entirely fake, it was false and unreal. But it did not matter that it was unreal, because the vast majority of those watching are already totally conditioned by the "screen in their pockets" and able to process the illusion, the deep-rooted unreality of the world in which we all now live.

Truth and illusion have now merged, and even merged in the kingdom of God. Nor does it matter how fraudulent it all appears because what matters is that the technique confirms our conquest over the circumstances, we are always in control. Lewis Mumford writes about the triumph of order which was pervasive: "Akin to that which a well-drilled regiment has when it marches in step. Creating the illusion of invincibility, the machine actually added to the amount of power man can exercise. Science and technics stiffened our morale."[34]

While it is a very unfortunate likeness, the church often in its practices mirrors the "well-drilled regiment," its people marching in step to the direction of the age, "squeezed into its mould" (Rom 12:2) J.B. Phillips, confirming Mumford's further observations,

> As substitutes for primary experience, the machine is worthless: indeed it is actually debilitating [What might these words have done for everyone who contemplated the art of "Zoom" worship?] . . . The machine cannot be used as a shortcut to escape the necessity for organic experience.[35]

The machine worship of "Zoom" will debilitate Christians probably for generations to come, another nail in the coffin of the eclipse of God. The Rubicon has been crossed . . . the point of no return.

---

34. Mumford, *Technics and Civilization*, 324.

35. Mumford, *Technics and Civilization*, 343.

CHAPTER 5

SEEING IS NOT BELIEVING

"What we use to interact with the world changes the way we see the world. Every lens is a tinted lens"

MICHAEL HARRIS REFERENCING
MARSHALL MCLUHAN'S LENS

Now we see things imperfectly, like puzzling reflections in a mirror, but then we will see everything with perfect clarity.

1 CORINTHIANS 13:12 (NLT)

THE BIBLE, EVERY CHRISTIAN MUST acknowledge, is a lens, a divinely tinted one. From the point of view of those who profess an evangelical faith the Bible is the only means of acquiring a *perfect* spiritual vision. It is through this lens that we view God, ourselves and the world in which he has placed us. There are other lenses available, some of them are excellent, but only this one is flawless. This lens is God's great provision to enable us to see ourselves, not as we perceive ourselves, but as we *actually* are. The world likewise, only appears as it really is when subject to these optics. Lenses have a way of focusing what we are looking at, and sharpening our vision, especially if we are not blessed with twenty-twenty. John Calvin comments: "The Scriptures are our spectacles of faith: we don't merely look at but *through* them at God, the world and ourselves."[1]

The lens helps us to see what is otherwise blurred, and seeing things in sharp relief after years of poor eyesight can take us by surprise. In reality God wants us to see as he sees; he wants us to see himself in his way, ourselves in his way, and our world in his way. This is ultimately his way of revealing to us the divine world view. This lens,

---

1. Vanhoozer, *Pictures at a Theological Exhibition*, 166, quoting Calvin, *Institutes of the Christian Religion.*

though not exclusively, is intended so that the Christian can interact with the world where God has placed him, with this clarity of sight, with a honed perspective it is a privilege to do so, then the journey of life is not only possible but deeply pleasurable.

Of course a perfect lens like this results in an entirely changed view of life, visually everything is subject to a new "depth of field." Once we see (with eyes of faith) Jesus Christ and him crucified, the depths of our very being are changed forever, status quo in this regard is outlawed once and for all. Handel saw this and included it in his "Messiah," "I will once more shake the heavens and the earth, the sea and the dry land" (Hag 2:6, NIV). God is in the business of shaking us up.

Lenses are wonderful having a huge variety of uses, not least to assist eyesight. Mumford says, "Glasses not merely opened peoples eyes but their minds: seeing was believing."[2] Surely to have sharper eyesight and more informed minds, is in all our interests? But lenses do more than this, they magnify with extraordinary power, giving an "authority to the eye" in microcosm, and as Galileo found, in macrocosm. Mumford observes the effect of the lens like this, "The naive conceptions of space that the ordinary man carried around were completely upset."[3] The lens changed perspective.

For years I used a professional photographer for my studio work, he preferred an old 10x8 inch plate camera, which needed to be viewed with a black cloth covering the camera and viewer, a novel sight to say the least. To enter that tiny dark space was not only special but very beautiful. The world was shut out and one was left only with the image as it was projected on to the plate glass. This image was presented upside down, a little disconcerting, but it didn't seem to matter, the whole experience was mesmerizing. With the world shut out I was able to enter a new one, entirely created by the medium and I can understand why some people describe it as being quite magical. Perhaps we can think of the lens like this; it creates its own world which removes all else, i.e., it isolates, and eliminates. I like to describe it as being "ignorant" of everything else, it deliberately ignores and pays no attention whatsoever to anything outside of the frame. It is selfish, it is disinterested in the wider world, it is an eliminator.

If we think of the testing circumstances of Adam and Eve our first parents, the subterfuge in the Garden of Eden was by and large partly about elimination. The picture presented to them by the serpent was a picture of themselves, the "new" selves, the peripheral vision which included God (we are not saying that Adam and Eve could not enjoy everything else) was now ignored. The lens focusing in on the subject shut out all else which was extraneous, so as to focus on the center, the essential . . . himself. The lens which the serpent presented was quite specifically a medium which would realize the desired end: "The fruit was pleasing to the eye and also desirable." God knows that when you eat of it "your *eyes* will be opened, and you will be like God" (Gen 3:5–6, NIV). Adam and Eve gained sharper eyesight, that day their eyes were duly opened, "seeing was believing," the serpent's promise was realized.

2. Mumford, *Technics and Civilization*, 127.
3. Mumford, *Technics and Civilization*, 126.

The serpent's lens changed their perspective on all things, not least on himself. Nothing would ever be the same again. The strategy which engineered the success was to inform Adam he would discover himself through the lens provided. Calvin's commentary on Gen 3:12 and indirectly on Jas 1:14, explains how everyone is tempted by his own concupiscence. Concupiscence is self love, meaning the earliest narcissism was in the Garden. Concupiscence moved Adam from loving God to loving himself, we would say "taken up" with himself. Calvin's commentary on Romans 7 explains this further. "The sin of concupiscence is more secret and deeply hidden. For this reason men never take it into account, as long as they judge according to their own sense."[4] The devil was saying to Adam "think about yourself for once, put yourself in the frame, why not be at the center, focus on number one . . . you are number one." Calvin's intentions when commenting on Romans 7 are not in fact brought out so clearly in english, as he was not conveying the idea of covetousness nor lust, but the more graphic concupiscence. Here we are dealing with revolt, concupiscent desire was Paul's problem expressed in Romans 7, "puffed up." Being "Puffed up" with self, Adam viewed himself through the Satanic filter, lest we forget, the medium was the gateway to the opening of his eyes. Every lens is a tinted lens. The devil knew the medium was the key, Adam's eyes were opened through the act of eating. If only Adam had been able to say with the apostle Paul: "We are not ignorant of his devices" (2 Cor 2:11, KJV). Instead he was made ignorant of God!

It is useless to try and distance ourselves from our first parents, as we are certainly not superior to them in any way. Surely their vulnerability to concupiscence is ours also. When Mumford assesses the influence of the mirror in its popular form he says,

> Self consciousness, introspection mirror conversation developed with the new object itself. This preoccupation with ones *image* comes at the threshold of the mature personality, when young Narcissus gazes long and deep into the face of the pool.[5]

Following on from Adam and Eve, Narcissus saw himself through the tinted lens. Having observed them closely we have also learned their decorum, we have studied them long and hard and now we are perfecting their practices.

The mirror, the glass, has changed the inner man, it has profoundly altered the personality and is no less an influence in our own time. If we did not know, it is a means to "talk" us up. As Martin Buber puts it: "Something has stepped between our existence and God to shut off the light of heaven . . . (and) that something is in fact *ourselves*, our own bloated selfhood."[6] It may of course have the adverse effect, but our need of it is to confirm what we *want* to hear. "Mirror, mirror on the wall who is the fairest of them all?" Silently hoping, please say me! We love to be talked up and we

---

4. Rolston, *John Calvin v The Westminster Confession*, 51.

5. Mumford, *Technics and Civilization*, 129.

6. Gay, *Way of the (Modern) World*, 196, quoting Buber, quoting Torrance, *God and Rationality*, 29.

even have the defensive expression "Don't talk down to me!" Talking him up the devil promised Adam, "You will be like God" (Gen 3:5, NIV) meaning you will go beyond what and who you are. Clearly we know the devil was peddling lies, his was the ultimate tinted lens which Adam found irresistible. From experience we know the mirror has this awful ability just to "tell it as it is." In its brutal way it exposes reality, our age, our weakness, our journey through atrophy, however it is just as willing to spell out health, vigor and beauty, and in this regard it is an incredible lure. Gyms are full of mirrors, to confirm that the members have bodies like gods or are on the right road to obtaining them. Building on this, the idol of the screen in its march to dominating our lives has caused us to be taken in, because above all else it has sold the idea that it is always possible to see or hear ourselves being "talked up," putting us at the center. Christians in the past would have been exercised and made to blush if they needed or sought flattery . . . not the case today. Consider the filters which can be used on smartphones, setting us free to be creative, every lens remember is a tinted lens. The filter is your friend, maybe even your best friend, the filter in a few clicks can deliver up the lie, but the lie doesn't matter, truth has vanished. The possibility of "another" you (not quite an avatar . . . yet!), but another more perfect self is the lie of the devil, "*You* shall be as God." The screen assists you in your aspiration to be bigger, better and more beautiful than the real you, as you live in your quiet make-believe world, and the wicked Queen's answer . . . you are the fairest of them all!

The problem is that this "make-believe" world is like a matrix, and as such the truth becomes blurred, so much so that people cannot distinguish between what is real or false anymore. This has extremely serious consequences in more ways than one. Susan Greenfield paints an alarming picture for the church: "When we come to consider how the digital technologies could be impacting not just the generic brain, but the individual mind, beliefs and states of consciousness."[7] Yes, she says "beliefs." When we add to this one of the most terrifying texts of Scripture, the apostle Paul speaks of "those who would not receive the love of the truth, . . . and for this cause God shall send them a strong delusion, that they should believe a lie" (2 Thess 2:10-11, NIV). If people cannot navigate a way through this morass of confusion and plot a course to see the truth about themselves by means of special grace, how on earth will they do so by God's common grace? It is as if all emergency exits out of our troubles have been boarded up, we are trapped in a place of our own making. The lie reigns supreme. This is a rabbit hole which the whole world has willfully, yet blindly gone down, but as we know Alice encountered strange and frightening anthropomorphic creatures there; but this is nothing like the rabbit hole into which even Christians have descended. We may only wonder what terrifying creatures of the mind lay in wait in this dark place.

7. Greenfield, *Mind Change*, 99.

The Merry-Go-Round

God deals in "real life," his currency is reality which the gospel endeavors to bring us face to face with. The false belongs to our ancient enemy who we have blindly followed on to the endless spinning merry-go-round, it is spinning faster and faster, so much so we cannot get off. We know that to attempt to do so would threaten serious injury, but it is equally fatal to stay on. Adam's nemesis and therefore ours, has thrown a "curved ball" not merely to distract us but ultimately to destroy us. The devil's up-to-date idol, like the Trojan Horse, looks harmless, this is why Paul speaks of him as one who appears as an "Angel of Light" (2 Cor 11:14, NIV). The tech, the screen, the entire world's ethos, appears perfectly kosher, no one is in the least bit alarmed, certainly not the Christian church. To bring computer screens and television cameras into the worship of God and join them to the stainless perfection of the God of Heaven was almost seamless. It could not have been easier. Mercifully when this was thrust upon the churches there were a few who saw the issue clearly, but the vast majority of Evangelicals, who were themselves so totally signed up and dependent in their private lives upon this yoke, did not think twice of imposing it upon Christ's church . . . it was natural, as natural as the air we breathe.

It is hard not to imagine the church displaying anything other than a pugnacious spirit when confronted with the question of "natural." Might it not be safely assumed that when the church opted for "Zoom" worship it did not in fact think spiritually at all but thought "naturally"? The lens which informed this action was one which had already been adopted, was unquestioned and probably conformed to. The tinted lens had already become well established long before the experiment.

It is surely not a case of conjecture to state the obvious influence which the simple environment of a home and upbringing might have upon any one of us. In many homes a particular political persuasion might dominate where a particular emphasis is the constant mantra. Added to this a particular newspaper with the same outlook may find its way also into the home, along with just the right news channel proclaiming the same emphasis. It is "naturally" likely that in such an environment, the one subjected to the "cause" may potentially be affected for life, of course it may be for good or ill. A church which forcefully presses the need for abstinence and promotes teetotalism must have in the same way presented a particular lens through which to view the question of alcohol. Furthermore, it would be no surprise if those growing up in this environment developed a "natural distaste" for the consumption of such beverages. In contrast there is the acceptable lens of Christians drinking wine in Europe and just as established is that of smoking cigars amongst the Dutch Calvinists. These are all established because of the lens adopted and once this is overlaid, it is almost impossible to view a given subject without the tinted glasses. We are "locked" in.

Two of my three sons love football (soccer), and one of them has no interest in the "beautiful game" whatsoever, which in fact has always pleased me. Not surprisingly the two who love the game are passionate about the team which I have always been passionate about, like my father before me. This is the work of the "natural" lens, it is inescapable, every lens is tinted.

In Thomas Watson's *A Body of Divinity*, he considers man's chief end, which is to glorify God. He then labors to set out the many ways this may be achieved; seventeen in all, the Puritans really knew how to squeeze a thing dry! His thirteenth point touches on "natural" actions: "We glorify God, when we have an eye to God in all our civil and natural actions, and do nothing that may reflect any blemish on religion."[8] For Watson "natural" actions take in eating and drinking, but also buying and selling, he was keen to express his view about the Christians handling of commerce where those of faith must spend a huge part of their life. It is here where he focuses on the need to take care in the "natural" sphere, so that religion is not blemished.

If we need to take care and be alert about the "natural" in the world of commerce, then we must surely exercise the same gravity in the life of the church. The Christian life is not divided nor compartmentalized, the Christian life is "spiritual life" 24/7. The danger though is obvious, when it suits us we will switch off the divine lens to look through the acceptable lens of this world in which we live. If we did not know it, "mere natural instincts" (Jude 10) must be one of our greatest enemies. It is in these "natural instincts" that the world boldly declares its proclivities to be free. Placards abound proclaiming freedom for just about everything and anything. The truth is, the world is caged, shackled to its "natural" instincts and the worry is that the church has misread this explosion of so-called freedom. The deified nature of tech has duped us more than anything else to view its "beauty" through its own lens. Horrible as this is and in danger of sounding irreverent, the text we know so well might be rendered for our benefit "if the tech sets you free you shall be free indeed." The lens has set us free but tragically, free to follow our "natural" instincts. The result, the "lens of freedom" sanctifies the medium (the screen) confirming we no longer have the ability to notice the obvious. Thomas Watson's blemish.

If this medium is not an idol causing a blemish upon the Holy Worship of God, then it is hard to think of one that is. It is tempting to wonder what Thomas Watson's take would have been on all this, would he have thought this to be a blemish? On the subject of worship Kevin J. Vanhoozer quotes Ronald Byars: "In shaping worship, the question must aways be, "Are these materials worthy of a BIG God?""[9] Is "Zoom" worthy of a big God? Vanhoozer says, "Trivial music and trivial words trivialize the divine."[10] Here we are with the screen at the center of worship, the question must surely be, what could be more trivial, what could possibly leave a more lasting blemish? We need to check the lens which the church has become accustomed to and extremely

8. Watson, *Body of Divinity*, 16.

9. Vanhoozer, *Pictures at a Theological Exhibition*, 119, quoting Byars, *Christian Worship*, 112.

10. Vanhoozer, *Pictures at a Theological Exhibition*, 118.

comfortable with. It appears to be murky and in need of a good clean, only then can we examine the materials rather more meticulously.

Vanity, Vanity, All is Vanity

Sophocles with sage-like awareness said: "Nothing vast enters the life of mortals without a curse."

It could be reasonably argued that the digital age dwarfs all other powers which have entered the life of mortals, artificial intelligence has surfaced and presents all manner of questions which in the next years must undoubtedly impact our world. These are developments which the Christian has to reckon with and which the church must be willing to grapple with. The idea that the digital age will stand still and leave us all to make our minds up is frankly fanciful. "Zoom" has taught us that if it is there, it can be used and equally used for the kingdom of God. The question at the present time is: Are there alarm bells to alert us to the curse which Sophocles highlights? To be sure the blemish of the tech experiment will have stained the churches for years to come and the association with illusion will not be so easily laundered.

More than this there will be collateral damage in lives, probably similar to that which affected so many who encountered the mass evangelical experiment through the middle of the last century; and an unequivocal signal will have been sent. If Christians who are Bible-believing think that their evangelicalism is well defined, they may discover that the new lens or lenses cleverly overlaid, rather than sharpening the image, will blur it forever making it so ill-defined as to be unrecognizable. The tinted lens of the screen entering the worship will confirm Sophocles to be a "prophet" in this regard . . . and *sola scriptura* will give way to *sola cultura*!

Naturally those who introduced the screen to worship, see little to be concerned with. However, if we add Heidegger's[11] observations to Mumford's and draw some real life accounts, we see quite the opposite. For Mumford, being completely whole and at one, at ease with the world, makes the mirror superfluous. If only we were at ease, instead life is a perpetual encounter "everywhere and always" with oneself, (recalling Matthew Crawford's observations in Chapter 3).

Nowhere is this more apparent than the 'cultural fetish' of our times which is here to stay, but what has created it? Professor Frank Furedi suggests overwhelmingly the evidence points to, "The unprecedented concern with the emotional needs of the self . . ."[12] and naturally self esteem. "The fragile character of emotion-based identities dooms the self to a continuous quest for affirmation."[13] Recently a member of my family, aware of what I was writing, drew to my attention something which alarmed her. She had received into her phone a "post" from two young girls who once

11. Martin Heidegger, *Question Concerning Technology and other Essays*, 33.

12. Furedi, *Therapy Culture*, 152.

13. Furedi, *Therapy Culture*, 152.

CAN WE ZOOM INTO GOD?

attended our church, both interestingly have made professions of Christian faith. On viewing these "posts," apart from my personal sadness at what I saw, it was important to remain objective. The overwhelming impression was that the girls were exhibiting themselves, but in truth not themselves, instead only an illusion of themselves. Their look was fabricated, it was a new identity which they wished others to applaud them for. The tinted lens enabled them to leave reality behind.

Unsurprisingly there is no caution in this, caution is abandoned, there is no hint of shame, it is pure undiluted, unabashed exhibitionism, which comes up from the emotional needs of the self. At all costs they want to be seen, they need to be seen, but not just seen, but they require adulation. The boundary lines are now re-drawn, the lens is not only facilitating their behavior it is the director, and the "worshippers" which they seek are duly provided in almost the "blink of an eye." This might be described as Kenneth J. Gergen does in *The Saturated Self*, "the fully saturated self becomes no self at all."[14]

They not only seek genuflection from their admirers naturally they return it, so as to complete the circle of flattery and those who fawn over them repeat the adulation: "So beautiful," "Perfect," "Perfect," "Perfect." Idols ordinarily draw out idol worship and the gushing praise is reciprocated. By now this kind of behavior must be considered entirely normal, not even alien to so-called Christians. As the astronaut I have to wonder what has the church ever tried to do about this? Recognizing the danger of violating Ecclesiastes 7:10, NIV "Why were the olden days better than these?" but taking care, there is some purpose here in reflection.

Martin Bell the legendary War Zone Journalist recalls the early days at the BBC when in 1954 at the Alexandra Palace TV news began. Bell recalls, "The newsreaders themselves . . . did not appear in vision."[15] Richard Baker (one of the newsreaders) wrote: "We were not to be seen reading the news because it was feared we might sully the pure stream of truth with inappropriate facial expressions."[16] When this new medium first arrived, Bell says, "Winston Churchill, who mastered the microphone but not the camera, dismissed it as a peepshow."[17] This is what the girls were engaging in on their phones, and so much of "screen worship" as they practice it, is just that "worship." This is a full-blooded narcissistic peep show. By now this lens overlaid in their lives means they can only discern life through it, their vision is sullied and tinted. Their search for reality is only a moment of yearning for affirmation, leaving them empty because in fact the affirmation they know is unreal, as much as their exhibition of themselves is untrue. It is all an illusion to try to meet the "unprecedented concern" with the emotional needs of the self.

14. Gay, *Way of the (Modern) World*, 197, quoting Gergen, *Saturated Self*, 7.

15. Bell, *War and the Death of News*, 79.

16. Bell, *War and the Death of News*, 79, quoting Baker, "50 Years of BBC Television News," 5.

17. Bell, *War and the Death of News*, 80.

Staying with the two girls let us watch them closely, they now swap the screen in their pockets, where they have indulged themselves and feasted on a diet of flesh. William Barclay commenting on the difference between body and flesh explains how this has to be understood. "The body can become the instrument of the service and glory of God; the flesh cannot. The body can be purified and even glorified; the flesh must be eliminated . . . The *sarx* cannot please God (Rom 8:8)."[18] This is what the girls, professing faith in Christ are ignorant of, which may be no fault of their own, after all the Corinthians needed to be told about their own dreadful practices. In the same way both parents and the church need to examine themselves and evaluate the now acceptable behavior, even as it touches worship and in turn subject everything to the scrutiny of Scripture. Without this, *sarx* will be allowed unfettered to dictate in realms which now are considered to be "off limits" for Christian analysis.

With a little effort we can get to the heart of the matter more effectively, we need only a change of words and this is achieved when considering J.B. Phillips-Weymouth and NEB, where *sarx* flesh is translated as "lower nature" (Gal 5:13, 5:16, 5:24, 6:8). This clarifies for us that what the girls are doing is not "just fine" after all, but profoundly harmful to them. It is true that "lower nature" proposes by implication that there is an opposite, namely a "higher nature" which total depravity denies. Perhaps we are hitting the mark if we say the flesh, the "lower nature," is what human nature has descended to, becoming what it is by virtue of sin in its members.

Barclay has mastered the sense of all this when he says (We) "can neither avoid the fascination of Sin nor resist the Power of Sin. Hence the need of a renaissance by the Power of the Holy Spirit." To then turn up at a screen worship meeting via "Zoom" or some other online worship service, where the church prays into a camera, celebrates the Lord's Supper, looks into a screen of pictures which not surprisingly in many cases reveals . . . themselves, these girls are living in the world of illusion, reality eat your heart out!

Peter Berger, et al concluding the Homeless Mind (1973) helps us to grasp this in more depth.

> Modernity has accomplished many far reaching transformations, but it has not fundamentally changed the finitude, fragility, and mortality of the human condition. What it has accomplished is to seriously weaken those definitions of reality that previously made that human condition easier to bear.[19]

I have argued throughout this book that images of ourselves are outlawed in any act of Christian worship; the girls now not surprisingly discern no difference whatever between what they do in the world and in the church. It seems grossly unfair to come down on the fourteenth century worshipper accessing images painted on a church wall, and then decrying this as a dark thing, at least we can say they accessed the

---

18. Barclay, *Flesh and Spirit*, 20.

19. Gay, *Way of the (Modern) World*, 107, quoting Berger, *Homeless Mind*, 185.

image of another. Our journey into self is complete, our concupiscence has reached its logical conclusion, the tech/screen enables the worship of God to be shared by the "boasting boy" or "girl" who are here to stay.

The Danger of Sight

While it could be legitimately argued that the tinted lens applies as much to "Ear-gate" as to "Eye-gate," it is undoubtedly the case that the eye renders us more completely vulnerable to the self. In the Garden the temptation came first through the ear, but was only completed by the workings of the eye. Without the eye the devil could have talked Eve's ear off with little effect. The eye was the key to realize the nefarious proposition. She saw, and what she saw "was pleasant to the eyes" (Gen 3:6, KJV). She could have hardly taken of the fruit if she had been blind! A.W. Pink observes "Satan *works from without to within.*"[20] Calvin says "This impure look of Eve, infected with the poison of concupiscence, was both the messenger and the witness of an impure heart."[21] The heart was affected by what the Conspirator proposed to Eve but to realize the subterfuge the eye was indispensable: without this unique wonderful gift the enterprise of darkness might never have got off the ground. What we look at can change our world forever.

Like someone who visits the gym every day and develops their biceps my eyes could be described as over developed, I have worked them assiduously since childhood. It was there they were first trained on the image. My parents thankfully acceded to the "powers" of a door-to-door salesman and bought for the family a set of encyclopedias, amongst them was a book of world famous paintings, I will always recall how pleasant they were to my eyes. Cézanne was there, Botticelli, Rembrandt, Titian, Michelangelo and the rest, through them I journeyed into another world, to Paris with Degas, the South of France with Van Gogh, to Tahiti with Gauguin, to St Mark's Square with Canaletto. These visual treats created a lens through which I could view the wider world, I was no longer confined to the remote Pennine cottage where I had been born, suddenly my world was altered forever. These images have never been erased from my memory, even my early distaste for a Cézanne is still as fresh as the day I passed my childish judgment on the Great Master. Their influence remains and when appearing before my mind's eye, which often occurs, they always do me good. I am enriched by them, the lens is still working.

Alongside this early experience of beautiful images in my book, I also saw my first cinema film, my first moving picture in color no less! "Ben-Hur" played by the actor Charlton Heston, portrayed a unique moment in the film which is also etched upon my mind. One thing I remember as stand out was the pathos of the presence of the one playing the role of Christ. Christ's face uniquely was not depicted, even as a

20. Pink, *Gleanings in Genesis*, 37.
21. Calvin, *Genesis*, 151.

child I remember recognizing the profound nature of that statement, it made a deep impression on me. It was a piece of film-making genius, that evening at the cinema I learned "less is more."

In the last century the church has abandoned this principle "less is more." If we did not know it the worship is not meant to be a visual delight, instead the crucial part is the "message" itself, "Ear-gate" is the focus, not eye. When the minister is a star and the choreographed sideshow is employed, the church has fallen to the poison of concupiscence, the worship service is then designed to be "pleasant to the eyes." Of course this is the full blown variety of this demise, but "screen" worship cannot avoid playing into the same narrative, where the "worshipper" is as intent on watching as much as listening. They have to be. Did it ever occur to those who first threw themselves into the arms of "Zoom" that so-called worshippers via this tinted lens, would find watching to be in direct competition with listening? One is much easier than the other, especially for those now trained daily in looking at images on a screen.

It has been more than a little instructive to hear the first hand account and honesty of my research assistant. When the lockdown came and the fog descended leaving the lie of the land uncertain, she of her own volition being under no compulsion, ventured into the world of "screen" worship. And while she tells her story of feeling somewhat reticent, nevertheless perhaps in a sense of "bereavement," she began her exploration. Her ability to clearly recollect the visual came easily, more telling by far, was her inability to clearly recollect the spoken word. The spoken content, whatever it was, lacked the power to oust the influence of the visual. She discovered that the screen rules. Thankfully when her sensibilities were revived (certainly not by me) the red flags appeared, the gravity of the practice made its impact. She explains how this was achieved. It was the overwhelming, visual consciousness of the self, the medium had forced her to be on display. Naturally the screen of any kind changed her, and all the others into performers. Of course, she needed to check her screen appearance. The so-called worship was far removed from being lost in wonder, love and praise for him who is the head of all things (Col 1:18). Instead like all engaged in "Zoom" worship they had to be concerned about their own heads and how they appeared on the TV screen. Ordinarily, in an act of worship where all participants "actually" gather together, where word is the dominant medium, no one is engaged in watching. They look at the one "who's feet bring good news" (Rom 10:15, NIV) but so long as he does not exhibit himself and draw undue attention to himself, everyone is engaged with the message; "Eye-gate" is quite dormant, as it should be.

The Imagination is Lost

The danger of letting sight loose is that the imagination is not only underdeveloped but gets to play no part at all, it is crushed and the desire for sight grows and grows! It strikes me that in our times of needing to see everything, of being inundated with an endless stream of images, we lose what powers of imagination we ever had. In our over-developed need of all things visual, "less is more" is probably something the modern world by now is frankly incapable of. This exposes us and makes us indulgent in a myriad of ways. We cannot wait for anything, we lose access to patience which thrives in the realms of the imagination which transports us to where we want to be without the thing itself being realized. Kevin J. Vanhoozer supplies the very best insight here to the merits of the imagination, he says, "The imagination also has a second function to play in theology: it enables us not only to synthesize but also to participate in the biblical text. Whereas analytic reason excels in "looking at," the imagination allows us to look along the grain of the text, indwelling it rather than remaining at a critical distance." This is what I have always called the "smells and sounds" of Scripture, the imagination is no danger to truth when we consider the reality in which the truth was forged. Christ had nowhere to lay his head, his beard was plucked out, he wept, these are not cold facts but to be engaged with, as Vanhoozer says "along the grain." For our purposes he also adds . . . "the imagination is the power of the 'synoptic' vision: the ability to see things . . . without recourse to images."[22]

It will inevitably be argued that the imagination is a dangerous thing, such as that exemplified in Gibson's film *The Passion of the Christ* and "vain imaginings" let loose can result in confusion such as he directs upon a gullible public. The answer to this, the Scripture must anchor our imagination at all times. But evidently Eve was not misled by her imagination but by her sight. Pornography may have its roots in the imagination but when sin is fully fledged, it becomes a graphic empty illusion available on any computer screen.

The imagination remains somewhat contained, the image on the other hand is let loose. Also the imagination may thrive in the abstract, this is where God's revelation of himself is so impressive, no one has ever *seen* God at any time. God said to Moses "You cannot see my face for no one may see me and live" (Exod 33:22, NIV) only the back of God was permitted for Moses to see (verse 23). What could be more abstract than God appearing in the burning bush? (Exod 3). We may let our imagination loose but all we will have at the end will be a burning bush!

Neil Postman says:

"The God of the Jews was to exist in the Word and through the Word, an unprecedented conception requiring the highest order of abstract thinking. Iconography thus became blasphemy so that a new kind of God could enter a culture. People like ourselves who are in the process of converting their culture from word-centered to image-centered might profit by reflecting on this Mosaic injunction."[23]

22. Vanhoozer, *Pictures at a Theological Exhibition*, 166.
23. Postman, *Amusing Ourselves to Death*, 9.

Though we may not have grasped this concept, picture is more, but in fact it is less. Word is less, but in fact it is more. The "toolbox" of faith may well include the imagination which Vanhoozer describes as "Good faith: the Evangelical Imagination." However, it may not ever rely on images or pictures for worship. Sight is a dangerous thing especially when influenced and altered by a tinted lens.

In our world where so much is mechanical, the danger is that the church will also descend to the place of zero imagination, as defined by Vanhoozer. Even in Christ's church the "Zoom" image has emerged to help us out of our predicament, imagination is now eliminated. The girls who shared their narcissistic illusion are quite unaware that they have entered into the most shallow of places, their imagination underdeveloped or not developed at all, they are prey to the fruit that looked delicious (Gen 3:5,6 NLT). Quoting "The Shallows" by Nicholas Carr, Michael Harris says:

> "The Internet fundamentally works on our plastic minds to make them more capable of "shallow" thinking and less capable of "deep" thinking. After enough time in front of our screens, we learn to absorb more information less effectively, skip the bottom half of paragraphs, shift focus constantly; "the brighter the software, the dimmer the user."[24]

Harris goes on to say, "For now it's easier to tell that something has changed in our minds, but we still feel helpless against it, and we even feel addicted to the technologies that are that changes agents."[25] Harris who is a self-confessed user of modern tech speaks of feeling helpless against it, feeling addicted and something having changed in the mind. If such a lens can make us shift focus constantly it is easy to see its application, in any shape or size, in any setting, it is not fitted to the worship of God. Words, not pictures, are the annunciation of truth.

In the garden where the fruit looked delicious the lens was the most tinted ever, and without putting words in the mouths of the two girls posting images of each other, it would certainly not offend them if someone were to respond, "delicious." What power do they now possess to secure any kind of mortification in their vulnerable lives? In "screen" worship the church is no help, in fact quite the opposite, the girls receive a mixed message and fail to realize that their behavior is that of concupiscence i.e.: self love with a good mixture of covetousness so as to produce, as Paul says, "idolatry" (Col 3:5, KJV).

J.I. Packer in his helpful book *God's Words* deals with mortification (to put to death) and gives this pithy visual: "you can't stop the birds flying over your head you can stop them nesting in your hair."[26] The birds are not only building their nests in the lives of professing young believers but in the very life of church worship, hatching their eggs.

24. Harris, *End of Absence*, 38, quoting Carr, *Shallows*, 216.
25. Harris, *End of Absence*, 39.
26. Packer, *God's Words*, 188.

In a hotel room in the USA I have often tuned into the TV during a night whilst suffering from jet lag, and accessed services of worship. Am I therefore a worshipper *with others*, sitting on my bed in the middle of the night, or am I just watching a screen of pictures? What would it take in that situation to make me with those pictured, into a worshipper? In reality I may be watching a recording of yesterday's worship, or last week's worship, for that matter. To many who use this they see no problem. Equally those who tune into their church worship via "Zoom" seem to be at ease, comfortably praying into a screen camera as they join in with a so-called prayer meeting. NB: we must not forget prayer is an act of worship. Those who participate may confidently tell themselves that they are joining in with the prayer meeting, but this is purely an illusion. A meeting demands corporeal presence. The reason this is called "virtual" is because "virtual" means "not actual" no one is present at an "actual" meeting, there is no "assembling," there is no "coming together." Paul's words in 1 Cor 14:20 are impossible to realize. Everything about this is like the football match with fake noise (Chapter 4), it is simply not real, it is not true. God on the other hand demands *truth* in the inward parts (Ps 51:6, KJV). Having drunk for so long at the well of what is unreal, the church has seamlessly joined God's worship to it. Does the God who demands truth in the inward parts seem no longer to care how he is worshipped? In "Zoom" worship one may even contribute into the "worship" by talking to the screen if, as the saying goes, "a picture is worth a thousand words" it behoves us to be extremely careful about the message which the picture is conveying. Twenty years ago, if we had suggested that we might find ourselves talking into a screen, we might have pronounced ourselves, "mad."

Is Anyone Out There?

It is hard to escape the thought that when COVID-19 hijacked the world, where else could the church find help? Naturally "Zoom" was the answer. It appears we have almost certainly confined the wonderful words, "Help of the helpless Oh abide with me"[27] to the confines of salvific application, and we have had the attitude, though unwittingly, that in our time of need we can "help" ourselves. It is equally hard not to see a desperation in the lightning fast rush to join worship to the world's medium. Perhaps Lennon and McCartney's hit song sheds a cryptic light upon the mentality with the screeching refrain calling out for "help." The reader might like to recall the words from the well known song, and ponder them carefully, since the church in its desperation fits this description. The song speaks volumes of insecurity, feeling down and "needing," just "needing" someone to be around.

Cryptically or not, the lyrics of this song seem like a fitting commentary upon the subject. They speak of a changed mind leading to open doors and, by inference,

27. Lyte, "Abide with Me," Hymnodist 1793-1847

to new practices. Why did the church suddenly change its mind and open the door to the act of worship via a medium, something it would never have countenanced even ten years ago? Was it because it had quickly lost its moorings and needed to get its feet back on the ground, or was it that the church with a well developed sense of self assurance was found wanting? It discovered that self-assurance was failing, leaving people as the song says feeling "insecure." COVID-19 was going to make lives change in unimaginable ways, resulting in the cry, "Please help me."

It would be no surprise if this analysis brought up some considerable ire in certain readers, however if the purpose of "Zoom" was not called upon in an emergency to "help," then one is left wondering why was it called upon at all? The desperation for "help" appears to have been so profound that the new "open doors" failed to reveal the true size of this unprecedented action. In a later chapter I ask the pertinent question, whether Christians would have been so enthusiastic for this "helper" to come to their rescue and deliver their desperate need for worship, if persecution had been attached to the use of it, or if it had been on the pain of death, or if it had resulted in criminal prosecution and a criminal record?

It is true that there were many components which contributed to this call for "help," but it looks impossible not to identify one of them as insecurity. Lennon and McCartney sang about insecurity, and of the feeling which comes from "being down." Certainly, this has been voiced by the suggestion that people just could not have made it through the lockdown without "Zoom" assistance. Glaringly obvious is the truth that "Zoom" (as previously stated) enabled no one to "actually" meet, no one "actually" assembled, no one "actually" gathered together. Christians might feel an affinity with the song's sentiments of appreciating someone coming around, being "together" in times of trial, not realizing in "Zoom" worship no one is "around" and to suggest otherwise is only an illusion. Lennon and McCartney intended to point to someone being present who they could reach out and touch, someone (as Postman puts it) in the same room, not a mere pseudo-encounter. Desperate for help the church opened the door to a world of unreality, but this nonetheless satisfied people because in their daily lives they are sated on a diet of illusion. As so often is the case, the "help" promised in the glossy brochure failed to deliver what was promised. Paul's words (1 Cor 14:20), have no gloss, just reality.

Help!

'Zoom" worship was entered into by the church when it needed "help" generally but specifically because, being cut off, it needed sight once more, and "Zoom" could facilitate it. This only confirms that people who chose this medium, needed to *see* one another, the image was paramount. Logic demands such a conclusion or else one would have expected Christians to be encouraged to take up some private audio means. As a form of worship this would at least have presented a time of devotion where images were relegated, but the desire to see something was just far too tempting, confirming that word is no match for image "a picture is worth a thousand words."

Had an option been given to Christians by their church, to listen to a recording of the Ministry of God's word alone, quietly in their own homes, where providence had confined them, or to watch pictures on a screen of church members in a so-called act of worship, one wonders what the choice would have been? If pictures of people were seen engaged in a so-called act of worship would this mean *de facto* the ones watching would also be worshippers with them "together?" This would be "help" indeed! However, since the medium will not stand down and demonstrably stands between, it is unlikely "together" that the holy act of assembled Christian worship was ever carried out. The act of *seeing* in worship is a catastrophic hinderance, an impediment of gargantuan proportions, because "Eye-gate" needs to process an overwhelming amount of information. In this there is little room left, if any for God, who, if we had not forgotten, the entire proceedings were intended for and not for ourselves. If the worshipping mind is to give God the first-fruits, then it is impossible to do so whilst assimilating images. This is quite impossible. What remains is a pseudo-image of pseudo-worshippers looking at one another, naturally they are very much in the picture, sadly God is not.

If this reasoning looks hard to accept, let us consider someone attending the church worship in the normal sense, coming bodily into a physical place with the sole intention of devoting themselves in a worship service, giving the first-fruits of their faculties so "that in all things He might have the preeminence" (Col 1:18, KJV). What shall we say then if this person brings their knitting, can they knit and worship? One hopes the answer is an emphatic "No" and this parallel needs to be kept at the forefront of our minds when analyzing and assessing so-called "Zoom" worship.

Seeing is not believing and if believing is not at the center of worship then it is rendered null and void. COVID-19 created a desire to *see* this was a cry for "help," "help" with insecurity as much as anything, but it did not get anyone's spiritual feet back on terra firma. Instead it provided the necessary social contact which I suspect was the deepest need of all. Instead of crying out to "Zoom" for "help," the church should have gone directly to God and offered private, humble closet-worship, or alternatively offended the state and the powers that be by breaking the law and returning to "actual" worship. Either of these would have been far better than to risk offending God, artistic license in worship has no place. No matter how insecure the people of God may feel, they need to be thrown back not upon themselves but upon God himself. The danger is the church looks as though it has become our salvation. "Help of the helpless Oh abide with me" is a reference not to the church but to God himself. Lennon and McCartney sang "Help." Our need is not just anybody to carry us through, it must always be God himself.

From all this must grow the conviction as to the danger of "screen" worship, it is manifold, but the matter of illusion is perhaps the chief. "Seeing" is not necessarily

SEEING IS NOT BELIEVING

"believing." I wonder, if like me, the reader of this book has ever shared their holiday photographs with friends, only to feel the need over this one or that one to add an explanation that the photograph as good as it is, falls short of the glory of the sunset and the drama of the Grand Canyon. Followed by the natural and heartfelt wish "if only you could have been there," "if only you could have seen what I saw." The truth captured in the photograph is the truth in part, but only in part. One might ask is this down to the equipment alone? Greater by far is what Camille Lauren explores in her charming book, she helps us to understand what is "actually" happening. She cites Roland Barthes about photography, he says: "It certifies, if we can put it this way, that the corpse is alive . . . The photograph is the living image of something dead."[28] It was, it has been, it is no more. The "moment" of the image is dead. We may be deeply affected by what we see on a screen but it is not real, it is not actual, as explained earlier "virtual" means "not actual," it is by definition an illusion.

Some years ago whilst visiting the wonderful Pergamon Museum in Berlin, into one of the galleries rushed a slightly out of breath young woman with her camera. Click, click, click as she rushed from one masterpiece to another, click, click, click. She managed not to *actually* look at any one of them. She barely gave the real paintings a moment's attention, and that only enough to navigate herself through the gallery space safely. The camera, the lens, had become her eye, she forfeited the "living," the "real" the "actual" image for a dead one. So desperate was she to hold on to everything in the end she got nothing but an empty experience, and forfeited what should have been so full and rewarding. We must wonder if she ever did go back to look at all the images she had so assiduously accumulated? Perhaps when and if she did, her encounter then would be with death and not with life. In his foreword Boorstin explains what his book is about "it is about our arts of self-deception, how we hide reality from ourselves."[29] Fifty-five years separate the young photographer from this notable author, she might benefit if she had the time to read him:

> He says: Early in the autumn of 1960, I received an elaborate color brochure advertising the Chevrolet for 1961. Inside, the only full page illustration is a brilliant portrait of a man in the front seat of a *deluxe* new model. His hard top convertible (advertised for its unobstructed view) is parked near the edge of what seems to be the Grand Canyon, a background of indescribable natural beauty. The man is not however, peering out of the car window at the scenery. Instead he is preoccupied with a contraption in his hand; he is preparing to look into his "Viewmaster," a portable slide-viewer using cardboard discs holding tiny color transparencies of scenic beauty. On the seat beside him are several extra discs. Standing outside the car are his wife and three small children. The eldest of them, a little girl about ten years old, at whom his wife is

28. Laurens, *Little Dancer Aged Fourteen*, 115, quoting Barthes, *Camera Lucida Reflections on Photography*.

29. Boorstin, *Image*, 11.

looking, is herself preoccupied with a small box camera with which she is preparing to take a picture of her father seated in the car. Here, if ever, is a parable of twentieth-century America. All the ingenuity of General Motors, Eastman Kodak, generations of Fords, Firestone, and Edisons, the accumulated skills of fifty years of automative engineering, of production know-how and industrial design, all the imagination and techniques of full-color printing, of junior and senior executives, and the whole gargantuan paraphernalia of the American economy have brought us to this. An opportunity for me to be impressed by the image of a man (with the Grand Canyon at his elbow) looking at an image, and being photographed as he does it![30]

In the winter of 2021 I witnessed a man on a sledge with his child coming down a snowy incline, a lovely sight. Sadly, rather than enjoying the *actual* moment, seeing what was before him and taking it all in, this man filmed himself and the child with his mobile phone! It would seem one is more interested in dead images than in living life itself. Has the church realized when it puts itself out on a screen of any kind it is trading in death not in life? "Zoom" is not even "death warmed up." As Kevin Vanhoozer states, "Images are simply the icing on the cake of the imagination, but there's little nutritional value in sugar."[31] Sugar, as we now know is really quite addictive, it rots the teeth and damages much, much more. The sugar of screen images I expect will rot the church for generations to come, and the nutritional value to the kingdom of God will be in the negative.

The screen's orientated "daily existence," as Dr. Susan Greenfield describes it, is "radically changing not just our everyday lifestyles, but also our identities and even our inner thoughts, in unprecedented ways."[32] What you use to interact with the world changes the way you see the world, because every lens is a tinted lens. This tinted lens of the screen has been overlaid on the most holy thing the church possesses, namely, the worship of God. Children and young people who have been exposed to it will, in my estimation, be altered forever and their understanding of the character and nature of God might never recover. "A detestable thing was once spoken of as having been done in Israel" (Mal 2:11, NIV). I wonder in the future if the same will be said of this.

Is Nothing Sacred Anymore?

There is a common view that the British are no longer a worshipping people, this is probably due to the fact that our church attendees are by now, 2021, falling exponentially. Britons may have little time any more for the worship of almighty God, but it would be a mistake to think that worship has gone to the wall. In vast numbers they love to devote themselves and pay large sums of money to sit and stand in adoring

30. Boorstin, *Image*, 251-52.
31. Reinke, *12 Ways*, 141.
32. Greenfield, *Mind Change*, 1.

wonder, come rain come shine, to watch their heroes, their gladiatorial performers, in an array of different sports. These "worshippers" cover all ages, men, women, and young people, it is also very egalitarian if you have the money to pay for it. The fact is, in the last twenty years, the cost of watching sport has greatly increased and often costs far too much to be *actually* experienced in person. The sport's industry in partnership or, might I say, in cahoots with TV, have "compassionately" come to the rescue, recognizing the need of the "worshippers" (fans). A solution has been devised at a fraction of the cost of both travel and admission to a game of football/soccer and now the "worshippers" can access their game "live" on TV. Even those "dyed in the wool" have gladly fallen into the hands of their beneficent providers.

As I write a football match can be watched on TV, a computer or smartphone, it all appears to be so very democratic. But naively most "worshippers" had not bargained for the trade off, as we know no one ever gets anything for nothing. During the first year's of TV's involvement at this level much remained the same, the game was untouched, there was not much of a noticeable difference, but then not surprisingly, came the advocates for change. Giant screens appeared in the stadiums which allowed the stars the possibility of indulging themselves, to check out their hairstyle after scoring a goal. Cameras soon covered every blade of grass and managed to focus on everything, and I mean everything. The crowd also was now "in the frame." Some years ago at one of the World Cups, it was decided to "Zoom" in. The game being watched between France and Brazil was no longer on the screen, it became acceptable, normal even, to turn the camera from the "real" event, to focus in on the crowd; particularly focussing on ladies of exceptional beauty. So now you could take a break from the game and even indulge in a form of armchair voyeurism. This has undoubtedly proved so successful and appears to have become standard practice at all major competitions. This is also standard practice in televised church worship, where the camera pans around to look at the congregation. In *actual* worship this would involve individuals at random turning around to look at other worshippers in the church.

In some Christian circles it can often be heard said, "our age is bereft of any values" and from one perspective this is easy to appreciate, though this is not really accurate, nor is it entirely true. What our age is deprived of is an "absolute," one beyond ourselves, some would call it a "moral code." Values in fact are surprisingly well established, but bear the hallmarks that they are of our own making. Not only this but they are entrenched, the author Frank Furedi acknowledges along with Ralph Fevre, that a "demoralization of western culture"[33] has taken place. "Instead of a moral code that provides experience with meaning, we live in an age of 'values.'"[34] The church co-existing with the world in this age of relativistic values, probably little realizes how closely with it these values are shared. Whether we know it or not we are being conformed. Furedi quotes J.D. Hunter, *The Death of Character: Moral Education*

33. Furedi, *Therapy Culture*, 162, quoting Fevre (2000).
34. Furedi, *Therapy Culture*, 162.

in an Age without Good or Evil: "Values are truths that have been deprived of their commanding character."[35] "Values are orientated toward the individual self."[36] "Values are personal preferences, inclinations and choice."[37] (The matter of inclination and choices is dealt with more fully in Chapter 10). It is not surprising that in our western culture where values are orientated toward the "individual self" we witness an ever deepening drive toward an acceptable drug culture. A tinted lens if ever there was one! One of the astonishing facts about those who operate in that culture where they possess and utilize their own set of values, is that there is "honor amongst thieves." They have their own moral code, which in truth is just a value system with their own preferences and inclinations. Those who run the cartels are unlikely to permit their sons and daughters to become degraded by drug addiction. These are the people who see the dangers of dependency, rather like those witnessed in the documentary *The Social Dilemma*, who equally will not permit their children to access the tech which they have developed to be used by everyone. They know the screen and the camera are addictive . . . enter their personal value system. But whatever else drugs do they bring a sense of empowerment to the individual in a life of impoverishment. The city trader in need of his cocaine shot is no different from the heroin addict in his derelict bunker, both feel empowered. Certainly the need to facilitate the individual self is at the fore; duty to oneself calls the shots. "What we use to interact with the world changes the way we see the world." Be it illegal substances of any kind or tech, drugs change the way we see the world.

Frank Furedi quoting Ulrich Beck says, "One of the key components of the therapeutically influenced value system is the principle of "duty to oneself.""[38] The girls alluded to earlier are evidently under the influence of the tech drugged culture to which they cannot extricate themselves. The value system of this culture has put the squeeze on and it is crushing them to death. What is more any "moral compass" they may have gleaned from their church attendance is made null and void, the narcissistic lock on them is equal to a narcotic. What should be of great concern is that from church and parents alike comes the message that they do not need to worry, since they possess "values." These values are truths which have been deprived of their commanding character, being orientated toward the individual self. Suffering from a continuous "high," it is the tech, the camera, the screen, the software, which the syringe delivers and as a consequence cultural sensibilities are altered forever. In the absence of a moral code, which not even the church possesses under the power of "tech deification," the girls are left only with a "self" centered value system. With sensory stimuli working day and night, 24/7 through the new dependency, duty to oneself becomes the "norm." The screen and camera work rather like a drug and all the evidence points

35. Furedi, *Therapy Culture*, 162, quoting Hunter, *Death of Character*, 76.

36. Furedi, *Therapy Culture*, 162.

37. Furedi, *Therapy Culture*, 162, quoting Hunter, *Death of Character*, 76.

38. Furedi, *Therapy Culture*, 162, quoting Beck, *Individualism*, 38.

to society, indeed the whole world being under the influence, this means the sacred from a moral standpoint, is subject to a mere value system. This value is as much a tinted lens as any, it just cannot be discerned but it can easily be tested . . .

The Assault on "Sabbath Keeping"

Let us consider the question of "Sabbath keeping," which many Christians with good conscience adhere to, or try to adhere to. This is in keeping with the view that the moral law, the Ten Commandments, is at least part of the rule of Christian living. In practical terms this would mean the TV along with many other things, being outlawed on the Sabbath, certainly eating out at McDonalds would be forbidden. But where the TV and the newspapers could not make the Sabbatarian bend, nor the "culinary delights" of McDonalds work its magic; the image-driven tech, with its own value system of personal preferences will have found this a "walk in the park." It is to be wondered how many good Sabbatarians open up their phones and computer screens to yield to unnecessary text messages, emails and the rest on the Sabbath day! The author is not indulging in stone throwing, only observing what the new drug is able to do to the moral law by replacing it with "a duty to oneself." In this it is surely eye watering to read the words of Michael Harris who says, "we still feel helpless against it, and we even feel addicted to the technologies that are that change's agents."[39]

This tech drug dependence of the world is present in the church and therefore cultural sensibilities have been very significantly altered. Where people could not be tempted to defy the moral law of Moses by turning on their TV, they can easily use the modern tech and justify it. These of course are plain and simple personal preferences. The truth is the camera, the screen, aided and abetted by *sarx* is well and truly in control, the addiction, the control, is plain for all to see. Nothing is sacred anymore!

Cameras Everywhere

The camera and the screen have confirmed that nothing is sacred any more. This ubiquitous "tool" has become the master of our culture and if the delight which it serves was to be removed, we would be at a loss. The only real dissatisfaction seems to be when it captures speeding motorists, only then is it a nuisance and even when it exposes the most outlandish sights it is still revered. A woman sits on the toilet and uses her mobile phone (multitasking no doubt!) to chat to a friend, but fails to turn off the phone at the end of the call causing embarrassing and fateful results, but who cares! (an actual scene). The Mayor of Antwerp was caught with his trousers down when he conducted a meeting from his home during lockdown. He was dressed as normal with shirt and tie for the "Zoom" meeting, giving the illusion he was fully dressed, but

39. Harris, *The End of Absence*, 39.

he had forgotten about an ill-placed mirror in the room, enabling all the onlookers to view the graphic picture of him sat in his undershorts. The mirror does not lie, he was not quite "the fairest of them all!"

In its nascent infancy the camera was the preserve of the rich and famous, the movie stars, who knew how to take a bow, and were even trained to do so. They were trained to play the role, they understood the illusion, they "knew" they were performing. Those who appear on the "red carpet" at the Oscars are skilled in the same art. The beautiful Tippi Hedren, made famous by her role in Hitchcock's *The Birds*, had never acted before she was invited to star in the film. Previously she had been a model and therefore knew how to present herself before the medium of the camera, but then she says, "Hitchcock taught me everything." In the past only these professionals could genuinely take a bow, now we can all take this stance by virtue of the camera and purloin without expectation of action against us. No one is going to prosecute us for our dishonesty and second rate performance in front of the lens. This of course is the camera duping us into the acceptable illusion, where we cannot help ourselves but engage in some kind of role, having watched closely the performance of the "stars." The screen is unnatural, the camera directed towards us and our response confirms this. On the whole those who perform in front of the mobile phone do so very badly, but nonetheless feel compelled to execute their "art." If what we see on the "red carpet" is not *sarx*, then it would be hard to know what is. Our two girls have studied their role models in depth.

At least in some measure being on camera, on screen, seems to present the opportunity of "levelling up," it is a form of democratizing of fame: "Hey I can get a slice of that!" (Andy Warhol's point exactly). Christians, like everyone else "squeezed" as they are by the drug "camera/screen allurement" produce the goods: "duty to oneself," providing equal opportunities for all in the age of equal opportunities . . . who can argue with that? Everyone has a "right" to a slice of the "red carpet," and in this way a "nobody" is miraculously, through the medium, empowered and transformed to become a "somebody," the desire of James and John the "Sons of Thunder" (Mark 10:35-45).

Furedi very helpfully provides insight, saying "Popular culture communicates the message that wider external demands are illegitimate if in some sense they thwart individual self-realization. Therapeutics is fundamentally a self-referential ethos."[40] He goes on to quote J.S. Rice: "the self's overarching moral significance, expressed by the claim that every person has a right to autonomy from social and cultural proprieties, is psychotherapy's central organizing principle."[41] This is the woman on the toilet, the mayor of Antwerp, the church in front of "Zoom." Furedi concludes: "The assumption that if it feels right . . . it ought to be pursued is informed by an ethic that

---

40. Furedi, *Therapy Culture*, 147.

41. Furedi, *Therapy Culture*, 147, quoting Rice, *Disease of One's Own*, 30.

depicts self-expression as an end in itself."[42] The church fell for the "gilded bait" of self expression. The camera "felt" right, the screen equally "feels" just the right medium to carry the worship of God and join hands to convey sacred worship. Drugs do blur reality, and it is worth repeating "what we use to interact with the world changes the way we *see* the world."

If only we had listened to Mr. Bunyan. He warns in his book "The Holy War" against Mr. Feelings who is a menace to "Mansoul" but we have evidently not listened closely enough. Feelings have opened the door to the zeitgeist in the kitchen, in the bedroom and office, in the garden and even in the church. Our love affair with the camera and the screen is like a dependency, and for this reason we could not see the need to protect the sacred from it.

As we have come a long way in our use of the camera and the screen, our need of therapy has significantly developed with it. And while the Freudian variety has long since been dismissed by Christians, we evidently belong to an age, a culture, which is sadly a drug dependent one. We are as Abraham Lincoln put it "a nation [a people: emphasis mine] so unhappily distracted." He would have concurred with the scriptures:

> But just look at you! You are putting your confidence in a false belief that will not deliver you (Jer 7:8, NET)

> 'But am I the one they are provoking?' declares the Lord. 'Are they not rather harming themselves, to their own shame?' (Jer 7:19, NIV)

When the football (soccer) authorities were presented with the possibilities of wall-to-wall screen coverage of the game, on hearing the offer from the broadcasters promising them untold riches, their eyes lit up. But perhaps what they did not bargain for was that in no time at all the "worshippers" stopped *actually* attending the matches. The stadiums were often half full, where were the fans now? In huge numbers people were sat at home in the comfort of their chairs, they did not have to face the inconvenience of traveling to the game in cold and inclement weather. Contented now they could cheer on their side while enjoying pizza and a bottle of beer, which not surprisingly the ad men were swift to show us the possibility of a new reality. The screen had "done a number" on the game and those who loved it were powerless to stop it. The artificial in the ascendency rode roughshod over them, without realizing it, the game we loved was no longer. Without a whimper, it had sold its soul. The "fluid line" which is how Guardini puts it had been crossed . . . "A line on the far side of which living closeness to nature has been lost."[43] Those who love the game of football know something of its original beauty has been lost forever, never to return. To

---

42. Furedi, *Therapy Culture*, 147.

43. Gay, *Way of the (Modern) World*, 96, quoting Guardini, *Letters from Lake Como*, 5.

confirm the loss of the fluid line, here are just a few of the plethora of "on-line" services the churches are offering post lockdown . . .

Live Streaming Services—Livestream church online
Join us this Sunday for church online. *Live* worship & dynamic relevant message. Join us! Connect with God who doesn't do social distancing.
Be blessed & uplifted. Join us!
Sign Up. How it Works. About Us. Support Center. View Features
We are open and live streaming—Stay home watch the livestream
From your big comfy couch you can watch Heartland Services.
Eat breakfast and enjoy church. Our children's church *live streams*
also so visit the website for times! Support Groups. Media Library. Online
Giving
Online Worship—The Life Church
Worship in the comfort of your home. For about an hour.
On your schedule. 24/7. Multiple *services*. Running continuously. Back to
back. Amenities: Faith, Bible, Word. Give. Mission
How to Livestream Your Church Service: A Practical Guide
When it comes to *livestreaming*, start slow and grow with time. Allow your
first attempt to feel like a disaster, but be sure to debrief . . .
Live Streaming Frustrating You? Get Better Results Today
There's no need for extra cameras and expensive equipment to *stream* great
live video. Tips, tricks and more that makes you look like a *live streaming* pro
on your first try. Coaching.
The Ultimate Guide to Live Streaming your Church Services
It'll help you reach specific church goals. While Livestream found that one
church's online donations increased by 70% after live streaming services.
"What's a Watch Party?
We're glad you asked. A Watch Party is a group of people who live in the
same local area and participate in the worship experience together. Whether
it's meeting in a living room, apartment, or community space, you don't have
to do church alone!
Your responsibility as a member of the Media Church
As a Member of Family Worship Center (FWC) Media Church, we will
expect you to look at FWC as your Church. Irrespective as to where you live,
by the means of the Internet and Radio, you are worshipping together with
us, and are just as much a part of our Church as those who live in the city of
Baton Rouge."

Simon Jenkins reveals that the lockdown (re: COVID-19) has not been all bad news:

Dynamic churches have turned the online boom to their advantage. Zoom praying, live streaming and social media posting have soared. Almost 17,000 services and events were added to the website . . . Time to Pray podcast has had 200,000 downloads so far this year. Only holy communion was a challenge, met by some churches via drive-in services in the open air . . . Many parish churches have become film sets with production companies attached. My local vicar has seen her meagre attendance at daily morning prayers more than double on Zoom . . . The question of what is normal could clearly be traumatic for the church. Churches are in the same bind as other institutions in the local high street. (Notice here Jenkins sees the church as a business like any other on the high street). Why drive and park when you can surf and click?[44]

Why indeed! The mistake here would be to think that we are more spiritual, when in fact we are just more religious. It is easy to recall Paul's observations in Athens when he observed not their spirituality "I see that in every way you are very religious." (Acts 17:22, NIV).

Jenkins acknowledges that things have been difficult for the churches, but what he is really saying is that by virtue of the tech, they are better off now than they were before, with more interested customers "virtually" than when they "actually" gathered. The Evangelical churches which have been so quick to boast of their soaring numbers of online device access to worship, might be wise to ask this question: if it was so successful in lockdown why not continue it? The customers will demand it![45] Pragmatism would certainly demand it. Pride and the quest for soaring numbers being shouted from the roof tops will prove too tempting to resist. How times change, as this is exactly what Billy Graham said about his power to reach the masses via television in the 1960s, which so many Evangelicals were critical of.

Jenkins also quotes the Church of England statistician, Ken Eames:

(Who) accepts that no one can tell the true value of such online "worship." It stands to reason that not having to dress up and travel to church is a huge convenience, especially for families. There is no social commitment to place, but so what? Eames says that COVID "may have permanently changed the way attendance is recorded in the future," and wonders "when, if ever, churches will return to normal.[46]

Whether we like it or not the "new normal" is now with us to stay. "What we use to interact with the world *changes* the way we see the world."

---

44. Simon Jenkins, *Guardian* columnist, 26 December 2020

45. This practice is now in fact established in the church. Since COVID-19 was cracked by the vaccine, churches have returned to "in service" worship, but understandably kept their "Zoom" worship to run alongside it.

46. Simon Jenkins, "If the Church of England Worship Online," *The Guardian*.

CHAPTER 6

THE NEW IDOLATRY

Idolatry is not simply the worship of a physical object, but rather any form of devotion that is judged to be incorrect.[1]

CARLOS M.N. EIRE

The huge modern heresy is to alter the human soul to fit modern social conditions instead of altering modern social conditions to fit the human soul.

G.K. CHESTERTON

Mortify therefore . . . evil concupiscence, and covetousness, which is idolatry.

COLOSSIANS 3:5 (KJV)

IF IT CAN BE REASONABLY shown that the modern screen/tech, along with a good dose of self, amounts to an idolatrous coalition, then the way is not only open to discuss the idol, but it becomes imperative to do so.

Although image has risen to proportions which appear almost stratospherical, placing it in the mainstream of our culture, we probably struggle to make connections with its historical roots. This chapter endeavors to help regarding its religious context, apart from anything else this gives the possibility to consider the fact that we easily allow ourselves to be cut off from the past. Whether we realize it or not, this makes us vulnerable to viewing life, and in particular spiritual life, only in the context of the present. The present is all that matters. On the other hand, if we do not know where we have come from how can we know where we are going? The result is the narrowing of our field of vision, as a consequence we routinely fail and life is then out of focus. We have already seen our convenient visual recognition of the Queen of Heaven, hopefully by now we can apply the same rules to the screen/tech.

1. Eire, *War Against the Idols*, 5.

The New Dictionary of Theology provides the necessary clarity: "In the Bible and the history of the Christian church, 'image' is closely associated with 'idol' and 'idolatry.'"[2]

> An image [Lat. *imago*; Gk. *eikon*) is a likeness of someone or something, most often in another medium. An image represents and symbolizes, but it is more; it is the similitude (see Hosea 12:10, KJV) of something, reflecting or mirroring it.[3]

What we may say with some authority is that while there is precious little spirituality in our times, religion on the other hand proliferates. There is an abundance of devotion, and at the center of that devotion is the idol of self. In this we are deeply idolatrous and the tech is our equal in its quest for honor.

The Numbers Game

Paul noted in Athens not that the people were very spiritual, but very religious (Acts 17:22). Simon Jenkins' report on what took place following the COVID-19 lockdown in Britain confirms this: "There has been a huge growth in people turning to on-line worship, to Zoom and the rest."[4] Jenkins, who views the church like any other high street business, naturally sees this as success. Apparently his only real concern for the church lies in his affection for ancient buildings, which he is entitled to feel passionate about. His grasp of the kingdom of God, of Christ's true church, is not remotely considered. To his way of thinking it is purely a numbers game, and if numbers are our aim then "Zoom" is impressive. But might we not mistake numbers in the way the Graham campaigns did in the 1950s and 1960s? The numbers were very impressive. Mega "churches" in America and Korea today are impressive in numbers, but should we read this as spirituality or, as Paul observed in Athens, merely "religious" leanings?

Let us assume the best and try to be constructive. Let us concede that the intent is genuine, and not just a "social fix" and this signals, in a most difficult time, a kind of turning point (it has already been reported that many will not return to their former patterns of worship) to God, a revival of kinds. After all if a church had only a handful of worshippers, but attracted hundreds during lockdown by "Zoom," or thousands in some cases, would it not be churlish to fail to recognize this as "revival," even if not in the strictest sense? Where, we might ask, did this upsurge come from? Equally we must wonder why these people did not come to church pre-COVID-19? It may be argued the only thing that matters is that they come. Some churches boast of thousands now connecting to their "worship." It is surely not difficult for any true Christian to recognize that ordinarily people come to church for a variety of reasons; and for a

---

2. *New Dictionary of Theology*, 330.

3. *New Dictionary of Theology*, 329.

4. Simon Jenkins, "If the Church of England Worship Online," *The Guardian*.

variety of reasons sadly they stay away. This increase in numbers may be genuine, but it may also be social, and this would not be surprising considering the unprecedented times we are facing, and the social network of which everyone is a part.

History Lesson

It may be helpful to draw a lesson here from a period of church history which many of us may be unfamiliar with. In the late medieval period, scholars agree, there was a religious intensity which emerged. Carlos Eire quotes,

> In his essay, "Piety in Germany Around 1500," Bernd Moeller points out that the principle characteristic . . . was its consistent churchliness, and says it was "one of the most churchly-minded and devout periods of the Middle Ages.[5]

It is recognized this was a kind of "lay fervor"[6] and it is spoken of in terms of "religious saturation."[7] But Carlos Eire points out the sinister side of the apparent success.

> Late medieval religion sought to grasp the transcendent by making it immanent: It was a religion that sought to embody itself in images, reduce the infinite to the finite, blend the holy and the profane.[8]

Apart from the destruction of a sanctified worship this could not fail in making the "divine commonplace."[9] Bringing this right up to date, here is our clear and present danger.

It is a well voiced criticism and understandably so, churches appear to have shoveled the common place out of the door. The complaint which may be leveled at the church and its religion, is that it is too highbrow; the preserve not of the common man, but very definitely of the educated older middle classes. Certainly this is difficult to argue with, and there is an obvious case to answer. It is vital for those who make this criticism to appreciate God is not above the common place, in fact God is more than interested in the common place. Obviously in the late medieval period the ordinary man or woman in their village, who saw the erection of a new image connected it with a wider religious democracy, in this they were reassured they were not alone, they were not excluded. Rome might have been the headquarters, a thousand miles away, but she was not impervious to the needs of a village community. Here was the benevolent mother church looking after everyone. Furthermore, we can easily appreciate the

---

5. Eire, *War Against the Idols*, 10, quoting Bernd Moeller, *Reformation in Medieval Perspective*, 1971.

6. Eire, *War Against the Idols*, 11.

7. Eire, *War Against the Idols*, 11.

8. Eire, *War Against the Idols*, 11.

9. Eire, *War Against the Idols*, 11.

sense of gratitude felt for the benevolent, caring eye which was cast over them by the newly erected Virgin Mary. This sense of community care, democracy, of all being included, all involved, is a natural one, no one is left out, no one is forgotten. In the same way we might not be far off the mark if we conclude that the modern medium of "screen" worship essentially builds on this psychology. It appears at first sight to democratize, it fixes a level playing field; perhaps this can be traced as the reason for the fervor. In medieval times everyone, church and community, had their crucifix, their statue to call on. This would have given a shared identity, everyone was joined in a common bond. No one fell outside the pious gaze of the Virgin, rich and poor alike enjoyed her tender interest in them. So in "screen" worship no one who wished to "attend" need feel forgotten, or out of touch, community could at least be *seen* to be functioning as normal. The tender intent of the church could be felt "through" the screen.

A Veneer of Virtue

Definition of a veneer: A veneer, a thin layer, often of wood or ivory, just microns thick covering a substrate of entirely different material not associated with it; giving a superficial, valuable, desirable appearance.

Quite possibly all of us can attest to the endeavors of our parents attempting (kindly as they saw it) to instruct us in their personal history, trying to compare their own "life journey" with ours. Unfortunately, and very often, theirs and ours did not seem to match up quite so seamlessly. We struggled to connect their story and ours, the relevance of their experiences so "long ago" with our own! In an attempt to do deference to parents and give them the benefit of the doubt, most probably they were simply, lovingly, trying to smooth the way through the tricky paths of life for their kids. The truth is, knowing better, much better, (it is the prerogative of the young to be opinionated) we quickly dismissed their wisdom . . . author guilty as charged! Perhaps years later viewing life from an entirely different perspective, gaining much needed experience, we were able to reflect and humbly acknowledge, and appreciate the merit of their advice. What takes place in all families also takes place in the family of the church, and there are voices which come up from the past to help us if we are only willing to listen to them. In our own day we may not know where we are going because we do not have much idea where we have come from. Getting this right is vital if we are to navigate a path into the future, because a "future" for the church there must be. Very often our parents' history lessons were genuinely meant, they were trying the best way they knew to point up their own mistakes and failings in the hope that we might not make the same. Church history is replete with examples of painful journeys, and much has been written if only we would read it. But history is often brutal in its re-telling and deliberately even foolishly, we turn up our noses at its lessons, desiring a sweeter kind of medicine.

"Don't Know Much about History"

Because of the nature of this enquiry it would be wise not to sweep history under the carpet, nor should we attempt to, since the parallels of the past and the present are too closely defined. It is from the past that a light shines, which, if we will be instructed by it, we may be delivered from the fog. History records that the church from the earliest times right up to the present has been burnt by the "image," from which the prototype always suffers, regardless of the image. Idolatry is as Eire observes, "any form of devotion that is judged to be incorrect."[10] Our devotion to screen is by now ubiquitous, we are sated even intoxicated . . . we need some help from the past to give us a perspective on the present.

Remarkably though there is little evidence of any crisis of conscience as the church has blundered in to its faustian deal with the idol.[11] But then this should be no surprise since *we* are at the center of it all, the idol has kindly invited us in.

To gain a perspective and view of our situation we need to go back in time, rather like Steven did in his history lesson (Acts 7). History lessons can be derived from the most unlikely of places, and though many Bible-believing Christians will be shocked, Erasmus, the Dutch Philosopher and humanist, is able to provide a partial guiding light—"beggars can't be choosers!" Erasmus is a "mixed bag," but to some extent we all are! Carlos Eire generously attributes to him the ability of, "a unique flair for blending his support of traditional beliefs with criticism; and for being able to distribute praise and blame at the same time."[12] While he must have been prone to fits of pique delivering his "barbs" and "acerbic comments," he certainly does not appear to suffer from a craven spirit. Rather, his willingness to assault reliance on "image" looks as clear and brave as anyone. He makes Luther the "great man" look rather feeble as touching the question of externals. Luther gives the impression of being indifferent as to whether these things should "stand or fall." Dare we say, Luther might even have come down on the side of today's "screen" worshippers?

Forever Friends . . . not!

On the one hand, we find him criticizing church adornment as "mere shadows and tokens of reality and childish things."[13] On the other, Eire informs us further, that "Carl Christiansen shows that Luther moved from an originally critical and even somewhat negative opinion of church decorations to an ultimately positive one."[14] This painfully provides a much-needed commentary on our forays in to "screen" worship. Prior to

10. Eire, *War Against the Idols*, 5.

11. A Faustian deal: spiritual values which are sacrificed for power and knowledge.

12. Eire, *War Against the Idols*, 49.

13. Eire, *War Against the Idols*, 67, quoting Christiansen, *Art*, 62.

14. Eire, *War Against the Idols*, 67.

lockdown many churches and Christians were quite partisan in their rejection of "the world." In fact anything that had the odor of "the world" was to be resisted fearlessly. Nothing of "the world" could be joined to the worship of God, in any shape or form. Nothing could be allowed to ingress the "Holy of Holies," the spirit of Josiah was upon them. This is where history does not gently nudge us, but bites us. Image was the incendiary which would explode in the face of Luther and Karlstadt altering their relationship. Luther descends to a place where he calls his old friend "our worst enemy." "Doctor Andreas Karlstadt has deserted us, and on top of that has become our worst enemy."[15] Fighting talk indeed! Eire interprets this as arising "from different interpretations of the nature of worship."[16] Karlstadt seems to have made himself an enemy of Luther as Paul did with the Galatians by doing no more than telling them the truth (Gal 4:16). In a treatise of 1520 Karlstadt expressed his "opposition to externalized worship," (in it he proposes) "that material elements are unable to convey spiritual benefits."[17] He viewed images Eire says, "as part of a religious atmosphere whose function was to retard the intellectual and spiritual growth of the laity." Having recently viewed an article put out by the *New York Times* highlighting "Zoom" worship, my very worst fears have been confirmed, the spiritual and intellectual are retarded. The idol looks to have fulfilled Paul's words: "Although they claimed to be wise they became fools" (Rom 1:22, NIV). In an array of shocking images and comments from so-called worshippers "kicking over the traces" so to speak, they confirm how the "benign tool" with consummate ease has been able to manipulate them.

Once it was the "stage star" performing the manipulation, now it is the mechanics of "Zoom." Luther on a better day would have generously called these "childish things," "Zoom" worshippers have clearly fallen under the "spell" principally by falling foul of the image, only this time images of themselves. When this happens, "The image and the prototype often become indistinguishable in the mind of the supplicant"[18] . . . game set and match!

John Calvin's insight into the dangers of idolatry follow a particular thought which dovetails perfectly with the introduction of "Zoom" into the churches. Eire interprets Calvin this way "Calvin's attack on Roman Catholic "idolatry" is a condemnation of the improper mixing of spiritual and material in worship."[19] What kind of commentary does this supply on our contemporary worship scene, where screen, the undisputed idol of our age, delivers worship? Could this be referred to as mixing? Eire says:

---

15. Eire, *War Against the Idols*, 65, quoting Luther, *Against the Heavenly Prophets*, 40, 79.

16. Eire, *War Against the Idols*, 66.

17. Eire, *War Against the Idols*, 56.

18. Eire, *War Against the Idols*, 21.

19. Eire, *War Against the Idols*, 197–98.

Because Calvin sees human nature as inherently prone to idolatry, he constantly warns that it is dangerous to accept even the most insignificant form of material worship in the Church, for "men's folly" cannot restrain itself from falling headlong into superstitious rites.[20]

Calvin's principle was based on *Finitum non est capax infiniti*, but *Soli Deo Gloria* was equally fighting his corner for him. Glory to God alone would be a Savior in the modern day church if we could only employ it. "Erasmus insists that religion is best when it does not depend on visible things"[21] (presumably of any kind). Translating this for us today would certainly mean that dependence on a dead saint, painted on a church wall (an image), conjuring inspiration is no different from dependence on a live saint (an image) conjuring inspiration pixelated on a screen. Though Christians will be loathe to admit it, in fact in truth these are strange "bedfellows." This complete opposition to mixture would also compel Calvin to deliver his own "barbs." "Thus, the first step of man's audacity is to ignore the prescriptions of God."[22]

Plaster and Pixels

The danger for those uninitiated in the power of image is that as the world is embodied in *it*, might not also Christians allow their worship to be so embroiled? If it has happened once before it can and will happen again, the danger is we are already "en route" as having *permitted* it we have *promoted* it. Those now who might like to distance themselves from the experiment have already provided it with much needed impetus. By an act of choice, entirely volitional, "screen" worship is now a new established art form in the church. The church unwilling or unable to risk "together" so as to do "corporeal," fell for the "opium of the people," and because of the stimulant that it is, it will be near impossible to break its hold.

In medieval times "harmless tools" were issued by the church to help the poor and needy, these came in all shapes and sizes, but could be accessed by one and all. A medieval worshipper in a mountain village might well have faced a predicament not unlike that which confronted people during COVID-19 lockdown, cut off, stuck in a place miles from anywhere. Who could he reach out to in his lonely location? Who could lift him up, encourage him, offer sympathy, succor and encouragement? Who could stir him and put fire into his belly? Who could assist him to reach that sublime abode? In fact he had no reason to fear, the church had his need in hand, the remote valley pathway could be illuminated, he had access to the mountain shrine. The gilded plaster cast of the saint or the Virgin so beautifully decorated, invited him in and then assisted him in his worship. Access to the divine transcendence was now within

---

20. Eire, *War Against the Idols*, 225, *Institutes*, I.11.3.

21. Eire, *War Against the Idols*, 36.

22. Eire, *War Against the Idols*, 205, *Institutes*, I.11.4.

reach, immanence had made this possible. He was no longer cut off, no longer alone, no longer feeling feeble, instead he was now empowered, now enabled. The image was blessed with remarkable powers. This blessing succeeded in exciting the needy by establishing a dependence. The fresco possessed the power to achieve the same; just as any encounter with the art of stained glass might; whether that was accessed in a village church or in the salubrious surroundings of a great cathedral. These when left entirely to themselves possessed the capability to translate the worshipper to an entirely different place from "here to there." These were not merely provisions by which the laity mighty fly away impressed by works of art, this art was intended to be used and perhaps most importantly used at their convenience. Refreshment through these visual delights was extremely democratic . . . that is if you had legs to get you there and eyes to see with. What is more these were sanctified, "a clean bill of health" was pronounced over the "wonderful provisions" which the church, with God's blessing, had fashioned for the good of everyone. "Authority" was stamped all over them, and no one could doubt, these were "tools," "God's tools." Because they worked (medieval pragmatism), everyone used them in their time of need, and who could deny people in their time of need? This "root," as Calvin observes, is in us all, meaning no matter how protracted, the "War against the Idols" will continue. This war which stretches from the golden calf to our present day computer screens and beyond, as the "veneer of virtue" will forever recommend such accoutrements to us.

The fundamental point here is that "plaster and pixels" in the form of images will always amount to the same thing (see Chapter 10, the calibrated weighing scales). These are called upon, depended upon in time of need. Why? They provide immanence. It has been rather clumsily argued by some that "screen" worshippers above all else are seeking access to the preached word of God, but this is misleading, word can surely be accessed by audio means, no one needs pictures (images) to facilitate it. No, the "screen" worship is about accessing images in the name of worship, something impossible to achieve "together" through a computer monitor. The reason images are needed today is just the same reason they were needed in medieval times, they dial up the temperature of the heart, the fire is kindled, the soul encouraged, not by meeting, but by seeing pictures (images). The result, the worshipper is translated to another place and immanence has done its work. In this, it is impossible to separate the mountain shrine from that of the "screen" as both assist worship. There may be a fundamental antithetical difference which separates "then" and "now," but the medieval worship was always confronted with reality. The statue, the image, was obviously made of paint, wood and plaster, it had an entirely worldly feel about it. The modern "screen" worshipper is by contrast drawn into an unreal world of "hyper-reality," with reality television aiding and abetting the framework of the illusion. Reality is re-drawn, the lie is believed. Of course "then" and "now" do have some similarities, Erasmus saw the baseness of such worship and Eire comments, "The images, in short, had come alive."[23] Plaster and pixels possess the same power. Sadly, very sadly, even if such religious practices reduce the divine in our understanding by their embodiment in images, whether that is plaster or pixel, the "veneer of virtue" will continue to recommend them to us.

It should be reiterated all images exist to be "used" i.e. employed, they are used for one reason only, they are *needed*. When the sport stars of today negotiate their eye-watering contracts, image rights are a major part of the deal. They treat their image as a commodity, becoming protective of it due to it being a commercial entity. They know that if their image is employed it can lucratively promote them. This means the basketball player, the soccer star or tennis superstar who has reached divine status, become common place so everyone can have a piece of them. Historically in this way the infinite was able to become finite; the reversal of *finitum non est capax infiniti*. The Cross in the Middle Ages was ubiquitous in every church, in every village, along with the Virgin they imposed themselves, they were the masters of self promotion. The Divine and the commonplace met and became fused. The Goddess Diana at Ephesus became an "image" which was able to support an entire industry, this is "as old as the hills." Again Eire says "The growing cult of images (like our own, emphasis mine) had no safeguard built in to prevent the people from confusing the image and what it sought to represent . . . images could acquire a life of their own."[24] The vividness and new magic nature of the image in the period of the late Middle Ages was bound to impress, "Eye-gate" was moved and how could it not be when much of what was presented was contemporary and modern?

During the early years of the sixteenth century Swiss workshops had their order books full, Zurich saw the commissioning of church art explode, it increased Eire tells us "a hundredfold between 1500 and 1518."[25] Not surprisingly guilds and other organizations devoted time, and more importantly money to the projects. These were "aids" to the worship of God, but in truth here was business at its most effective. This most significantly fulfilled an external need, this was Madonna's "material world," and the church the "material girl" but not unsurprisingly it did not bring God or spirituality into closer proximity, it only corrupted so as to serve the creature more than the Creator. Eire quotes one scholar who has observed "The Christian church had never displayed such visual splendor as it did in the late Middle Ages."[26] What else would this produce except a breathtaking sight, obviously added to this was the novelty of it all. In its own way it possessed a modernity with magic-like powers. Keith Thomas, also quoted by Eire, "has made the blunt, perceptive observation that much of late medieval religion was magical."[27] The danger of magic is further exemplified by R.C.

---

23. Eire, *War Against the Idols*, 21, Allen, ix.

24. Eire, *War Against the Idols*, 14.

25. Eire, *War Against the Idols*, 13, Garside, *Zwingli*, 87.

26. Eire, *War Against the Idols*, 14, Hans Preuss, *Die Deutsche Frommigkeit im Spiegel*, 122.

27. Eire, *War Against the Idols*, 11, quoting Thomas, *Religion and the Decline*, 49.

Trexler who observes the extensiveness of "the belief in powerladen natural objects . . . magic . . . does give some assurance of control over fate."[28] Gay also quotes Keith Thomas, "A reservoir of magical power which could, at the discretion of the priests, be made available for secular purposes."[29] These observations are apt, if rather "too close to the bone" as touching our own digital magic.

The apparent danger for the church of the twenty-first century is that the "image" which is so dominant, so magnified, so glorified in our culture, cannot fail to work a deep confusion in those who depend upon it. The magic of the medium becomes a drug, it creates a dependency, an idol all by itself with which people become transfixed and besotted. Eire points out what should be obvious to us all,

> Pictures (of any kind, emphasis mine) are not a good medium by which to convey qualitative distinctions in worship. The growing cult of images had no safeguard built in to prevent the people from confusing the image and what it sought to represent.[30]

This confirms Calvin's comments: "Though all men do not worship the *same* (emphasis mine) idols, they are all nevertheless in bondage to idolatry."[31] "All modes of worship fabricated by men are rejected as unsavory."[32] If "Zoom" worship is not a fabrication of our artistry then we have become entirely blind to our contemporary idolatry.

The case has already been set out in this book that the approach of worship through a screen (a tinted lens) will affect the perception of it, especially in the young as they try to comprehend divinity. The account of the reformer and mentor to John Calvin, Guillaume Farel, illustrates this; he recalled his childhood experience of his encounter with a *material* object. The *material* object was a "web of fraud, deceit and priestly avarice."[33] In the huge numbers who have encountered the same through "screen" worship, we cannot imagine anything but confusion and fragmented thinking. What a deeply damaging psychological experience, especially for the young and impressionable. What was Farel to make of the image presented to him? What are children to make of the Worship of the one true God through a computer screen set up on Sunday morning on the kitchen table, which may also include the service of the Lord's Supper? The transcendent has been eliminated, the imminent rules. What damage will have been done when they realize, if they ever do, that this medium was the world's number one idol? We must remember that vast numbers of people blighted by the worship of any false religion struggle to gain their freedom, because the idols

---

28. Eire, *War Against the Idols*, 25, quoting Trexler, *Florentine Religious Experience*, 9.
29. Gay, *The Way of the (Modern) World*, 109, quoting Thomas, *Religion and the Decline*, 47.
30. Eire, *War Against the Idols*, 14.
31. Miller, *Calvin's Wisdom*, 157.
32. Miller, *Calvin's Wisdom*, 386.
33. Eire, *War Against the Idols*, 8; Farel, *Du Vray Usage de la Croix* (1560).

and images are never completely dealt with, never expunged. They leave a deep and indelible mark upon the consciousness, and remain stubbornly resistant to truth.

Material, Material Everywhere

As anxiety builds, people often caught in the vortex of it, try to navigate a way through. Anxiety forces their hand, leading to considerable hurt thereby making matters worse. When, in the spring of 2020, COVID-19 forced the UK into lockdown, many churches almost immediately followed the lead of business and turned to tech to solve its problems; in this way much of "business" could continue as usual, a very unfortunate likeness indeed. Such action somewhat recalls what Eire observes about worship in the Middle Ages, "Seeking divinity through more immediate means."[34] Late medieval religion only succeeded in making it ever more distant. This is worship conducted via the *material*. In the case of the contemporary church, that *material* is the screen/tech, the mechanical is called upon to bridge the gap which exists so as to bring worshippers together. Yet in reality the *material*, the "tool" (so-called) is in fact unable to perform the gymnastics. Church "meetings" online are a misnomer, no one is "meeting," no one is doing "together," no one is in "assembly." In *reality* the distance between individual worshippers remains the same, while it must be feared, the distance between the worshipper and God is greatly enlarged, just what Farel experienced. The reason being, any *material* object must of necessity place distance between God and the supplicant because it is *needed*, it is *depended* upon in an attempt to join the two together, it is an indispensable "tool."

Steven Ozment when assessing the affects of medieval iconoclasm explains that this "was the response of a people whose piety had been sincere, but who suddenly realized they had been hoodwinked."[35] Carlos Eire makes an observation about medieval worship, a most uncomfortable link with our present entanglement. "Popular devotion was externalized"[36] this was perfect for the terribly dry and arid conditions of the soul in the late Middle Ages. He goes on to say, "The image and the prototype often become indistinguishable in the mind of the supplicant."[37] In our dry and arid days, it is to be wondered what effect "Zoom" worship has had, and will continue to have on thousands who suddenly became attracted to church. In much the same way, many of those who reflected on the techniques of the mass evangelistic campaigns, knew, but far too late, they had been "hoodwinked."

The pertinent question has to be this: Can a comparison be drawn between then and now? It is possible, and indeed likely, that idolatry will arise in any age, during any period of the Christian church. Why should we think we are incapable of it now?

---

34. Eire, *War Against the Idols*, 25.

35. Eire, *War Against the Idols*, 26, quoting Ozment, *Reformation*, 44.

36. Eire, *War Against the Idols*, 15.

37. Eire, *War Against the Idols*, 21.

Do we think our modernity has driven it out of us? What would make *us* more astute in steering a course through life without this becoming a stumbling block? Perhaps in our sophistication we consider ourselves above such base admixture. Let us test . . .

"The" Hammer Blow

There are many ways to describe the religious conditions which prevailed in Europe before the Reformation as a force broke the stronghold of the Roman Church. One description is simple, it was materialistic. A religious mindset prevailed which, on the face of it, was beyond any hope of change, the depth of this is brought out by Carlos Eire, he makes it plain that western Christendom diffused the sacred in with the profane. The spiritual was joined to the *material*, but as we know one must give way to the other, and it did. This was the religion of *material,* the cult of saints with its images, relics and Catholic Mass. Immanence held sway by holding all the cards, it was a controlling power from which the poor people under its influence could not break free. "Transcendence" came to the rescue, "Lutherans, (and) also championed the principles of *sola fide* and *sola scriptura,*"[38] these were the double hammers which delivered the fatal blows.

But alongside these was another assistant just as weighty but little known about, a "third principle" is how Eire describes it, "Finitum non est capax infiniti" (the finite cannot contain the infinite)."[39] Here was the pincer movement guided by this battle cry, the reformed focused on piety which would hopefully be the death blow to immanence. It was just here though that issues arose between the crusade of the Reformed and that approach of the Lutherans who sailed rather too close to the wind of historical Catholicism. Eire tells us, "While some Protestants cast down the "idols" of Rome, Luther cast out the image breakers from Wittenberg. The redefinition of the sacred, then, became the watershed that separated not only Protestant from Catholic, but Lutheran from Reformed as well."[40] Lutherans seem to have been somewhat ambivalent as touching the question of *material* and therefore necessarily immanence. Eire again observes the difference between the Lutherans and the Reformed lay in the fact . . . "they (the Reformed, emphasis mine) paid much more attention to the way in which the divine ought to be approached."[41] Here is the heart of our contemporary issue, the concern of this book . . . *the way*. Have the boundaries of *the way* been re-drawn by "Zoom," albeit in a very subtle *way*, so that churches have turned to immanence without even realizing it? The fear must surely be that no hammer can smash this new found idolatry.

---

38. Eire, *War Against the Idols*, 3.

39. Eire, *War Against the Idols*, 3.

40. Eire, *War Against the Idols*, 2.

41. Eire, *War Against the Idols*, 3.

The Finite Cannot . . .

The problem for Christians is the issue of the "dark ages," being long ago, these are now "out of sight," therefore "out of mind." Some will never have heard of the questions raised by the Reformation, never mind that of immanence. If they had and understood the dangers of it (which those of a Charismatic persuasion look to have fallen for), then they might have been more alarmed at the thought that the finite, the "screen," is able to contain the infinite, God himself in the form of worship. In Eire's introduction to his book *War against the Idols* he explains his reason for writing, his aim is "to analyze the interrelationship between circumstances and ideas."[42] This is just what this book deals with. Circumstances by virtue of COVID-19 have forged partnerships with ideas which led to invention, which in turn has led to behavior. Lutherans seem to have been somewhat ambivalent as touching the question of *material* and therefore necessarily immanence. "Admixture of spiritual and material in worship"[43] is how Eire describes it. The Reformation clearly threw up a conflict which in truth was as old as that entered into by Aaron. The distinction between the Reformed approach and that explored by Lutherans was that one paid particularly close attention to the "way" that God in worship should be approached, the other less so. This was one of the principle concerns of Reformation thinking: ideas lead to actions. Eire puts it this way (the) "correlation between ideas and situations."[44] Idolatry is a combative word which forces the question (now as in the past), what is true and what is false, what is permissible and what is forbidden? This combative can be seen as it arises between Moses and Aaron after the tragic forging of the golden calf. Idolatry necessitates, even demands, the combative.

The situation which resulted in the creation of the golden calf was realized by the means of a "good idea," circumstances led to it. The goddess Artemis/Diana, like all other idols emerged out of a desire for immanence. These were born in a situation which called forth ideas, which in turn led inevitably to practice. The chain is unmistakable and inevitable. Neil Postman suggests, "The form in which ideas are expressed affects what those ideas will be."[45] Fast forward to the foot of the mount . . .

The Image of Compromise

When, because of circumstances, Aaron (the magician, Exod 32:24) exclaims "I just threw this in and out came this calf." . . like a poof of smoke, he turned to the *material* he clearly had not weighed the moment as to the consequences. There was "fall-out" just as there was in the Reformation. Interestingly Aaron tries to mitigate in some way

42. Eire, *War Against the Idols*, 4.

43. Eire, *War Against the Idols*, 24.

44. Eire, *War Against the Idols*, 7.

45. Postman, *Amusing Ourselves to Death*, 32.

the axis of error, he attempts to join God to the profane. "When Aaron saw this, he built an altar in front of the calf and announced, 'Tomorrow there will be a festival to the Lord.' (Likewise "Zoom" was offered up to the Lord). So the next day the people rose early and sacrificed burnt offerings. Afterwards they sat down to eat and drink and got up to indulge in revelry" (Exod 32: 5-6, NIV). Undoubtedly this was an attempt to sanctify the "idea," that is to cleanse something, all this was rooted in their need for immanence. When Moses returned to survey the scene he realized these actions would make them "a laughing stock to their enemies" (Exod 32:25, NIV).[46] The ultimate upshot of all this was that the people were struck down with a plague. *Material* is always a plague to worship and causes division. Luther learned this to his cost.

Many Christians will be familiar with the name Martin Luther, but few will know about his colleague at the University of Wittenberg, Karlstadt (alluded to earlier in the chapter) making himself odious to Luther. This illustrates as with Moses and Aaron, issues touching worship may reach explosive levels. Carlos Eire considers the outward fundamental which divided the two men in 1521-22. The "issues of religious policy, not so much of theology, (i.e.: doctrine, emphasis mine) but inwardly their disagreement stemmed from differing interpretations of the nature of worship."[47] Circumstances had led to ideas which naturally led to practice, the outward expression of their inward exploration.

Today, though very uncomfortably, we do share a likeness with our forebears, we are facing similar questions which hinge on *the way*. It is helpful to know that others have been on this journey before. To put it bluntly the questions hinged on those *material* outward things, externals imposed upon the act of worship. Eire points out that Luther's early position on these matters demonstrates his skepticism and quotes Luther:

> See, that is the proper worship, for which a person needs no bells, no churches, no vessels or ornaments, no lights or candles, no organs or singing, no paintings or images, no panels or altars . . . For these are all human inventions and ornaments, which God does not heed, and which obscure the correct worship, with their glitter.[48]

Not much later Luther's tone alters: "Outward things . . . are really indifferent and can do no harm to the faithful if they are not trusted in."[49] This has been exactly mirrored by evangelical churches in the present day.

Luther says religious artworks are "neither here nor there, neither evil, nor good," and adds, "we may have them or not, as we please" (benign tools).[50] We can easily see

46. Giaver, "Can You Gather with God Over Zoom?" *The New York Times*, 22 May, 2020.

47. Eire, *War Against the Idols*, 66.

48. Eire, *War Against the Idols*, 67-68, quoting Luther, *The Church Postils of 1522*

49. Eire, *War Against the Idols*, 68, quoting Luther, *Third Lenten Sermon* (1522).

50. Eire, *War Against the Idols*, 68, quoting Luther, *LW 51*, 86.

how this led to a struggle within the ranks of those expressing their evangelical beliefs, in fact much the same as we are experiencing now. For Karlstadt and Zwingli what appeared to be at issue was the need to separate out very clearly the earthly and the heavenly. The medieval church had its worship directed to the *material* world, it was an externalized piety. *Material* was at the center, *material* "pulled the strings," *material* forced the compromise. Zwingli moved to demonstrate this more thoroughly. For him we may say that the greatest issue at stake was between true and false religion. At the heart of this problem was the manner of true worship. Worship is the ultimate "touchstone." Zwingli's insight comes right into the present when he observed with great clarity:

> that man cannot respond to God properly because of the corruption of human nature. In fact, he says that man persistently fails to acknowledge the supremacy of God in the spiritual life, substituting a multitude of "ends" in his worship.[51]

Jesus the Iconoclast

Zwingli went further and traced a psychology in all of this (which is apposite to this subject) he differentiates between the inner god and the outer idol. The inner god he says always comes first. This means in practice if we turn to *anything* outward, *material* (*dem gotzen*) the idol, it is because it was already a "strange god" within us "*der abgott.*" Our idols in all their various forms have first of all been established in the heart. Jesus says, "out of the heart come evil ideas" (Matt15:19, NET). What is "in us" emerges; and *material* is what we are. We belong so completely to the *material* world, we cannot escape the call in all its various forms, and therefore we easily and quickly establish idols. Heinrich Bullinger saw it clearly when he said "Man is tied to the earth and that it is this adherence to *material* (italics mine) things that prevents him from worshipping God correctly . . . men seek the divine and infinite in the *material* (italics mine) and visible."[52] It was by means of the *material* that Adam was struck down. The *material* always stands full square in our way, it asserts itself. This was in part the truth of Jesus's teaching in John 4, Jerusalem and the mountain represent the *material* god and as such they assert themselves, his teaching is that they must be gone, eliminated, removed forever, so as to establish true, internal heart worship. In fact Jesus confirmed it would all be gone, and so it was in AD 70 (Matt 24:1, 2). This is only accomplished when the *material* is totally abolished, mediums have no place in worship. The problem with both Jerusalem and the mountain is obvious, both are a visual delight (a lure), but equally an undoubted stumbling block. Being earthly they have everything to attract the worshipper, Jesus in this sense was the most gracious iconoclast, the

51. Eire, *War Against the Idols*, 83-84.

52. Eire, *War Against the Idols*, 87.

material needed eliminating . . . here is the divine voice to persuade us, but because of our allegiances we are still unsure. Weaning us from "the mountain" and the "city of Zion" is proving very difficult indeed!

It seems strangely ironic that in all this the church looks to have been "hoodwinked." This is obvious when we consider that in many conservative evangelical circles over the years, there has been a robust rejection of *material* in worship. Particularly there has been a resolve to reject what might be described as "contemporary worship," for want of a better description, the worship led by the "pop band" at the front of the church. The guitars, drums, saxophones and the rest were seen to be worldly, fleshly, and had no place in the worship of God, even a certain dress sense was "outlawed." While individual churches themselves could give their reasons for this, one dare hazard a guess as to an unspoken reason. Such visual displays of *material* appear as an "art form" and this is what makes the images of the Middle Ages so easily identifiable to the critical eye of the Evangelical; these we recognize, no problem, we are in no doubt, they shout out, "This is art!" This is *material* used in worship (more on this subject in Chapter 10).

Nifty Footwork

Equally to our rather simplistic but neatly accommodating way of thinking, the Queen of Heaven and her kind, are undoubtedly idols, images, upon this there is no discussion, no debate. How then does the screen/tech elude this definition? Postman says

> Technopoly is a state of culture. It is also a state of mind. It consists in the deification of technology, which means that the culture seeks its authorization in technology, finds its satisfaction in technology, and takes its orders from technology . . . and of necessity leads to the rapid dissolution of much that is associated with traditional beliefs.[53]

Dr. Greenfield in her book associates the power of the tech with stimulation, not unlike that influence of addiction . . . "digital technologies could be impacting not just the generic brain, but the individual mind, beliefs and states of consciousness."[54] Yes, we need to pinch ourselves, she says "beliefs." The digital experiment may well alter our minds, it may well already have done so. These minds are the ones which the apostle instructs, "Let this mind be in you, which was also in Christ Jesus" (Phil 2:5, KJV). When viewed like this we may find in the next twenty years the new drug culture has altered precious minds, so that they are fundamentally damaged in an irreparable way, so as to lack any capacity to think outside of the digital model. The church also lending a considerable hand in its decline. Having idolized the tech it is

53. Postman, *Technopoly*, 71.
54. Greenfield, *Mind Change*, 99.

possible it will dismantle the ability to believe the most rational of all rationales, God himself (Rom 1:20).

Tony Reinke, not at all squeamish, is also willing to call out its danger as an idol. This and much more should convince us that these are the clues to identifying our modern idolatry. But why the church cannot see it is probably down to what Craig M Gay observes, "Science and technology foster certain habits of mind." He goes on to quote Peter Berger, as referenced in Chapter 3 where he points out the "pragmatic cast ... and deep skepticism" of its rigorous learning (emphasis mine). These habits of mind where science and technology collude and even enjoy glad embrace, convince us by virtue of their objective discipline that they are free of noxious substances! There is no danger here of one being hijacked and influenced in to superstitious genuflexion. As Gay further remarks, it possesses "the pragmatic cast ...matter-of-factness ... possessing a "skeptical bent." We should be in no doubt: "the scientific way of knowing the world is superior to all others." Science/tech makes its pitch with its *perfect* "health and no safety" warning, it does not even possess the possibility of being harmful, alluringly convincing us of its beneficent intent whilst clasping us all in irons. Yet under this disguise tech deftly, cleverly maneuvers itself out of the spotlight. These comments only confirm the obvious; the mindset, moulded, fixed by a construct which is pragmatic and naturally based on science, knows best. This mindset can easily identify idolatry which is "art based" but cannot see the idolatry "staring us in the face" which is the screen serving up images of ourselves.

George Bernard Shaw more than seventy years ago, wrote that the average person today is about as credulous as was the average person in the Middle Ages. People in the Middle Ages believed in the authority of their religion, no matter what. Today we believe in the authority of our science (a religion), no matter what. Shaw saw clearly what is seen today, definitely it is "no matter what." This is the result of a state of mind like those of the Middle Ages, who were blind to the idols due to their mental conditioning. We, though we cannot see it, are suffering exactly the same plight. It is a state of mind, it is a blind spot, we fail to discern its "nifty footwork." The British journalist Arthur Koestler said, "We are indeed a blind race, and the next generation, blind to its own blindness will be amazed at ours."[55]

The power laden natural object of the Middle Ages was loved and worshipped, venerated, depended upon. What was viewed as being perfectly harmless by most people, was in fact in control. Seeing this, Thomas à Kempis in his *Imitation of Christ* says "Learn to despise outward things, and to give yourself to inward things."[56] The screen/tech of our day is a "necessity," it organizes life for people, it is life, almost everything which is done, is done through it. Naturally we have come to depend upon it, because it serves us so wonderfully, and is undoubtedly good to us. It is loved, and because it includes us in its frame of reference, we adore it, we venerate it. Bringing up

55. Koestler, *Sleepwalkers*, 533.
56. Eire, *War Against the Idols*, 22, quoting Kempis, *Imitation of Christ*.

such adoration it is not at all difficult to join the dots, and draw the obvious parallels between "then and now." It is just this blind spot, or the "nifty footwork" which renders the church vulnerable and open to join this apparently benign "tool" seamlessly to "worship." While many people evidently struggle with the meaning of love, they need only look at the soul refreshment derived from tech to understand what love really is, in every way this is a "marriage of convenience." However, before we said our vows we might have heeded the words of Benjamin Franklin "Keep your eyes wide open before marriage, half shut afterwards." Instead we are "bamboozled," "starry-eyed," "love-struck," "hoodwinked," but why should we care when this lover gives its all to facilitate our every need, even . . . our need of worship! We are so completely besotted by the tech, so much so we see no reason why we cannot turn our "love affair" to our every advantage.

This means that when at prayer or whatever, we can view the interior of a Christian's home and wonder what on earth were they thinking about to choose such wallpaper or what were the titles of those books on the bookshelves and do they really read that kind of literature? Perhaps secretly we thought the "Zoom" prayer meeting was more of an opportunity for X, Y and Z to show off their new kitchen. In this way the devotion (so-called) turns into a playground of materialism, likewise the externals of medieval religion would have found voice as one village or town sported a new and more well appointed idol. With very little difficulty jealousy would have resulted. Carlos Eire quotes,

> Huizinga (who) argues that the medieval Church overlooked the danger involved in letting people learn from images: "An abundance of pictorial fancy, after all, furnished the simple mind quite as much matter for deviating from pure doctrine as any personal interpretation of Holy Scripture."[57]

Confirming the outspoken voices of men like Thomas à Kempis and others, "the material and the spiritual cannot be joined."

Beware the Serpent!

Finally God's word draws attention to the power of the *material* in the form of the brazen serpent. This confirms, along with Calvin, that images of any kind possess the power to develop a life of their own in our sinful, impressionable hearts. The brazen serpent (the bronze snake) in its original was not bad it was good, it was purposeful, it was made to serve a particular end, it was essentially an exercise in faith which ultimately was intended to point up the Savior, and faith in him who was lifted up to die so that all who look to him might be saved (John 3:14). It was evidently limited in its purpose, its useful time frame must have been fixed. Not forgetting this was not

---

57. Eire, *War Against the Idols*, 14, quoting Huizinga, *Waning*, 166

created by man's imagination but by God's command, for a specific purpose (Num 21:8, 9).

However, the bronze snake takes on a life of its own, which possessing only inanimate form it was powerless to do, but in the hands of the needy it emerges as an idol, something to be worshipped. This confirms that by nature we are all prone to the trick of our artifice. Hezekiah, the iconoclast, eliminated the high places, smashed the sacred pillars and cut down the Asherah Poles. He also demolished the bronze serpent that Moses had made, for up to that time the Israelites had been offering incense to it, it was called Nehushtan (2 Kgs 18:4, NET). How quickly we pervert things! Eire commenting on medieval practices says, "The growing cult of images had no safeguard built in to prevent the people from confusing the image and what it sought to represent."[58] In the same way how often has a very good and graphic analogy been used by the minister attempting to explain the gospel in his message, yet its spiritual meaning was entirely lost, and all that was retained was the analogy itself. The ministry that was intended for good, turned out to ill effect. I am quite sure I have been guilty of this myself, endeavoring to help I may well have proved to be a hindrance. It is as if the analogy itself comes alive, and succeeds in obscuring the substance, the heart of the matter, namely that which is spiritual.

As the brazen serpent recommended itself creatively to the people, we should recognize it for what it became, a kind of magic charm, an oversized amulet. It possessed the power to implore the people, to recommend itself to them in this sacrilegious action, to pressurize even. If this is true of a bronze snake, what shall we say of the magic of screen/tech? It beckons us, it draws us in, just as the sylph-like image of the Queen of Heaven . . . irresistible. This thought is explored in the well-known film Jurassic Park, when Hammond (Richard Attenborough) needs to sell his idea of the park to his invited paleontologists, but also to the rough and ready mathematician Jeff Goldblum. Hammond when challenged delivers the only answer: "How can we in the light of discovery not act?" In other words he is saying the tech compels us, we have no option but to comply. It demands that we act, we are not free to turn it down; what we have discovered has to be used. Goldblum says, "you don't see the danger inherent, you wield the power like a kid that's found his dad's gun. There is a lack of humility before nature here which staggers me, the scientists were so preoccupied with what they could do, they didn't stop to ask the question if they should."[59] The idol, whether Nehushtan or the Queen of Heaven, whether the iPhone or any tech is always offering intimacies whilst holding a gun to our heads, we are left beguiled with no choice but to willingly conform. This, the church has gladly acceded to. The worldly technopoly is, as Gay puts it, "an overemphasis of human agency at God's expense . . . may be said

---

58. Eire, *War Against the Idols*, 14.

59. *Jurassic Park*, Film

to be worldly by definition."[60] Not unsurprisingly, as a consequence, "The elevation of one god requires the demotion of another."[61]

Spiritual Relativists

Postman further observes "technology does not invite a close examination of its own consequences. It is the kind of friend that asks for trust and obedience."[62] When the church engaged "screen" tech for worship, it did not invite close examination, in fact it invited none at all. This "friend" is even viewed by Christians as a "divine provision," perhaps these Christians should listen to Dr. Greenfield and those who are the tech experts and inventors, who are now in some respects its detractors; tech is deified like the bronze serpent, thankfully they can see and confirm this. Nevertheless the church blind to its inherent dangers has "bought into it," no questions asked, with the intention of trying to irrigate the bone-dry hearts of those who worship at its "screen" altar, leaving the church paralyzed, and unable to warn against the idol which is "joined" to God. Consequently the church is caught between a rock and a hard place. The church cannot speak out against it, or send out a warning message, because God uses the tech like everyone else! In the Middle Ages "everyone" was "on board," "everyone" was a signed up member of the cult, and if you were not, you were probably in prison, or without a tongue, or dead. It did not make sense in any way to be outside the cult. Business life, social life, eternal life, life depended on it. One's health and well being, family, security, hope was all tied up with the *material* god. If we did not know it, this is the tragic picture of us today. The minds of the sixteenth-century worshippers were undoubtedly programmed, and whether we realize it or not, we are in Huxley's "Brave New World," just as programmed in the 2020s.

The all powerful idol in our times has our lives in its grasp. The squeeze is on, and we have no power to extricate ourselves, nor it appears do we care to do so. At least we could have said up until recently, God is not tarnished by all this, but sadly, not any more. As Neil Postman observes, "A preacher who confines himself to considering how a medium can increase his audience will miss the significant question: In what sense do new media alter what is meant by religion, by church, even by God?"[63] He also believes our only hope is for our minds to be "deprogrammed." I find myself agreeing with this remarkable sage of the twentieth century, but without such a work of "deprogramming" we are left only with the stark reality set out by the psalmist. The idols of our invention and of our use will reshape us, if they have not already done so. "Those who make them will end up like them, as will everyone who trusts in them" (Ps 115:8, NET).

60. Gay, *The Way of the (Modern) World*, 88.

61. Postman, *Technopoly*, 165.

62. Postman, *Technopoly*, XII.

63. Postman, *Technopoly*, 19.

CHAPTER 7

UNPACKING

The means are just as much a part of the truth as the result. The search for truth must itself be true; true research is truth unpacked whose scattered elements are reunited in the result.

KARL MARX

For the message of the cross is foolishness to those who are perishing . . .

1 CORINTHIANS 1:18 (NIV)

The Medium is the Message

MY WIFE HAS AN EXTREMELY organized mind, and when it comes to holidays she excels, this is how it seems at any rate set against my own feeble efforts. When she arrives at the destination she immediately empties her suitcase, neatly placing her clothes in the drawers and cupboards. In this way she can easily access them just as she likes. I on the other hand have a different approach, (inherited my wife tells me by our three sons) and much to her chagrin I have always holidayed out of my bag or suitcase, thinking I can grab clothes, etc., just as easily from my bag as I can from any closet! Her point is, it is difficult to see what we have when one thing is on top of another. Although I am sure she is right, I am still a work in progress! Clothes are relatively easy to unpack, the truth however is another matter, for my own part I think it is worth the unpacking.

Marx says "the search for truth must itself be true." It is plainly set out in Scripture that rigor is essential in the soul of the one who comes to faith in Christ. "And you will seek me and find me when you search for me with all your heart" (Jer 29:13, NKJV). No one ever finds the Lord Jesus Christ whose heart is not true, whose search is not genuine. Marx was right, the means are as much a part of the truth as the result.

In a year where truth has proved elusive to governments and scientists around the world, there has nonetheless been the need to go on "unpacking."

Counting the cost

As I write, the British government has announced the need for a further enquiry into all aspects of the Pandemic. However, before that inquiry sees the light of day we already have the benefit of some remarkable facts. In October 2021 a cross-party group of Members of Parliament, the Public Accounts Committee, reported on the single aspect of "Test and Trace." They were searching out the truth trying to "unpack" the scattered elements, especially scrutinizing "Test and Trace." The BBC's Health Correspondent, Dominic Hughes, says that "the evidence could hardly be more damning." The Public Accounts Committee which examines value for money of Government projects says, "the program's outcomes have been muddled and it hasn't achieved its objectives despite costing the tax payer billions. The National Health Service, "Test and Trace" program has been one of the most expensive health programs delivered during the Pandemic, it has cost thirty-seven billion pounds, equal to nearly a fifth of the entire NHS England budget. When it comes to test results just 14 percent of six hundred and ninety-one million lateral flow tests distributed by "Test and Trace" were registered." Dame Meg Hillier MP, Chair of the Commons Public Accounts Committee said:

"We found it very difficult to see what it had achieved for thirty-seven billion pounds. It set out very bold aims, it failed on many of its own terms . . ."

Thankfully our system of government opens a door to such scrutiny. Only pride or a "cover up" could prevent the necessary "unpacking," so that we can all feel satisfied that due diligence has been done. Like governments, the church was caught completely "off-guard" when COVID-19 struck. The situation was unprecedented, there was no model, not since World War II had the church faced a crisis of such national proportions. In the future individual churches will be able to give their account as to how much truth was "unpacked" before the "lightning speed" actions brought on the experiment of "Zoom" worship.

We Are On Your "Case!"

Perhaps it is too much to expect that any church will carry out an investigation like that of the Public Accounts Committee, and examine whether the "new worship" was not in fact muddled and more importantly, what the legacy of such an experiment will be. Now that eighty percent of churches have participated in the experiment with, to their mind, a degree of satisfaction, it is hardly likely that any of them will countenance an investigation. Searching out the truth takes time of which there is precious little in our world of rush and haste, and this will probably preclude any enquiry in the future as to what took place and how this developed. The author has no way of knowing if churches in the 1950s and 1960s ever conducted such an inquiry into the affects of the Graham Evangelistic Model which was taken up so enthusiastically by countless churches, and whose influence still lingers to this day. "Unpacking" the truth exposes what is at the bottom of the trunk, but we will never know unless we are prepared to take everything out, thereby revealing its contents in full.

Buried Treasure

Maybe if an attempt had been made to "unpack" the truth, a vital discovery might have been made which would have altered the course of this moment in church history. "The medium is the message," the unavoidable message! But it was hidden, buried at the bottom, completely out of sight and out of mind. This is what we need to "unpack" now and consider its ramifications on the worship of God. Christians who like to demonstrate a catholicity of spirit are glad to recognize, on paper at least, the homogeneous nature of faith. There is more that binds us than separates us, the creeds were meant to help establish this, and these have proven to be wonderful but very often, wonderful only on paper. When the creeds were "unpacked," it was then that difficulties were encountered, difficulties which should not merely be attributed to seemingly obstructive people. Regardless of creeds, history records for us a vast array of disagreement amongst God's people, but at least they seem to have attempted to "unpack" the truth. Some, we might think have been tolerant, others may appear intolerant, it all depends on which side of the fence you sit!

One man's meat is another man's poison

It is hard not to think of Calvin and Zwingli as bigoted, while Luther was the reasonable, tolerant reformer. However, viewed from an entirely different perspective, Luther looks tolerant of externals which were plainly wrong, while the other reformers are intolerant of the same. One looks compromised, the others quite firmly set for the defense of the faith. In all this we gain some vital insight into the complexities which arise when we address the questions of a "practiced" faith. We would all say a justified man/woman is a sanctified one. It is not possible to be a Christian theoretically with faith unpracticed. However, let that faith out i.e., express it, perform it, use it—do it, and it is just at this point we are easily undone and certainly meet formidable obstacles. It is known that Origen, one of the church fathers, was willing to accept gradations of faith expressed by Christians. Calvin was ready to accept the perpetual virginity of Mary, and Luther was able to play fast and loose with imagery. We have to wonder, would any of them find acceptance into our church memberships with such baggage? To compare Luther and Calvin for a moment is helpful in our attempt to "unpack" our own actions in order to discover the truth.

Luther Pro-Screen, Calvin Anti-Screen

Luther clearly believed he could rationalize his approach regarding "outward things," and was ready to risk very much in the defense of this. He quotes the apostle Paul and says, "without a doubt he (Paul) wanted to show that 'outward things' could do no harm to faith, if only the heart does not cleave to them or puts its trust in them." He says, "This is what we must preach and teach."[1] It is tempting to ask the obvious question: If Luther was presented with our situation would he "unpack" the truth and become a delicately balanced, moderate "screen" worshipper, allowing room in the worship of God for images of the screen, using the medium of our age? Equally with our vivid imagination we must wonder what John Calvin might make of it all? What would his response be? The historian Diarmaid MacCulloch may be able to assist our experimental enquiry. He writes pointing out Calvin's dissatisfaction with images.

> Calvin's single-minded hatred of anything which could be regarded as an idolatrous obstacle to the worship of God skewed in a negative direction the delicate balance of attitudes to Mary which the Lutheran and Zürich Reformers had managed to sustain.[2]

The delicate balance was not maintained. Looking at circumstances from a distance it is hard to see how a delicate balance was possible at all with what was at stake. Calvin it appears, saw "obstacles" to that which was at the heart of the reformation endeavor, namely worship which is the expression of faith. Upon this piety hinged so much, the mixture in the worship of the people was the result of obstacles, the mediums which were employed in that worship. Carlos Eire explains how Calvin only ever wrote to Luther once, but it was not about doctrine that prompted Calvin, he says it was the "occurrence of dissembling behavior among Protestants."[3] Calvin wanted Luther to lend his support to those who were wavering to the point of compromise, and clearly saw that the progress of the Reformation would be set back by the obstacles of church creativity. Images of any kind, any shape, any size, are obstacles, hurdles which must be overcome. Sadly church history reveals they have not been overcome, and even to this day remain stubbornly, resolutely fixed. Countless souls have lost their lives falling at these hurdles.

It is surely stretching the imagination to think that Calvin with his stance on obstacles would have joined today's modern evangelical church in its experimental worship, using images as it does, to facilitate this. This reveals the struggles of the present are in fact those of the past, only in different dress. Generosity demands an acknowledgement be made, that we are all trying honorably before God to offer him the worship of which we think he is worthy, subject as that worship is, not primarily

1. Eire, *War Against the Idols*, 68.
2. MacCulloch, *All Things Made New*, 43.
3. Eire, *War Against the Idols*, 234.

in the light of the individual conscience, but subject to the word of God to which the conscience must be bound. It is undoubtedly true that we are able in some measure, to tolerate the nuances of doctrinal expression, yet up until now we have found it beyond us to shape-shift when it comes to piety, the expression of our faith. Our theology above all else, works its way out into our worship, as we "unpack" the truth one thing follows another. As we get to the bottom of the suitcase we now discover precious garments once hidden, now revealed. Did those who entered into "screen" worship consider the thorny question, the delicate matter of "the medium as the message" as touching all aspects of worship, or just some?

Mad Men

What of the Lord's Table, the breaking of bread service, was this considered? Whatever our individual church practice, the question must be: Can this service of worship before God in the remembrance of Christ's death be conducted through a screen? Can we break bread and honor God by participating through a medium, or does the medium negate it? (see Chapter 12). From the point of view of this book, it seems clear and obvious that if *worship,* shall we say in the form of a prayer meeting, may be "performed" through a screen, then so might any other element of Christian worship? It is all or nothing, the Lord's Table, baptism along with everything else.

At the time of writing I was aware only of the Church of England's practice of screen assistance in the communion service, in what appears to me to be the "ultimate magic trick." But now I am reliably informed that Evangelical, Bible-believing Christians subjected the Lord's Table to the computer screen. The Church of England also practiced drive-in communion services, and why not when we have drive-in McDonalds and Starbucks? The tech makes all this possible, why not harness it? Obviously this would be taking matters too far for many conservative Evangelicals. The problem is clear there is a certain recoiling at the sight of worship reduced in this way. Yet how illogical, if one form is acceptable the other must be also! It appears this shrinking back on certain matters for some obscure reason, is only for aspects of worship which we have decided are "too holy" for the screen. We can imagine the quicksand into which Luther slipped as he tried to navigate his way, holding on as he did to the use of imagery. The church today will undoubtedly struggle with the same quicksand regarding "screen" worship.

Erasmus believed "religion is best when it does not depend on visible things"[4]— this is my point. In "screen" worship there is not only a dependency on the image, but image, more dangerous by far is at the very center, it becomes indispensable. Such "screen" worship, it should be remembered, can in fact only proceed by employing the use of the image. But the voice of reason which has obviously arisen in the church

---

4. Eire, *War Against the Idols*, 36.

sends out the calming message "fear not blending," "disregard mixture," and all will be well, and alluringly as always, "profit is the promise." Erasmus understood that spiritual pluralism was an enemy. We, on the other hand, have been blindsided in a most subtle way.

Craig Gay points to the joint authorship of *Secularization and Pluralism*:

> Indeed, we have been left largely to our own devices in trying to construct our own identities. This has left us highly vulnerable to fashion, however, and to the seductive claims of various mass-marketed products and techniques that have been developed in recent years to facilitate private self-construction. (This is before the internet, emphasis mine). Authentic individuality, which has such a distinguished intellectual history in the West, has thus devolved into mere individualism and conformism. Put somewhat differently, individuality has been an unintended casualty in the rationalization of social order. Religion has, for the most part, been relegated to the private sphere of subjective autonomy.[5]

Individuality has been lost to individualism and conformity is shaping our structures . . . cultural pluralism has driven us mad!

A Golden Opportunity

Is it possible that our individuality has given way in our thought processes to mere individualism? This in turn promotes the private self which is vulnerable to fashion and conformity, so that we are demonstrably impressed by anything, as Gay says, quoting Romano Guardini, who noted, "As long as men are unable to control themselves from within . . . they will inevitably be 'organized' by force from without."[6] Such forces are able to introduce entirely new and fascinating experiences neatly extolling the virtues submitted by Schleiermacher. In the blink of an eye individualism and ego were presented with a golden opportunity to flourish on screen, the force from without, while the church seems unable to grasp the reality that the medium is indeed the message, whilst others like Postman, outside of the church suffer no such problem. Christopher Dawson, in *Progress and Religion* says,

> We have entered on a new phase of culture—we may call it the Age of the Cinema—in which the most amazing perfection of scientific technique is being devoted to purely ephemeral objects, without any consideration of their ultimate justification. It seems as though a new society was arising which will acknowledge no hierarchy of values, no intellectual authority, and no social

---

5. Gay, *Way of the (Modern) World*, 210-211, quoting Berger and Luckmann, *Secularization and Pluralism*, 73-84.

6. Gay, *Way of the (Modern) World*, 72, quoting Guardini, *End of the Modern World*.

or religious tradition, but which will live for the moment in a chaos of pure sensation.[7]

Max Weber, in his analysis of the influences in which religion has impacted capitalism, makes a similar point in his author's introduction: "He who yearns for seeing should go to the cinema."[8]

"The medium is the message", and in this case a medium of illusion of sensation. In so far as Christian worship is concerned, the experience must be ephemeral, a mere transitory encounter, since image is just that. Of course this ephemeral in the world of tech is accepted as reality, and remarkably seems acceptable in the church, it is just here where our unpacking capabilities have come adrift as we have entered into a "new phase" of our spiritual culture.

The Medium Has Always Been a Dangerous Message

It is all too easy for non-conformists like myself to judge "high church" worship as a wooden formality. We wonder how such worship could have ever been established, and we are equally bemused as to how it is maintained. From my own wing of the church (Baptist), we like to think of ourselves as those who are committed to a pattern of worship laid down in New Testament revelation, but does this mean that every vestige of the human will has been eradicated? Certainly the recent introduction of the "screen" raises a serious question. Looking at the church, high, low or middle, through the eyes of a casual visitor, we must wonder what would be seen. "See" is the operative word because such a casual visitor knows nothing, and cares even less about the theology of a given church. I suspect the minutiae is of no interest to them but what matters is the visual, their focus inevitably must be on the medium which at all times is "center stage." Many Roman Catholic worshippers will unreservedly recount the sheer delight of the visual feast which is accessible in their form of worship. The entire visual involves an extremely impressive dress code, and alongside this there is the choreography, well-measured, well-rehearsed, well-practiced, enabling a perfected performance. All this helps to create the ambience, the *effect* so as to *affect*. If we had not noticed, this is to a greater or lesser degree a form of theater, a medium which captivates and compels, inviting the visitor to linger a while . . . sometimes forever.

If the high church has its theatrics, then so also do the Pentecostal and Charismatic churches, with their expressions of "modern" worship employing all manner of different attractive mediums, relevant to the various visceral needs of the visitor. Worship leaders vie for center stage with musical groups and dancing girls, the preachers literally "strut their stuff" across the stage with yet more refined choreography. Perhaps from the view of the non-conformist it is easy to see this as "will worship," but what

7. Gay, *Way of the (Modern) World*, 181, quoting Dawson, *Progress and Religion*, 228.
8. Weber, *Protestant Ethic*, 29.

about the Baptists and Presbyterians? Some have choirs and extensive musical accompaniments, others have pianos and organs, whilst still others have no accompaniment at all. Then there are ministers with their ministerial gowns, and other churches make the case that their worship centers on the public reading and preaching of God's word, prayer and the singing of psalms, hymns and spiritual songs, yet even in these churches there is often an unspoken dress code, e.g., the suit and tie is good, denim jeans are bad! There are pulpits and lecterns where sermons can often appear like dead lectures, and to the Charismatic, Pentecostal worshipper this all must look rather lifeless. All the aforementioned are merely an acknowledgement of the obvious, we have all contributed visually to the worship, we have all left our mark on it for good or ill.

The mediums which have been employed all carried a message. A piano is no less a medium than an electric guitar, and only someone who is unable to "unpack" the truth could ever disassociate the message from either of them, since by and large both have been used by the world, both must carry worldly connotations—an inescapable fact. It seems ludicrous to argue that the electric guitar is "worldly" while the organ is "sanctified." Choirs are a medium with a message, buildings likewise, and buildings which churches meet in have all been *designed,* they could not escape artistry because our hands have been laid to the task, mediums of bricks and mortar speak. These are never purely functional and utilitarian, and they cannot help but impress the worshipper by inspiring, encouraging and giving confidence. Yes, they do stand for something, because they go beyond mere functionality. The glory of a great cathedral may have been foolishly pilloried in ignorance by a non-conformist "purist," while many churches update their interior, redecorate and redesign one thing after another so as to give a "good impression," because who, after all, wants to give a bad one?

Stone-Throwing

Evidently we are all prone in our own way to our preferences, that is to our own aesthetic. That aesthetic is impossible to deny, it means necessarily we all accept that "the medium is the message." What we use we are interacting with, and all these prove to have a voice, and while some of the voices of our creating are very loud indeed, others have a quieter voice but the truth is that they all call out to us. The electric guitar can have the effect of making feet tap but so can the drums, saxophone, piano and even the recorder. The point being made is that it would be straining to try to argue that the screen is not purveying a message, clearly and loudly. However, we must beware in all of this not to carry an air of superiority or of self-righteousness, because he who is without sin in his choice and use of any medium should remember Christ's words about throwing stones! Don't forget that, as we say, "those in glass houses should not throw stones." Like Luther and Calvin we are all making a journey in our service to worship honorably and serve God "in Spirit and in truth." Nevertheless the question remains: What are the ground rules which allow *"things"* into the holy of holies. More unpacking needed!

Delusion

While it is true, as Mumford explains, that the Benedictine monks invented the mechanical clock in the twelfth and thirteenth centuries, marking seven periods each day to serve their regime of prayer, but it went further, much further, becoming a medium redirecting their lives, and in turn all of ours. Keeping track of the hours of the day for service to God and fellow man might have been the motive in using the clock, but it inevitably went on to control the actions of men. Might we say, "you cannot keep a good thing down?" But such a good thing was always going to refuse to be confined, it had to break out, and as we know it has! This could be seen as the church's early tech at work already imposing itself, and eventually evolving a controlling power.

David Berlinski, writing in *The Devil's Delusion*, includes a short section titled the "Seeing Eye" where he sets out the necessity which was laid upon Islam to harness its own issues of time. This would have been an obvious requirement with its own Koran commanding five-fold prayers each day. He goes on to explain how Islam through various means regulated its times of prayer. He concludes: "In Islam, as in no other religion . . . the performance of various aspects of religious ritual has been assisted by scientific procedure."[9] Religion has not been slow in harnessing the inventive processes of our acumen. What became necessary to Islam in its scientific procedure, we have harnessed in our modern day tech. The churches of Christendom ring their bells to "summon the faithful" to worship. Initially this would have served those without a timepiece. The medium of the bell is a message!

Innocently, Gutenberg thought his advances in tech would aid the church of Rome, in truth it aided the printing of Luther's books and pamphlets. What seemed like an obvious advantage to Catholicism needed only fifty years for Protestantism to turn to its own. The difference of course, between these dependancies which come to be relied on, and the purely visual stimuli such as that of the late Middle Ages, appears to be obvious . . . One was always practical and useful (rather like the screen) it could impose itself on the religious community without consequence. It would be a win-win situation, but as Mumford explains the clock imposed itself and altered our lives forever. The clock hath given and the clock hath taken away. The medium of the clock was and is its own message. We could say it has taken over the world, it dominates our lives. It cannot be closed down, it cannot be silenced. Sadly, even in churches it dictates to the Holy Spirit the exact duration of our service to God, even the exact length of the ministry, fitting in with the broadcasting schedule. The clock has invaded God's church at every level and we can do nothing about it . . . we are powerless.

9. Berlinski, *Devil's Delusion*, 14.

Clean and Unclean Animals

Postman said, "I believe I know something about what technologies do to culture, and I know even more about what technologies undo in a culture."[10] The delusion comes when we are blindsided by the "usefulness" of something. We then assume that the thing as a "tool" is neutral, especially if it sits neatly on the scientific tech side of the fence, (as outlined in Chapter 10). We see it as one of the "clean animals" of Leviticus which God instructed Moses to tell the people of Israel they were permitted to kill and eat. These were easily identifiable, God made it clear to Moses. However, the rabbit and the pig were out of bounds, and when God had finished he said to Moses, "You must distinguish between the unclean and the clean, between living creatures that may be eaten and those that may not be eaten" (Lev 11:47, NIV). Quite clearly the church appears to possess no such help and specificity when it comes to "clean" and "unclean." As stated earlier, the piano is perceived as "clean," the saxophone and electric guitar are "unclean." The Fresco in the fourteenth century church is definitely "unclean," the screen/tech providing images to aid and abet worship is given a "clean bill of health."

It should not be difficult for anyone to realize that all of these possess the power to undo our spiritual culture. The worrying part is that most Christians are unable to comprehend that all are in fact mediums, and as Marshall McLuhan said in 1964, "The Medium is the Message what you use to interact with the world changes the way you see the world." In the same way what you use to interact with worship changes the way you see worship. If someone taps their foot to a piano tune or to a guitar, the medium's message is clear! A hammer is a medium it carries with it an obvious message—it can drive in nails, and if it has a claw end its additional message is, "I am also an extractor of nails." A violin does not need to be played with the notes of Vaughan William's "Lark Ascending," piercing from its remarkable body, to convey its message, but it is obviously distinct and different from that of the trumpet. The medium contains within itself its own message because it is the embodiment of the message, these cannot be separated. "Zoom" on the internet is a medium, the screen is a medium, as is the camera. The mediums and their messages are one. They cannot be disenfranchised, they are conjoined.

The Knack

In just the same way a machine in the form of the screen/tech embodies its own abiding message, and which some believe that, amongst other things, is plainly both fraudulent and evanescent. This medium without a second thought has been joined to the worship of God, and with a loud voice it speaks, it cannot, it will not be silent. The danger to the church will be its inability to see the object, the "tool" of the machine,

10. Postman, *Informing Ourselves to Death*.

failing to comprehend its product. It has already been noted that our weakness is to forget *procedure* and focus only on *product*, but surely we know the machine is the master of this; to quote Mumford once more, "The machine thus appeared purely as an external instrument for the conquest of the environment."[11] The message of the machine is "I produce with a capital "I." "I conquer the environment." As Max Frisch put it so succinctly, "Technology . . . the knack of so arranging the world that we don't have to experience it."[12]

Witching Hour

When Saul engaged the services of the Witch of Endor, he engaged a medium, who with her own brand of technology had "the knack of so arranging the world" (1 Sam 28). She is a producer, a conquerer even, but also a go-between, an intermediary rather like the Queen of Heaven. Saul is unable to reach Samuel, she is indispensable to him, he needs her and she *seems* to have the power to bring the two parties together (whatever that actually means). However, the reality is Saul and Samuel were miles apart, worlds apart, the distance between them is life and death, and without the Witch of Endor, Saul cannot *see* Samuel. He remains cut off from him. She alone is able to join the two parties, only she can produce the goods, she is the Master of Ceremonies. A medium is a middle state, or a condition of halfway between extremes. A medium in art is a carrier, crucially it is a bonding, glueing agent or adhesive, fixing disparate materials together which otherwise would be apart so they can then be used. Lance Strate explains it this way: "A final point about the concept of medium is required, which is that it should be understood as representing not a *thing*, but a process of mediation, a relation or relationship."[13]

Duped

'Zoom" worship is misleading in its impression of reality, much like the work of the witch. In this the illusion persuades the worshippers that they are *actually together* with other worshippers. Were Saul and Samuel really *actually together*? The medium is capable of delivering this lie, demonstrating what a dangerous creative force churches have employed by turning to a medium which is no less dangerous than the creative force of a Fresco. Mumford thinks it is a "third estate midway between nature and the humane arts, that it was not merely a quicker way of achieving old ends but an effective way of expressing new ends."[14] Here is the profound danger for Christian worship: the machine introduced a new way of living, an indispensable way of living. The witch

11. Mumford, *Technics & Civilization*, 322.
12. Boorstin, *Image*, inside cover, quoting Max Frisch.
13. Strate, *Amazing Ourselves to Death*, 49.
14. Mumford, *Technics & Civilization*, 322–23.

was essential, requisite to Saul. She was most significantly his means of being able to *see*. She was the effective way for him to explore new ends, "seeing is believing." The king said to her, "Don't be afraid. What do you *see*?" (1 Sam 28:13, NIV). Without her as his medium he is blind. She is the message, the carrier who was cardinal to success in this venture.

Consider the priest . . . the ultimate medium! He is the screen (the confessional box is only the physical form of himself). He is the interface and the absolutely indispensable component. We should not think that the content which comes out of the priest's mouth is the message (only in a secondary way), rather *he* is the message itself. The worshipper needs him and is entirely dependent upon him. The priest is the one who can translate the worshipper from "here to there."

The medium being a message all by itself must of necessity be heard, indeed it cannot be silenced, it will not be silenced. The priest's role will long be remembered, and what is true of any priest is equally true of the screen, both are indispensable, as mediums they naturally possess independent existences apart from the user. Frances Haugen, "whistleblower," exposing the practices of Facebook, reveals the power of the independent algorithms which determine what appears first on the screen. This is machine "expertise"; a camera informs the user there is insufficient light to make a successful picture; a car with "lane assist" gently guides the car back to the correct position, with its onboard computer; drivers trusting implicitly in satellite navigation have been led in to impossible situations. The medium is indeed a message all by itself.

Absorbed by our Tech

By casting an historical light, Lewis Mumford further explains the point. He writes about the "assimilation of the machine," that is, the absorption of it and adaptation to it. Mumford observes: "The tools and utensils used during the greater part of man's history were, in the main, extensions of his own organism: they did not have—what is more important they did not *seem* to have—an independent existence."[15] He suggests this resulted in something profound, it affected him in his relation to his environment by securing a closer harmony to it. This meant, though he may reshape his environment by the use of his tools, the harmony "made him recognize the limits of his capacities."[16] This idea of limitation is almost anathema to us. In every sphere of life, in food, sex, exploitation of resources, exploration . . . you name it we can have it! Even worship when incapacitated needs to bend itself to technological capabilities so as to deliver what we need when we want it. Harmony i.e., agreement between ourselves and truth is forfeited.

Whatever technologies were present at Babel, one thing is for sure: there were no limits, their powers must have extended way beyond the task of making bricks.

15. Mumford, *Technics & Civilization*, 321.
16. Mumford, *Technics & Civilization*, 321.

Mumford says: "In dream, he (man) was all powerful: in reality he had to recognize the weight of stone and cut stones no bigger than he could transport."[17] This meant the environment could "neither be intimidated nor be cajoled." At Babel, the opposite was true: God could see there was nothing that man's inventiveness would not control. Mumford thinks that mankind learned during the period of the "written record" that not only could the environment not be intimidated but one had to "learn the laws of their behavior, instead of petulantly imposing one's own wishes."[18] Relating this to our own enquiry is both uncomfortably easy and painful. Charting the progress of the machine and what it inflicted, Mumford further observes,

> As production became more mechanized . . . more impersonal and the work itself became less rewarding, apart from such slight opportunities for social intercourse as it furthered, attention was centered more and more upon the product: people valued the machine for its external achievements, for the number of yards of cloth it wove, for the number of miles it carried them. The machine thus appeared purely as an external instrument for the conquest of the environment: . . . We assimilated the objects rather than the spirit that produced them.[19]

He is saying we became utilitarian and the product of the machine was all that mattered. The machine functioning purely as an external instrument in the church worship focused upon the product (worship becomes a product). In fact, product is everything. "Zoom" conquered the environment which COVID-19 had uncomfortably forced on us and we assimilated the objects . . . "the medium is the message"!

Complete Amalgamation

Churches everywhere have now given proof of this, and many have assimilated the object. In this it does not matter that the organic is robbed in worship and that the mechanical exerts an independent power, the machine has made its conquest of the (spiritual) environment. The machine opens the door for a new creativity in worship which can be experienced in a variety of ways. Mumford realized this and wrote:

> That technics had become a creative force, carried on by its own momentum, (aka "Zoom") that it was rapidly ordering a new kind of environment and was producing a third estate midway between nature and the humane arts, that it was not merely a quicker way of achieving old ends but an effective way of expressing new ends—the possibility in short that the machine furthered a new mode of *living* was far from the minds of those who actively promoted it.[20]

17. Mumford, *Technics & Civilization*, 321.

18. Mumford, *Technics & Civilization*, 321.

19. Mumford, *Technics & Civilization*, 322.

20. Mumford, *Technics & Civilization*, 322–23.

Many of those who endorsed and experimented with "screen" worship were deluded by the possibilities and power of the tech. While it is true they had not anticipated the "new way of living," as stated previously, the "genie" is out, the amalgamation is complete. Billy Graham's "genie" of "decisionism" has never gone back into the bottle.

A New Way of Living

Churches now realize the creative force, a quicker, more profitable way of achieving old ends and expressing new ones, the machine has "done a number" on us and we walked blindly into it. In the rush churches attempted to make the "object" (the worship) appear to be something other than the product of the machine, all was quite normal, natural and organic, nothing to worry about here! But they had not cognizance of the reality. The machine furthered a "new mode of spiritual living." As long as our culture is glued to the screen, "screen" worship will only further evolve, and because of it new spiritual values will emerge as they must. To lean on Mumford once more, "a whole series of new values that had been called into existence by the development of the new technics."[21] The new technics of the future in the form of Metaverse and the like will be unstoppable . . . "the medium is the message"! It is a pity, in our impulsiveness, that we could not "unpack" the truth, instead we hastily launched upon an experiment, and like Saul we must await the terrifying results. One employs a medium at one's cost. Mumford deserves the last word: "One does not make a child powerful by placing a stick of dynamite in his hands: one only adds to the dangers of his irresponsibility."[22]

What is Prayer?

Undeniably, whenever a church sits at prayer it is engaged in an act of solemn worship, often articulating matters of profound sensitivity. However, if the information provided by Google is correct "Zoom" even collects any information you upload during meetings, and the group chat happening within the meeting. The obvious question: Is "Zoom" able, one way or another, to make merchandise from our prayers? Naturally, if the church thinks and operates like a business, this will be of little concern to it. Kate O'Flaherty, a cybersecurity journalist, has misgivings about using Zoom. (I have no way of knowing whether she has any interest in the civilization which is God's kingdom). She says:

> On one side are those who are very suspicious about Zoom. And rightly so—the video conferencing app's privacy policy makes concerning reading. That's on top of the serious risk of "Zoom bombing," news that data was being sent to China, people's video calls being leaked online . . . It's already led many

21. Mumford, *Technics & Civilization*, 323.
22. Mumford, *Technics & Civilization*, 325.

organizations to publicly dump Zoom . . . New York schools, NASA and Elon Musk's Space X to name a few."[23]

Presumably none of the churches have seen the light, and we must wonder whether they care to.

No doubt the church can comfort itself with the fact that it is joining the huge number who are signed up to this medium, ten million a year ago, today two hundred million. We must remember: "Zoom" was initially designed for business. O'Flaherty quotes Jake Moore, Cybersecurity Specialist at ESET, who says: "Privacy isn't a strong point of many of the video conferencing platforms, including Zoom. If data privacy is extremely important to you, then you should probably consider a more secure method of communication."[24] To conclude, O'Flaherty says, "So while you are on COVID-19 lockdown by all means, take that exercise class, have a chat with a group of friends or family—even use it for online learning if the subject matter isn't sensitive."[25] Prayer outside of the market is sensitive.

Sound the Alarm

Yet, given all this it appears the church is unlikely to listen to the alarm bells. Danny Fortson of *The Sunday Times*, recommending Jaron Lanier's book, writes: "An eloquence that is hard to argue against . . . Every time you log on, you are adding to a fire that is burning your house down."[26] The reason is almost certainly because the mindset is conditioned to see the machine at all times as a beneficent ally, possessing the power to work quantity, quality not being the first cause. This concept of quantity first is an enemy to the Christian and to the church in some measure, which is dealt with by Jesus's teaching in Matthew 6. His warning, of a fundamental kind, is against the need to be seen; *NB:* this is exactly what the screen trades in. We all have a built-in flaw, to a greater or lesser extent: we like to be noticed. The medium's message is *you* can be seen. Pride will seek out anything which can be employed to this end. Pride in the hypocrite seeks to maximize the moment, seeks extension, turning the spiritual act of prayer into something which could be merchandised to his advantage. He could *gain* by his performance, he could *increase* in quantity, he is farming himself out. Such hypocritical prayer cares nothing for quality. The performance of the "show off" praying in a public place was to gain mileage out of the act of prayer, prayer out in the open had become a utilitarian tool. Instead Jesus teaches that prayer can be conducted in a cupboard, in the secret place, but "Zoom" hardly looks like the secret place whilst data could be sold off to China or wherever. God forbid that prayer should become a

23. Kate O'Flaherty, "Zoom," *Forbes*, April 15, 2020.

24. Kate O'Flaherty, Kate O'Flaherty, "Zoom," *Forbes*, quoting Jake Moore, Cybersecurity Specialist ESET

25. Kate O'Flaherty, "Zoom," *Forbes*, April 15, 2020.

26. Lanier, *Ten Arguments For Deleting*, inside cover, quoting Fortson, "Sunday Times."

marketable product! The thought must be that the hypocrite operates like an automaton, machine-like. The organic, the natural, the real, the authentic is non-existent, it has been lost in his desensitized approach to God. This is mechanical prayer. Jesus has no use for it.

Long Way Round

The impersonality of the machine cannot cease to be what it is in its nature. Therefore it cannot be a carrier of direct communication between oneself and others (together) and God. More crucially, and just as importantly, it presents itself as an *indispensable* tool, a bridging device attempting to bridge the impossible gulf, and without it, "together" we are unable to get to the other side. Nowadays, the "long way round" is of no use, nor of any interest to the church where its focus is *quantity* and instant instrumentality. Our conditioned modern thinking will not permit us being stalled, not by anything, no, not for one moment. Why? There is no time, since quantity is always dictating the program. Here is the flavor of secular market reasoning influencing the worship of God.

A Ladder up to Heaven

If the medium is in fact the message, then the message is deafening and unmistakable. Beware! Here is the problem: the machine as a human product obtains a much louder voice than all others, God's included. We are naturally hooked, after all, it is the work of our own hands, it is *our* workmanship! The Bible's words at Babel echo down through the ages: "Come let us build a great city for *ourselves* with a tower which reaches into the sky this will make *us* famous" (Gen 11:4, NLT). God knew what the outcome of this would be. "After this, nothing they set out to do will be impossible for them!" The medium of the tower bespoke its message—man is a god. Although the tower was destroyed, the seeds of the gods have lived on in our tech, we are masters of the universe, we can do anything, even devise objects which will help us to scale to heaven itself.

While on the one hand the machine exalts its own prowess so as to produce soft obeisance, on the other hand it exalts its creator. The Tower of Babel proclaimed its master, loud and clear. Our tech, more than its equal, must always steal the show by its powers and the enabling with which it provides us. Invariably, all these stand as a monument both to ourselves and to the work of our hands. Remember Brunelleschi's Dome calls out his name, not the name of God. If the prestige of improvement, success and power resided with the machine as Mumford suggests, then it was only natural that we would share it, our ego would demand it. The ancient peoples of Babel, just as in the present day, needed the therapy which it administered. In this, self is satisfied, all of our striving is seen to come to fruition, our autonomy is established, our god-like profile cast forever, nothing will be impossible for us.

The Model T, which Ford built, is always quite rightly going to carry his name, equally Penicillin belongs only with one name. The medium carries its message and it cannot help but exalt us, but as we all know, this is of no use whatever to Christ's gospel. Every medium sings its own praises, carries around with it its own Nobel Prize (an award for ingenuity, brilliance and power). The fresco carried the genius of the Renaissance master who created it, the two cannot be divorced, and it is more than tempting here to imagine many Christians saying, "Well why not?"

Lock, Stock, and Barrel

I do not apologize for criticizing the use of this indispensable medium called upon and employed to serve the worship of God, a medium with its distinct message, or more accurately messages. Naturally it engineers space and attention for itself, but there is only room in Christ's church for one message, no other must be allowed to be heard: Here is a Babel-like construct which points to fame and recognition, exalting us the gods of its creation, turning the eye, seducing and ensnaring. It is the undoubted number one idol which leaves its own imprint, and crucially helps us to establish our own. More than twenty years ago Gay observed:

> Protestants have prided themselves on their resistance to modern ideas and assumptions and on their preservation of the gospel from a "modernist adulteration." While this is undoubtedly true to some extent, especially relative to their "liberal" counterparts, it is important to stress the conservatives have also accommodated typically modern ideas and assumptions within evangelical theology in a number of material ways, and not without profoundly damaging results for evangelical churches.[27]

Today we see the Evangelical church appearing, by and large, to have sold itself lock, stock, and barrel to the *material*, the world's number one idol, and because it is its own message, it will, humanly speaking, always come out on top. Luther believed that "outward things" could do no harm if only the heart does not cleave to them or puts its trust in them. This medium already has the hearts of everyone, including Christians, so surely only the vainly naive could agree with Luther? History is now against him and watch this space, it will be against us also.

The Medium is the (Embellished Indispensable) Message

In an old English church a most unusual treasured artifact displays itself, fashioned ingeniously to carry and exhibit four books. This unusual book stand is quite original

27. Gay, *Way of the (Modern) World*, 249–50.

as it swivels at its base, allowing the viewer/reader the facility of remaining in a fixed position while accessing all four books. The books are the Bible, *Pilgrim's Progress*, *Book of Common Prayer* and *Foxe's Book of Martyrs*. This impressive artifact takes pride of place, being *seen* by all who enter there for worship, though I suspect its uniqueness now makes it protected from the fondling public. To my keen aesthetic eye it is both an object of great beauty and ingenuity. It celebrates the books which have shaped the church in our land, and I assume the motive for it being placed in the church must have been very honorable, pointing as it does to the word of God above all else, whilst acknowledging the very profound part others have played in our spiritual history. To the modern worshipper who sees it Sunday by Sunday, it must represent something unique and a "thing" so obviously to be proud of. However in the church where this object is found, it is probably just one of many artifacts which make the place stand out.

Our Innate Creativity!

Art is competitive: stained glass, flying buttresses and vaulted ceilings have a way of bringing all other contributions down to earth. The embellishment of the mediums we use in worship is well established. These embellishments increase their effectiveness, and in turn alter our appreciation of them. A good example would be a great family church Bible, like the one we have in our home which has come down through my wife's Dutch family, dated 1738. What an extraordinary work of meticulous printing, even containing a concordance. With its fabulous hand-stitched leatherwork, the binding is held by ornate brass fasteners, and caution is needed not to drop it on one's toes! Only sixty of these Keur Bibles ever existed. It is clear and obvious that this Bible was made to be read, but more than that, those who made it believed it deserved its own kind of unique embellishment. After all they must have reasoned in their own Protestant way, the Bible above all else deserved to be elevated. But wait, such a word brings back thoughts of the elevating of the cross and the host in the Catholic mass. Nevertheless a good sixteenth century Protestant could have presented many arguments to justify their embellishment of the Bible.

Interestingly however, the inside pages do not include any color, being as plain as plain can be, unlike so many beautiful, meticulously painted manuscripts, offered up by the artistic merits of Rome. It seems the embellishment was needed to draw the eye to call the book to our attention. Once this was achieved, once inside, nothing else was required. The word of God, pure and simple, could be trusted to do its work, yet even knowing this, the engravers embellishing art was still required, providing a compendium of illustrations!

Pleasing On the Eye

The definition of embellish is to beautify, to adorn, to enhance. This is what a woman might do to her eyes or lips, this in turn makes her, she hopes, more attractive, more noticeable, more desirable. Jezebel painted her face (2 Kgs 9:30). (Nothing is implied here about the rights or wrongs of Christian ladies using make-up or that they are related to Jezebel!) When Esther entered the world of Xerxes she was subject to the King's desires, and so she underwent beauty treatments (Esth 2:3). This was her embellishment, she was perceived to be in need of something to attract the eye. Whether people or buildings we are not only capable of beautifying a thing, we feel a deep need to do just that. Though we will never know, this could be to do with a sense of our fallen world and the desire to improve our deep-rooted imperfections. Paul says the whole creation groans, and this may be in part a reaction to that groaning.

Out in the Cold

Unfortunately the need to embellish the medium is not the preserve of the secular world it breaks out into our worship, it was this that particularly exercised the Swiss side of the Reformation. While this placed a vital seed into protestant worship it would only be a matter of time before the need arose for help which came in the form of endless kinds of embellishments. "The medium is the message," but what if the message which was given off by the externals was cold and austere? Today people will speak of cold, dreary uninviting church worship, not unlike the worship of bygone days where buildings were frigid and colorless, where black dominated, where the utilitarian spoke loudest and where the preaching dealt with hard facts of the gospel. Not surprisingly, in that situation, the fleshly sensibilities came to life.

Question Time

Why should the walls be whitewashed when they could equally be duck egg blue with delicately added darker accents? Why could the pulpit not be lifted up and thereby the minister of the eternal gospel be exalted? Along with this, why not give a little gold leaf to the edging of the lectern that would certainly draw ones wondering eye back to the center, which after all everyone needed to focus on, namely the message, the word of God? Often the pews were utilitarian, simple souls could come to worship and should be glad even of a wooden bench to sit on, but then why not place a cushion on them, is comfort a crime? Why not choose a bright fabric to cover those cushions? Surely no one is going to be misled by the cushions under the bottoms of the worshippers! Here in Yorkshire, in the North of England, someone said

> There is a gifted wood carver in the parish so why don't we ask him to embellish the new pews for the church? His droll calling card is a sweet little

mouse carved into all of his work. What could harm the worship by providing creative decoration, bringing sweetness and light to the new seating and communion table?[28]

Feet of Clay

The church I attended as a student in London saw no harm in displaying at least three rather elaborate flower arrangements for Sunday worship. Personally, if I was to choose decoration of any kind this would be my choice, but the question is what place do they have in the church? Dr. Lloyd-Jones seemed to believe the ministerial gown should be worn by the one standing in authority proclaiming the word of God. Lloyd-Jones goes on to justify this:

> I believe it is good and right for a preacher to wear a gown (Geneva gown emphasis mine) in the pulpit. The gown to me is a sign of the call, a sign of the fact that a man has been "set apart" to do this work. It is no more than that, but it is that.[29]

Is it at all possible to think of the apostle Paul being embellished with such a gown? Even if all this rather amusingly demonstrates our interest and preferences for the visual, it nevertheless confirms that none of these touch on any particulars regarding sound doctrine, or any doctrine at all for that matter, but only on things external, things *material*. What this demonstrates is that we can never entirely preclude the medium, and what is more, in some respects, we are always slaves to adornment. No doubt Dr. Lloyd-Jones's ministerial gown was designed to hide his clothes underneath so as to prevent distraction, only succeeding in providing its own by virtue of curiosity, and it must be said peculiarity. Try as we will to prevent the medium from ensnaring us, be it a building or whatever, we seem to succumb to the charms and allurements of our innate creativity.

Considering all this is so easily observable, it seems all the more strange that those who have maneuvered the screen so deftly into the center of worship, could fail to recognize it as an embellishing "tool"; an embellished medium embellishing. On the other hand if its work is in the main to embellish ourselves, then it stands to reason that we would be blinded, our narcissism unable to call it out. Like nothing ever before brought into the church, it claims a kind of unique diplomatic immunity, shouting, "Untouchable!" Neil Postman's observation captures the sense of this when he suggests, "Technopoly's key symbol is now the computer, toward which there must be neither irreverence nor blasphemy."[30] In this we see how the Queen of Heaven achieves the same for the Virgin Mary, she must suffer no irreverence nor blasphemy.

28. The Wood Carver Mousey Thompson (7.5.1876-8.12.1955)
29. Lloyd-Jones, *Preaching and Preachers*, 160.
30. Postman, *Technopoly*, 179.

After all she exists innocently to exalt the original, and in doing so deftly side steps any criticism, since she is merely a "servant," a humble "tool" like the screen willing to point up the original, seeking no glory for herself. In reality we know otherwise, like a magnet she draws people to herself and as she is painted and decorated she becomes alluring, an embellished, irresistible image—this is creativity once more. In much the same way the screen is art, the idol has to be embellished for us to be drawn to it. Once lose the sense that this is art, its magic will have enticed us. This is its power and we are naturally spellbound.

The Indispensable Holy Spirit

Socrates said: "The unexamined life is not worth living." He would have endorsed the work of "unpacking" the truth. The Bible constantly holds its divine torch to our souls, examining us regardless of how uncomfortable we find it, because all scripture is given for correction (1 Tim 3:15). When the screen was introduced into our churches evidently it did not undergo any rigorous testing, there is both a philosophical and practical reason for this. When placed under a reasonable light (no microscope needed) we discover not only is "the medium the message," but what is more it is a medium dealing in images, pictures which are prohibited by the great confessions of faith, and also a medium whose message embellishes the worshippers themselves. While such embellishment of ourselves by now feels quite natural, it renders the worship null and void, it is dead.

Food and water are basic necessities, indispensable, life depends upon them, unlike holidays and golf, however much we enjoy them, are not indispensable. For Protestant Evangelicals, there are things which are deemed to be indispensable, the Bible and faith are dependent upon each other: "Faith comes by hearing and hearing by the word of God." Jesus explains the indispensable nature of God's word when he tells us, "Man shall not live by bread alone but by every word which proceedeth out of the mouth of God" (Matt 4:4, KJV); "Without faith it is impossible to please God" (Heb 11:6, NIV). In every way we realize that God, Father, Son and Holy Spirit are indispensable to us; the Trinity is indispensable to the individual Christian and to the church, yet the challenge presented to us is that anything might suggest itself as equally indispensable, usurping the truly indispensable.

Seventy years ago A.W. Tozer, critiquing the state of the church of his day, illustrated its deep fault by recalling how the great locomotive steam trains could be stoked up to reach maximum speeds, but even when the boilers were spent of fuel they could still run for seventy miles on momentum. To his mind the danger to the church lay in its power to generate its *own* power rather than depend on the power of the Holy Spirit. This highlights the fact that the church may at any time resort to its own strength, its own understanding, its own ingenuity, its own rationalism, its own worship. It can resolve any problem by its own initiative, rendering faith unnecessary because it can extricate us from any predicament, vis-à-vis Abraham. If in Tozer's day the church, independent of God could travel on momentum, one shudders to think how far it can travel as a business entity today.

The Trimmings

Perhaps we never realized before that everything we engage with and which the church employs as a medium, is dispensable and in fact it has to be. In our modern church we have convinced ourselves for a church to exist it is impossible to function without certain things. Even the building is dispensable for worship as Christians have proved down through the ages from New Testament times to Whitfield and Wesley. Consider the piano, the pulpit, even the seating are all in fact dispensable. Of course we may prefer them, but the worship of the one true God does not depend on any of them. The car, the toilets, the lighting, all these and more are obviously dispensable. God can and has been worshipped out in the open fields and by hundreds and thousands. J.C. Ryle in his book *Christian Leaders of the Eighteenth Century* recalls the great distances people were prepared to walk to attend the worship of God. Naturally conditioned as we are, we cannot conceive of such a "ridiculous" suggestion that we should rise two or three hours earlier on Sunday morning to walk several miles to gather as the church. A horse and trap were dispensable . . . the worshipper had two legs. If we had not realized in our present age of consumerism, we have painted ourselves into a corner of convenience one of our own making. We have trapped ourselves by being convinced that our worship cannot possibly go ahead without our own requisite form.

What It Is to Be Needed

It is therefore natural that the indispensable medium of the screen enters the worship to rescue us, but its indispensable nature is in fact the one and only thing which is *true* about it, it is utterly indispensable to "corporate" worship, as used by "on-line worshippers." This kind of worship, if it may be called that, relies entirely on a machine which means without it there will be no offering to God. Without the screen nothing will happen, the screen has the whip hand, the screen rules. If it shuts down (by its own choice the signal drops and the internet fails) the church has to shut down its corporate worship. The church does not realize it has blundered into a Faustian deal, the worship of the only true God subject to will worship, now in tow to a machine, an indispensable machine at that. "The medium is the message," with its message loud and clear: "If you want to worship your God *together* you need me, you cannot do without me!"

Outlawing the Prefix

It is difficult to read 1 Chronicles 16:29 and think of anyone's head bowed toward a screen:

> Give unto the Lord the glory due unto his name: bring an offering, and come
> before him: Worship the Lord in the beauty of holiness. (1 Chron 16:29, KJV)

This text alone should rein in our actions. However I recognize that it has not had this effect on those Christians who moved to screen, which should both sadden and surprise us. Had many of us thought about the "medium as being the message" perhaps a brake might have been applied. One must assume that the great majority of Christians never gave this consideration. Can the worship be prefixed? Can we speak of Baptist worship, Presbyterian worship or Pentecostal worship? Has the church realized what it is participating in? Because in reality there is only worship, worship of the one true and living God in Spirit and in truth. The prefix "Zoom" should have been a warning. "Zoom" worship can have no place in our vocabulary. However, having secured an established status it must be analyzed against the truth of God's word, and since it has clearly been legitimized, it will become a fixture, not just in actions but may in time find its way into the dictionary.

Into the Light!

It is alarming but obvious that the "will" is the greatest threat to true worship. Paul uses this prefix regarding worship (Col 2:23), when he speaks of those who have a show of wisdom in "will" worship (KJV; Berean Bible, "self prescribed;" NET and NIV, "self imposed"). Here is a prefix constituting worship of their own kind, of their own making, i.e.: that which they desired, which pleased them. By contrast, Jesus speaks these emphatic timeless words, never to be forgotten in the church . . . "the *kind* of worshippers the Father seeks" (John 4:23, NIV). This is the fixed criteria, all that matters is what the Father wants, our own wishes are irrelevant. God does not ask us for our view, our opinion about worship. We wonder how even the apostle John could make the most dreadful error as he fell down at the feet of the angel to worship (Rev 22:8, 9). This confirms that we are all prone to get worship wrong, we must beware of any prefix added to our principle offering which we render exclusively to God, Father, Son and the Holy Spirit.

Location, Location, Location

When Jesus spoke these immortal words to the woman at the well, John 4, he was pointing her to the *only* worship, that is worship without the need of a medium. He was inaugurating a worship which could not be bound by time or place. For herself, like many today, she could not help but think of worship at places, specific places. Still today people consider worship being carried out "uniquely" in a church building. She thought of "Jerusalem" worship and "Mount Gerizim" worship at the Samaritans' temple. Today churchgoers easily think along the same lines, regarding worship as that which is conducted in a specific place by singing certain hymns, using particular Bible versions, or by lighting a candle, kneeling, or approaching God with a specific posture. In truth none of these are *needed* at all. Jesus said that neither Jerusalem nor Mount Gerizim would be *needed* any longer, they were to be abrogated because they were mediums. On to the present day, we must be equally persuaded that there are no special places, nor special times to worship God. By tradition alone, we have established, at least in our English churches, two services of worship on Sundays, as if this was God's requirement laid down in Scripture. This is no more of a requirement than the "Geneva gown" worn by Dr. Lloyd-Jones.

Confusion

The remarkable Congregational Minister, John Angell James, the Minister at Carrs Lane Congregational Church in Birmingham, who preached there for fifty-five years, would probably have something to say about this as he conducted more than two services of worship on Sundays. Was he right? Were the humble village chapel goers in the 1950s who walked miles over the Pennine hills of Yorkshire, offering the right amount of worship in their solitary afternoon service? The Waldenses worshipped in their barns, presumably with all the smells and the sounds of livestock. James Montgomery Boice is correct when he says, "We must not confuse worship with the particular things we do on Sunday morning."[31]

All You Need Is . . .

Obviously when COVID-19 struck, many churches could not escape the confines of their established Sunday morning worship "together" which was denied them. In their haste, without forethought they chose to employ the screen, even though this did not make "together" possible at all. In point of fact, it was just pseudo-worship, an illusion. People find it difficult, very difficult, to get "Jerusalem" out of them. For many of us to worship God is going to a place, a specific place even at a specific time! The woman at the well saw *only* the geographical places as the medium. She had grasped the medium's message, which not surprisingly was, "You need me and without me there will be no worship." Jesus is saying all mediums are dead, defunct, one must not be dependent on anything. All need is met when worshiping in "Spirit and in Truth." What must be remembered is that our very lives are intended to constitute an act of worship (Rom 12:1, NIV). This is "proper" worship.

31. Boice, *Gospel of John: Vol 1*, 296.

In His Steps

C.S. Lewis, as only he could, helps us here. Lewis was used to Church of England worship with its particular liturgy, Boice says,

> Lewis did not plead for liturgy. He asked merely for what he called "uniformity," on the grounds that "novelty" in the worship service at best turns our attention to the novelty.[32]

Lewis wrote,

> As long as you notice, and have to count the steps, you are not yet dancing but only learning to dance. A good shoe is a shoe you don't notice. Good reading becomes possible when you need not consciously think about eyes, or light, or print, or spelling. The perfect church service would be one we were almost unaware of; our attention would have been on God.[33]

The screen completely eliminates the possibility of this as the worshipper must be conscious above all else of his dependency upon the medium . . . Lewis could not have been a "screen worshipper."

Jesus was saying Jerusalem is null and void, you do not need to see it, to hear it to be in it. A.W. Pink says,

> We cannot worship by admiring grand architecture, by listening to the peals of a costly organ or the anthems of a highly trained choir. We cannot worship by gazing at pictures, (this for him would have precluded the camera and "Zoom") smelling of incense, counting of beads. We cannot worship with our eyes or ears, noses or hands, for they are all "flesh," and *not* "spirit."[34]

"Worship, then, is the occupation of the heart with a *known God*; and everything which *attracts* the flesh and its senses, *detracts* from real worship."[35] Again "the medium is the message," it is needed, depended upon, relied upon. "Screen" worship centers naturally upon a "screen" which is the center of attention, a "tin novelty." Surely it is impossible for us to envisage C.S. Lewis, or for that matter A.W. Pink, employing such a medium or endorsing it. Jesus tells the woman, true worship, is that which is offered in Spirit and in Truth. The "screen" deals in illusion, truth is not associated with it, nor can it be. The conclusion, prefix and worship are outlawed, beware the witching hour! Now to the serious task of "unpacking" . . .

---

32. Boice, *Gospel of John: Vol 1*, 297.

33. Boice, *Gospel of John: Vol 1*, 297, quoting Lewis, *Letters to Malcolm*, 4.

34. Pink, *Exposition of the Gospel of John*, 209.

35. Pink, *Exposition of the Gospel of John*, 208.

CHAPTER 8

The New Influencer

Warning!

The Neon God

For as he thinketh in his heart, so is he.
PROVERBS 23:7 (KJV)

WHEN MY WIFE WAS A child growing up in Holland she recalls visiting her grand-mother in Friesland and enquiring, in her childlike way, to every move which she made. She remembers the curt answer to her question, "Where are you going now?" It was the unforgettable "*Ik ga naar de plaats waar zelfs de Keizer alleen heen gaat!*" Translated being, "I am going to the place where even Caesar goes alone!" In our old school home we have just such a small, private, downstairs room where there hangs an old black and white photograph, taken approximately a hundred and ten years ago, of this school as it once was, and in fact not much over the years has changed. However, it is not the school in the photograph which draws me back to it again and again, rather the gathered children in that historic moment. I like to think they were in so many ways just like us, but it was customary in that day for them to wear hats; their clothes were slightly different, yet they must have been like us, alive to their world, their time, their tastes, life's joys and sadness, its frivolity, cruelty, health, sickness, its life and death. How very sobering to think that they all once walked about this old school we call home, and sat within its walls to be shaped by the education presented to them. They are all dead now.

Every Picture Tells a Story

This is a touching image which continues to affect me, adding an air of great beauty and indeed dignity to that room where "even Caesar goes alone." I am especially touched by the smiles which can be discerned on some of the faces, even the grumbling expressions worn by those who clearly felt the inconvenience of the occasion, as the man with the camera must have demanded their military-like attention. Looking at that photograph, the question keeps coming back to me: How did they think? Furthermore how were they *made* to think? I suspect like us, they would have reflected the thinking of their day as much as it managed to filter down into their parochial village life. In our imagination at least, we can see the older boys not long after the picture was taken, would have had their young minds awash with thoughts of war. In a matter of years someone persuaded them to take up arms and journey to a strange foreign place, where they lived in filthy trenches, where they were prepared to kill and be killed for a king whom they had never seen nor heard, and for a country which to most of them was no more than the size of a few square miles around their village. Their minds had been shaped, altered by those with the power of influence, and consequently many were anxious to get at the "Hun" as soon as possible, thinking departure from their normal established order and tradition would soon be over as they would have the Germans "licked" by Christmas and able to return to their idyll. Such blind idealism has often been seen in those with noble intentions who sadly set out on a path of no return.

Under the Influence

In this chapter I want to explore the thought of "influence." How, why and by whom have we been influenced to think the way we do? Without sounding too sinister I wonder who has "got" to us, who or what has "shaped" our thinking and directed our minds? This is something Dr. Greenfield believes is easily possible. Certainly the poster of Lord Kitchener pointing his finger at the young "would-be" conscript, appealing to him with the words "Your country needs you" must have had a little impact and worked its influence. It is remarkable how easily we are persuaded, the ad-men, "The Madmen," knew this equally then as now. Recently there has arisen a new phenomenon, the "social media influencer." Hard as it is to comprehend, this is now seen as an acceptable occupation. Obviously a climate which can embrace this will naturally embrace almost any kind of influence.

Hammer and Chisel

No doubt many of us will be familiar with the influence of the cults and their power to shape and re-orientate the vulnerable mind. The apostle Paul equally wanted the mind to be altered, he appealed to the Christians at Philippi to adopt the same humble mind of Christ: "Let this mind be in you which was also in Christ Jesus" (Phil 2:5, KJV). The gospel, in its very nature is "mind bending," it has to be since the Bible suggests powerful forces have twisted our thinking away from its original. The gospel has a formidable foe which must at all times be acknowledged, Paul reminds the Roman Christians, "Don't let the world around you squeeze you into its own mould, but let God remake you so your whole attitude of mind is changed" (Rom 12:2, J. B. Phillips). Note: the whole attitude of mind! To be a Christian is to have experienced "mind change," and ongoing mind change. The truth is we have all been "got at" in our home by parents, in life at school by teachers, in tertiary education by professors, at work by colleagues, in social life by friends and even in the church by its teaching. While the Christian may like to think that the whole attitude of mind has been changed by the gospel, it may be found on closer analysis, that individual churches and Christian writers have taken "hammer and chisel" to form and shape us into their own likeness. This is not to say it is always detrimental. Being a Calvinist I confess openly that Calvin's school of thought has deeply, profoundly affected me most of my Christian life. Calvin himself was profoundly influenced by Augustine, Luther by Erasmus and Zwingli also, who attributed his conversion to a piece of poetry (art no less) written by Erasmus. The "chisel" of the Puritans, John Wesley, Billy Graham and countless others may have shaped us more than we care to admit. Not surprisingly these have often fashioned us to look like themselves, as Elisha longed for a portion of Elijah's spirit and received his mantle (2 Kgs 2:9).

Without being aware, many of us wear a cloak with the embroidered names of those we have often followed rather too closely. Probably many admirers of Dr. Lloyd-Jones took up his authoritative, but thoroughly romantic notion of the "Geneva Gown," and may remain influenced to this day. Instead Christians should all strive to be unconscious Calvinists, Baptists and Anglicans, because only then can it be said in an unalloyed way, that they are striving to be the living image of him whose likeness they long to reflect above all others. However, Calvin's influence is one thing and Elijah's another, but consider the transformation which screen technology is having on us. Dr. Susan Greenfield says "A still deeper issue is how computers and iPads can also provide information in an utterly different, non-verbal way, and thereby perhaps actually *transform how we think* (italics, emphasis mine). If inputs arrive in the brain as images and pictures rather than as words, might it, by default, predispose the recipient to view things more literally rather than in abstract terms?"[1] The reader might like to consider Vanhoozer on this, as he also makes relevant and valid observations.

1. Greenfield, *Mind Change*, 46–47.

Shape Shifting and Resistance

It may be uncomfortable for the church to acknowledge that it is far more worldly in its orientation than it perceives itself to be. Some churches have fashioned an identity as those who fight on all fronts a war of attrition with the world, but in fact this turns out in reality *not* to be a "war" reflecting Paul's "attitude of the mind" but merely a "war" on externals. These are easily observable, especially to the judgmental who masquerade under the banner of "Mr. Valiant for Truth." In his 1998 foreword to Craig Gay's book, J.I. Packer puts his finger on this with his typical clarity:

> Worldliness meant smoking, drinking, ballroom dancing, novel reading, theatre—and movie-going, makeup for women, deodorant for men, mixed bathing for adults, and late nights for children.[2]

Packer says he was bemused by it all as a young eighteen-year-old Christian. He goes on to say that what is needed in the church is an appreciation of our current situation:

> Without it, deep-level worldliness cannot be avoided. There is far more to worldliness today than was dreamed of at the "fagend" of the Christendom culture of the West fifty years ago, and a far more radical view of separation from the world has now to be thought out.[3]

Packer notices that our thinking is pulling us all out of shape, the attitude of mind is being changed, but not by Christ's gospel, but by the world we live in. This is where our level of appreciation needs to be focused, not on the make-up and theatre-going. Forget these!

"Natural" Thinking

It is my contention that a particular attitude of mind, a "mindset," was needed to open the church up to the experiment of worshipping God through a screen. Initially when I wrote about this issue in July 2020, I suggested to those experimenting that they had not "thought" this matter through at all. Today I would retract this, because I believe it was in fact the most natural thing to do, for those who are affected by the world at the "deep level." What I mean is their thinking in this was already established, their thought processes were fixed unalterably, and this is why "screen" worship was entered into without a second thought, simply because it did not need one, that way of thinking was quite innate. It arose principally from a loss of control, a breakdown in communication, not with the head, Christ, but socially with one another. The thought of isolation was unbearable.

---

2. Gay, *Way of the (Modern) World*, Foreword, Packer.
3. Gay, *Way of the (Modern) World*, Foreword, Packer.

No Limits

The above condition can probably be traced to what James R Beniger has explained in considerable depth in *The Control Revolution*. He quotes Emile Durkheim, French sociologist (1858–1917) who wrote about the "Crisis of Control," not just at a societal level, but also where it touched individual psychology. Commenting on this Beniger says, "Here he found a more personal but directly related problem, what he called *anomie*, the breakdown of norms governing individual and group behavior."[4] To be clear and accurate, Durkheim was speaking specifically about the developing industrialization, the growing "systemness" of society. Interestingly though he noted that in such a world of (the "organized" type) the producer . . . "he can no longer see limits, since it is, so to speak, limitless."[5] Be it "complex systems," "machine technology," Beniger sees the resolution of the crisis (any crisis emphasis mine) demanded new means of communication. The limitless power of the medium, namely what it can achieve for us, its power to extricate us from our dilemma, whatever that might be, did not need a second thought, certainly not spiritual thoughts. This meant the "norms" of our tradition never really stood a chance, this is "deep level thinking" as the world thinks. Durkheim noticed that the breakdown was not just with the action of the individual but also of the group.

The Drug of Our Times

When the Coronavirus struck, the world was caught off guard, sadly many had no immune resistance to it, and the loss has been both grave and considerable. In the same way it exposed the deep vulnerability of the church, which equally had no resistance to the latent worldliness within its borders. It appears to have instantly capitulated to the demands exerted by the screen. This is not difficult to diagnose, as people already dependent on screen/tech for life have virtually no power to find fault with it, spiritual objectivity has no voice. Indeed it would appear God can find no fault with it, because it is seen as wholly benign. It seems that the church was unable to put up any resistance to the power of the modern secular age, bedazzled by what the medium could achieve. It must not be forgotten that the work of influential recruitment had already been established, practically everyone by now is a "social media animal," craving the "social" because, whether we like to admit it or not, it is the "opium of the people," the "drug" of our times. "Zoom" only needed the sign of the cross or the holy water of religious acceptability to sanctify it. Evangelicals though had their own means to sanctify and make the practice acceptable. It became possible because it was something innate, being in them at what Packer calls the "deep level" and manifesting itself . . . it was "rationalism," the greatest "influencer" of our times.

4. Beniger, *Control Revolution*, 12, quoting Durkheim, *Division of Labor*.
5. Beniger, *Control Revolution*, 11, quoting Durkheim, *Division of Labor*.

Misshapen

Gary Gilley, in his book, *This Little Church went to Market,* quotes Os Guinness who thinks that ". . . in our time, the change was not 'so much from Calvinism to Arminianism as from theology to experience, (Schleiermacher's brain child, emphasis mine) from truth to technique, from elites to populism, and from an emphasis on 'serving God' to an emphasis on 'servicing the self.'"[6] This confirms, if it is true, that we are being pulled out of shape or have already been reconfigured.

I remember as a young student experiencing this to my cost, and how easy it is to reshape something so as to affect it forever. I recognize in my upbringing, much to my embarrassment, my mother had looked after me far too immaculately and meticulously for my own good, washing, drying and ironing all my clothes, including socks! So, when as a complete novice, I decided one day to wash a sweater, and then hang it up by the sleeves to dry, I found the garment was only going to be of any use at the zoo in the gorilla compound! The Christian lady who ran our lodgings, quite rightly berated me for my folly. I have never forgotten it or her!

When is a door not a door?

The church can be pulled completely out of shape never to return to its former likeness. It is true that history teaches us that the church has always been morphing, but very often with dire consequences. I remember thinking when I looked at my "gorilla sweater" why had not some of the other students warned me of my folly, but then I realized they were probably as uninitiated as I was! Schleiermacher in his day was pulling the church out of shape, Billy Graham likewise, but not enough of the church really noticed until it was too late. Gary Gilley's book, *This Little Church went to Market*, tries to deal with some of these questions. He says, "the real issue is how this philosophy is changing both the message and the essence of the church."[7] In other words it is impossible to truly separate our methodology from our message, for to a large degree they hinge on one another. After all a door is nothing without the doorframe upon which it hangs and depends, the message and the method go together. If a door in a doorframe is not "plumb" and "true" the door will never function as it should, however much it looks like a door![8]

Merger or Blip?

Too often evangelicals have concerned themselves with the *content*, the doctrine, the method on the other hand was thought of as being a matter of individual "church

6. Gilley, *This Little Church Went to Market*, 55, quoting Guinness, *Dining with the Devil.*

7. Gilley, *This Little Church Went to Market*, 48.

8. "We must be as concerned with the truth of the message as its means of presentation." (Augustine).

taste." Praying to God *together* through a computer screen becomes just a matter of taste, like the electric guitar, drums, the choir and all our wider creative capabilities. Only in our shapeshifting age, as we do obeisance to tech, can we comfort ourselves so as to masterfully make the merger possible, enabling God and machine to hold hands affectionately. Paul Simon and Art Garfunkel act as most remarkable seers from the sixties, and prophetically sing of those who "bow to the neon god they have made which flashes out its warning that it is forming." There will be those who tell us that this blip of contortion is only temporary. But this, to put it mildly, is naive, the tech greedily eats up what might be called tradition, it has no limits. Mumford, Gay and Postman all recognize this; it is no respecter of persons or conventions.

If today we can buy a car which will park itself and reverse into the tightest of spaces, eliminating all possibilities of scrapes, scratches and insurance claims, then the rationalism in us will dictate it as our next purchase. The tech is reshaping the parking of cars. "Zoom" has already reshaped the church, there is no going back, the neon god has shaped the shapeshifters and the "deep level" worldliness is there for all to see.

Eureka!

While some of these things may be clear and obvious, a sinister influence always lurks ... underpinning the whole is a philosophy which makes the actions seamlessly possible. While on the face of it the seismic shift is in the *practice* of the "screen" worship itself, the *willingness* to use the tech to reach God is the real shift, and is rooted in a profound place which needs a little technical illumination, as dark places almost always need illumination. This is a very dark place. When the church wakes up one morning and says, "Eureka! Let us use Zoom to worship God!" it is not born, though it may appear to be of the moment, rather it comes to birth through ages of thought and conditioning. "Screen" worship is above all else an act of rationalism, and rationalism employs many parts, which in turn are used to convince and persuade us that what we are doing is right. Our blind spot is this: We mistake the need to be rational human beings with an "ism" ... subscribing to an ideology, a way of life.

Rational rationalism

Jacques Ellul in *The Technological Bluff* says:

> And what is so reassuring as the rational? It is reassuring because it is both understandable and certain. Implying the development of a series of linked operations, it can be fully grasped. If, then, the world is to be grasped (i.e., understood and mastered), it must be rational. All that we ask of people in this society must be rational. It is rational to consume more, to change immediately what is worn out, to acquire more information, to satisfy an increasing number of desires. Constant growth is rational for our economic system. We

can take the ordinary actions of 99 percent of the population in a so-called advanced country and we shall find the key to them is always rationality.[9]

It was rational for Europe to depend on Russia's oil and gas, that was before the invasion of Ukraine! For example: it is rational to use the fossil fuels currently available, riches which China, India and Australia are sat upon and unwilling to give up, but will it be good to us?

This 99 percent sadly includes the church. Owen's *Thinking Spiritually* did not find a voice when the COVID-19 restrictions were imposed, because rationalism trumps it every time. Billy Graham employed the same rationalism seventy years ago. Gay remarks, "Rationality . . . is in the eye of the beholder."[10] What is rational from one point of view may well be irrational from another. It would be very interesting to poll the churches which pursued a rationalism which led to "Zoom" worship asking how many have in the past been critical of Graham's "rational" methods of evangelism? Gay makes an observation which relates exactly to this point:

> Of the other lines of historical development overwhelmed by the process of rationalism, the most significant in our own Western context has been the Christian. Whereas Christianity had provided *the* interpretive grid for Western European society and culture for many hundreds of years, with the onset of modernity aspects of European social and cultural life began to be surrendered to purely pragmatic, calculable, scientific, "rational" judgement.[11]

In such an environment religious ends are not in view, society instead functions with the consideration of efficiency, effectiveness and viability. A.K.A, coal! Gay writes of "practical rationalization of our *whole* (emphasis mine) outlook on life."[12] The church, "under the influence," turns out to be first of all practical rather than spiritual, the kingdom of God bows to the kingdom of this world.

Iron Cage . . . Market Thinking

'Zoom" provided efficiency, it provided effectiveness and as we shall see, viability, it enabled us to adapt to our entirely new social environment. The root of all evils pulling the purse strings is never far away. The Christian grid providing interpretation in the unique "unprecedented" circumstances was gone, it disappeared in a flash. In an instant the church woke up one morning reconfigured its worship practice and embraced "Zoom." It was calculable, it was highly systematic, it was a means-ends tool. It could deliver for business to keep it afloat and profitable, to keep its customer

9. Gay, *Way of the (Modern) World*, 139, quoting Ellul, *Technological Bluff*, 161.

10. Gay, *Way of the (Modern) World*, 139.

11. Gay, *Way of the (Modern) World*, 137.

12. Gay, *Way of the (Modern) World*, 156, quoting Schumpeter, *Capitalism, Socialism, and Democracy*, 123–124.

base, it was effective, here was ingenuity which rationalism suggested to a church that "leaned on its own understanding."

The church, while thinking this way did not realize that it belongs to the 99 percent i.e. the world's thinking, and as such it demonstrated that it is locked inside the iron cage which Weber described as far back as 1904. This is market thinking, nevertheless this does not seem strange because such rationalism can always be justified, "if it works it must be right." Should it not strike us that there is something of the dehumanizing taking place when the kingdom of God becomes so inextricably linked to a means-ends philosophy? "Whoever knows the world as something to be utilized knows God the same way,"[13] wrote Martin Buber.

It is very heartwarming to read Craig Gay's analysis of this when he says "Christian faith does not permit us to treat our neighbor as an object to be manipulated for the sake of practical purposes, or to reduce his or her "worth" to a digit within the economic calculus."[14] When so-called "Zoom" prayer meetings operate by giving each person a number and place to offer their prayer through the medium, it can be seen *nature* as described in an earlier chapter, has been lost. The rationalism denotes a process which is impersonal, the outcomes are sure because they are planned, which suits us "down to the ground," it is "highly systematic." As Thomas Luckmann observed Weber's own analysis, he says: "In Weber's view the outstanding characteristic of modern society is its 'rationality' . . . In modern society he discerned the prevalence of a highly systematic, anonymous and a calculable form of law, he found an economy guided by its own principles of calculability and means ends rationality."[15] Weber, though not exclusively, saw the process of this rationalization. Eduard Shils also writes:

> Rationalisation denotes a process in which social action ceases to be determined by traditional wisdom and/or custom and comes instead to be determined by abstract, calculable, and often impersonal, "rational" criteria. It entails the elimination of all decisions that cannot be shown to contribute to planned outcomes, outcomes that have themselves been rationally defined and determined according to generally valid empirical laws.[16]

The New Testament has left us a vivid picture of just such a mentality . . .

Jesus and the Religious Rationalists

Let us be generous and say that many churches and individual Christians "threw their lot in" with experimental "screen" worship in innocence and even with honorable

13. Buber, *I and Thou*, 156.

14. Gay, *Way of the (Modern) World*, 178.

15. Gay, *Way of the (Modern) World*, 137, quoting Luckmann (quoting Weber), *Theories of Religion and Social Change*, 13-14.

16. Gay, *Way of the (Modern) World*, 136, quoting Shils, *Tradition*, 291.

motives. But then tens of thousands of Christians in the fifties and sixties did the same as they followed the Billy Graham Campaigns, only confirming it is possible to be sincere but sincerely wrong. As already indicated "Zoom" was designed for business, and all too often the church in its history has proved to be of the mercantile cast, and that no less today. Certainly Gary Gilley's book title, *This Little Church Went to Market*, leaves little to the imagination. When Max Weber broke down the kinds of rationalism which have invaded the entirety of life, he recognized practical rationality as the means to achieve self-interest. Gay observes from this that:

> Not surprisingly, the practical and self-interested cast of mind has historically been most characteristic of merchants and businessmen. Those engaged in commercial activity do not, as a rule, tend to be philosophically inclined and tend instead to be concerned with practical results, with the proverbial "bottom line." . . practical rationality says in effect, "and get down to business."[17]

When the churches made their snap decision to "get down to superficial business," entering into "screen" worship, it was not at all tested, that would have required some philosophical thought; Paul's counsel would not have gone amiss: "He does not make his plans in a worldly manner." He does not make his plans "according to mere human standards" (2 Cor 1:17, NET). By contrast, the church driven by "the bottom line" needed to keep the machine moving, and we know growth and progress are driven by the need of "the bottom line" This views the church, and even tragically souls, as an economy (Rev 18:13). Peter Berger observes it is, "a rationally calculating and planning manner. This individual is also animated by a strong sense of ambition and the goals of this ambition are to be reached by way of competitive achievement."[18] All of this appears to have been the mindset of the churches and Gay helps us to see that such a mindset cannot really be challenged. He says:

> The burden of proof today thus falls upon anyone who would dare suggest that there ought to be some other basis *besides* that of rational self-interest on which to make business decisions. After all, individuals and firms *must* pursue their own self-interest in a rational fashion for the market system to function efficiently and for the economy to continue to grow.[19]

It is just this self-interest (not God's interest) which propelled the church into "Zoom," and naturally for growth in the future because it will not permit its tight grip ever to be loosened. Who would dare suggest to a church in the future that "Zoom" should be abandoned since it has attracted large numbers of "worshippers," many now gladly contributing to the church coffers . . . "the bottom line" rules!

17. Gay, *Way of the (Modern) World*, 140, quoting Weber, *Protestant Ethic.*
18. Gay, *Way of the (Modern) World*, 157, quoting Berger, *Capitalist Revolution*, 107-8.
19. Gay, *Way of the (Modern) World*, 147.

Those Who Know the Price of Everything and the Value of Nothing

Thankfully we have one who has dared to challenge the mercantile mindset in a religious setting. Christ by his actions at the Temple (John 2), questions "self-interest," "the bottom line" he does not surrender to rational methods, practices and techniques, but he places them under his divine scrutiny. Jesus confronts the works of the merchants, for them "traditional wisdom and custom" had little or no influence. Jesus had gone up to Jerusalem for the Passover which appears remarkably to have changed hands, John calls it the *Jewish* Passover, or the Passover of the Jews. This seems strange when it was originally called The Lord's Passover (Exod 12). By the time Jesus encounters this grotesque scene the Passover has changed hands, its ownership is no longer seen as belonging to God but to men. We must confess that far too often this is how Christ's church appears, the power, the influence, the direction is with men and not with God, a subtle exchange has taken place, but no one noticed. In this regard the church looks to be under new ownership, meaning it is possible anywhere and at any time for Christ to be the head of the church in name only. Equally, two thousand years ago, Jesus confronted a situation at the temple, where even the name of God had been removed from the Passover. Men had come to rule by their own outrageous schemes, God had been seamlessly stripped from the proceedings.

Yeast . . . a powerful influence

Perhaps this subtle, almost innocent imperceptible change, "harmless" many might have said, was responsible for the ease by which God's House of Prayer was turned into a market place. It is hard for us to see how this could possibly happen when we consider the safeguards which were in place. The Passover historically was viewed strictly so that the substance of yeast/leaven within homes was outlawed. Paul borrows this image for his own purposes and says, "a little yeast works through the whole batch of dough" (Gal 5:9, NIV). When he speaks of covetousness, extortion and idolatry in the church, he sees it like that of yeast influencing the whole body of Christ. Hodge puts it this way "It is the nature of evil to diffuse itself. This is true with regard to individuals and communities."[20] Hodge was saying evil works to extend its territory, to extend its borders of influence.

When Jesus caught sight of the merchants and their practices ingressing the Holy Place, his holiness dovetailed with it, so that what it was, he was. He clearly saw evil diffusing itself and if it was not confronted, it would spread. Someone needed to put down a marker to question what no one else was willing to confront. A.W. Pink thinks the dealers, "would have argued that these moneychangers and cattle dealers, in the temple courts, were there as a convenience to those who came to the temple to

20. Wilson, *Commentary on 1 Corinthians*, 80, quoting Hodge, *Commentary on 1 Corinthians*.

worship."[21] A church observer today might even say "what could be more commendable!" And practical rationalism would almost certainly demand such a response. Far from these being pernicious actions they were in every way good and positive, advancing the cause of God's worship. Pink quotes Dr. Dods: "Yet although many must have lamented this, no one had been bold enough to rebuke and abolish the glaring profanation."[22]

If a complainant had dared to suggest that this was out of order, the reply one might have expected would be, "We are facilitating what God has commanded, we are making possible that which does honor to God." These actions are merely a pragmatic response to a need. After all, in addition to this, when God has instituted something we are bound over to make sure his will is obeyed. Seemingly what matters is that it *is* carried out and not the "how" of it! From this perspective these merchants were friend not foe; they were positively on God's side, they were "doers," "activists" in a holy prescribed work . . . only they were not! Christ sees beyond this into a world where holiness is stripped down, the utilitarian, the market, the machine-like process has come to dominate. Yet undoubtedly here was the logical way, the means-ends, the calculated and efficient, the viable and of course, the profitable. The pro-market men would have kicked and screamed as is their want when challenged, but Jesus meets this with his inflexible, excoriating righteousness and sees it for what it is, compromise, resulting in idolatrous commercialism.

How could any one of us fail to see that coin was at the center of the enterprise? For the Temple tradesmen money was calling the shots, and while we might have expected the holy backdrop to work its influence upon their thinking (perhaps the way we are affected when entering a great cathedral) the environment of holiness was no match for "a root of all kinds of evil" (1 Tim 6:10, NIV). The pure thing was made to give way, to submit, by those who knew the "price of everything" and the "value of nothing." In this way the profane could be joined to holy practices and "good reason" given for it.

Disturbingly, but not remarkably, no one seemed to notice or cared to notice, no one but the Lord of Glory, "whose eyes are like flames of fire" (Rev 1:14, KJV). Only he recognized that this was out of order, out of place, and God was dishonored.

Money, Money, Money

Of course the merchants were money men, and the money men have never been far away from God's civilization. Some might even say money has been the cause of much of its troubles, and it is hard to argue with this when Paul calls the love of money "a root of all kinds of evil." If money gains its voice in the church then its demands will stress quantity over quality. Naturally quantity will point to further profits, larger

21. Pink, *Exposition of the Gospel of John*, 94.
22. Pink, *Exposition of the Gospel of John*, 96, quoting Dr. Dods.

yields, "bigger barns," (Luke 12:18) which might even be seen in the numbers who frequent our churches. Karl Marx, cited by Lewis Mumford says, "Everything becomes saleable and purchasable . . . not even the bones of the saints are able to withstand this alchemy; and still less able to withstand it are more delicate things, sacrosanct things which are outside the commercial traffic of men."[23] When one reads these words it is impossible not to think of the churches at so-called prayer, or celebrating the Lord's Table, one of the most delicate, sacrosanct, inviolable practices in the Christian life, all rendered by "Zoom" so as to look like a commodity, recalling "Church Live Streaming Worship," which not suprisingly had produced a 70 percent increase in donations (Chapter 5). Worship, then, instead of coming up "smelling of roses," has the deleterious effect of something harmful to spiritual health, appearing as it does, "dressed to kill" in its mercantile garb!

Speedy decision making

Glenn Tinder comments on money as a root of all evils: "Holdings in money can be indefinitely increased; one's barns become infinitely capacious. And since money is readily convertible into a variety of physical possessions and personal services, it adds to the charm of ownership the allure of power."[24] It would surely be stretching credulity to think that these dangers are the preserve only of a fallen world and not God's civilization. "Zoom," amongst other "tools," enables business not only to stay afloat, but to make gains and undoubtedly this has been true for churches, and some have even boasted of it. This is where "screen" worship scored so highly, and why it did not require nor welcome investigation in the kingdom of God; in every way it would prove profitable. Here was holy enterprise, the church was staring a "gift horse in the mouth," it is impossible not to believe that this informed the decision making.

A church with twenty members of staff having considerable salaries to be paid, is essentially the same as the business down the street, enterprise during lockdown would be needed for survival. Not only this, there was no time to evaluate it because the need was immediate, the COVID-19 circumstances meant that the churches, like everything else, were put into lockdown, "business" was bound to suffer. The requirement was, as the saying goes, to "think on your feet," and to act quickly. The warning of Scripture, "he that believeth shall not make haste" (Isa 28:16, KJV) found no voice where rationalism boomed out its pragmatic solution.

Craig Gay provides the meaning for the term "bourgeois:"

> The typically bourgeois individual is one who tends both to value and to exhibit a high degree of individual autonomy, and to place a premium on worldly, practical rationality . . . by functional rationality, by sober, no-nonsense,

23. Mumford, *Technics & Civilization*, 24, quoting Marx.
24. Gay, *Way of the (Modern) World*, 155, quoting Tinder, *Political Meaning of Christianity*, 184.

problem-solving attitude to life in general and, of course, to economic life in particular . . . This individual is also animated by a strong sense of ambition and the goals of this ambition are to be reached by way of competitive achievement. Finally, here is an individual who is open to innovation, as against one bound by the past. Indeed, there is a tendency within this individual to regard anything as better just because it is new.[25]

In the circumstances of lockdown the innovative, the novel attraction, the "new" could not be resisted and importantly, it being the "tool" of life in everyone's life, it was "crying out" to be used. Whatever test it needed to pass, it had already "passed with flying colors." The historic practice of the church patiently bearing its cross in the midst of trials, quietly leaning upon its God, in the sure and certain hope of his deliverance, was not even remotely considered.

Gay's observations apply: "The practical, activistic, and this-worldly bourgeois outlook is not particularly conducive to the religious view of life, especially to the extent that religion occasionally enjoins contemplation and the cessation of activity."[26] But as we know, contemplation requires time which the anxious soul and bourgeois establishment "problem solvers" could not possibly countenance.

Naturally in a "moment" of introspection the church could easily legitimize its decision to use the "screen," monetization could make an undoubted case for it. At the conclusion of the documentary film, The Social Dilemma, the tech experts seem sure that the greatest obstacle to change is monetization. Money and mercantile thinking are "joined at the hip," nothing can separate them, by their power we are locked in. The reality: Christ's church is also uncomfortably connected at the deepest level, which makes retreat from the present experiment very unlikely indeed.

Tracing our Pathology

In 1650 Oliver Cromwell wrote a despatch from Dunbar, it read, "God hath a people here fearing his name though deceived." In his book Religion and the Rise of Capitalism, Professor R.H. Tawney charts the development of Puritan thought as it touched on the economic spirit, like Weber before him he believes that their thought and action enabled them to "serve two masters."[27] In actual fact, in this, the most influential, most profound period of spiritual history found itself deceived by men who failed to grasp the most fundamental in the spiritual life . . . You cannot serve God and Mammon. It would not be surprising if this kind of intellectual criticism raised the hackles of some Christians, nevertheless we should nerve ourselves to test all our forbears as we must test everyone. J.I. Packer, no mean authority and admirer of the Puritans,

25. Gay, Way of the (Modern) World, 156-157, quoting Berger, Capitalist Revolution, 107–8.

26. Gay, Way of the (Modern) World, 157.

27. Tawney, Religion and the Rise of Capitalism, 245.

encourages this, a robust analysis of those he describes as "seraphic Baxter, dreamer Bunyan, and elephantine Owen."[28] To Packer the Puritans were giants compared with us, and it is impossible not to concur with him. He says:

> If we are to profit from studying Puritan teaching . . . our approach to it must be right. For it is all too easy for admirers of the Puritans to study their work in a way which the Puritans themselves would be the first to condemn. Thus, we can have a wrong attitude to the men; we can revere them as infallible authorities. But they would scarify us for such a gross lapse into what they would regard as papalism and idolatry. They would remind us that they were no more than servants and expositors of God's written word, and they would charge us never to regard their writings as more than helps and guides to understanding that word. They would further assure us that, since all men, even Puritans, can err, we must always test their teaching with the uttermost rigor by that very word which they sought to expound.[29]

Time is Money

We owe it to ourselves to demonstrate a spiritual probity about all our dealings, "test everything" is the apostle's mandate; Reformers and Puritans included. Paul would have tested them. To say, as Tawney does that the Puritans ("the schoolmasters of the English middle classes") have influenced us is an understatement, while it may be shocking to some it should come as no surprise that we have not only been compelled by their theology and emphasis on the spiritual life, but *life* itself, both the world and the church. Not forgetting that both church and state have often been co-extensive. It was Benjamin Franklin, a child of the Puritans, who coined the phrase, "Time is money." Franklin still speaks today, he is in our psyche, we appear not to be aware that the world at large has more of Puritan DNA in it than we realize. Is Franklin's maxim giving us God's view about time, or the world's view? Christians of all persuasions, even those who have never heard of the Puritans, sport the same DNA, though most are quite ignorant of it. Undoubtedly in our modern "business" thinking Machiavelli is obviously reflected and who, like Columbus, knew that gold constitutes treasure: meaning our business roots go back to Florence, the financial capital of medieval Europe and to Antwerp and the Netherlands of the Golden Age. But equally the Puritans have levied their economic model on us and made us *think* in a particular way. Having had a hand in shaping our "business" mentality, they are surely as influential as the shrewd Florentine analyst. "Where did we get this from?" "Who put this into us?" These are surely worthwhile and important questions. It is this profound picture of Puritan influence on our thinking which requires thoughtful consideration as it

28. Packer, *Quest for Godliness*, 16.
29. Packer, *Quest for Godliness*, 233.

impacts our inquiry. Professor Tawney's research leads him to conclude that "Puritanism, not the Tudor succession from Rome, was the true English Reformation, and it is from its struggle against the old order that an England which is unmistakably modern emerges . . . the revolution which Puritanism wrought in Church and State was less than that which it worked in men's souls, . . . (and) if the inward and spiritual grace of Puritanism eludes the historian, its outward and visible signs meet him at every turn, and not less in the market-place."[30] *NB*: By the "work in men's souls," Tawney does not mean regeneration by the power of the Holy Spirit. Clearly the effects were visible on those who were influenced by Puritan thinking and that manifestly in terms of "business," the market place. A pamphlet of 1671 confirms this—"There is a kind of natural unaptness . . . in the Popish religion to business, whereas on the contrary among Reformed, the greater their zeal the greater their inclination to trade and industry, as holding idleness unlawful . . ."[31]

If Tawney is correct and the revolution in the church was less than the effects upon people which their religious liberty had conferred upon them with considerable advantage, then we would expect to see it . . . and so we do. The church today which practices and tolerates mercantile worship of any kind, has little of the spiritual worshipping Puritan in them. Would these Christians conscious of the "painted bauble" (Chapter 3) have practiced such worship? These were Christians for whom Joel Beeke acknowledges "*everything* was important."[32] "Today the church is full of people who have been so preoccupied with one thing that they forget the importance of another. The Puritans did not forget the importance of anything in their churchly outlook; everything was important."[33] While on the other hand today's church is comfortably mercantile in disposition following and reflecting the Puritan discipline and mindset, rationalizing and systematizing life with a method which predates the Methodists by a hundred years. The Puritans are in us for good and ill.

The Coiled Spring

What is glaringly obvious, our churches do not have in their DNA, the spirituality of the Puritans but unmistakably their business "know-how." Tawney recognizing the driving force, which is probably no stranger in our own churches touches on this.

> For it is will—will organized and disciplined and inspired, will quiescent (will which had been dormant, emphasis mine) in rapt adoration or straining in violent energy, but always will—which is the essence of Puritanism . . . The

30. Tawney, *Religion and the Rise of Capitalism*, 199.

31. Tawney, *Religion and the Rise of Capitalism*, 206.

32. Beeke and Jones, *Puritan Theology*, 852.

33. Beeke and Jones, *Puritan Theology*, 852.

Puritan is like a steel spring compressed by an inner force, which shatters every obstacle by its rebound.[34]

Here is the spirit of the will, exemplified in today's church, which rushed to use a computer screen to worship the almighty God and even pray into it, and astonishingly attempt to celebrate the Lord's Supper. The coiled spring, Tawney says, "shatters every obstacle by its rebound. Sometimes the strain is too tense, and, when its imprisoned energy is released, it shatters itself."[35]

Who Got to the Puritans?

However let us rewind and remind ourselves of the major influences and players before the Puritans took up their mission, who put the energy into them? We need to know who influenced them, how and why. The danger for Christians may be their willing appreciation of the Reformation, but nonetheless to read only selectively concerning the issues of its wider influence. The world which the Reformation inherited was not only a crucible of religion but one ripe for change at every level, especially in the realms of the ethics of social organization. This would be, as Tawney agrees with Weber, (the age of) "influence of religious ideas on economic development. (which then he believes comes full circle) It is not less important to grasp the effect of the economic arrangements accepted by an age on the opinion which it holds of the province of religion."[36] If we perceive the Middle Ages to have been controlled by the power of a musty superstition which Rome exerted, we may attribute more to that control than was in fact the case.

Max Weber thinks that the control prior to the Reformation which people lived under "was very lax, at that time scarcely perceptible in practice, and hardly more than formal . . . The rule of the Catholic Church . . . is now tolerated by peoples of thoroughly modern economic character, and was borne by the richest and economically most advanced peoples on earth at about the turn of the fifteenth century."[37] This "rule," this "mastery" of life was confronted in the Reformation by what appears to have been an entirely "other alternative" but no less a "rule" and "mastery" and especially where it had its center in Geneva and Scotland. The theology i.e.: the foundation became, as Eire says, "a sociopolitical ideology."[38]

Under the tutelage of new masters a new theology (that of grace apart from works) brought its powerful spiritual influence. However alongside the interests of the "new religion" ran the need to impact and affect the totality of human interests. It

---

34. Tawney, *Religion and the Rise of Capitalism*, 201.

35. Tawney, *Religion and the Rise of Capitalism*, 201.

36. Weber, *Protestant Ethic*, Foreword Tawney, 11.

37. Weber, *Protestant Ethic*, 36-37.

38. Eire, *War Against The Idols*, 4.

did not matter that trade was one thing and religion another, nor that as Tawney puts it "Christianity has no more deadly foe than the *appetitus divitiarum infinitus*, the unbridled indulgence of the acquisitive appetite."[39] The whole of life was to be brought under the umbrella of what John Knox had described as, "The most perfect school of Christ that ever was on earth since the days of the Apostles."[40] Clearly though not all who hailed from Scotland shared the views of Knox. Tawney says, "In Scotland the views of the Reformers as to economic ethics did not differ in substance from those of the Church before the Reformation, and the Scottish Book of Discipline denounced covetousness with the same vehemence as did the "accursed Popery" which it had overthrown."[41] Plans for a new religious model were being fashioned from "an odious paradox to that of an unquestioned truth." The Reformation found it could not only live with the paradox of business and religion in glad embrace, but the one could not live without the other. This is vital to emphasize since the contemporary church possesses the same propensity for business modeling.

Church PLC

Craig Gay makes an astute observation:

> Calvinists . . . tended to be somewhat more pragmatic than their Roman Catholic and/or Lutheran counterparts in assessing the actual results of economic actions. If something worked and was useful, it was deemed Christianly acceptable. The Christian was not to be bound by moribund tradition in economic matters, but was instead expected to be open to practical-rational innovation in the service of his or her neighbor and in the interests of the common good.[42]

Here are the seeds of our business rationalism in the church which have also impacted our spiritual life, these seeds have come down through time and have survived right up to the present day. It is this powerful informant which wields an extraordinary influence in God's kingdom. If only we knew it, this was the principle thinking which essentially informed, and is still informing, the evangelistic campaigns of various kinds. In addition the entire contemporary "worship scene," "Zoom" worship included, is in our DNA. Calvin paradoxically is in the Arminian, the Anglican, the Pentecostal, the Charismatic and in the broader church. The church is an unashamed business!

---

39. Tawney, *Religion and the Rise of Capitalism*, viii.

40. Tawney, *Religion and the Rise*, 126, quoting Knox.

41. Tawney, *Religion and the Rise of Capitalism*, 134.

42. Gay, *Way of the (Modern) World*, 163.

Illumination vs. Substitution

To grasp this we need to capture a sight of the people under the tutelage of their new masters. A new theology (Paul's old theology), that of grace apart from works, brought a powerful spiritual influence wrought by the Holy Spirit. The Reformation was undoubtedly all of this. Nevertheless alongside it ran the need also to affect the "totality of human interests." The "whole of life" was to be brought under the new umbrella, meaning that "economic appetites" were as much in need of reform as was the spiritual. The new world would need a new ethic, Gay commenting on Weber describes it as "*ethical* rationalization of the world wrought within Calvinist Protestantism that gave rise to an essentially new kind of practical rationality, one that was profoundly acquisitive . . ."[43]

Vast numbers of people who crossed over at the Reformation easily ditched their popish dress and exchanged them for Protestant clothes, their masters were no longer in Rome but in Geneva, where church and state would be reconstructed. The masses morphed and now wore a new ensemble, many hearts across Europe which now felt the force of the Protestant revolution remained naturally unregenerate, but this did not prevent the world of business being welcomed with enthusiasm in a way unknown before. Tawney says: "Calvinism endowed the life of economic enterprise with a new sanctification."[44](This is mirrored precisely in the new expressions of worship). The problem was that those in the fold were "not wholly weaned from the fleshpots of Egypt."[45] The unregenerate and those by new birth who belonged to the civilization of God's kingdom appeared now as one people, subjected to the one new rule; one which the natural man who "could not receive the things of the Spirit of God" (1 Cor 2:14, KJV), could nevertheless very easily receive and welcome with open arms the new social ethics. Tawney remarks on the age: "The religious revolution of the age came upon a world heaving with the vastest economic crisis that Europe had experienced since the fall of Rome."[46]The connection here with our own economic crisis arising out of COVID-19's assault upon the world's economies is both irritating and uncomfortable, to say the least.

Earthly-Minded

When Benjamin Franklin coined the phrase "time is money" he was not providing an ounce of what is spiritual, this is not biblical authority, rather it is Reformation thinking and Puritan mentality—Puritan authority. Let us not forget that Franklin was in

---

43. Gay, *Way of the (Modern) World*, 161, quoting Weber, *Protestant Ethic and the Spirit of Capitalism*, 171

44. Tawney, *Religion and the Rise of Capitalism*, 47.

45. Tawney, *Religion and the Rise of Capitalism*, 127.

46. Tawney, *Religion and the Rise of Capitalism*, 76.

fact a deist, who was brought up in a strict Calvinistic family. In his autobiography he reveals the impact of his father upon his thinking, and how he "got to him." Again and again in his youthful years he heard the mantra from the Bible, "Seeist thou a man diligent in his business? He shall stand before kings" (Prov 22:29, KJV). Weber thinks it was "drummed into him," the result—"time is money." To be more specific, it is hard not to imagine Baxter's influence prompting the thinking of Franklin beyond that of his father. This is the Reformation impacting lives at the most personal level beyond church theology. When we consider these words, "Keep up a high esteem of time and be every day more careful that you lose none of your time, than you are that you lose none of your gold and silver. And if vain recreation, dressings, feastings, idle talk, unprofitable company, or sleep be any of them temptations to rob you of any of your time, accordingly heighten your watchfulness."[47] Matthew Henry adds a similar thought: "Those who are prodigal of their time despise their own souls."[48] The reader will forgive my irenicism, but it is amusing to think of those today who consider Baxter's ethic to be almost a biblical ethic, who at the same time fritter away hours and hours "surfing the net" . . . what on earth would he have made of us? All of the above was almost certainly the thinking of the Reformation, it was "good" business sense, depending of course on which side of the business fence you sat. This impacts us today because quite rightly we extol the Reformers and Puritans so highly, but consequently we confuse the flesh with the Spirit. The business model which is followed today by both church and the world alike is right, but most of us would struggle to explain why, other than it serves us best, and it is the only explanation we know. Nor for that matter do we welcome the likes of Tawney and Weber trespassing on our territory, which by now wears a divine complexion.

Tawney makes this observation: "The law of nature had been invoked by medieval writers (Luther included, emphasis mine) as a moral restraint upon economic self-interest. By the seventeenth century a significant revolution had taken place. "Nature" had come to connote, not divine ordinance, but human appetites, and natural rights were invoked by the individualism of the age as a reason why self-interest should be given free play."[49] One has to pinch oneself when reading such a perceptive observation since we are evidently under the same influence. The rise of individualism, the "strain of the gods" and the tragic descent into the exploration of spiritual possibilities which the law of nature (even appreciated by the Medieval writers) might have suggested a warning to us. Tragically the worldly ethos of our day shouted the compelling voice of nature into submission. Not even nature can speak above the deafening voice of "economic self interest." Yet Paul appeals in Romans 1:19, 20 to the unmistakable voice of nature if we would just listen. Instead, self-seeking hubris and complacency coupled with an inability to question the past where we were born

47. Weber, *Protestant Ethic and the Spirit of Capitalism*, 261.

48. Weber, *Protestant Ethic and the Spirit of Capitalism*, 261, quoting Henry, *Worth of the Soul*, 315.

49. Tawney, *Religion and the Rise of Capitalism*, 183.

and raised with the business spirit of Reformers and Puritans, has left the church vulnerable and exposed. The pity is their remarkable spiritual DNA is missing, while their virtues of "rationalism," "diligence," "moderation," "sobriety," "thrift," "prudence," "economic enterprise" (time is money) and not least "asceticism" still grind the gears of the Christian conscience with, of course, our own caveats neatly reconfiguring these things to fit our times.

A Mixed Multitude

It is not hard to see how those who came under the influence of their new religious masters were inclined to listen to their "new" social ethic. This could not be separated from the new religion, an entire societal revolution was underway, making it relatively easy for a new secular way of thinking to become acceptable and ennobled. Thus wearing the new revolutionary spiritual clothing would triumph, but when put into practice by the individual, the religious element could be easily jettisoned. To such recipients of the "new faith," like new worship, the question: "What doth it profit a man if he gain the world?." . . .would be everything! The "form" emerged supreme, the spirit swiftly vanishing away, if it had ever existed. The Protestant unbelieving churchgoer now gained ascendency but thankfully with a regenerate business ethic! Undoubtedly such unregenerate churchgoers ("so-called Christians") fill English churches today, offering their "Sunday" worship to almighty god, while the almighty God of Commerce receives their ultimate offering. "As Xenophanes remarked twenty-five centuries ago, men always make their gods in their own image."[50] Neil Postman also provides an outsiders view of religion: "I think it both fair and obvious to say that on television, (any screen, emphasis mine) God is a vague and subordinate character. Though His name is invoked repeatedly, the concreteness and persistence of the image of the preacher carries the clear message that it is he, not He, who must be worshipped."[51]

What Is in a Man?

In the maelstrom of the Reformation it is evident that men like Luther, Bucer, Melanchthon and others were wrestling to achieve a coherent way forward, not just in religion but in social systems. After all how could one proclaim the gospel and not have a view on usury? Something which even the Catholic church viewed with disdain. In this, Luther's appreciation of Ezekiel 18 had more of the Bible in him and the Puritans apparently more of Machiavelli (1469–1527), (the modern father of political philosophy and political science). Bunyan in his own inimitable way was touched and despite his Puritan environment, was able more than most, to convey the iniquities

50. Postman, *Amusing Ourselves to Death*, 138.

51. Postman, *Amusing Ourselves to Death*, 125.

of the dead man "Mr. Badman"[52] who could press down on the poor with exorbitant prices and usury. It probably surprises us to discover that there once was a time when the city of Coventry in England fought the Prior on the question of usury. The Court Leet of that place deemed usury to be on a par with adultery and fornication, and those who had been practitioners were decreed as unfit for office as Mayor Councillor or Master of the Guild. While Luther's utterances on social issues demonstrate an attempt at what appears to be impartiality, they lacked the force and power which the new movement in Geneva could effect. "Luther's utterances" reveal a laudable insight, but according to Tawney: "On social morality are the occasional explosions of a capricious volcano, with only a rare flash of light amid the torrent of smoke and flame."[53] In other words not terribly effective.

Although Tawney recognizes in Luther's utterances a conception which dominates them, namely that all departments of life, the state and society, education, science, law, commerce and industry were to be regulated in accordance with the law of God. Therefore:

> So far from accepting the view which was afterwards to prevail, that the world of business is a closed compartment with laws of its own, and that the religious teacher exceeds his commission when he lays down rules for the moral conduct of secular affairs, he reserves for that plausible heresy denunciations hardly less bitter than those directed against Rome. The text of his (Luther's) admonitions is always, "unless your righteousness exceeds that of the Scribes and Pharisees."[54]

Evidently Luther's voice was not the overwhelming one which influenced the Puritans. Interestingly John Owen barely ever refers to Luther perhaps only observing him as little more than a capricious volcano.

Usury . . . Oh Dear!

Let us fast forward to Trinity College Cambridge 1909, there we find the very well-mannered and well-spoken William Cunningham D.D. writing, "An open letter addressed to his Grace the Archbishop of Canterbury, President of the Convocation of the Province of Canterbury." The title of that letter being: "The moral witness of the church on the investment of money and the use of wealth." On reading it a hundred years and more since first issued, it is evident on the question of usury alone that Cunningham is more a relative of Luther than he is of Calvin and the Puritans. Indeed he is very critical of the Puritans in this regard. His letter is an attempt to shine a light on business in the church (the Church of England). He is questioning it. He feels the

52. John Bunyan, *Life and Death of Mr Badman, 1680.*
53. Tawney, *Religion and the Rise of Capitalism*, 97.
54. Tawney, *Religion and the Rise of Capitalism*, 100.

need to explain to his eminent reader that questions of "right and wrong in business life"[55] are before them:

> In the foregoing pages I have indicated my grounds for thinking that the examination of the traditional Christian morality is a good starting-point for enquiring as to personal duty in the complex conditions of modern life . . . Parliament in 1570 recognized that "all usury, being forbidden by the law of God, is sin and detestable."[56]

At this time the term usury was not current in its modern sense (i.e.: 1909) of excessive interest, but was applied to the exaction of any interest on a loan.

Usury as a business transaction was considered to be a notorious crime and a scandal, receiving both secular punishment and ecclesiastical censures. After the Reformation with great skill and aptitude the Puritans were able to re-draw this map, and so it is re-drawn to this very day. Let us suppose someone in the life of the church today needing financial help, borrowed ten thousand pounds/dollars, they ought then to be expected to return the ten thousand by the allotted time, but ought they to be required to pay interest? Droll as it is such "naive" economics are the preserve of much earlier times when the darkness of Rome ruled the hearts of the people of Europe. How ironic! Since then the great operation of spiritual lobotomy has been undertaken and this was the immovable force which Cunningham was concerned with. The church to his astonishment, thought just as the world did, begging the question why? . . . because it was a veritable business!

The Influence Goes on Influencing

Tawney says:

> The characteristic which was distinctive of Geneva—"the most perfect school of Christ that ever was on earth since the days of the Apostles—was not its merciless intolerance (i.e.: pointed shoes, golden ear-rings and even knee-breeches) for no one yet dreamed that tolerance was possible. It was the attempt to make the law of God prevail even in those matters of pecuniary gain and loss which mankind, to judge by its history, is disposed to regard more seriously than wounds and death.[57]

Evidently pecuniary gain, usury and many other practices, suffered far less censure during the Reformation than did other misdemeanors. Perhaps this has always been true in the church right down to the present. Tawney writes:

55. Cunningham, *Open letter to His Grace the Archbishop of Canterbury*, 18.
56. Cunningham, *Open letter to His Grace the Archbishop of Canterbury*, 38.
57. Tawney, *Religion and the Rise of Capitalism*, 124, 126.

The magistrates . . . had seen without a shudder an adulterer condemned to be hanged, and had mercifully commuted his sentence to scourging through the town, followed by ten years "imprisonment in chains." He contrasts this with the "godly proposal to make capitalists die the death of Achan" (which not surprisingly) their humanity blenched.[58]

The reformed authorities could make the rules as suited them best. Tawney says: "The religious community formed a closely organized society, which, while using the secular authorities as police officers to enforce its mandates . . ."[59] This would make the acerbic remarks and observations of Beza almost flattering, "what would the people say? That they are dumb dogs . . . As to the question of causing scandals, for the last two years there has been unceasing talk of usury, and, for all that, no more than three or four usurers have been punished . . . It is notorious everywhere that the city is full of usurers and that the ordinary rate is 10 per cent or more."[60] Going on to highlight these inequalities, Tawney observes the practice of the French synods, as they showed "the persistence of the idea that the transactions of business are the province of the Church, combined with a natural desire to avoid an impracticable rigor."[61] Here we find exemplified the skill and alacrity with which churches were able to accommodate the world as it pleased them best, and which few were able to find a voice to question. It is important to be reminded that this chapter deals with influence. The church influenced the magistrate and vice versa, the church was in the world, the world was in the church. Making the connections as we must, Tawney bravely lays a glove on the New England form of Puritanism to demonstrate the power of influence.

> Of English-speaking communities, that in which the social discipline of the Calvinistic Church-State was carried to the furthest extreme was the Puritan theocracy of New England. Its practice had more affinity with the iron rule of Calvin's Geneva than with the individualistic tendencies of contemporary English Puritanism. In that happy, bishopless Eden, where men desired only to worship God, "according to the simplicities of the gospel and to be ruled by the laws of God's word," not only were "tobacco and immodest fashions and costly apparel," and "that vain custom of drinking one to another," forbidden to true professors, but the Fathers adopted towards that "notorious evil . . . whereby most men walked in all their commerce—to buy as cheap and to sell as dear as they can.[62]

---

58. Tawney, *Religion and the Rise of Capitalism*, 132.

59. Tawney, *Religion and the Rise of Capitalism*, 132.

60. Tawney, *Religion and the Rise of Capitalism*, 131-132, quoting Beza.

61. Tawney, *Religion and the Rise of Capitalism*, 134.

62. Tawney, *Religion and the Rise of Capitalism*, 135, quoting Winthrop, *History of New England*.

To which Augustine had offered his own thoughts, "to buy cheap and sell dear is common, but it is a common vice."[63] One minister early in the establishment of that Eden, makes a searching observation:

> The old Adam—"profit" being the chief aim and not the propagation of religion"—and Governor Bradford, observing uneasily how men grew "in their outward estates," remarked that the increase in material prosperity "will be the ruin of New England, at least of the Churches of God there."[64]

The danger for us today is that we fail to make the connection and application to ourselves, we close our eyes to the relevance of historical church error. What is more it would be all too easy to explain this by applying it and confining it to those in our times sold on the "prosperity gospel," but this would be far too narrow an application. Like ourselves our remarkable, old, best, spiritual relatives were both a force for good and ill.

Calvinism in Arminianism

If Luther influenced Cunningham, he also influenced John Wesley. Compare then Richard Baxter's voice to that of Wesley and ask which of these two have more influence in Christ's church today? Baxter (1615–91) says:

> If God show you a way in which you may lawfully get more than in another way (without wrong to your soul or to any other), if you refuse this, and choose the less gainful way, you cross one of the ends of your calling, and you refuse to be God's steward, and to accept His gifts, and use them for Him when He requireth it: You may labour to be rich for God, though not for the flesh and sin.[65]

Did this include usury? Would this be a lawful way to "get more," to "labour to be rich," or would this be "flesh and sin?" Furthermore how would the natural man, the one still without the Spirit of God, who did not belong to Christ, receive this piece of "inspired" wisdom? Fear certainly might strike into his soul at the thought of missing his "calling," (whatever "calling" meant, when applied in this way). Terror might have struck him down as he contemplated refusing to be God's steward, a subtle form of blackmail. Laboring to be rich would have easily gained his attention. The notion of "flesh and sin" would have been an alien concept to him. Here was an economic's tool to whip the people into shape dressed appropriately in the ensemble of God's kingdom, but in truth it was worldly wisdom at its most effective.

63. Tawney, *Religion and the Rise of Capitalism*, 216.
64. Tawney, *Religion and the Rise of Capitalism*, 135–36.
65. Weber, *Protestant Ethic and the Spirit of Capitalism*, 162.

John Wesley, fifty years after Baxter's death, seems to run counter to Puritan thinking:

> I fear whenever riches have increased, the essence of religion has decreased in the same proportion. Therefore, I do not see how it is possible in the nature of things for any period of revival of religion to continue long. For religion must necessarily produce both industry and frugality, and these cannot but produce riches. (Remembering Calvinism glories in frugality and in asceticism emphasis mine). But, as riches increase, so will pride, anger, and love of the world in all its branches. How, then, is it possible that Methodism, that is a religion of the heart, though it flourishes now as the green bay trees, should continue in this state? For the Methodists in every place grow diligent and frugal; consequently, they increase in goods. Hence they proportionately increase in pride, in anger, in the desire of the flesh, the desire of the eyes, and the pride of life. So, although the form of religion remains, the spirit is swiftly vanishing away. Is there no way to prevent this—the continual decay of pure religion?[66]

As stated earlier the Calvinists were in the Arminians!

"The clock is a god"

Thomas Luckman points out:

> The "rationality" (rationalization) of modern society was perceived by Weber as the result of a unique line of historical development which—as soon as it became welded into the structure of society—became divorced from the conditions of its origin and either overwhelmed all other lines of historical development or came to serve as a model for them.[67]

Weber was observing the glaringly obvious, that although the Reformation and Puritans engaged their world as spiritual combatants they did so employing their own philosophies of life, ones which quickly divorced from the spiritual. "The flesh wars with the Spirit" (Gal 5:17). "Time is money" is meant to harness a rigorous intense individualism producing activism, making the clock a god, but it has nothing to do with God or his word, it is a human construct.[68] Cunningham must have seen this working its way out, not only in individual Christian lives but also ingrained in both the church and society, just as it is today.

66. Gay, *Way of the (Modern) World*, 133, quoting Wesley cited in Weber, *Protestant Ethic and the Spirit of Capitalism*, 175

67. Gay, *Way of the (Modern) World*, 137, quoting Luckmann, *Theories of Religion*, 13-14.

68. Paul's "redeeming the time" (Eph 5:16, KJV) is less about time, i.e. the clock, and more about opportunity.

Seamlessly Welded

This rationalism is now completely welded into place and virtually holds all of life together, including the kingdom of God, where it is more sinister, unquestionably more sinister. A good weld in a superstructure can last hundreds of years and be completely depended upon, and those who make use of such superstructures may not have the slightest awareness of the powerful adhesive itself, and its ability to keep the entirety together. The world is in the church, welded to it in a most profound philosophical sense; this is Packer's "deep level worldliness." Tragically when viewed like this we are faced with the stark unhappy reality, it can never be broken. We may fear the comparative religions and the cults, but in fact our enemy is not at the gates but already inside, welded to the kingdom of God . . . a permanent fixture. Over time things do emerge to confirm the deep solid hold which this weld exerts. Recently it has been the "weld" of "screen" worship, just another "tool," a business model, bonding us, promising us freedom whilst enslaving and imprisoning the church in the world of business.

How Do You Read It?

If we are infected with this most subtle form of worldliness it must, it will reveal itself, but what if we have no capacity to see it for what it is? What if we are totally blindsided, unable to think in any other way than that dictated by the cage which is our only recognizable environment? Here I offer an illustration which is a personal account remembering that Luther had said "the teacher exceeds his commission when he lays down rules for the moral conduct of secular affairs." Luther traced a heresy and was prepared to vent against Rome and others if he sensed inequality. He was no respecter of persons, we on the other hand appear to have quite a different philosophy.

Some years ago I had the pleasure of meeting a gentleman who was a lover of the arts. During our conversation he told me of his unusual profession, he was a professional gambler, this was his job in the way that anyone might find gainful employment. Formerly he had been a tax inspector but now employing his considerable skill and knowledge to determine, as he saw it, the way to read the potential outcomes of horse racing, boxing, basketball, football and the many varied sports. How fascinating it was to hear his in-depth knowledge of worldwide sporting events. His preparation and study were meticulous, becoming very successful, making a handsome living. Afterwards, I thought, "Could such a man be a Christian while engaged in this world of gambling? Would he have to give up his job if he was converted to Christ?" Knowing our civilization as I do I felt quite sure most Christians would reject out of hand the very thought of it, but why? Would the same Christians outlaw someone from their church working on Wall Street or in the City of London, on the trading floors, laying off bets against copper, gold, sugar, euros and dollars, gambling with hedge funds stocks and shares, risking millions, tens of millions on the markets? The truth is both are gambling, but in the church one is unacceptable, whilst the other is good commerce and emerges "as clean as a whistle." This is our "business cage." However in God's sight there can be no difference since we know he is impartial. In the church one of these professions receives a scornful resounding "No," the other a slap on the back, a righteous confirmation that what they do is God honoring and worthwhile. The truth, as Dr. Greenfield suggests, is the mind can be re-shaped, re-configured, and this is what I consider has happened to us. The human brain she says "will adapt to whatever environment in which it is placed; the cyber world of the twenty-first century is offering a new type of environment; the brain could therefore be changing in parallel, in correspondingly new ways." She likens this mind change to that of "climate change (which) is not only *global . . .* but also *unprecedented, controversial* and *multifaceted.*"[69]

The Reformers and Puritans were the great architects of mind change, and as such worked a climate change which is still impacting Christ's church to this day. A climate change of thought which went beyond the theology of grace, was unprecedented, multifaceted and controversial. We are all under their influence! Tawney's parting shot assessing the Puritan movement offers this throwaway remark: "So little do those who shoot the arrows of the spirit know where they will light (land)."[70]

Quantity versus Quality

Uncomfortably for the church, it was Stalin who said "quantity is its own quality." Without being too brutal (and as a confessed lover of the Puritans) it is nonetheless hard to read Baxter's well known words and not think of this as an endorsement of quantity, which also comes out in Franklin's "time is money." Baxter's interest is in pursuing the "gainful" but in doing this (by contrast) John Wesley sees danger, recognizing the consequences, namely the "religion of the heart" must suffer. Baxter in this regard is a "quantities" man, he would have argued, "God is up for quantity," and in addition one could also gain something for oneself (subtle works). By this one could secure the knowledge of good stewardship and the blessed knowledge of one's calling, confirming the responsibility to "make one's calling and election sure" (2 Pet 1:10). Baxter sees quantity as a "win-win" situation. In truth it is cold calculated rationalism, to the Machiavellian spirit this is a full-blooded works religion. It is fundamentally important to remember the natural man will not, cannot hear the spiritual message which Baxter and the wider Puritan fraternity were at pains to make known. Weber and Tawney trace this as if a deadly poison, though both are evidently not Christians yet they are able to see the monster let loose. Tawney again helps to draw the threads together: "In reality, as in the case with most heroic ideologies, the social and religious aspects of Puritanism were not disentangled; they presented themselves,

69. Greenfield, *Mind Change*, 13.
70. Tawney, *Religion and the Rise of Capitalism*, 226.

both to supporters and opponents, as different facets of a single scheme."[71] Weber grasping (and who can blame him) the shell of Calvinism sees what many of us have seen. "The God of Calvinism demanded of his believers not single good works, (as the priest had formerly demanded) but a life of good works combined into a unified system."[72] The problem here is not the good works, which Jas 2:18 (NIV) exhorts, but Calvin's "unified system" of good works, and none of us can know how many poor, unbelieving souls were trapped in it, to coin an expression . . . they were "out of the frying pan and into the fire!" Coining another expression: "we have never been able to unscramble these eggs!" In this sense the Church of England seems to be one huge business, and the eggs appear to have turned bad a long time ago. The poor people of that denomination "do not know their right hand from their left" (Jonah 4:11).[73] By and large, like those raised under the teaching of Rome, they are mistaken in trusting in works rather than grace. Nevertheless the business models of these churches and many others simply rumble along.

George Simmel provides helpful insight and shows how much of Baxter's thinking is in us. In *The Metropolis and Mental Life* he says: "the preoccupation with calculation has given rise to that distinctly modern attitude captured in the term "blasé." It is an attitude in which all qualities have been flattened out into calculation of quantity."[74] The "blasé" attitude which Simmel observed is the subjective reflection of the money economy. In such an environment quantity squashes quality, like the pugilist in the ring, it flattens its opponent and quality is "out for the count." Jesus saw the duplicity of the merchant men in the temple who no doubt possessed this cold-blooded rationalism in abundance—the cash nexus being the only consideration. When "screen" worship was joined to the churches it flattened the quality of worship which had always eschewed any idea of sight, medium or pictures ever being employed to any end.

Market Traders

The qualities of holiness in the "House of Prayer" were met head-on, being flattened and along with additional blows of pragmatism, rendered the *coup-de-gras* to quality. These sagacious dealers were in the temple courts for one reason only, unalloyed self progress. Everything must bow to the utilitarian mindset. Today we would expect Richard Baxter to berate a Christian for taking a job which they enjoyed and loved, but which paid twenty thousand pounds/dollars a year less than the job that was meaningless and loathsome. Why so? Because he thinks utilitarianism, man becomes utilitarian, a mere "tool" in God's purposes, his focus is purely one of gain. It is this

71. Tawney, *Religion and the Rise of Capitalism*, 234.

72. Weber, *Protestant Ethic and the Spirit of Capitalism*, 117.

73. Whilst the above is indisputable there remains in the broad spectrum of the Church of England (Anglican) lovely expressions of genuine faith in Christ, where he is worshipped in Spirit and in truth.

74. Gay, *Way of the (Modern) World*, 155, quoting Simmel, *Metropolis and Mental Life*, 414

soullessness which may be traced in Christian thought, and as the church today is more engaged in the market then ever before, quantity wages war on quality and the developing picture of all denominations at worship confirms this.

Is it pressing the point too far to suggest our soullessness, in so very many aspects of life is winning the war, and the evidence of this is manifest for all to see? Christians more than most might be expected to care deeply as they observe quantities warfare on quality, though by now it is to be feared that we are so desensitized it seems we cannot capture the power to feel the depth of loss anymore. The world has beaten us into its shape. As crass ugliness triumphs, both world and church alike appear to have lost all sensitivity. Jude speaks of those who "slander whatever they do not understand and the very things they do understand by instinct—as irrational animals do—will destroy them" (Jude 10).

Out For the Count

In the USA and the UK our eating habits have burgeoned to treat as "normal" over-sized meal portions, leading to habits of epidemic proportions and at such a cost to health—we have lost all sensitivity, but does anyone notice or care? We have the look of irrational animals about us, so in our desperate quest for more, quantity is a heavy-weight and has delivered a fatal blow to sensitivities. "Black Friday" as BBC News reported in 2015: "Last year saw scenes of mayhem erupting across England as shop-pers scrambled to get their hands on cut-price goods. As the American institution becomes firmly established as a feature of the shopping scene on the other side of the Atlantic, we ask how UK retailers plan to fend off scenes of violence."[75]

Even if the aforementioned quest is a race to the bottom, becoming an addiction to mediocrity, we have learned not to care as there are bigger economic "fish to fry." Offer most people one garment of real, genuine, exceptional quality, costly perhaps haute-couture, (therefore special and lasting) precious even, and alternatively offer ten garments of mediocre quality, perhaps even manufactured in questionable condi-tions, more often than not the ten will be chosen over the one. Our sensibilities to quality are invariably crushed by quantity, hence we know "the price of everything and the value of nothing." This way of thinking, this approach to life presents as a rul-ing principle, nor do we have any capacity to free ourselves from it, as it has become our default mechanism, invading every aspect of life, even our most sacred act of Christian worship.

Mumford was able to illustrate this by no one less than Galileo where even he blindly sees "primary" qualities as the only thing that matters, he dismissed "second-ary" qualities. Reading between the lines, Galileo could only see merit in size, shape, quantity and motion—these were "primary." Tastes, smells and sounds were only

---

75. Kayleen Devlin, "Black Friday: Responding to last year's mayhem," BBC, 26 November 2015.

secondary and spurned for their subjectivity. Mumford casts his perceptive analytical eye over this, and shows just how critical the sense of smell was for survival, as it could determine whatever food was fit to eat. Galileo had his "primary" qualities fixed in his mind because above all else "he possessed a measuring stick," by which to quantify them. Joined to utilitarian thinking this is a formidable influence on our approach to life, and even our approach to God.

As Plain as the Nose On Your Face

Alarmingly what appears when these issues are examined, is that the world and the church enjoy the self-same outlook, Baxter's ethic is in our spiritual DNA. This means when the question of the garments is considered it comes under righteous judgment, the judgment being that one of them panders to the flesh and is a dreadful display of aggrandizement, while the others are modest, good, utilitarian and astonishingly godly! It appears quantity even has God on its side! Quantity is now able to wear the mantle of "true" spirituality, it can afford to "look down its nose" at those who fail to produce on the "grand scale" thereby confirming we have been influenced, we have been "got at," and have learned to think as we have been instructed to think. Considering all this, it would be natural for anyone with a basic knowledge of the Bible to site Paul's instructions to the ladies, who attended the worship, not to go out of their way to draw attention to themselves by employing gold, pearls, expensive clothes and elaborate hairstyles (1 Tim 2:9) (*haute couture* is definitely forbidden). In truth Paul is not attacking gold, pearls or expensive clothes per se, rather that these should not be allowed to "speak" in the worship with a "loud voice." Indeed this passage has much to say about our proclivity to turn to things seen in our corporate acts of worship, bringing the world into this sacred time. Who or what has the "loud voice" today? . . . *naturally* the "screen" is louder than most.

These women and their actions bring to mind a Shakespearean quote "empty vessels make the loudest noise." They were probably in the business of elevating themselves in the act of worship, where only One is to be elevated, but they were drawing attention to themselves. This passage of Scripture makes no comment whatsoever, it is not a pointer to asceticism or a fillip to those who believe in its merits. Even less in this passage is it a green light to extol the "excellence" of a Reformed and Puritan ethos, which appears sadly "to know the price of everything and the value of nothing." "God hath a people here fearing His name though deceived." . . "For as he thinketh in his heart, so is he" (Prov 23:7, KJV).

It's All in the Mind

Perhaps it is too easy to have a simplistic view of church life before the dawn of the Reformation, one where a spiritual and social solidarity glued the common life of the people together. The complexities of the politics of that time, even if they could have been grasped, were almost certainly for the masses, "out of sight and out of mind." The people knew they "belonged," and the sense of "a controlling power" supplied the security, however tenuous.

Max Weber, as stated earlier, thinks that the control which people lived under prior to the Reformation "was very lax, at that time scarcely perceptible in practice, and hardly more than formal." He adds this thought that . . . "The rule of the Catholic Church . . . is now tolerated by peoples of thoroughly modern economic character, and was borne by the richest and economically most advanced peoples on earth at about the turn of the fifteenth century."[76] This rule, this mastery was confronted in the Reformation by what appears to be an entirely other alternative. But was it in fact an *entirely* other alternative? In theological terms no one would argue with this, the theology of Grace confronted and replaced that of works, but did this mean that *works* were gone from lives altogether? Apparently not: "the Reformation meant not the elimination of the Church's control over everyday life, but rather the substitution of a new form of control for the previous one."[77] Clearly the controllers now wore a Protestant ensemble rather than the garb of Rome. But it was not so much the dress sense which influenced the people as the thinking of the "social influencers," "there is nothing new under the sun." "For as he thinketh in his heart, so is he."

76. Weber, *Protestant Ethic and the Spirit of Capitalism*, 36-37.

77. Weber, *Protestant Ethic and the Spirit of Capitalism*, 36.

CHAPTER 9

WHO IS REALLY ON THE THRONE?

If you can meet with Triumph and Disaster
and treat those two imposters just the same . . .
"IF," RUDYARD KIPLING

For every complex problem there is a simple answer, and its wrong.
H.L. MENCKEN

Heaven rules.
DANIEL 4:26 (NIV)

Control

IN HIS BOOK *Technopoly*, under a chapter heading "The Broken Defences" Neil Postman writes,

> Technopoly is a state of culture. It is also a state of mind. It consists in the
> deification of technology, which means that the culture seeks its authorization
> in . . . orders from technology. This requires the development of a new kind
> of social order, and of necessity leads to the rapid dissolution of much that is
> associated with traditional beliefs.[1]

At 8:30pm on the evening of Monday 23 March 2020, the British Prime Minister,
Boris Johnson, addressed the nation; nothing with such solemnity had taken place
like it since 1939 when Neville Chamberlain's voice crackled out over the radio broadcasting the unhappy news: "We are at war with Germany." With Johnson's statement
it was difficult not to come to the same conclusion, warfare lay ahead, as a nation we

1. Postman, *Technopoly*, 71.

were being put on a kind of war footing. The third world war which many had feared, was upon us, just not in quite the way we had all expected. We were under attack but it was by a new "super power" which had emerged on the world stage.

Inevitably in the age of post truth there were detractors, the fake news (not a new thing and well established) did not help people to navigate their way through the sea of information. However anyone who trusted in our information overloaded society, thinking that this would help us gain some coherence, was in for a shock, things were about as "clear as mud." The only clear fact was that COVID-19 or "Coronavirus," as it was called, had made a dramatic and sudden entry on to the world stage, and in doing so had upstaged all of its combined powers. It was both a remarkable and fascinating sight, the status quo was undone. As the apostle Peter confirmed two thousand years ago in the living word, "they say everything goes on as it always has" (2 Pet 3:4). Here was something to stop the world, to halt its never-ending march without a moment's thought. Some calmly considered this might be the time to stop and weigh matters, take stock, look at life from a different perspective, to consider not just the present but the future also, and to ask what God was doing. Life was definitely not about to go on as it always had.

As the governments of the world floundered, their pride in themselves like that of the Titanic, seemingly unsinkable, were now no longer in control. Something which they depended upon was, in measure at least, wrested from them, and now a microbe was flexing its muscles, exercising its power. Noticeably in the early days of COVID-19's emergence, there was some remarkable evidence of irreverence, even slapstick comedy in which a few politicians traded. Could this perhaps have been an attempt to lighten the mood thereby adding an air of calm, or maybe to give assurance that "all was well," the powers that be were in control, even if they were not? No-one need be unduly alarmed . . . it would be business as usual!

Global Panic

When Neville Chamberlain's message reached the British people in September of 1939, it made no difference whatever to the strategic masterclass of the Third Reich, Hitler's machine just rolled on. At that time the average citizen was helpless to stop the relentless onslaught, one country after another fell and Europe was reshaped. In the same way, regardless of government statements, COVID-19 was steadily taking charge. Italy and Spain were no match for its powers and soon the USA "the super power," admitted even with clenched teeth, that this was very serious, with its trajectory being certain. As I write, India is suffering dreadfully and recording half the world's COVID-19 deaths.

There was a shared panic around the world. Desperation was seen from Australia to Canada and also here in the UK where, amazingly the chief concern, was bottoms! Yes, there was a mad dash for toilet tissue! Panic-buying of essentials soon followed, and government ministers felt the need to reassure us that we were not suddenly going to starve to death! It was particularly disappointing to hear of Christians who responded to this in exactly the same way as the world. The machine, the cogs of life so reliable, so dependable were unable to run, and as the saying goes, "the wheels had come off." How sad when even Christians were in a state of panic. The *control* we so much depended upon looked profoundly suspect.

With the specter of lockdown came the loss of freedom; curfews were employed; workplaces shut down; all non-essential shops were closed; doctor's surgeries/clinics were out of bounds; education was put on hold; holiday plans were scrapped; the entire sports industry shut down; even the Olympics postponed; entertainment such as theatre and cinema were forced to close their doors. Life as we knew it was suspended, piece by piece our control was being wrested from us.

In Britain the most serious threat appeared to be to the National Health Service, (health care, free at the point of need) the fear was that it might fail and become overwhelmed, especially in its provision of intensive care. The predictions were very stark indeed, so much so "Nightingale" hospitals were quickly commissioned to provide for the expected flood of COVID-19 patients. Thankfully these were not needed. Certainly the pictures of emergency morgues and cremations reaching capacity looked alarming. It was described as a "global health security emergency." Here we were, the world's powers, masters of our destiny, held hostage, and for the first time since the war years, uncertainty hung over our lives. What would the future be? Not even the Cuban Missile Crisis of the 1960s could match this.

Bowls of Wrath

As to what the future would hold, the church unlike the world could say with confidence and mean it, "God alone knows!" The way of life as we had previously known it, was on hold, but more sinister by far, it was threatened. Essentially the virus was able to spread at will and did so at great speed, leaving the world feeling vulnerable, since COVID-19 was an unseen enemy. All of this meant we began to re-draw the way we did life, as the hold which the pathogen had on us was such that practically all noticed how life itself had slowed down.

Surely it was not hard to see the sovereign loving hand directing God's judgments. The "bowls of wrath" are not reserved, as some suggest, for a moment at the close of history, they are continuously poured out onto the earth, to remind us, if for no other reason, *we* do not rule. God is in control of all events.[2]

God does not allow the world to have the "peace, peace," which it so much craves, rather he directs his judgments graciously to save us from the more important eternal

---

2. Paul confirms this when he tells the Roman Christians: "the wrath of God *is* being revealed not will be" (Rom 1:18, emphasis mine). For further excellent commentary see John Murray, *Epistle to the Romans*.

lasting pain. "The clouds you so much dread are big with mercy and shall break with blessings on your head."[3] This re-drawing of the way we were to "do life" confirmed that the world was now sharing control with another. Interestingly, this was a time when experts could see no particular benefit from mask wearing, when groups were not permitted to sit together on a sunny day in the park for a picnic, and yet were encouraged to go to work the next day crowding onto the London Underground! When our Chief Scientific Adviser, Sir Patrick Vallance suggested "it would be a good outcome if we could escape with 20,000 deaths," official figures suggest it currently stands at 218,405 (approx. February 2023). Uncertainty, lack of clarity from our leaders was hanging heavily over us all. It was hard to think how the national mental wellbeing and even its psyche would not be tested and altered by this new "normal." What would the church do, how would it deal with this "unprecedented" moment?

Lex Rex

The churches, like everyone else, were required to go into lockdown, to close their doors. The church was not seen by the state as a special case, there were to be no exceptions to the rule. To the thinking of many Christians however, these kinds of actions belong only to totalitarian regimes. But the argument was "well made," for the need to love one's neighbor as oneself, as it would be selfish not to consider everyone, since this existential threat was literally "in the air."

In view of such "reasonable" sentiments, the church did not stop to think and challenge these restrictions, but rather easily decided to follow government law, which senior members of government themselves clearly failed to keep. Perhaps today many Christians would not countenance the questioning of their God-given government, yet on scrutiny it might be found that Christians are more inclined to "fall into line" depending upon the political ideology which at the time is in the seat of power. It is tempting to ask whether "a little knowledge" of Rutherford's *Lex, Rex* (The Law and the Prince) might at least have provided an intellectual challenge to such willing subservience. That being said, the churches by and large offered compliance and agreed to accede to government directives, even if the ordained worship of God, which must be the church's principle work above all others, had to be forsaken. From some quarters this must have been seen as very "reasonable." But not all "fell into line" so amicably and obediently, whether they knew of *Lex, Rex*, or not. The answer for some was obvious, above the need to look after one's neighbor, God must be first, as stated by the commandment, the spiritual responsibility to obey God rather than men must be the supreme authority. As a result some refused to follow the government's requirements and continued to meet corporally to worship God, even in secret locations. In some parts of the world this became headline news, and it was a brave individual who

3. Cowper, "God moves in a Mysterious Way," hymn.

observed and criticized these actions; but criticism there has been, noticeably by some in the church who themselves had turned to "screen" worship.

On the face of it there were only two options for the church, the church could either close its doors and wait to re-open, or break the law. It was easy to see how this might cause division and even splits in congregations. COVID-19 was going to present one of the greatest challenges to the church since the onset of World War II. Emerging quickly though there appeared another option, almost in the blink of an eye, a new impulsive approach to worship was to unfold, one which had never been explored or tested in the UK before. Along with elbow bumps (the new way of greeting each other) there was also to be a new way of conducting corporate worship, worship through the camera lens and a screen.

Mind Change

For some Christians the capacity, the ability to wait (they that wait upon the Lord shall renew their strength (Isa 40:31) was their first most ingrained influence, but for others this worked no impact whatsoever. The reason, as stated earlier, was deep rooted rationalism, the "business sense," utilitarianism, an unspoken rule in our secular society and in the church. Craig Gay says that "modernity is characterized by the three inter-related themes of *control, securit*y*, and anxiety.*"[4] Naturally the latter is served by the former, and in an age where deep rooted anxiety is well established, even ingrained, the need to be reassured by some form of control was evidently what "screen" worship provided. Pinned down by COVID-19, life as we knew it was spiraling out of control. The secular world turned to Zoom to alleviate its anxiety and failing business, but so did the church. Does the church have so much secular thinking in its DNA? Evidently! Perhaps this was the moment when God exposed and revealed where the hope, the security of Christians really lay . . . was it in the church, the meetings, the program of events, the people, or in himself?

Obviously the anxiety which Christians felt, should have been alleviated, not by a computer screen, but the reassuring voice which comfortingly says "Peace be still" (Mark 4:39). Instead, in anxiety, the rational, needing to feel control, bowed without thinking to the solution which tech had already exerted upon almost everyone's life. Frightening as it is, Dr. Greenfield chose well the title of her book, *Mind Change*. It was this "mind change" which enabled the deed to be done, with no one questioning it, no one could possibly think about challenging it because now control was back where it should be, with ourselves . . . Phew!

It would seem this anxious secular thinking was no different in Christ's church to that of the world at large. The screen with which people were obsessed could relieve the anxiety like nothing else, it was a no-brainer, who could contest it?

---

4. Gay, *Way of the (Modern) World*, 308.

H.L. Mencken's famous quote comes to mind when we look at this action which, without examination, the church embarked upon. "There is always a well-known solution to every human problem—neat, plausible, and wrong."[5]

Had loss of control, deep ingrained anxiety and uncertainty, amongst other things propelled the churches in those early days to go in the "neat, plausible, but wrong direction?" It appears so. Instantly COVID-19 had drilled deep into our anxious age, and just as the people of today live at their doctor's surgery for the least little ailment, in fear of what might be "killing" them, the virus struck fear into lives who had their focus more on church, than they did on the God of the church. This led to a rapid dissolution of much that is associated with traditional beliefs, and the "techtonic" worship shift was the result.

Permission to Hug

In recent days we have seen the depths to which control can extend itself. On the 9 May 2021 the British Government opened the door and gave people "permission" from the 17th of May to hug one another! Our anxiety even needs this kind of instruction! It would not be surprising to hear of Christians who literally followed this to the letter. I site this because it reveals our "plastic" brains, as Dr. Greenfield suggests the human brain along with that of "a whole range of animals are astonishingly plastic . . . and superlatively so. It is constantly adapting physically to repeated types of behavior."[6] Hence it can be reshaped. We need at all times to be told what we should do, how to do it, as someone else (especially in authority) always knows better. We dare not detract from those who "know best." We appear to be afraid, to be alone, and this is where the constant contact with the screen in the pocket "comes into its own." With control so well and effectively delivered, but not from heaven, our dependency is keenly felt and our uncertainty alleviated. In my local doctor's surgery there is a notice which illustrates a thirteen point plan to show me how to wash my hands. Here we are in an age which devoutly "believes," moreover this is needed in an anxious world. When COVID-19 struck, the church took control and instantly introduced the screen to its anxious flock, who immediately did what they were told. If it had been a thirteen point plan they might have been even more willing to follow it to the letter and rejoice in the control which it provided!

Muscle Waste

Craig Gay identifies three interrelated themes, these are highly significant, having a bearing on this chapter. Anxiety is a state of apprehension, sadly it may even present as

---

5. Mencken, "Divine Afflatus," *New York Evening Mail*.

6. Greenfield, *Mind Change*, 71.

mental disorder, as fear paralyses. When control was lost as COVID-19 took over, our world of certainty upon which all our hopes are built, came crashing down. For many, hope was gone. At least in the West, the substance of life is built around this hope, because we all crave assurance, we are wired with the alarm which rings immediately at the sight of its disappearance. Hundreds of years ago we would have found the church to be quite different as it faced uncertainty on all sides. Life was fragile and they knew it, permeating their very existence. Assuredly to assist the Christian of that time was probably the highly developed muscle of faith, well used and exercised. This muscle today looks as though it has shriveled up and wasted away. Gay goes even further in his analysis: he suggests that faith has somehow been emptied of the possibility of any real encounter with the living God, and so has really ceased to be faith at all. In truth it is to be wondered, when the control (our control) disappeared, was there any encounter with God by faith or was it the "will to power" conjured up by our own ingenuity?

However none of this coldly suggests that loss of job or home or loved ones can easily be dealt with by stoicism. We read of the early church being "seized with fear." Fear provides some necessary tools such as "fight or flight." Archbishop Cranmer's fear makes us all tremble, knowing we would not have responded any better. Fear is where anxiety lives, breathes and is fed, which is where it is at home, established in a secular age, not merely as an occasional nuisance but a fixture, and one which increasingly and alarmingly needs medication (recognizing medication is often paramount to the saving of lives). Anxiety is all around us, it flourishes but being so enthralled with the control of the secular age, dependent on it, in vain we hope for deliverance. This gives voice to Weber's "iron cage," we are prisoners and often trembling ones.

A Still Small Voice

What the church actually needed to do when the pandemic appeared, was first to see the events in terms of judgment. But it was far easier to attribute events to the "sinister" Chinese hand, some even said possibly assisted by "US funding," rather than the hand of the Almighty. If a sparrow cannot land on the ground apart from God's will (Matt 10:29), we can be sure COVID-19 could not lay a finger on us until the God of love saw fit. We needed the truth of Scripture to direct us in the first place and not our human wisdom, despite how vulnerable we felt. Our first place of help should have been to discern the new circumstances as part of God's judgment. The psalmist writes: "Thou didst cause judgment to be heard from heaven, the earth feared and was still." (Ps 76:8, KJV). The NIV renders this: "From heaven you pronounced judgment and the land feared and was quiet."

It is possible that the church, for only a moment, flirted with the idea of this being judgment, and very quickly would be able to re-establish the status quo. Soon enough everything would return to normal, control would be back where it should be, in our own hands. If this was the case, then there was no time to be still, no room in our restless fear and anxiety to be quiet. It was noticeable how almost immediately Christians were falling over themselves with text messages and emails, establishing a facility for "one-anothering." There was no talk of judgment and even less of the need to remain still, it was all about the "game plan" which we ourselves could devise, and it was hard not to read this as a "state of panic." Being still, being quiet would have given the church the time to consider and weigh God's purposes, after all he was clearly on the throne orchestrating all events. Surely we needed in this "unprecedented" moment to be still and listen in to what he was saying by his providence. However, it appeared that God's organization of events would not give the necessary peace of mind, it would be *our* organization which we could really trust and depend on. This reveals that both church and state ultimately believe and practice similar things, they "lean on their own understanding." If both cannot organize their way out of a situation, any situation, then no one can. When on the edge of what looked like a precipice, with no time to rest, nor to be quiet, the church machine of organization swung into action. The "screen" worship however compromised, was compelling as it came up out of our "own understanding," out of our own ingenuity.

And . . . Action!

James R. Beniger says, "Organization is more than mere order; order lacks end-directedness: organization *is* end-directed . . . (the) purpose of organization is the essential property of *control.*"[7] It has been rather easy for the people of the West to view critically the lives of "poor souls" living under dreadful regimes where they suffer excessive control, while failing to grasp, we ourselves are also under the same. The "cage" which we have chosen to live in, boldly marked "freedom" is one which we are all so thankful for, since it provides such organization giving peace of mind. But one way or another we are all being controlled. George Orwell's *1984* and Aldous Huxley's *Brave New World*, in a remarkably prophetic way, peered into the future (our present), and whether we like their findings or not, no one can deny both their accuracy or their penetrating discernment. Our education system, our health, our employment, our banking, our liberty, the whole of life is one huge organized process which is driven by end-directedness. Indeed, if this was not the motive, what would be the point of it all? Crucially the church has decided to "drink at the same well."

It may be true that many Christians fail to see their lives being guided, even regulated by the church where this end-directedness holds sway. To be sure for many it is not God the Lord as director, but the institution of the church; ominously mirroring the ancient church of the Middle Ages which wore its infallibility so respectably and authoritatively. Christians, being under such power might not in the first instance think God's thoughts by his word, rather their default mechanism is instantly

7. Beniger, *Control Revolution*, 35.

the church, which comes dangerously, perilously close to infallibility, so that 'ordinary' sheep should just follow its control. This has been highlighted in earlier chapters where it was observed how countless Christians unthinkingly supported the Graham Campaigns. It looks as if Christian believers are unable to think, making themselves vulnerable, subjects first of men and only then possibly of God.

When COVID-19 invaded life, the church needed to assert its control to an end-directedness, which ostensibly could (like the Graham Campaigns) be justified for the spiritual benefits which would accrue. In the Graham Campaigns this resulted in tens of thousands of "decisions" for Christ. Under the new COVID-19 jurisdiction, the church needed to proceed in what it perceived to be a straight line to manage its affairs, the alternative oblique possibilities were clear and laden with loneliness and anxiety. Left to themselves how would any of them survive, with control gone, the church acted fast. Loss of control and organization coupled with fear, and vitally with impatience, the door was shut firmly on the quality control of the Holy Spirit. He could not be permitted in quietness and stillness to direct. Pragmatism sat in the director's chair and bellowed out the instruction in real Hollywood fashion . . . "And . . . Action!." . . Enter the computer, enter "Zoom" worship.

The saying: "Nature never hurries, atom by atom, little by little, she achieves her work," is very instructive but it is tempting to think that while this may be true of nature, it is not true of the spiritual nature. Perhaps Neil Postman's words provide a commentary as to why this is the case. He says: "the computer compels respect, even devotion, and argues for a comprehensive role in all fields of human activity."[8] In the anxiety and uncertainty, the computer, the screen tech, highly respected as it is, compelled the church to lean on it and even obey it. After all it was the benign "tool" which everyone was most enchanted with, and like nothing else it commanded the power to supply the necessary salvation.

The Pill

Postman says it argues for a comprehensive role in *all* fields of human activity. Some of us, innocently perhaps naively, would immediately respond and say, "surely not the church," but Postman is right—"all fields." Nothing can prevent its onward march, it is an unstoppable controlling power. Naturally to those who were seasoned worshippers at the "altar of the screen," narcotized even, who were very much controlled by it in their daily lives, instinctively turned to it for help. It is not difficult to trace out the thinking which invited the tech into worship. When COVID-19 began to rule there remained one supreme "invincible" which the microbe could not master . . . technology. This would solve all our problems from vaccines to worship!

8. Postman, *Technopoly*, 119.

In the early days the overblown confidence was easy to discern as governments around the world highlighted the need for "track and trace." Although the approach was questioned, "the powers that be" were quite fixed. Arguments were made for employing the traditional "tried and tested" method, methodically going from door-to-door, but slow. The Government's tech solution also raised ethical questions which were dismissed as insignificant, and not surprisingly, belligerence won the day. At great expense it proved to be unsuccessful. Even the later more sophisticated versions of it which were employed deep into the pandemic in 2021, were still being called out for their failures, and the eye-watering cost to the exchequer of billions. Yet, all this notwithstanding, it provided the vital insurance, the sense of security which everyone yearned for, even if it did not work. The human race is very easily convinced, willfully credulous.

I recall an amusing scene around this time, a threesome attempting to enter a coffee shop in a department store. Right in front of me, they spent an inordinate amount of time trying to transfer, from their phones, the vital details to the store computer, so as to gain access. My traditional approach was a little simpler . . . pen and paper! I was enjoying my cup of coffee before the others had barely taken their seats, but perhaps they sat quite contentedly, the tech had everything under control, all was well with their world. This is written somewhat tongue-in-cheek, but the bigger point illustrates the dominant place in our psyche which technology plays; working confidence in it; what we expect of it; our inalienable trust in it.

It was this trust and belief which turned the church towards the tech. Our age believes there is no affliction for which we cannot devise a pill, and here was the pill to soothe our spiritual anxiety and fear . . . the screen.

Pain Control

Dr. Anna Lembke, Director of Addictive Medicine at Stamford University, explains very helpfully in a recent interview how pain is viewed today, contrasting how it was viewed one hundred and fifty years ago. It will surprise no one that we have come a long way. However, coming a long way in Dr. Lembke's view is not necessarily entirely healthy, pain today is seen almost as the number one enemy, and at all costs (even addiction) it must be expedited. In America it is well documented how opioids have deeply impacted the country in what has been called "The Crime of the Century."

Pain comes in all forms and someone has said the most painful pain of all is that of the emotions. C. S. Lewis tackles the problem of pain, as only he can, with his unique mastery. Pain is complex and profound, and there is no making light of it. The judgment spoken of in Psalm 76 must surely of necessity, bring on pain, but the reaction needed is quietness and stillness. We must wonder what will be the response at the ultimate judgment, surely it will be as every voice is stilled. God's judgments require a humble quietening of the soul. Yet pain, forces us into action, to expedite it immediately, as today we consider any kind of pain to be dangerous, when in fact pain may be a valuable barometer. The pain of lockdown, the closure of the churches was unparalleled, but what was this pain the result of? It could not possibly be the pain of the loss of access to God in worship or fellowship with him, unless we are saying worship is only essentially composed of a structured gathering of ourselves together in certain meetings, once or twice a week. Is this the only time when Christians pray, sing, rejoice and consider the deep, deep mines of God's word, lost in wonder, love and praise? God forbid! Nevertheless it is to be feared that much of the church lives its Christian life in this manner, being dangerously part-time, nominal even!

Did John Bunyan during his long incarceration (twelve years) lose his love and devotion and worship of God because of his painful circumstances? The evidence from what emerged out of that dark confinement is that he did not, no doubt he would have said, "I triumph still if thou abide with me."[9] This is not to make light of the deep pain which he must have suffered. The same may be said of the brave Dietrich Bonhoeffer, and many others, who proved Christ in what we would describe as impossible circumstances.

God or Church?

Dr. Lembke's opinion is that the view of pain in the past was along the lines that, "what didn't kill you made you stronger."[10] Of course we might come to the conclusion that these folk of bygone days were made of stiffer stuff, more robust by far, able and willing to endure some suffering and difficulty . . . This is certainly hard to argue with. By contrast, we today are made of much softer material and very easily bruised! In this, we have to admit former generations have the measure of us, acknowledging our instant solutions have shaped us, not least in the alleviation of pain. Our age has done nothing in this regard to inculcate the grace of patience which is the fruit of God's Spirit (Gal 5:22). Patience may have to live with circumstances being out of our control for a while, giving faith time to develop.

We may safely assume that it was pain of a particular kind which must have worked in the rank and file of the church, which, in turn, persuaded most churches to sign up to Zoom. Certainly bereavement of a kind was the experience but also the pain of loss of "social," being alone, being by oneself, was painful. Gay wonders whether conditions have given "rise to the possibility that historical—social change might also become the object of worship."[11] If Gay was to assess this currently he would surely be unequivocal. It would be very interesting to ask "Zoom" worshippers the question: If the worship of God, "no matter what," was the heartfelt motive, the "deepest desire," and people were so "desperate" to achieve this end, could we expect

9. Lyte, "Abide with me," hymn.
10. Dr. Lembke, *Crime of the Century*, Netflix film.
11. Gay, *Way of the (Modern) World*, 259.

the same people to "meet" on "screen" if the prospect, the expectation of persecution loomed large as a consequence for participation in such a practice? That is, if it was potentially possible for engaging in such worship, it might result in the worshipper going to prison? I rather think ingrained rationalism, pragmatism would have given the definitive answer to this. In our age of "easy bruising" the "screen" worshippers would quickly work out that a social gathering by "screen" was not worth the persecution, furthermore, to quote the apostle Paul, this would only be testing sincerity.

"No Man's Land"

In a conflict arena it must be unnerving to enter "no man's land," an ambiguous place where no established control exists and where guidelines are unclear. Anyone in such a situation might understandably find themselves on the "horns of a dilemma" . . . which way to go? COVID-19 changed the landscape, secular and spiritual alike, government on one side—God on the other. Previous to the invasion of the virus, the church could always exult in the greatness of democracy, God's "provision," but now democracy was not quite so benign and friendly to God nor his church, which was caught between two fires, it was a case of "picking your poison!" It was just here that the *test* would be applied: The church had always made impressive statements about God's Sovereign control, but did it really believe them? Perhaps this belief was only equal to belief in itself, COVID-19 would expose the truth.

If rationalism was the tutor providing education so as to introduce "online" worship then its teaching would certainly provide the navigational aid needed in the new virgin territory, where quite evidently control was either gone or in very short supply. Though as stated above, it is hardly likely that this navigational rationalism would allow for any "risk taking." Worshippers, so "desperate" to "do" church (any way possible) would hardly under such tutelage take "silly risks;" that is if the new engineered mode of worship carried serious penalty. Worship "together" is important, but is it *that* important? While writing this the extraordinary bravery of a young Russian woman has emerged as she forced her way onto a newsfeed protesting against the war in Ukraine. She has risked very much for her beliefs; testing her sincerity is not difficult! The nagging question remains: does the "screen" worshipping church believe with the same passion and commitment as the brave young Russian? Would anyone be prepared to give up their freedom to stand up for this new experiment and appear on "screen," and as a consequence suffer loss? This would confirm whether it was God, the man of love, the crucified, who the church was desperate to meet with, or was it the church, the meetings, the program, the institution of church itself? In other words, the desire for "one-anothering." If the social was flexing its not inconsiderable manipulative controlling powers, then the "screen's" welcoming arms could not have been a better provision. It is easy to appreciate the help which "screen" could afford those suffering with waning certainties, subjective certainties, which have always been sought by Christians plagued by a lack of assurance. More is the pity that even true Christians may be drawn to things visual to remedy their malady.

Not all those who became participants in "screen" worship were by any means needing the comfort of "whistling in the dark," but nor were all the participants believers. The new control did not suit everyone, yet nonetheless many joined in, being uncertain of the territory marked out in "no man's land." But what could possibly persuade them to venture out into such uncertain terrain? Perhaps voices from the past worked on the conscience as they delivered a shrill note of warning against "idolatry of the flesh" which lazy non-participation might imply. Weber recognized Puritan "moral book-keeping has . . . the most important psychological sanction for care and exactitude"[12] What a controlling influence! Yet when controls of this kind exert a pressure on us, it is more likely to be the hand of man at the controls, rather than the hand of God. "Zoom" worship turns out to be good management control, which cannot fail to provide rewards and since control and rewards are bound insolubly together, the success and longevity of the project is assured. Humans are greedy for rewards, if they can acquire them, and will prefer to be controlled to secure them, rather than to be free and forfeit them. From Eve in the Garden to Elisha's acquisitive servant Gehazi, to Judas' pursuit of thirty pieces of silver, the Bible shows the danger of such a quest; but as Mecklenburg points out: "We only see the rewards and ignore the costs. But there can be no rewards without costs, a law that nature ordained."[13] A law which Eve, Gehazi and Judas all discovered to their cost, submitting to control in pursuit of rewards may be a poisoned chalice.

But the attraction of the new worship had sufficient rewards on offer, not least safe passage through "no man's land." Also it would secure an independence, a controlling independence, enabling the church to rise above its enforced circumstances. Mecklenburg quips: "we think we can be independent and dependent. But we cannot."[14] The independent-minded Christian often demonstrates his dependence not in God but in himself, leading to the dark but very real possibility which is Craig Gay's assessment: "The logic of practical atheism may well be more deeply ingrained in the evangelical tradition than conservatives perhaps have realized."[15] This is the form of Christian atheism which with chameleon-like ease can pass itself off as genuine. Max Weber astutely observed the roots of this, writing of the Puritans quoting Wesley he said:

> Those great religious movements, whose significance for economic development lay above all (else) in their ascetic educative influence, generally came only after the peak of the purely religious enthusiasm was past. Then the intensity of the search for the Kingdom of God commenced gradually to pass

---

12. Weber, *Protestant Ethic and the Spirit of Capitalism*, 238.

13. Mecklenburg, *Philosophy of Size and The Essence of Enough*, 107.

14. Mecklenburg, *Philosophy of Size and The Essence of Enough*, 107.

15. Gay, *Way of the (Modern) World*, 71.

over into sober economic virtue; the religious roots died out slowly, giving way to utilitarian worldliness.[16]

Such utilitarianism, such worldliness is manifest in Christian atheists throughout a kingdom (the UK) which was once graced by the great truths of God's word proclaimed no less by the Puritans themselves.

All Hail Rote!

Rote learning may not have originated with the Puritans but in this regard our western culture has certainly been influenced by them, their desire to catechize has been bound to us like another limb. Those who know of Twain are aware of his humorous sideways swipe at this practice in "Tom Sawyer." While Twain was no friend of God, he recognized something which hopefully all of us can see, rote learning, rote worship is void of the soul, and allows no room for it. Mecklenburg though takes his own swipe at it: "Critical thinking, once the bastion of liberal education, has become rote thinking . . . education should be less about creating robots and more about creating humans who can exist without following an operating system, one that teacher and the state programmed."[17]

We are living unquestionably in the *ultimate* programmed age, and perilously comfortable with it also. The world and church alike accede to it without a second thought, the mechanical and robotic render us dumb to sound the alarm. The rote mentality seems to fit us very well indeed, "controlled," "mechanistic," "rational," "secure," "foolproof," "programmed" is just how we like it.

In the world of "no man's land" Mecklenburg provides his own brand of navigation:

> When we are pondering a path, we cannot merely determine which costs we like most; we must determine which costs we dislike least . . . In life, we must know what we like, and we must know what we dislike; and, in choosing a path, we must choose what we like most and what we dislike least.[18]

God's word should have been the satellite navigation through uncertain territory, Christ's likes and dislikes confirming the safe route in a world of questionable *control*.

Wake Up

More concerningly, this "screen" worship has been introduced to the young. Again Neil Postman provides his own form of analysis for us to consider: "Children are the

---

16. Weber, *Protestant Ethic*, 176, quoting Wesley.
17. Mecklenburg, *Philosophy of Size and the Essence of Enough*, 109.
18. Mecklenburg, *Philosophy of Size and the Essence of Enough*, 107.

living messages we send to a time we will not see."[19] Only time will tell what their perception in the future will be of the one true God who was first encountered through a medium, a "tool," a modern day idol. Even without this new additional screen intrusion, the burdened minds of the young look terribly vulnerable, exposed as they are daily to the neon god. It is particularly sad to personally hear harrowing accounts of children from Christian families who feel trapped, mentally imprisoned by the idol in their pockets. Children in their early teens, twelve and thirteen year olds, suffering at the hands of the tech, and yet this seems to strike little fear into some Christians who constantly feed their children the drug of our age. Do we really think this "Zoom" is God's provision? Perhaps the same people might like to suggest tobacco equally deserves the endorsement, "By Royal Appointment to the King of Heaven!"

God's work by his Spirit is plainly to fashion, by his grace, the "new man," of which the mind is at the center. Have we forgotten that God and God alone, is to be the divine sculptor of the mind? It seems the church is unaware of another dark hand which has taken up the artwork. We are all (astronauts excluded) being fashioned into a likeness which is only gradually emerging. Like the deposits of nicotine in the lungs, it does not kill immediately, but eventually the skin goes sallow, the arteries clog, the cough starts and gets worse, and the cancer becomes incurable. Before Christians in such a cavalier fashion, attribute to God the authorship of "Zoom" and its accomplices, they might like to remember who is the god of this world, and consider rather more seriously the one who, not surprisingly, appears as an angel of light (2 Cor 11:14).

Be Still and Know that I Am God

In our frenetic, control-driven secular age, disfigured as it is by anxiety, fear and pain have demanded a door be opened for instant relief. Patience and quietness with stillness have been all but banished, as if they were enemies to all, even to God's kingdom. Reflecting on my Christian life, I am indebted and appreciative that my spiritual mentors came to me in the early days of my "life of faith," these were often the elderly ladies of the church who reminded me in the most reassuring way "The Lord is on the throne," He was and is still in control. This was not the sovereignty of God expounded as mere theoretical knowledge, but absolutely believed, being observed in lives which were evidently at rest, quiet and still. God's judgments did not alarm them. It was very impressive, I have never forgotten this kind of "living faith," which I like to think in measure is mine also, and is still shaping me. Those ladies exhibited what this civilization should really look like. Heaven rules . . .

---

19. Strate, *Amazing Ourselves to Death*, 133, quoting Postman, *Disappearance of Childhood*, 1.

CHAPTER 10

The Blur God Project

Conscience: the inner voice which warns us that someone may be looking.
H.L. MENCKEN

Take heed brethren, lest there be in any of you an evil heart of unbelief . . .
HEBREWS 3:12 (KJV)

Vital Components

"PUT THOU MY TEARS IN thy bottle" (Ps 56:8, KJV) was a thought which evidently for the psalmist proved a source of great comfort. Thankfully God sees our tears, he knows about our individual suffering. One of the ultimate comforts in this life is to know that tears will one day have had their day, they will be no more. Sadly for now we must witness the pain which produces them, and this is especially uncomfortable when observed in children, but even harder when we recognize it was often inadvertently inflicted. No doubt families have always engaged in their own form of child psychology, trying to get to the source of the characteristics and behavior of their offspring, yet all the while failing to analyze their own. However, we must assume that most caring parents want to try to work things out, especially when the task of raising children presents challenges, as it does all too often.

It does not take a genius to know that much of the hurt and pain experienced by children is done *to* them, this not only in the form of elements introduced into their lives but also vital components denied. My father's unhappy, painful story was that he was forced back into a urinated bed as a punishment for his weak, childhood bladder, and denied any real loving affection. What a dreadful composition! When I repeated the same habit as a child in the 1950s, I experienced only compassion and tenderness, with an abundance of love. What a wonderful composition! Far too often we struggle to find the right balance, the very worst of actions gain ascendancy while the vital components are missing and even denied. Which one of us can doubt that nature and nurture are inextricably linked?

Listen Up!

Essentially this is about commission and omission. Of course achieving the correct balance with children is a huge challenge, I should know I have three of my own. This balance is quite an art form, and there are few of us who can testify to producing masterpieces! Nevertheless, the vital ingredients are just that, vital, the balance is crucial. The same can be said about the functioning of the immune system. When cancer strikes there is something malfunctioning in the body, the T-cells, the soldiers, have abandoned their post, becoming sleepy and needing to be "chivvied up." Cancer is on the march in our day, and it is said one in two will be diagnosed with this disease in their lifetime. We know a diet of fast food (commission) and zero exercise (omission), along with many other toxic components, is a recipe for disaster. The questions now posed are: Will we wake up and heed the warnings? Will we alter our lifestyles to the saving of our lives?

This picture of things "vital" being absent while others, of such a harmful nature, being present is illustrated in Christ's letters to the seven churches. The Lord of the church says "Take my advice" (Rev 3:18, NET). Some of these churches had a spiritual diet of fast food and zero exercise, here is omission and commission at work, as indeed we must admit is the case in our churches today. Their lifestyle choices were evidently a clear threat to their spiritual prosperity, and drastic measures were called for—or else! These churches were introducing practices which were damaging and harmful, but also were ignoring and refusing the "vital" necessities for their spiritual progress.

To the church at Laodicea, Christ tells them, gold, new clothes and eye salve (ointment) are needed, these were lacking, and as a consequence their spiritual health was failing. The Lord of the church says, "Take my advice." It is just this kind of advice which we today have failed to heed. This chapter now considers not just what we have willfully ingested, namely the preferences of our time, soft atheism included (read on), but also what we have rejected, the vital role of the conscience. Where was the conscience when the coup took place, when "screen" worship so smoothly impressed our senses and affections? The conscience, or lack of it, must now be considered.

The final part of this chapter will look at what is most significantly missing in our churches. We have no aesthetic to speak of to curb the slavish subservience to our culture, which bows so readily and submissively to the mesmerizing technopoly. Hopefully this investigation will throw even more light upon our study.

Of course some will see no need for analysis, but it is probably safe to note that these are the same people who believe all that matters is "getting down to business"; an unfortunate expression given the seriousness of this subject.

Now and Then

It is a great pity that John Bunyan's 1678 meticulous masterpiece *The Holy War* is unknown to most Christians, since it represents by far his most accomplished work, and probably the most important Christian "picture" book any of us will ever read. In an age saturated with image and picture, this finest of books sets out to convey the most profound of scriptural truths and concepts. If it is pictures we yearn for, then *The Holy War* can meet this need like no other, though it contains no pictures whatsoever, yet if carefully considered, its imagery will remain for a lifetime! Bunyan possessed a unique skill to bring home truths which have a graphic quality, but where the truth has not been lost in the image. What a remarkable skill!

Early in the book Bunyan draws attention to something we now need to consider, which touches vitally upon our main subject. He writes,

> As for Mr Recorder (the conscience) before the town (the soul) was taken, he
> was a man of courage and faithfulness to speak truth at every occasion: and
> he had a tongue as bravely hung, as he had a head filled with judgments. Now,
> this man Diabolus (the devil) could by no means abide, because, though he
> gave his consent to his coming into the town (the conscience was complicit in
> allowing the ruin of Mansoul) yet he could not, by all the wiles, trials, strata-
> gems, and devices that he could use, make him wholly his own.[1]

Bunyan goes on to say that while the conscience had yielded to Diabolus, yet "now and then (Mr. Recorder would) think upon Shaddai" (The Lord God Almighty).[2]

On observation many of the failings in the Christian life must be traced to this spiritual malaise, regrettably, and far too easily, we think upon God only "now and then." This is undoubtedly a great weakness to which every professing Christian is prone. It is far too easy to go through the motions, God may be far from our thoughts, yet the outer shell is well established, the institution of the church, the meetings, the external becomes the life and not God himself. How dangerous! There once was a time when this was labelled "nominal Christianity," "Sunday Christianity." Today it might be called "Church Christianity" and perhaps all too readily and easily, very acceptable Christanity.

My Delight

In his book *God's Battle Plan for the Mind*, David W Saxton leans heavily on the Puritans to encourage his readers to address the question as to how the mind is used, especially in the acts of meditation and contemplation. He quotes Thomas Watson:

---

1. Bunyan, *Holy War*, 19-20.
2. Bunyan, *Holy War*, 20.

"He who delights in God's law is often thinking on it."[3] Unfortunately, history shows how this *delighting* in God's law became, for many churchgoers, only a legal matter, the life was not in it. This was done at the expense of *delighting* in God, in Christ himself. People learned to delight in *something* and not *Someone*. This is not meant to speak disparagingly of Watson's motives, only that this *delight* undoubtedly became a thing of the letter not the Spirit, and was therefore rendered lifeless in the lifeless practitioner. My father-in-law, brought up in the Dutch Reformed Calvinistic Church, studied at the "Free University Amsterdam" and became an expert in Greek but he was actually a lifeless professor of religion, until Christ was formed in him. His *delighting* in God's law was only a mechanism, and as such had hidden the grace of Christ from him (his words not mine). This *delighting* was in *something* and not *Someone*, as was the issue at Galatia for which Paul was willing to become the enemy of the church (Gal 4:16, NIV). Undoubtedly it is the case that scores of people today are raised in churches devoted to *something* and not *Someone*. Furthermore it is perfectly possible we are here uncovering and exploring a significant part of the present demise in Christian worship, rather than Christians thinking upon "him," they think upon "it." The obvious danger is that the church may be construed as an "it," the worship as an "it," the meetings as an "it." This will be considered in more detail later.

What is undoubtedly true is that as churches turned to this world's medium, they were *naturally* thinking the thoughts of *spiritual business* and *spiritual commerce*, indeed the medium demanded this. The result, the meeting, the worship, the breaking of bread in the Lord's Supper, was reduced to a "thing," an "it," whilst musing, contemplation and meditation upon the holiness of God and his character may have arisen, but only "now and then!"

As "screen" worship is an untested experiment, nevertheless it has certainly won the gold medal for hubris, it seems only fitting to consider another experiment, albeit a hypothetical one. In this way the two may be compared and if both survive analysis, then both can be legitimately experimented with by the church. By employing this trial the conscience can be scrutinized to find out what it will tolerate, and this in turn may reveal our predilections, our preferences. We may be surprised to find that "screen" worship answers more to preferences than to anything else. Let us see!

Knock Out!

A computer, a camera, a lens, a screen, we have already established are all mediums, and "the medium is the message," not forgetting as far as the message of the Christian Gospel is concerned, there can only ever be "one" message. There must never be any tug-of-war between God's message and that of the world. Competition can never be allowed in the church, especially in the worship of God. The medium of the camera,

---

3. Saxton, *God's Battle Plan for the Mind*, 26, quoting Watson, *Christian on the Mount*, 11

the lens, the screen, all vie for space, for attention, needing to communicate to us . . . all mediums do this. Their success rate is seen by the near saturation levels of their presence in our modern life, and clearly have no equal in human history. God versus "screen" when joined, is like putting a featherweight in the ring against a heavyweight; the competition is equally unfair, there is only ever going to be one winner, the "screen" is a knockout!

Tabloid Worship

Now let us turn to the experiment and call on the old traditional newspaper (a medium) to be a carrier of the things of God. Let us imagine a center spread in a well-known Sunday tabloid, featuring an order of a worship service in which thousands, even millions, are exposed to Bible readings, a written prayer and hymns with suggested tunes which could be accessed on the internet, or on a mobile phone, and along with these the all important sermon, a message proclaiming the Savior. Of course this would have to fit the medium which is being employed, not forgetting the newspaper, just like the computer, has its own intrinsic inseparable voice. Indeed if it ceased to have this voice it would no longer be a newspaper. The message of this tabloid is now "joined at the hip" to the worship of almighty God. The worshipper, as he must, interacts with the medium, then as the saying goes the two, God and medium, will now have to "slug it out" . . . let the contest begin!

Cheek by Jowl

Naturally, many Christians reading this will feel squeamish, because the downside to the experiment is that the holy and profane are joined. By association the sacred act of worship is made to share the medium of this world. Let us also consider that the medium is the essential indispensable carrier. On one page, the soft porn appears, which I understand, with the click of a button, may be accessed by any computer, (apparently the addiction to pornography through the screen is now endemic), holy and profane together, "cheek by jowl." I am informed that one could even split the screen, pornography and worship together, and though this may be abhorrent to us and make us retch, this is reality. This is not just reality, but has already been exposed as a practice.

Nevertheless, the "newspaper" worship could be carefully navigated avoiding the "trivialities," the "lies" and "stories" of pure invention and sensation, the "innuendo" and sheer weight of crass reporting. Of course the project might be rescued by the emergence "here and there" of a smattering of truth, and possibly, just possibly, something of merit. Presumably Christian pragmatism and rationalism would provide the support and the go ahead for this "noble" means-end-experiment, making it look in every way like a triumph with which no one could possibly find fault.

In its favor, the argument might be made that this "tool" enables the church to introduce worship to the un-churched, to those who find it difficult to engage in spiritual life and should any discomfort arise, rationalism will do its work and overcome any conscience-driven obstacles. What is more, the gospel in this way would be reaching people who hitherto might never enter through the doors of a church. No doubt this will become a major argument in the future for the experiment of "Zoom" to become a mainstay, no longer a visitor, but a welcome guest (and why not?). By now the discomfort with this uncomfortable experiment is probably sinking in, perhaps even the conscience beginning to be stirred a little?

If a defense can be mounted, it might be along the lines that the two mediums may not be fairly examined and compared, on these grounds alone it might be argued there can be no comparison made, since there appears to be no similitude. The protest, one imagines, is that the newspaper does not allow for presence, whereas the "screen" does. The truth is the "screen" does not allow anyone to be "actually" present at anything, hence the need for it! The very perceptive Marshall McLuhan noted that "the electronic media allow us to be everywhere and nowhere at all at the same time, a center without margins."[4] In addition McLuhan's associate Tony Schwartz (1983) referred to the electronic media as "the second god, which man has created."[5] The second god enables us to pretend and give the lie that we are present. The pseudo-event enables the pretense to be sold as reality. The result is, as Boorstin notes, "More and more of our experience thus becomes invention rather than discovery."[6]

A Custodian without a Conscience

Strate's observations are worthy of any true Christian who displays a conscience which works beyond "now and then," as he explains why the "screen" worship and that of the newspaper propositions are both failures for exactly the same reasons. Strate amplifies all this when he explains:

> The problem, as always is one of context. Participating in a religious ritual places us in a special context that is different from all other contexts, situating us in a distinct semantic environment, one that asks us to play different roles and play by a different set of rules. Whether the location is a church, synagogue, temple, or mosque, or outdoors, at home, or in a rented hall, religious experience, as Eliade (1959) explains, is characterized by a sense of sacred space and sacred time, as separate and distinct from profane space and time.

4. Strate, *Amazing Ourselves to Death*, 119, quoting McLuhan.

5. McLuhan and McLuhan, *Laws of Media*. Strate, *Amazing Ourselves to Death*, 119, quoting Schwartz, *Media: The Second God*.

6. Boorstin, *Image*, 257.

Indeed, the deep meaning of sanctification and consecration, traced back to the Hebrew word *kadosh*, is to set apart and differentiate.[7]

Under this spotlight the "screen" and the newspaper are evidently equals, to allow either of them the distinction to be carriers of the worship of the one true God is a testament to who we believe him to be.

Strate continues,

> What happens, then, when religion is moved out of its particular context of the sacred, away from contexts that have been carefully chosen and prepared to communicate the seriousness of religious ritual and create a sense of separation from the everyday, profane world? What happens when religion is framed within a new context created by electronic media?[8]

Lance Strate certainly appears to possess more discernment and insight than many in Christ's church whose cognizance of these things is found glaringly wanting. God, thankfully, is able to raise up stones to praise him (Luke 19:40). Conscience clearly failed to bring home the plain obvious truth, the sacred act of worship composed on a screen, of any description, beamed into a bedroom or kitchen to "watch" (remember as stated earlier, no corporate act of worship is "actually" taking place), is being shared by an unholy medium with its own agenda, identical to the pages of the tabloid. The church, which should be the custodian of this civilization, the kingdom of God, looks in many respects to be bereft of a conscience.

Digital Duplicate

Strate explains . . . "the religious website may be one of several pages or tabs opened at the same time, so other programs may be running as well, not to mention the presence of background images . . . text messages, voice messages and cellphone calls may interrupt the experience at any moment."[9] (I am reliably informed how during certain "Zoom" worship meetings people had to get up to answer their door to take a delivery or to respond to a need). Strate confirms this when he observes this is: "a profane environment that may contain many distractions and imposes few special restrictions on behavior, (the cat may need to be put out during the worship of God, emphasis mine). Simply put . . . (the) real physical situations cannot be duplicated through the electronic media."[10] Astonishingly Christians insist on calling their "Zoom" practices "acts of worship," in other words they see no distinction between "corporeal," "actual," "physical" and "coming together" (1 Cor 14:26, NIV) all delivered through the medium of a "screen" employing images. This means, for all intents and purposes, the

7. Strate, *Amazing Ourselves to Death*, 114.
8. Strate, *Amazing Ourselves to Death*, 114.
9. Strate, *Amazing Ourselves to Death*, 115.
10. Strate, *Amazing Ourselves to Death*, 115.

mechanical "Zoom" is capable of duplicating digitally exactly what we do when we meet in person. Daniel Boorstin offers this insight assisting every Christian to access reality.

> A dream is a vision or an aspiration to which we can compare reality. It may be very vivid, but its vividness reminds us how different is the real world. An illusion, on the other hand, is an image we have mistaken for reality. We cannot reach for it, aspire to it, or be exhilarated by it; for we live in it. It is prosaic, because we cannot see it is not fact.[11]

In the light of this, by any analysis or judgment the conscience has clearly failed, the inner voice did not send out its warning, the "bravely hung tongue" was stuck to the roof of the mouth, courage and faithfulness, so vital, failed. We need to explore some of the complex reasons why this has happened.

Someone and someone

Shakespeare's line, "Thus conscience doth make cowards of us all" seems to be the Bard's way of pointing up the truth that we are all on the run from what we really know and sense internally to be right. Conscience finds us out and painfully displays how prone we are to a craven spirit. Tragically, when we reject the arms of conscience we fall swiftly into the arms of another. By rejecting the voice of *Someone* we turn to the voice of *someone*.

Sigmund Freud seems to have distanced himself from the concept of conscience and saw it as merely a notion, inculcated by parents and society, both harmfully and repressively. Certainly from a Christian perspective, which along with Bunyan believes that this property belongs to God's creation, Freud's narrow confines of its origin fail to provide solutions. Nevertheless, his analysis is not entirely found wanting. He points to "interiorization of the norms of parents and society."[12] This is not so far away from Paul's concern that the world should not be allowed to "squeeze us into its own mould" (Rom 12:2, J.B. Phillips). Freud may have been wrong in his conclusions about the conscience, but that we are socially and psychologically shaped and conditioned by our parents and environment, seems almost foolish to argue with. We find it difficult to shake off the mould! The world, whose arms we so easily embrace is the *someone*, not forgetting that the conscience only recalls God "now and then." The result being, we, others and society fall prey to the thinking of our times and what is deemed "standard practice."

The tragic story of the North Atlantic Slave Trade provides some insight into this. If we assumed that the majority of those who traded and profited from the slave trade had no conscience, then we would be wrong. Undoubtedly, their consciences

---

11. Boorstin, *Image*, 241.

12. *New Dictionary of Theology*, 161, quoting Freud, *Psychology of Religion* .

worked perfectly well on a wide range of other matters and informed their behavior and actions accordingly. Slavery was not going to keep them awake at night as their pernicious trade was above all else an acquisitive one, and the conscience is rendered a weakling by "a root of all kinds of evil" (1 Tim 6:10, NIV).

Lies My Teacher Told Me

Furthermore, the conscience is significantly put at ease, duped even, when society endorses a "thing," when politics and economics bring a "thing" into the mainstream and, even better, when the church gets "on board" endorsing it . . . Now everyone can "sleep easy at night!" Uncomfortable as it is, wearing our modern clothes, schooled in our age, the question has to be asked: Would we make the claim today that we would never have endorsed slavery as they did? After all we are no less subject to "group-think," to the influence of the majority, the herd, which they say "is always right." The result is the bending of the knee in willing compliance, the conscience naturally, understandably feels at ease, and any pangs of distress are quickly extirpated. "The conscience doth make cowards of us all!" Nor should we forget, having a "clear con-science," having good motives, does not excuse us or exonerate us from our errors and ill-judged decisions. History is littered with crimes, but crimes committed with good motives.

The New Dictionary of Theology helpfully identifies one side of the conscience, exploring the meaning of conscientia, that is the ability to relate general rules to par-ticular cases. But if history teaches us anything, it has been the failure of this ability to relate general rules to particular practices. The limitations of the conscience are there for all to see, leaving the field open to society, to the spirit of the age to direct us; even the democratic voice, the politics and economics neatly confirm for us that we are indeed on the "right path," no need for doubt, while quite reasonably "pressing us into its mould." We can now understand how those who seek the termination of life might "reasonably" apply these fixed acceptable "norms" to confirm their practices, ensuring the conscience is not awakened. Society, economics, politics, democracy, power, all exert their pressure.

The Slave Trade

The conscience can be tricked, fooled, beaten and bludgeoned, soothed and coerced into willful submission so that the true identity of events are hidden, reconfigured, or even disfigured. In his exhaustive work on the Slave Trade, Hugh Thomas identifies the power of economics and society to impose itself. How might a commodity like sugar impact the Atlantic Slave Trade? How could sugar impact man's inhumanity to man? Thomas astutely observes in the "age of sugar" "the fat faces in the portraits of the beauties and the kings, of the ostlers (stableman at an inn), and of the actresses."

He goes on to inform us that, "In 1750, already, 'the poorest English farm laborer's wife took sugar in her tea.' She baked sweet cakes, and spread treacle on her bread, as well as her porridge."[13] He says: "in the case of England sugar was the most valuable single import . . . and, of course, sugar . . . depended on the imports of African slaves into the Caribbean."[14]

The evidence for the emergence of sugar's importance appears in a famous cookbook of 1747, and also in Jane Austin's "Sense and Sensibility," where anxiety is felt when the purchase of sugar looks to be put in jeopardy. This is the voice of *someone* in the form of sugar, and it can shout down every other voice, even if it is the anti-slavery voice. What does the conscience do when the Queen speaks in favor of something? Here are the words of Queen Anne in her speech to Parliament on the 6 June 1712. "I have insisted and obtained the *asiento* or contract for furnishing the Spanish West Indies with negroes shall be made with us for thirty years."[15] (As recalled by the Duke of Clarence, quoted by Hugh Thomas). No doubt the Queen, like many in her realm, had a sweet tooth! Dowden has remarked: "a good conscience simply became one of the means of enjoying a comfortable bourgeois life."[16]

Eighty years passed before Parliament heard the "bravely hung tongue" of William Pitt saying: "*No nation in Europe . . . has . . . plunged so deeply into this guilt as Great Britain.*"[17] Society's booming voice backed by that of Royalty who were in favor of sugar, demanded that the conscience stand down, shut up, get into line and comply. [18]

When the occasional conscience is stirred to question things, and to cease from man (Isa 2:22, KJV) it is not unusual that society, the tribe, brands them as "mad." At *extremes* of the conscience scale we observe this with the self-styled prophet and freedom fighter John Brown, whose actions were instrumental in initiating the American Civil War, a war attempting to end slavery.[19] Also William Wilberforce, the Christian Politician, whose noble warfare, different from Brown's, nonetheless accepted the voice to his soul of *Someone* rather than *someone*.

It is not too difficult to see how a disposition to sugar might lead to its necessity to flavor every cup of tea and every bowl of porridge. The very fact that lives were being traded to facilitate it was no match for the habit which would rot the teeth, and so much more! Now the conscience languishes. It struggled *then* with society,

13. Thomas, *Slave Trade*, 263-64.

14. Thomas, *Slave Trade*, 264.

15. Thomas, *Slave Trade*, 236.

16. Weber, *Protestant Ethic*, 176.

17. Thomas, *Slave Trade*, 235.

18. It is duly noted (April 2023), an announcement was made that King Charles III has now expressed his support for research into historical links between the monarchy and the transatlantic slave trade.

19. The author's view: there never was/is a more just cause than the attempt to end all slavery. Freedom is at the heart of the Christian gospel.

with politics, with the majority, with popular opinion and with rational, reasonable economics . . . it struggles *still*.

No doubt Christians of that day were swept along with the tide, and "squeezed themselves neatly into the world's mould" and it was after all, the sweetest of moulds which everyone had developed a taste for, and complacency was just a part of their vocabulary! Now here we are today with our own complacency, our own sweet tooth, our own addiction, our dependency . . . it is called modern tech, the "screen." The manipulating mould just goes on moulding and the "bravely hung tongue" does not warn us of our newly developed shape, only confirming the stark truth, unwittingly Christians may be burdened with society's standard patterns . . . but who cares when they are so sweetly imposed?

Worse than Inconsistency

It is possible that this line of inquiry is too narrow, perhaps the failure of the conscience might be as much about preferences as anything else. Preferences, which we must admit are framed and endorsed by our age, by politics, by society in general and by popular opinion. Only now in the UK is sugar under the spotlight as being potentially harmful, especially in the lives of children, and only now is legislation thought to be a tool to employ against its powers . . . just three hundred years after the Queen signed up to the Slave Trade to ensure the commerce of sugar (Rev 18:23, NIV). Presumably up until recently the sugar industry has been too big to fight. The slave trade of the Southern United States was backed by a political consensus, well established economically, and while there were dissenting voices, the conscience of the slave owners evidently was largely untroubled and angst if there was any, was controlled by preferences, these "set in stone." This is not to say that they had no pangs of conscience at all, no doubt it was pricked on a number of issues, just not slavery.

Weighed on the Scales and Found Wanting

During the writing of this, some people have freely told me of their inherent discomfort with their forays into "screen" worship; "something was just not right," the conscience was speaking, but the preferences, the established tribal order called out with its booming voice, like sugar of old, and this must have been a factor in the huge numbers who took up this new practice. What is obvious is that the conscience forbids and permits, and permits rather too easily. Preference implies favor, favor of one thing over another. This means a favorable bias, a partiality is employed, we might even say a weighing scale of our own making. Hence Luther's conscience is not bound by his conscience, but by an infallible external to it, namely the word of God. It seems impossible not to see the slave trade as adopting its own "weights and measures," this must have enabled the conscience in that economy to be silent, comfortable and undisturbed. It must be admitted that such scales have undoubtedly always been used by the church.

I recall a story, which has both its serious and amusing side, to verify the truth of these scales, still in use everywhere today. The Christian who is condemned and called out for smoking a quiet cigar on Sunday afternoon (much appreciated still by the Dutch Calvinists) is soundly condemned for his worldly pleasures by the "clean living" American family who leave church after Sunday morning worship to take lunch at McDonalds, thus breaking the Sabbath of the Dutch Calvinist! Apart from the fact that these two are probably as bad as each other, (though personally I think the cigar is the safer!). It does not matter because the scales have already decided, and established for us how we should think. In truth these always decide, our preferences are fixed, "set in stone."

Do we realize we possess the same scales for evaluating so many practices, including worship, and to a greater or lesser extent we are subject to them? Remember these scales will not only weigh Bible perspectives but the conscience as it is subject to personal preferences. This is easily observed as we watch the "cogs drop into gear" in the conservative evangelical mind regarding practices which are "clearly" right and wrong. Let us suppose that such a Christian was asked to assess the worship of the Russian and Greek Orthodox and Roman Catholic faiths. From my perspective all these participants are merely "watching" worship, the visual is at the center. While much is said and acted out in these various expressions of "worship," nevertheless above all else, the appeal is that it is a "good watch." Our proctor from the evangelical tradition, like the sniffer dog, has a trained nose for error, and picks up the fact that this kind of worship is essentially about externals, even mechanical, a mere process of going through the motions which is painfully evident. Notice at the center of all these acts of worship there is a dependence upon *something*, something irreplaceable and indispensable to the act itself . . . the medium. For instance, in Catholicism the priest is this "indispensable" medium. When all this is keenly observed by the supervisor, judgment falls swiftly and easily, the worship being recognized as unmistakably focusing on *someone* and not *Someone*. It could be said the show itself stole the limelight, and our judge and jury found it glaringly obvious. This so-called act of worship has been instantly "weighed on the scale and found wanting" (Dan 5:27). In all this we see the clarity and ease with which error can be diagnosed, the enthusiastic evangelical eye picks up on the "*use*" of the requisite tools employed to make the worship possible, inevitably the judgment swiftly follows.

The "Inner" Man

Across Europe we might find it just as easy to arrive at the same conclusion as we watch someone entering a church, standing, gazing, transfixed in front of an impressive wall painting, a fresco, which perhaps has served others for centuries. It need not be an image of Jesus, nor of the Virgin, nor even one of the so-called saints. Furthermore this may not be an act of genuflexion, but only one of appreciation. This fresco may create a sense of awe in the one who interacts with it, in warming the heart, as many things do. Encouragement might be derived, and as a result, invigorating strength be found, the trembling coward spirit helped to find a voice. The result, God is glorified from the inward parts which is where he seeks the truth (Ps 51:6). Now some would argue that here is nothing to be frowned upon, the worshipper is not an idolator, and like all of us in some measure he looks to the earth for some tokens of help. While generosity forces us to be gentle with this worshipper of God, there is no guarantee the aforementioned judge and jury will be so lenient. In fact, with cast-iron certainty, the well-schooled, self-righteous proctor will call this out as a "dark practice," and undoubtedly as "will worship."

My interest in this book is in part to assess our current preferences and however painful, expose them. It is indisputable the image of the fresco is just that, an image, an undeniably beautiful one. It is more than a thing of beauty, it is stimuli, an "aid," a "tool," an "assist," which is used, i.e. employed toward a given end. Nonetheless, generosity compels us to note the content of this man's worship, the reality and truth of it is known to him alone, which may not be judged by any man: "Before God we stand or fall" (Rom 14:4). This, however, we can be sure will not be kindly received by those who are ready to judge others.

Seek and Enjoy . . . Not Seek and You Shall Find!

Having said all the above it has to be admitted that the external is always speaking and offering its influence, it must be because it is being called upon, even relied upon. The framers of the historic church confessions saw this when they wrote about worship, as they anticipated the possibility of this being impacted and corrupted by imagery. (See the Baptist and Westminster Confessions). Our judge and jury may well agree with Neil Postman: "In every tool we create, an idea is embedded that goes beyond the function of the thing itself."[20] Despite the fresco's alluring beauty and naturally any predilections towards it, it is still a medium like any other, being invested with meaning, conveying ideas. It is born of a philosophy, so its purpose is therefore neither neutral nor benign. Neil Postman says, "Each technology has an agenda of its own."[21]

The fresco demands that we look at it because it is *there,* inviting us to linger a while, compelling us. In fact it possesses a *magical* touch, like other visual mediums, and who could ever think anything ill of it? But whilst compelling us we lose sight of the fact that all this is secondhand, producing "secondhandness." No matter as Boorstin observes "We make, we seek, and finally we enjoy, the contrivance of all experience.

---

20. Postman, *Amusing Ourselves to Death*, 14.

21. Postman, *Amusing Ourselves to Death*, 87.

We fill our lives not with experience but with the images of experience."[22] All of this forces us to ask the question: If God is not partial (Jas 2:1, Rom 2:11), how can we be?

In the willingness to unthinkingly bow to the neon god, the churches appear to have thrown away their own rule book, this is not just "worse than inconsistency," it is much, much worse. On close examination the church at large, and even conservative evangelicals, have a highly developed set of weighing scales, which when deployed, are able to discern minute discrepancies. Certainly the *someone* and *Someone* of Christian worship can be identified without much difficulty by them and it would seem when the scales are balanced and calibrated "correctly" one's conscience can always be set at peace. Comparing the fourteenth century worshipper leaning, depending on the fresco with the "screen" worshipper leaning on digital images for the same purpose, it only becomes difficult to square if the scales are corrupt, not forgetting God hates unjust scales: "I do not condone the use of rigged scales or a bag of deceptive weights," (Micah 6:11, NET). Earlier, when the merits of the tabloid newspaper and that of the screen were weighed, they were found to be of identical weight.

If we dare compare "like-with-like" we will find both sets of worshippers seeking soul therapy, and what could be wrong with this except where and how one goes looking for it. It may be reasonable to assume that the digital "screen" worshipper is already "hooked" on the screen's daily social fix, therefore the "Zoom" worship above all else presents as an extension of what in truth is just routine, a way of life. In this there is little distinction between what is done before the "worship" on the screen and what is done by the same screen when a so-called act of worship is conducted.

Hijacked!

In his book *The Intolerance of Tolerance*, D.A. Carson has a searching chapter, "Worse Than Inconsistency," in which he quotes Jean Bethke Elshtain who remarks on "the kind of self that has accompanied "the triumph of the therapeutic culture.""[23] The "screen" worship is most likely a response to the need of a therapeutic culture:

> It is, she says, a "quivering sentimental self that gets uncomfortable very quickly, because this self has to feel good about itself all the time. Such selves do not make good arguments, they validate one another."[24]

In fact "screen" worshippers when placed on accurately calibrated scales, weigh exactly the same as the fourteenth century worshipper who is dependent on his fresco. In both cases the self has to feel good. Indeed the modern "worshipper" much more so, he/she is the one who needs to feel good all the time, hence the 24/7 social media

22. Boorstin, *Image*, 254.
23. Carson, *Intolerance of Tolerance*, 94, quoting Miller, *Alone in the Academy*, 31.
24. Carson, *Intolerance of Tolerance*, 94-95, quoting Miller, *Alone in the Academy*, 31-32.

requirement. The quivering, sentimental self gets uncomfortable very quickly, thus needing constant confirmation from the screen that "all is well."

The suspicion must be that those who "turned to the screen with such unmitigated haste" did so for a variety of reasons, but surely the drive for the "feel good factor" must have been a major influence as feelings are able to exert an unusual pressure on us. Since God can never be worshipped through any medium whatsoever, nor through an interface, it was not haste to come into God's presence that was deeply desired, it had to be about self, the sentimental self. By these actions the conscience is *sated, supported* and *conveniently sanctified* by the environment of the now entrenched, accepted and dominant culture of tech. To add further peace of mind, all of this suggests a harmless disposition, so it must be God given! Yet in reality the conscience is "press-ganged," hijacked, even being made a hostage to fortune, the fortune of the world.

When Whitefield and Wesley decontextualized their service of God in worship, by and large they did so by separating themselves out from the religious status quo. In doing so they undoubtedly altered the established appreciation which was firmly embedded—namely, a human construct of the church which had existed for ever. The two great evangelists by their actions would differentiate between the flesh and the Spirit. When Finney introduced his "anxious seat" (no doubt with good intention) into evangelism, the context of true evangelism was altered, an invasion of sorts had entered in, just as with Billy Graham's approach to "reaching the lost!" But there is a significant difference between the earlier and later evangelists, whilst all were concerned for the kingdom of God, Whitefield and Wesley's work of deconstruction (departure from the "norm") did not trivialize religious encounter. In reality it was able to breathe a new liberating air, gaining traction. The conscience of the people was at last set free from the cage called "church" Did Wesley or Whitefield blur the sacred by taking it into the open field and valley? Did the elements of nature stand in the way of the Holy Spirit and exert pressure on the individual conscience? We may presume none of these were ever in danger any more than the elements of the river proved a danger to Lydia, as God graciously and sovereignly opened her heart (Acts 16).

But what happens to the conscience when the majority (eighty percent of the church) turn to a medium which is indispensable to their own offering of worship *together?* What happens when the medium "sanctified" as a "holy thing," needs no further investigation? Now the conscience of the individual is mastered by the majority. Lance Strate reasons:

> In traditional communities, (like the church, emphasis mine), there is always some pressure to conform, and it is also true that individuals with different points of view, interests, and motivations have to find a way to negotiate with each other, accommodate one another, in order to live together, the alternative being to leave and join or create another local community. The electronic

media's ability to tie like-minded individuals together at a distance, makes it possible for extremists to create a large-scale movement.[25]

In this situation, with the conscience manipulated by the majority, the new worship marches unhindered . . . it just waltzes in. Even if the worshippers, in a most unholy way, bow to the neon god, nothing feels out of place because as the church bows, it simply joins the world in mimicking its posture. In addition, so as to ensure that conviction does not arise in the soul disturbing the peace, the rigged scales will always leave the modern "screen" worshipper unmolested. The conscience is fooled, but the truth is we are uncomfortably and embarrassingly found out, our duplicity is exposed.

The Identity Parade

The subtitle to Craig Gay's book *Why It's Tempting to Live as if God Doesn't Exist*, is not so much a hand grenade, as an atom bomb. It suggests the unthinkable: latent atheism in the church. No matter which way we like to paint the picture, regardless of the digital spin, those who do not *live* as if God exists are in fact atheists. The explosive question which Gay posits is very uncomfortable since it is directed in his book to the church and professing Christians. If indeed the conscience is deeply subject to the age in which it operates and functions, it will of necessity be a servant to the preferences of that age. It will be hamstrung. Could its greatest enemy be latent atheism?

Dormant atheism in the soul is disguised in a variety of ways, and was sown in the sin of our first parents, resulting in the blurring of God. What a pernicious masterstroke dealt by the "enemy of our souls!" Satan, knowing God could not be eliminated, sought to blur him and make him indistinctive. As God became blurred, Adam and Eve were brought into perfect focus. Self was exalted: "*you* shall be as gods," and this remains true. While it is wonderful that our spiritual cataracts are cured in the renaissance which the Holy Spirit engineers by his almighty power, this is by no means the end of the story . . . Oh, if only it were!

The Key

The Holy War introduces us to Atheism who, with other enemies of the soul, is apprehended and placed in the custody of the gaoler, Mr. True-Man. When questioned, he pleads "not guilty." But more significantly, Mr. Incredulity breaks out of prison, and after a search, could not be found. However, we read, "he ranged all over dry places."[26]

---

25. Strate, *Amazing Ourselves to Death*, 121. The reader may like to familiarize themselves with FWC Media Church and decide if this variety of "screen" worship fits the New Testament model for God-centered worship (112). Since the office of prophet is now obsolete (Heb 1:1-2, 1 Cor 13:9-13) Strate is unable to wear its mantle, but the accuracy of these comments is truly astounding.

26. Bunyan, *Holy War*, 177. Bunyan shows how Incredulity is able to give life to any nefarious character who lurks in the soul . . . Atheism included.

For this reason the Christian must be in for the long haul, not just be a "good time" disciple, rather one willing to wage war against this ancient enemy. In this, atheism must be thought of like any other antagonist who assaults the town of Mansoul, with greed, jealousy, pride and unbelief (soft atheism) to name a few, these are never far away, never completely absent from the life of the Christian, never mastered entirely in this life. If greed must be mortified, along with the rest, then we would expect soft atheism to need the same constant attention; attention is the key. With typical honesty, one of the Puritans lends his voice to confirm even his realization of this enemy. Under the heading "Humiliation" *The Valley of Vision* records this prayer: "Sovereign Lord, When clouds of darkness, atheism, and unbelief come to me . . ."[27] Perhaps the church today thinks it is done with atheism, but it must think again, taking a leaf from the book of the Puritans.

Camouflage

With such observation it is not difficult to associate with Craig Gay, since some of us have suspected for a long time that atheism has "done a job" on the church, yet this is a malady which Christians appear not to be aware of, because it is latent, like an undiagnosed fatal disease, it is influencing the whole constitution, killing us while we live. Very surreptitiously, it is able to go into hiding, camouflaging itself in pragmatism and rationalism, thereby making it nearly impossible to identify, root out and mortify (kill). It occupies a neat, ideologically "pigeon-holed" place ensuring that it is not easily detected, if at all. I suspect the church may be laboring under an old, convenient, overly simplified, truncated view of atheism. This textbook atheism is easily seen in the communist east, or much popularized variety of the West, that of Bertrand Russell and others. This is easily identified, the "them" and "us." The danger is that we seem unable to grasp how we have in so many ways become the "them." We need to move away from the strict stereotypes, look at ourselves, and conduct a rigorous examination, just like the Puritans mentioned above, and only then can we hope to deal it the necessary death blows.

Identity Parade of the Soul

In the UK and in the USA "church going" is still a national pastime, but do we suppose all these people really believe in God? Perhaps theoretically, but this hardly satisfies what may be regarded as believing and faith. The concern here is that this may be much more representative than we realize. Is it merely in "nominal circles" that the "form" the "mechanics" are performed, the "outward" of a Christian profession, while the *summum bonum* is absent? The radar we employ may identify our unbelief, but

27. *Valley of Vision*, 142.

when do we admit and acknowledge this unbelief for what it really is? When does it, as the text at the head of this chapter suggests, become "an evil heart of unbelief"? It is obvious we struggle to identify atheism and call it out for what it is, being more squeamish about this perhaps than anything else. We are easily fooled. We need the "identity parade of the soul." In the past, and still today, the identity parade is employed, while recognizing it is possible to get false positives. Nonetheless, the apostle is quite clear: "Let a man examine himself to see if he is in the faith" (2 Cor 13:5). Enter . . . the identity parade. The Christian needs to exhibit the qualities of the sleuth so as to eliminate suspects of an alleged crime, equally trying to put the finger on someone under suspicion, though while this may not be foolproof, the detective in us should be sufficiently developed to solve more cases than to fail. It is important to note here the detective work is with reference to ourselves and not our neighbor.

Under the Spotlight

Here are the questions: How innocent is our unbelieving? Dare we subject it to deep scrutiny? The Bible's assessment needs to be ours, or we will fail to properly identify this cruel enemy. The spies who returned in trepidation from Canaan were overwhelmed by *sight*. It was *sight*, not God which informed them, rationalism beating faith out of them with the most dreadful consequences for themselves, and the whole community. These atheists may escape lightly by our own weights and measures, but the measure of their crime is reflected in their punishment and the life long loss. God's measures are different from ours. The things which happened to all these people, Paul recognizes as having happened for the teaching benefit of the church (1 Cor 10:8-12).

Aaron at the foot of the mount, along with the anxious Israelites, displayed the same atheism. With Moses gone and the benefit of *sight* lost, panic sets in and, no surprise at all, the idol steps into the breach. Atheism's vital breath (so to speak) to mix metaphors is *sight*, "seeing is believing." The disciples in the imperiled vessel, as they perceived it, were flush with *sight*, the Lord of life was actually, *corporeally* in the boat, but anxiety overwhelmed them, and they did not, at that very moment believe in him (Mark 4:35-41). Thomas is an atheist following the resurrection, he believes but only by *sight*, "Unless I see" (John 20:25, NIV). Judas is an atheist and what shall we say of the others in the hall of shame?

Paul says we *live* by faith not by *sight*. It is only reasonable to ask: can the same be applied to us today, because it is apparently deeply "tempting to live as if God does not exist"? In the light of all this, should not God's civilization employ the most rigorous identity parades, questioning everything which points up *sight* above faith? Distressingly without this, the world of pictures, of images, will grow ever more powerful and their invasive influence will kill faith which alone is able to please God (Heb 11:6). Cheap bowls of soup are not worth exchanging thoughtlessly for a priceless birthright (Jacob and Esau).

Master and Commander

Craig Gay chooses the word "tempting": "Why it's tempting to live as if God doesn't exist." All around us we face the most challenging circumstances which threaten to overthrow faith. Personal faith in Christ as Savior is always under assault, always being questioned, always opposed, and understandably this alarms us, as it should. However, what appears to concern us rather less is the overthrow of faith which is the vital "living" by faith. The temptation is for the "life" of faith to be forever on hold, as stated earlier, a mere theory; this is not the faith which the apostle John speaks about, "a faith which overcomes the world" (1 John 5:4). The concern must be, that with such a mentality, the church may only treat God as a kind of figurehead, so that "life," daily life, is lived without him. This gives rise to the criticism of those who oppose God and Christ by looking at the church, accusing it of making God a convenience. Naturally these people do not look at God, they focus on those who purport to follow him. They are not fooled, and can discern clearly that the church, in practice, lives as if God does not exist!

By way of illustration, the church can be likened to a great sailing ship ploughing its way through the choppy waters. Such ships were remarkably well built of great oak timbers, soundly constructed to withstand whatever adverse conditions might prevail. What a nostalgic and beautiful image, drawing out our admiration. The powerful film *Master and Commander*, directed by Peter Weir, captures these images perfectly. At the front of the Acheron (the ship featured) there is a figurehead which suffers some degree of damage in a violent skirmish, and then immediately is lovingly restored, as if the figurehead was just as vital as anything which belonged to the vessel, even masts and sails. We observe the same kind of figurehead on the ship which conveyed Paul to Syracuse (Acts 28:11). Luke noticed "the heavenly twins" (NET) the pagan deities of Castor and Pollux. Now picture these giant ships with their sails filled, advancing with the figurehead at the bow, pointing the way forward giving the lead. Notice, significantly, despite the role of the figurehead, the mighty vessel is under its *own* power, unstoppable.

The reality is that the figurehead is a small insignificant token gesture without any real authority, "a nod and a wink," that if difficulties arise the deity can be called upon to help. All things considered the god would not be needed, as the power was in their *own* hands. Depending upon their training, expertise, ingenuity and intuition, with their "master and commander" at the helm, and their extraordinary seamanship, they "leaned on their own understanding" (Prov 3:5). Obviously the figurehead was unnecessary. It is to be understood the ship required the vital wind supplied by nature, but the rest was provided by themselves, unless they were to hit the doldrums. Christians may be tempted to rely only on their God absolutely, when absolutely necessary, when impossible circumstances force them, when all else fails, that is, when they hit the doldrums! When the doldrums of the lockdown struck, when God was absolutely necessary, a "figurehead" was called upon instead to alleviate the malaise.

We certainly need the Holy Spirit to work the supernatural renaissance to re-generate our dead souls, so as to speak life to the lifeless, which is what our theology teaches us. This is ingrained, as it should be, but it often appears as if the church can do the rest itself. Are we the "master and commander" of the vessel? A.W. Tozer alluded to this as he observed this condition in the churches of his day.

The unseen guest at every table

If the feet of rationalism and atheism are well and truly ensconced in the church, in a way like never before, then science was almost certainly the power which established them as a force to give faith "a run for its money." Science has won! It is science which has become the "unseen guest at every table!" The author, Mark Noll, charts the jour-ney and traces the gestation to the turn of the eighteenth century. It was then that American Evangelicalism in particular, held an admiration for modern science and willingly opened the door to it. Perhaps this explains the reason why Charles Hodge was ready to explore the question of evolution along with others. Noll seems to point to a "common sense philosophy" as a root. By the close of the nineteenth century a collision between evangelical and secular scientific thought had been forged, and as a consequence Hodge and B.B. Warfield were vested along with a number of others. (Incidentally Noll is not critical of this, indeed he rather applauds their readiness to embrace science the way they did and criticizes the modern narrow evangelical mind with its slowness to embrace the intellectually obvious).

Karl Barth's *Protestant Theology in the Nineteenth Century* explains what hap-pened. The guest was accommodated. He sees Protestant theology bending to ac-commodate the "liberal." "From the eighteenth century onwards, Protestant theology has acquired that obvious habit of looking round outside, at the circumstances and movements in the Church and the world, before venturing to speak, so as to be able to speak in a timely way, appropriate to reality and to the situation."[28] If it makes sense to say science has won, it is intended only to be understood in this way: science seems to have made Christians ashamed of faith as a "way of life," this has, in a large part, turned the church into a rational, businesslike institution which can be logically worked out on a spreadsheet . . . soft atheism.

Prove It!

The cause of this might come across with more force from the philosopher Kierkeg-aard: "When faith begins to feel embarrassed and ashamed, like a young woman for

---

28. Barth, *Protestant Theology*, 139.

whom her love is no longer sufficient, but who secretly feels ashamed of her lover and must therefore have it established that there is something remarkable about him— when faith thus begins to lose its passion, when faith begins to cease to be faith, then a proof becomes necessary so as to command respect from the side of unbelief."[29] As science dominated, faith shrank, and although science, as touching ethics, and particularly the doctrine of creation, is often rejected in conservative circles, all else is generally kosher, which is why we are slavishly devoted to modern tech. The church would have felt ashamed if it had not used its wisdom to engage with "Zoom," to the world the church would have appeared foolish because it needs to prove that it is always alive to that which is rational and reasonable.

Art vs. Science

Gay says: "Conservatives have also accommodated typically modern ideas and assumptions within evangelical theology in a number of material ways, and not without profoundly damaging results for evangelical churches."[30] Gay could not possibly have anticipated "screen" worship and "Zoom," but his remarks fit the present situation perfectly. Faith has shrunk, faith when ceasing to be faith must have *sight* at all costs, and the science behind tech makes the practice "common sense." "Zoom" is just this. If we were to conduct another simple experiment and subject congregations to look at frescos, works of art for help and inspiration so as to put fire into bellies, rather than digital, pixelated, screen images of the saints, there would be one almighty protest. Why? One is art, the other is science! The "unseen guest" helped to calibrate the scales. Looking back into history is helpful, because it is almost certain that some charlatans from the not too distant past would certainly have rubbed their hands at the opportunity to "get their teeth" into "Zoom" worship.

There is a link also in this chain with the practices of an evangelist like Finney, that is the collision of the evangelical and secular scientific thought. Gay says:

> Even faith and conversion would come to be seen in a scientific and mechanical fashion within American evangelicalism. In this connection, one need only recall Charles G. Finney's "new measures" for revival around 1830." Gay then brings this right up to date when he says . . . "the scientific spirit has surfaced most recently in the manipulative and technical orientation of the so-called "Church Growth movement."[31]

---

29. Gay, *Way of the (Modern) World*, 249, quoting Kierkegaard, Concluding Unscientific Postscript, 31.

30. Gay, *Way of the (Modern) World*, 250.

31. Gay, *Way of the (Modern) World*, 251.

It is just this "mechanical" which has become the engineering masterpiece of the church, backed as it is by science, the "tech made" "screen" worship then becomes a *fait accompli*. Furthermore, this is the open door to what Os Guinness describes as the:

> Holy Grail of the technologist (which he believes) . . . is the consuming search for the "one best way." (Finneys "new measures" were evidently the "one best way"). When this is found, the process immediately becomes self-directing. Everything that can be done must be done or the result is poor technology. At once human, moral and aesthetic values are either ousted or relegated to a lower position. Then only the technical is left to fight the technical .[32]

He goes on: "The debate over the Bomb illustrates this. During the national discussion in France in 1966, Jacques Soustelle expressed this view bluntly:

> "Since it was possible it was necessary." More telling still is the story of Robert Oppenheimer, widely known for his lack of zeal for the H-Bomb. What is not generally known is that he later changed his mind in favor of this super bomb because of the improved design he had been shown. Studying it, he exclaimed that it must be tried, because it was so "sweet and lovely and beautiful.""

Guinness concludes: "So when the best way is found, the procedure is automatic . . . To be in the possession of the lightening thrust of technique is a matter of life and death for individuals alike; no power on earth can withstand its pressures." As technology progresses, technique "modifies whatever it touches, but is itself untouchable.""[33] For all the scientists reading this, from the point of view of artistic expression, technique is, in many respects, anathema, it is the mark of the automaton.

Is "The One Best Way" Best?

"The one best way," if we did not know it, is wooden, lifeless, repetitive, unimaginative, soulless and deeply damaging, and comes up out of the machine mentality. Of course it is going to be "the one best way" to raise ten thousand chickens in one shed without the light of day, maximizing productivity, size etc, rather than allowing them to roam freely. Jacques Ellul suggests, "Technique cannot be otherwise than totalitarian. Technology (is) as a tyrant, in which "technique" is the psychology of the tyrant."[34] In this we see the soul is missing, the spirit, unlike technique, has no rapacious value, indeed who needs the spirit with technique? Technique empties a soul, it starves the soul, yet our God "desires truth in the inward parts" (Ps 51:6). In this we see the emptiness of mechanical love, mechanical giving, mechanical service, mechanical worship. In other words mere process may be "the one best way," but it is dead.

32. Guinness, *Dust of Death*, 133.

33. Guinness, *Dust of Death*, 133-134, quoting Soustelle, Oppenheimer, Ellul.

34. Guinness, *Dust of Death*, 135, quoting Ellul, *Technological Society*, 125.

Tragically, technique enables us to proceed with our eyes closed, Ellul again captures the sense of this when he says: "Our civilization is first and foremost a civilization of means . . . here man himself becomes the object of technique."[35] This is what I have often described as "emptying out," yet God's intention is to fill us up. Reading Ellul and others on this should fill the Christian with profound sadness and shame as it takes the children of this world to shed their light upon the church, God's civilization. "If then the light within you is darkness how great is that darkness!" (Matt 6:23, NIV). "And it is true that the children of this world are more shrewd in dealing with the world around them than are the children of the light" (Luke 16:8, NLT).

What is not at all appreciated is that where tacit atheism is established in the church, being undetected, the "technique," the "mechanical" will eventually win because it is manipulative and after all it is "the one best way." God being marginalized by the wonder, the power of a technique, and we see in our day how the doctrine of "creation" has become its victim. Apart from modern science's intrusion into matters theological and ethical, most Christians seem not to be aware that it has produced an objectification of our world, which is seen on display by wholesale utilitarianism in which Gay sees a link to modern technology. This objectivity he sees as an overgrowth resulting in the managed quality of modern life. "Zoom" worship is ultimately managed worship—managed, mechanical worship.

Insights

The exploration of this was in some measure touched upon by Martin Buber's "I-Thou" versus "I-it," (later translated as "I-you" versus "I-it") which is a very helpful insight as to what has emerged with "screen" worship. Worship can be managed, just as one would manage any business. Quite possibly the churches fell in love with "Zoom" so quickly because it provided just that management when no other could be found; Ellul grasped this in the 1950s when he wrote *The Technological Society* (1954): "To be in the possession of the lightening thrust of technique is a matter of life and death . . . no power on earth can withstand its pressures."[36] This gives sense to the speed of the experiment, it was entered into almost immediately, before we could even pronounce the word "COVID-19." If the world is viewed as an object then essentially our relation to the world is as an "it," then as McFadyen says, "The relation can only be exploitative and manipulative."[37] And Gay states this "prevents us from apprehending such things as beauty"[38] which for example would make burning the Amazon reasonable, after all its essentially a resource, a utility. The Amazon is "useful" to us in our utilitarianism as we recognize its "worth" principally in providing us with our vital oxygen, promising

---

35. Guinness, *Dust of Death*, 132, quoting Ellul, *Technological Society*, 19, 22.

36. Ellul, *Technological Society*, 21.

37. McFadyen, *Call to Personhood*, 123.

38. Gay, *Way of the (Modern) World*, 297.

within its vast array of unique flora and fauna, the pharmaceuticals to rescue us, and to eliminate our troubles. This is how we justify its worth, not in the first instance by its essential beauty, but its usefulness, Buber, a little abrasively and searchingly, asks the question, "Can mammon's slaves say You to money?"[39] The point is that our personal relations will be relegated, or as Gay says "subordinated to merely impersonal ones."[40] Who then cares if the Amazon is burned if "it" is manipulated? Equally the same might apply to worship, the church, the meeting in which we join *together* in the sight of God, and again this might be applied to reading one's Bible, which then becomes a task, a duty, similarly prayer, the worship service, or anything where the spirit in us points up "it", rather than "Thou". … "the flesh wars with the Spirit."

Finney's "anxious seat" is clearly tacit atheism, being mechanical, a technique, manipulation, as is Billy Graham's approach to "winning the lost" for Christ by employing his unique technique. Buber's searchlight exposes this: "The unbelieving marrow of the capricious man cannot perceive anything but unbelief and caprice, positing ends and devising means. His world is devoid of sacrifice and grace, encounter and presence, but shot through with ends and means."[41]

Beauty is Not in the Eye of the Beholder . . .

To clarify such objectification, this viewing the world as an "it," a "thing," we need only reference the obvious. Take the objectification which men have often displayed toward women, though not exclusively so. In this a woman may be viewed as a body, an "it" or a "that," her beauty may be even seen as a "thing," and consequently something to use. In this the woman is seen as purposeful. The sad explosion of pornography, which Tony Reinke exposes, also provides evidence for this, nor is it difficult to see the machine age of technique fulfilling the attitude of objectification, the soulless process of going through the motions. Reinke says: "Smartphones make free pornography easier to find than the weather forecast. Porn has always been the main driver in visual digital communications."[42] To confirm the near industrial nature of its exponential growth in our times, D.A. Carson in his book *Christ and Culture* confirms Reinke's assessment: "the income from the sale of porn in North America now outstrips income from the sale of alcohol, illegal drugs, and cigarettes *combined*."[43] This was in 2008! Gay says:

> The objective spirit is also quite obviously destructive of any number of relationships that it is possible to have with other persons . . . In the first instance,

39. Buber, *I and Thou*, 155.

40. Gay, *Way of the (Modern) World*, 300.

41. Gay, *Way of the (Modern) World*, 298-299, quoting Buber, *I and Thou*, 110

42. Reinke, *12 Ways*, 134.

43. Carson, *Christ and Culture Revisited*, 126.

the objective attitude essentially prevents us from apprehending such things as beauty, for anything that is appreciated only as a "resource"—that is, as something to be utilized—cannot really be apprehended as beautiful.[44]

"O worship the Lord in the beauty of holiness" must eliminate any vestige of "it" and only permit "Thou" to impress the occasion of Christian church worship as we actually engage *together*.

Aesthetics—Who's That?

In the civilization which is the kingdom of this world, the church of Jesus Christ is at once the richest (by virtue of the gospel), but also amongst the poorest. The church is undoubtedly poor, indeed the starving poor at a cultural level where it engages with aesthetics. In fact it is a moot point whether Christians ever specifically engage deliberately with aesthetics at all. This obviously gives voice to the impression given by the church that art is merely to be treated as an ancillary "thing," Christians appear to have little or no appreciation of the arts. Philip Ryken, in his book *Art for God's Sake*, gives a sad account of a young woman studying art as a major who became thoroughly sick of comments by Christians about art being "a waste of time, a field for slackers and weirdos."[45] This mirrors exactly my own encounter in the early seventies with church philistinism. Obviously none of this just dropped out of the sky, rather it is endemic, it is in the DNA of Christians, which some authors easily trace back to Puritan thinking; the inability to appreciate life beyond its utilitarian purpose.

John Marlowe, in *The Puritan Tradition in English Life*, says: "This attitude obviously prevented him (the Puritan) from regarding art as "useful.""[46] He thinks the arts were viewed merely as an "optional extra," but for our purposes, more significantly, he asks if: "this attitude towards the fine arts . . . has been injected into the English character? (by English Puritanism) . . . an exceedingly persistent residue."[47] It is impossible to avoid the overwhelming evidence for this in Christ's church, where the residue is to be found liberally. Wherever you go in the kingdom of God, this philistinism has been injected. Christians are not only ignorant of the arts, they are manifestly combative against them, being fearful of them.

Since the author's conversion to Christ almost fifty years ago, he has had the unfortunate embarrassment of listening to church people who speak boldly of Shakespeare as an idiot, and to hear the gasps and childish shrieks of those who anticipated encountering a Rembrandt or Rubens nude in one of our National Collections.[48] The

---

44. Gay, *Way of the (Modern) World*, 297, quoting Grant, *Technology and Justice*, 51.

45. Ryken, *Art for God's Sake*, 9.

46. Marlowe, *Puritan Tradition in English Life*, 102.

47. Marlowe, *Puritan Tradition in English Life*, 104.

48. Christians might like to consider: "Nudity is a state of fact, lewdness, to coin a phrase, is a state of mind." "To the pure all things are pure" (Titus 1:15, NIV).

ballet is dismissed as exhibitionism and the theatre as a place of degradation, the cinema as worldly entertainment, the TV, being the devil in the living room, along with art galleries where a subversive culture is to be encountered. Why read Plato, or *Meditations* by Marcus Aurelius, not to mention the danger of reading C. S. Lewis? Sad to say, when this manifests itself, God's people look like ignorant isolationists who may have more in common with the extremes of Islam; very uncomfortably Marlowe in the 1950s makes the connection with the Wahhabi Muslim. "We have then to distinguish between the basic iconoclasm which dominated the Puritan attitude towards all visual art, and which resembled, for example, the attitude of the Wahhabi Muslim today, and the incidental philistinism which was the result of the super-imposition, first of cultural isolation, and then of opulence, on to the basic iconoclasm."[49] However, Oliver Cromwell is a wonderful example of the opposite, when he moved to save Raphael's drawings and Mantegna's *Triumphs* of Caesar from destruction, which Charles II attempted to sell. But what is apparent Christians simply do not care, digging themselves ever deeper into holes of cultural darkness, where only a utilitarian emptiness awaits them.

All of this goes some way to point up the fact that we are profoundly deficient, empty of any cultural depth except that which science and tech serve up, consumed in vast quantities, and is naturally portrayed as entirely clean and beneficial for us. Malcolm Muggeridge saw the "void" created by all of this, leaving us all barren of anything which would speak to us outside of the objective spirit. This way of thinking is in the church meaning, when the sheer ugliness of bowing in front of a screen in the kitchen confronts the "worshipper," there are no reserves, no resistance … unable to fight even the alarm bells do not ring. The "beauty" of worship is lost, destroyed by the "one best method," but we cannot see it. Christians in their "screen" worship are unconsciously following, whether they realize it or not, the functionality given in huge part by Frederick Winslow Taylor in his celebrated treatise of 1911 "The Principles of Scientific Management" in which he identifies the "one best method," when he said "In the past the man has been the first; in the future the system must be first."[50] The system is the slave, a most willing subservient of the medium.

A New Environment

In the use of any medium we must admit an order, the medium always comes first, and our insensitivities to beauty and shallowness fails to halt proceedings, as the medium precedes everything. Strate clarifies this:

> In its most basic meaning, *medium* refers to something that goes in-between, and links elements together. And while a linear channel or pipeline fits this

49. Marlowe, *Puritan Tradition in English Life*, 101-2.
50. Taylor, *Principles of Scientific Management* 1911, 7.

definition, so does a substance that surrounds and pervades, that is to say, an environment. This is perhaps easier to understand in the age of the Internet, as that decentralized network has eclipsed older, more linear forms of communication . . . in reality, the medium has to come first. Before the source can create a message, there first must be a medium to construct the message out of, a medium such as a language or symbol system, and/or raw materials and methods such as paper and pen and the practice of handwriting, or electricity, a computer, and the ability to type on a keyboard.[51]

Before anyone thought of the content for a service of "so-called screen" worship, the first thought was not the content, not even God, but as always, the medium as the carrier is first.[52]

Since the medium is the dominant force in this worship, along with the absence of an aesthetic, no one is capable of asking the question as to whether beauty is being sacrificed. With no one feeling deeply, no one stops to ask how can we possibly engage with transcendence via a bunch of pixelated images. Because the medium is shouting, even screaming at the church to be used, "the one best way" makes it "common sense." Pre-occupied with the need for instrumentality, the objective mechanical spirit has no time nor the desire to consider beauty.

Both Craig Gay and Os Guinness are concerned about the loss of something in our objectified, technology-driven culture. On the one hand, the "Holy Grail of technology" which introduces "the Process," forces aesthetic values to be relegated or even ousted altogether, and on the other hand, the "overarching" objective attitude which renders beauty a "thing" is unable to be really apprehended. Indeed if Christians are culturally bankrupt of an aesthetic then the advent of "Zoom" left both them and the church exposed. The person standing in front of the Mona Lisa in the Louvre with the sole interest of capturing her on their *iPhone's* camera, to be able to say to friends, "Look at *my* pictures of the Mona Lisa" is not just behaving as a narcissist, but as someone for whom culture may just be another trophy. In many ways for this visitor to the Louvre the aesthetic means nothing, it might as well not have been there. In the same way, bereft of imagination and removed from the transcendent now possessed with a reductionist view of worship, the "Zoom worshipper" fails to see, like the photographer, what inevitably comes up is a projection of the self.

Beauty Vanished

Daniel Boorstin sees this projection of ourselves as a "declaration of conceit." A people raised daily, hourly on a diet of prestige are unable to grasp this for what it is: "old fashioned vice." We are gripped with the desire for "the means of fabricating

51. Strate, *Amazing Ourselves to Death*, 47-48.

52. In the created order, the sea (the medium) appears first followed by the fish which teemed and swam in it (Gen 1:9, 20).

'well-knownness.'"[53] Yet it does not register with us as ugly, there are no "tools" to confirm its ugliness, since there are no "aesthetic tools" to shed light on its darkness. Consequently, beauty in the beauty of worship has lost out. It is nonetheless true that beauty comes in all shapes and sizes, being as it is "in the eye of the beholder," and all that is written here is not to influence or shape our personal aesthetic view. A huge Jackson Pollock canvas can be viewed as beautiful (I think) equally a Mark Rothko, even a tiny droll watercolor by Paul Klee. Interestingly Klee's art, along with others, was labelled as "degenerative" by Hitler and his Third Reich. Klee's lovable diminutive work, beautifully and profoundly points to our humanness and imagination on a grand scale as he saw the world through unique eyes. When we encounter his work, *we* feel small, little wonder Hitler hated them. Hitler was consumed with the objective with "the one best way" . . . naturally his way! Perhaps if he had not summarily dismissed Klee and others, he might have gazed upon a different world, with an abundance of varied possibilities; we will never know. It is the varied possibilities of culture's riches which would adorn God's people.

I do try not to be too partisan about my dislike for Rossini's "William Tell Overture," or Ravel's dreary, repetitive "Bolero" which does nothing for me personally, but I am glad I have heard and know them, and I will continue to listen to them, as likely as not I am missing something! It must be stated others disagree and rave about them, beauty really is "in the eye of the beholder." But what if our eyes had been gouged out, and now we are unable to possess even a modicum of aesthetic to work on the soul, whilst at the same time, the soul itself is bombarded 24/7 with image after image of a never ending stream of inanities. What then? The answer, we become addicted to mediocrity, and as we plumb the depths of the shallows, there is no room in the soul for an alternative voice. The void prevails and uncomfortable as it is to highlight, for most Christians there is not even the option of "scraping the bottom of the barrel" for an aesthetic, because for them there is no "barrel."

This I confess is a gloomy picture, nonetheless an accurate one and more importantly realistic. When Os Guinness trains his analysis on McLuhan he traces in him conclusions which "leave us with a weary helplessness."[54] Uncomfortable as McLuhan's conclusions are they still smack of reality, the gospel of Jesus Christ is the only ultimate answer for helplessness. We need to wake up, the circumstances which tech forces, without any apology, leads to hopelessness, the addicted gambler and alcoholic will testify to the same. While offering considerable deference to Os Guinness, with respect, we must face reality. For myself I think both McLuhan and Ellul are more accurate in their pessimistic analysis, and in the present climate appear to be the most trustworthy prophets. We must face the fact there is no going back because there is a "before and after." Before the internet and after, before "Zoom" worship and after, the desperate scenes of weakness and vulnerability are of our own making. The gospel will

53. Boorstin, *Image*, 57.

54. Guinness, *Dust of Death*, 127

save our souls, but it seems it has no power to save us from the "god" of technics, in this I think it is right to be pessimistic. Having witnessed the "trajectory" of Christian worship over almost half a century, it is not at all unreasonable to be realistic. The "barrel," if one existed, would at least provide a chink of light, a moment's respite from the gloom. Like myself McLuhan held out some hope, he was not the "habitual pessimist" any more than Ellul before him, and as Guinness observes "he partially relieves this gloom by suggesting that in the person of the artist society has an "early warning system.""[55]

The Color Blind Church

When "Zoom" in its fancy dress came along, some Christian worshippers sadly strangers to imagination, became immediately "hooked" on the cheap novelty, but cheapness and ugliness found no warning voice, since our age is surgically attached to tech. Philip Ryken notes this about Christian bookshops, where a plethora of kitsch, of the cheap and nasty is to be found, where quality and depth are strangers, yet alarmingly the kingdom of God seems to possess no capacity to discern it. It is as if the age has swallowed us, in what Vanhoozer calls the "McDonaldization" of worship."[56] Instead we should have had the eyes of our hearts enlightened (Eph 1:18).

Maybe if we had learned in a healthy way to obsess over images of depth, greatness, and profundity, stretching our imagination, intellect and even our emotions, we might not have followed so closely in the footsteps of Narcissus. Boorstin comments: "The gods then decided to punish Narcissus: they doomed him to fall in love with his own image . . . When he saw his reflection his passion for this phantom so obsessed him then and there that he could not leave."[57] Bereft of a deeper seeing eye, without an imaginative aesthetic, the self is left alone and the narcissistic self gazes at the phantom, confirming we cannot leave, we will never leave, to our own degradation.

Sense and Sensibility

Kevin J. Vanhoozer further emphasizes the place of imagination: "Worship also requires the right subjective attitude: "spirit." The truth of who God is and what God has done for us engages not merely our intellects, but our whole being: not only our minds, but our hearts, hands and imaginations too."[58] God is the Father, God is the Son, God is the Holy Spirit and such truth must be received as truth, but such truth equally demands our imagination.

---

55. Guinness, *Dust of Death*, 127.

56. Vanhoozer, *Pictures at a Theological Exhibition*, 136.

57. Boorstin, *Image*, 258.

58. Vanhoozer, *Pictures at a Theological Exhibition*, 116.

The very presence and influence of a richer imagination might have saved the church from throwing itself headlong into something, about which even twenty years ago people would have felt a distinct embarrassment and unease. Now in our day not even the blush comes out, no doubt this has been eliminated by the constant feed of internet inanities. When we are void of sensibilities and sensitivities, the finer nuances, the rich tapestry of the exalted and transcendent God worshipped in the beauty of holiness, is reduced to a mechanism, an "it" ("it" and "Thou"). We have been bewitched! This is what happens when we lose sight of the fact that images of worship are but pseudo-events.

Surprise! Surprise!

Boorstin asks, "How can we flee from this image of ourselves? How can we immunize ourselves against its bewitching and allusive power?"[59] When our great art collections reduce the great art masterpieces down to t-shirts, coasters, sandwich boxes and the like, we know we are in trouble. They have become divorced from the soul and reduced to "it." When Monet's water lilies and Van Gogh's sunflowers appear on coffee cups and ties, our appreciation of the original, if we ever had any, is altered and the glory of the original is tainted. We are bewitched without care. Of course, there are those who tout the market mantra that this is good, this is democratization, egalitarianism, not to mention, in hushed tones, that this makes economic sense. Well, what a surprise!

Good Value?

Equally, it is no surprise that the masses who buy into it almost certainly care nothing for what is the original, and now the pseudo event, the pseudo-encounter, is all that matters; "here today gone tomorrow." In truth, the encounter with Messrs Monet and Van Gogh is flat and empty, being a pretense, a sham, inane, and only commercial. "Zoom" is all this and more, God commercialized. We are left with this question: who cares about the original? While people were "getting down to business," finding "the one best way" they lost sight of the hymn writer's words "O Worship the Lord in the beauty of holiness," because in the future the system must be first.

The "it" is in us

Our machine-driven age has made our world into an "it" more than ever before. The creation becomes an "it" at the hands of evolution. The grace of God in the gospel reduced to an "it" by the evangelists, the beauty of holiness to an "it," in "Zoom" worship, all three raped of their beauty and dignity being made to serve as a utility. In

59. Boorstin, *Image*, 258.

our besotted, rapacious culture we see anything, a woman, a man, a church, church worship, through acquisitive eyes, something to manipulate, something to be used. In this, "Thou" would be dead and the field left open for "it" to reign supreme, even in the church. The result: the glorious body of Christ becomes a highly functional machine, a utilitarian tool with a high cash value, out of which, by employing the right technique—any technique, we can grow a crop, even unto eternal life! The results will be incontrovertible and confirm the intrinsic unquestionable value of "it" over "Thou."

If exploitation is the natural result of such a mindset, i.e. a philosophy, then the native Africans were only a resource, the objective spirit bolstered by atheism could hear but one voice, its own, making "I" and "it" at the center unopposed, atheism is "I" at the center. In his book *The Call to Personhood* Alistair McFadyen says: "Intending someone or something as an object (God might be an object) is to intend the relation as a monologue . . . The relation can only be exploitative and manipulative."[60] When this monologue rules, anything can be manipulated "the one best way." Gay's analysis of the "overgrowth of an objective culture"[61] could easily be leveled against Christ's church. The worrying thing is it would not only be ignorant of such a condition, it would not care.

The extent of this philosophy is seen when even procreation is considered. It is no longer embarrassing for Christians to boldly announce, without any shame, their willingness to manipulate the military-like procedure in the conception of their children. This control technique gave the couple the advantage to even exploit the possibilities of achieving extended months of salary payments from their employers for maternity leave, depending on when the baby is born. Even the making of a child is seen in this partly for its cash value. The management, the control, the means end, "the one best way," the technique, the mechanics all are in us so completely. And whilst this is shocking, or at least it should be, evidently within the kingdom of God it is not. "Zoom" worship is simply following in a long line of acceptable, mechanistic thinking, this being one of the reasons why it was so easily embraced, and why it does not look at all out of place. Joseph A. Schumpeter draws a conclusion which sheds additional light on this: "for example, that it was the application of a kind of "inarticulate system of cost-accounting" to family life that accounted for the phenomenon of bourgeois couples having fewer and fewer children."[62]

Today it seems quite acceptable to see one's pregnancy as a utility, even the act of love making becomes a "thing" an "it" a mechanism, a utilitarian tool. This is the overgrowth of our objective culture and clearly J.I. Packer's "deep level worldliness." In reality this is the hearing of the "one voice" our own fallen one, this is the monologue.

60. McFadyen, *Call to Personhood*, 122-123.

61. Gay, *Way of the (Modern) World*, 296.

62. Gay, *Way of the (Modern) World*, 156, quoting Schumpeter, *Capitalism, Socialism and Democracy*, 24.

Gay pins it down perfectly when he says "The objective attitude is largely atheistic . . . spiritual relationality simply does not survive the process of objectification."[63]

The Revolving Door

In summary, joining the parts together as we must, the image of a revolving door serves the purpose best. I have often seen children from within a hotel lobby having fun in one, and amusing themselves. Unlike any other door, a journey is embarked upon, or so it seems, and it appears to have the ability to transport us, bringing us right back to where we started. Great fun! On the one hand, it is an inviting door, but at mid points we are decidedly locked in, stuck in the middle, especially so if the mechanism fails. But note, while we are required to do the walking in this revolving door, it does the pressing, forcing us in one direction, propelling us where we and it both want to go, there is no going back.

In the church where *"practiced"* faith turns out to be tacit atheism, this then is the place of entry, the driving force, the "master and commander," always tempting us to live as if God doesn't exist. As it presses on us in our frenetic age it forces the pace, this always propels us in the direction which requires sight, and since everyone is traveling in this same direction, the unbelieving world included, none of this appears strange. Above all else what matters is that we are getting to where we want to be, results are everything. Remember . . . this is "the bottom line."

At the mid-point of the journey, the conscience which only "now and then" thinks upon God, is hamstrung, the tongue sticks to the roof of the mouth. Although occasionally the revolving door might also get stuck, interrupting the journey with an unwelcome hiatus, there is no "well-hung tongue" to call out for help. The preferences of the age have so informed the conscience, making it powerless, so now society, politics, and the overwhelming majority in the church, all render it dumb. Once more this recalls J. B. Phillips words: "Don't let the world squeeze you into its own mould" (Rom 12:2). Unfortunately it appears we have done just this, and we are interminably locked in. There is now no way out of the revolving door, no escape, since the preferences are underpinned and endorsed by the scales of our own making, perfectly calibrated to deliver just the required reading. What on earth have we ingested, what have we joined to ourselves, what have we permitted and what have we excluded threatening our spiritual prosperity? The Lord of the church still warns us, "Take my advice" (Rev 3:18).

Where then does this leave us? Exactly where we started. The revolving door just goes on going round and round and, as we might expect, there are no surprises on this journey, since it is wholly mechanical and predictably utilitarian. All this causes not the least bit of concern, since all that matters is that the journey is made, and the

---

63. Gay, *Way of the (Modern) World*, 297–98.

machine will repeat this journey again and again and again. And because of the speed at which we are all spinning, the most alarming fact is that we are unable to see God is blurred by it all, but that does not seem to matter, since in this dizzy strife no one has even noticed!

CHAPTER 11

TESTING! TESTING! TESTING!

If a man will begin with certainties, he shall end in doubts, but if he will be content to begin with doubts he will end in certainties.

FRANCIS BACON

Again, I observed this on the earth:
the race is not always won by the swiftest,
the battle is not always won by the strongest:

ECCLESIASTES 9:11 (NET)

The Trojan Horse

UNFORTUNATELY WHEN "ZOOM" CAME CALLING at the church door, the locks were quickly unloosed to allow its entry, and in the nicest possible way like all tech, it demanded to be let in. As already explained, the "presence" of certain unfortunate "things" made access a formality, while the "absence" of others which should have kept the doors firmly bolted, meant any resistance simply melted away. Susceptibility to the world's thinking contributed to its installation, the conscience failed, fear and anxiety loomed like a dark specter. The business model applied its own kind of pressure to the door whilst the narcissistic, mirror possibilities "flashed their eyelashes" so the bolts were gladly unloosed. The entry of "Zoom" into the churches met with little or no opposition and while the average sheep trusted their shepherds to keep the doors locked and securely bolted, their hands would need the power of the Holy Spirit to do so. That power would have to come in the form of patience which is "the fruit of God's Spirit" (Gal 5:22, NIV); this patience in many ways would prove to be the most crucial factor in the experiment. Almost immediately the absence of patience unbolted the doors and the trojan horse was invited in. In years to come Christians may well ask "However did we come to this?" When the first significant test in modern times impacted the church, how did it wilt so easily? The answer will be the church had no patience, it failed in the vital hour when evangelical neurosis held sway. Along with this, our empirical powers, whatever they were, faded away. Not forgetting such thinking draws off both experience and testing. Observation, combined with examination through experiment delivers the result, or it should do. Ordinarily before we draw our conclusions we endeavor to subject our decision making to these processes. Strange as it may seem, or blithely ignoring the obvious, it may be just this empirical approach which has blinded the church to the biblical method of testing. When "Zoom" made its proposition (as the church interpreted it) to be the "divinely provided" carrier of lockdown worship, empiricism, as practiced by the wider world, convinced the church to become a "believer" and as such it was entirely unnecessary that it should run its own tests. Our vaccines, the food we eat, the water we drink, and a myriad of life's necessities must be implicitly trusted, all we need do is sit back and enjoy . . . no questions asked!

Trailblazers

Of course there are reasons why we lean so confidently on our laurels; the packaging possesses unlimited power and influence, things are dressed so seductively making the sale easy. Also we are "told" "what is good for us" and since everyone agrees (and they cannot all be wrong) we wilt at the knees. When something is scientifically "proven" (the Holy Grail) we may be assured "all is safe," "all is well" with the world, today whatever science touches is obviously given a "clean bill of health." Indeed one dare not question anything which has been authoritatively "signed off," to do so appears both backward and disrespectful. In this way whatever is being sold to us "holds all the cards."

We should be in no doubt, such a philosophy is merely a strain of humanism and while many churches may boast of its amputation, we can be sure it is alive and well, pulling the strings in Christian worship. Os Guinness thinks this brain child of the Renaissance, leading as it did to the Enlightenment, produced an "explosive confidence of the human mind . . . Man is the measure of all things."[1] He quotes the Renaissance thinker Leon Battista Alberti, "A man can do all things if he will."[2] The evidence is that in "screen" worship along with much more the church has surrendered to this humanism. When Guinness refers to the "wedge" between "reason and authority" speaking about humanism's "forward-looking thrust of science and the backward-looking stance of classicism" which Renaissance thinking delivered, it is hard not to recall Charles Hodge and others in their day bent to accommodate the "new" and "breathtaking" findings of science. In truth, those who readily accommodated science

---

1. Guinness, *Dust of Death*, 13.
2. Guinness, *Dust of Death*, 13, quoting Alberti, quoting Clark, *Civilisation*, 104.

were the trailblazers, making it possible to do what takes place in our churches today, and that with a smile.

When Mark Noll, who appears to be somewhat a champion of the "forward-thinking" evangelicals, extols what was achieved, he recalls Charles Hodge, along with William G.T. Shedd and B.B. Warfield and other notable names who had their disagreements: "They were however, united in believing that biblical interpretation needed a contribution from the day's best science, even as it exerted an influence on the application of scientific conclusions."[3]

In time humanism has forced the church to bend, but in truth it has shaped itself rather too willingly. These trailblazers, with their "breathtaking" scientific convictions liberally helped to deliver the church from its "backwardness" and the "shackles of its superstition." These in turn have brought us to a place where tech also enables us to completely "come of age." In time, as Christians evoked Hodge and others, evolution was near seamlessly joined to Scripture. In this, evidence was given (if any was needed) of further proof of the fact that, "Man is the measure of all things." One could easily imagine Knoll applauding the church of the 2020s for not being "backward in coming forward" as it experimented with science based tech. However, the church, inured by the possibilities, shrugged its shoulders and reaffirmed that it has the prowess if left unmolested, untested, to cross all the remaining unexplored frontiers: "A man can do all things if he will," thus making moribund tradition a thing of the dark past, divesting Paul's words so as to now say, "We can do all this not through him who gives us strength, but through our ingenuity which enables and empowers us" (Phil 4:13). Welcome in the Trojan Horse! We may be sure when hindsight is employed to reflect on the journey to which we are now committed, we will still remain puzzled as to how we ever got here. How did the Christian church arrive at this place so swiftly? How did it venture down the road of a completely new form of worship employing a medium which had never been seen nor practiced before? How was it introduced with relative ease, so seamlessly? My hope is that perhaps we do not need hindsight and the present enquiry will suffice.

Returning to the question once more, how could Bible-believing Christians (often renowned for their assiduous, scrupulous testing mentality) be induced to engage in a so-called act of worship through a computer screen, without anyone raising the alarm? Probably the answer lay in the fact that both the church and individual Christians possess as much "certainty" in themselves and their proven ingenuity, as they do in God himself and his word. Not least, if a fatal humanism is in fact at work in God's civilization, it must in the end result in "doubt," so that this one "small step" may turn out to be one "giant leap." But in every way this looks like a fateful leap into the unknown.

Another probable answer to the above question, though not necessarily definitive, is that digital dehumanization is already well underway, securing a critical foothold in

3. Noll, *Scandal of the Evangelical Mind*, 185.

our lives. It is exerting a profound influence, as much in the church as in the world at large. Recalling Postman's analysis, if correct, tech is untouchable, wearing as it does the mantle of deity. As the dehumanizing god gains greater traction within the church (which it must) it is only reasonable to assume that it will make further suggestions to God's civilization, by its very nature it must extend its arm of influence. Some may be reluctant to conjecture what the next "great idea" will be or the next "best thing," yet it would be naive not to think that the church will open its doors to more "light blinding" innovations.

The question as to how all this emerged is vital so that lessons can be learned for the future, so that mistakes are not repeated. Ordinarily when things go wrong in public life, enquiries are set in motion to get to the heart of the matter, yet to the obscurantists of the church such introspection might be deemed a waste of time. After all the "horse has already bolted" and there looks to be no way of retrieving it. But surely we can attempt to show future generations how to carefully lock the door so as to prevent further loss? For those unable to appreciate the scale of the dehumanizing role of tech in our world, one need only delve a little into the direction in which warfare is set to develop. Without most of us being made aware, the major nations of the world, the "key players" over the last five years, have been discussing the future of warfare as it moves ever closer to AI (Artificial intelligence). This is not about drones in the sky seeking out targets, but the chilling artificial intelligence making decisions as to who is to be killed. At the other extreme, but no less sinister and discussed already in these pages, is the sight of young people selling themselves through the medium of the screen. In addition there is the development of automated job interviews where employers use algorithms to assess applicants. Researchers of this practice reveal the obvious, job applicants feel dehumanized by the process of answering a set of questions whilst sitting in front of a camera . . . welcome to the future! This dehumanizing has a definite breadth to it and will certainly have its effect upon the church, the result will be a pejorative one. The "traditional," "real," "living," "actual" act of Christian worship will be undermined and the genuine reality of God himself lost in a mechanical maze.

Words of Wisdom

G.K. Chesterton once observed, "When people stop believing in God they don't believe in nothing they believe in anything." While this may not apply to all who make a Christian profession of faith, we should take care not to stumble at Chesterton's prickly words, dismissing them too quickly; they carry both a force and an application to what is written here.

If what has already been explored in this book conveys a semblance of truth, then at the very least it needs to be acknowledged that the church, in part, is not the work of the Holy Spirit at all, but the work of men. The Bible does not provide the injunction

"Cease ye from man" (Isa 2:22, KJV) for nothing. The "Hymn of Man" by Swinburne comes to mind as cited by Os Guinness: "Glory to Man in the highest! for Man is the master of things."[4] Guinness also speaks of, "The eruption of the importance of man."[5] Of course the point is that the pejorative effect is to "belittle," to make small, to depreciate. In warfare AI will belittle human decision making. Tragically this is happening to God, the church asserting its authority says to God, "Stand aside!" "Be little!" "Get back in your box!" while we organize things our own way. When God is skillfully "killed off" (by just a different method than that employed by Nietzsche) "people do not believe in nothing they believe in anything," but mainly themselves. As both the "golden calf" and the Tower of Babel could dehumanize, so also does our technology. It is surely impossible not to see that God is "belittled" when watching Christians attempt to "Do this in remembrance of me" (Luke 22:19, NIV) and recall the sacrifice of Calvary via a computer monitor, the result . . . we have not been "filled up" but "emptied out," dehumanized. The church is belittled, we are belittled, above all God is belittled.

As Chesterton's deafening words ring his timely warning, the church forces its fingers more firmly into its ears, confirming our susceptibilities and deep impressionability. Man, not God, is the conductor, and the church being the orchestra, delivers an uncertain sound and "screen" worship, like nothing else before it, plays an excruciating tune. Sadly, it is more than likely that this will fail to register, discussion will not take place, as the tech renders us "tone deaf." The tuning fork to test the pitch has been set aside and looks to be lost forever!

What Goes Around Comes Around

What is apparent is that history reveals failure after failure to test, at times shocking levels of credulity have worked unimaginable demise. Interestingly the church has been able to see through the "smoke and mirrors" of Charles Taze Russell (founder of the Jehovah's Witnesses) and of Joseph Smith (the Mormons), and others. Their outlandish claims of miracle wheat and stories of giant spectacles, both "divine provisions," no less (a claim sadly made for "Zoom," also) have been understandbly seized upon by critics. Not surprisingly, history does not look favorably on religious madness. But such claims are nothing new, as Diarmaid MacCulloch reveals some embarrassingly "toe-curling" accounts found amongst those of the "worthy" reformed faith. Practicing Protestants were not always free of the lunatic element . . . he explains.

> One Scottish minister was not untypical of Reformed preachers when in 1597 he brought to a climax the solemnities of his reception into his new parish of Gullane by demanding his congregation's "obedience to the voice of God in his

---

4. Guinness, *Dust of Death*, 17, quoting Swinburne.
5. Guinness, *Dust of Death*, 13.

mouth." Scottish ministers were indeed prima donnas of the pulpit, dramatic performers (perhaps the forerunners of today's church theatrics, emphasis mine) who might themselves claim or be awarded powers and popular reverence previously associated with the saints. The Reverend John Welch, minister of Ayr around 1600 (and John Knox's son-in-law), was reputed to be a frequent miracle worker, up to and including causing a sarcastic papist fellow guest at dinner to be struck dead, and on another occasion bringing a more godly young man back to life.[6]

These accounts, of which there are doubtless many, inevitably leave the church looking foolish, desperate, and credulous, difficult to trust and respect. More than anything they give voice to the on-going inability to "test everything," not only doctrine but also practices.

Christian Forensics Needed!

The most elementary of school science lessons taught that science is a discipline of knowledge, gained by ascertaining facts, deduced by testing. If we were in any doubt, the "test tube" confirmed this. The cancer survivor will give testimony to the critical place of phlebotomy, over and over again the blood is being regularly tested. It seems likely that blood testing will play a major future role in identifying the early development of many cancers to the saving of lives. The only obstacle to blood testing, carried out to ascertain the status of our health, will be ourselves: The fear of needles, discovering bad news, the trepidation of the treatment which may be required to save us from consequences which could prove fatal. It would have proved fatal for the New Testament church to have ignored Paul's command, "Examine everything" (1 Thess 5:21), and to follow the example of the Bereans, "who were more open-minded than those in Thessalonica, for they eagerly received the message, examining the scriptures carefully every day to see if these things were so" (Acts 17:11, NET). The thought is surely to leave no stone unturned, inspect, scrutinize everything, this is just what our medical examiners do to save lives. Paul insisted that the prophecies, proposed to the church, should be rigorously examined under the microscope. In this way truth could be identified from error, and if fault lines ran through the utterances they could be eliminated, not forgetting the words of Moses (Deut 18:22). Here was a safeguard to prevent error before it ever entered into the hearts and minds of the people, to poison the bloodstream of the church. The apostle John reveals this same testing spirit which was found in the church at Ephesus, "You have even put to the test those who refer to themselves as apostles (but are not) and have discovered that they are false." Revelation 2:2 (NET): "You have examined the claims." (NLT)

---

6. MacCulloch, *Reformation Europe's House Divided*, 1490-1700, 555.

All this was designed to be a defense, a safety mechanism to preserve the church for the future. The apostle John also makes clear the responsibility to test the spirits, "Do not believe every spirit" (1 John 4:1, NIV). Daniel in Babylon was willing to be tested for ten days to prove his theory (Dan 1:12). Here was a means which would bring confirmation one way or another. It would establish whether a vegetarian diet (in his case) was as good, if not better than the royal delicacies. He had no fear of testing! Thankfully, Fleming tested his penicillin because only then could he know its efficacy. The Germans tested their V2 rockets to great effect in World War II, and Londoners found to their cost that the Nazi testing program had paid off. Consequently the Kennedy Moon Missions, beginning with Apollo 11, owed much to the same German rocket scientists ensuring Armstrong's words will live on forever. Testing brings its rewards. Our cars are subject to rigorous testing, our food, water, and vaccines, much in the news today, none being permitted without certification arising from in-depth scrutiny. It is a great pity that while individual Christians have seen the need for this practice in all things worldly (perhaps the need for control and paranoia has a great deal to do with this) yet the church has avoided its God-given responsibility.

It may well be deduced from Paul's mandate to "prove all things" that he was in the first place establishing a safeguard against a dangerous form of individualism. His interest was the greater good of the entire church. The individualism of the itinerant prophets, then as now, needed careful observation and analysis. The individual independent thought, the egotism, all required complete transparency and, if necessary, were placed under the spotlight, and finally called out for their error.

The obstacle of credulity has always dogged the church, remaining a constant and ever present threat, especially as we believe unquestionably in the spirit of the digital revolution. As such it inevitably and, in particular, places the young, vulnerable believer in danger at the hands of the "all-knowing" guru who always knows best in everything and is trusted implicitly. These invariably possess the credentials like the first century mentors who were able to "breathe out" what was new and wonderful, to which the sheep gladly give their tacit approval.

Dare we say in this regard Paul would have preferred the church to begin with doubts as opposed to certainties, since the early church which began with certainties apart from God's word, breathed by bona fide apostles and prophets, might later result in doubt? Others who were unable to come to a knowledge of the truth suffered even more profoundly, "they believed the lie" (2 Thess 2:11), and "God sends them a deluding influence" (NET), a harrowing picture if ever there was one. "Better to begin with doubts than certainties" is Bacon's maxim and in this context a very enlightened one.

Patience Locked Out

As I write this chapter the sad and unhappy scenes of the Taliban taking control in Afghanistan are playing across our news channels, detailing how a new chapter in its turbulent history is about to unfold. How telling and revealing was an interview with one of the fighters who disclosed an Afghan maxim, they had arrived at this day because "while the West had watches they had time." Patience, practiced by an Islamic tribal power, had once more delivered the nation into their hands and this even in the face of the western "superpowers." Although the Taliban suffer western obloquy they demonstrate their own superpower patience, a power in which the church should have excelled, but in which it manifestly failed. We definitely had watches and we gave them far too much attention; God had time in *his* hands but we were not content with that, so without patience *our* hands were forced into a retrograde action. "The fruit of the Spirit" would have saved us from "getting down to business," "the bottom line," the "fear factor," the need for "social above spiritual," the "call of the idol," the "loss of power/control" While these unbolted the church door at a frantic speed, patience was locked out because patience would have demanded that the experiment be thoroughly tested. The tech, entirely at home based on science, had been given a "clean bill of health," a safe passage and for this reason patience was dismissed as an unnecessary intruder. It was as if patience had nothing to bring to the table. The church, driven by rationalism, gave the impression that patience was a nuisance, it was "a stone in the shoe." Understandably the obscurantists mentioned earlier, will no doubt deny this and argue that patience and its fruit was still at work. However, this does not explain why the bolts were loosed so quickly and doors flung open so readily to receive the new magic!

Postman's assessment of tech as a thing deified, gives us the most obvious clue as to how and why patience never caused the church to draw breath and test the experiment. It is hard not to be left with the impression that, because minds were governed, not by the word of God, but by tech-driven psychogenic processes, the appetite was in fact not for worship at all, but for church. Looking like the broken fragments of pre-Reformation times, the idol i.e.: the tech, silenced the means of the Holy Spirit to bring patience to bear on highly questionable expressions of faith. Consequently, it saw no need to test anything. Perhaps if Christians had been more conversant with the root meaning of patience they might have exercised it in this "unprecedented" moment.

The Long and Short of It All

The truth is when "Zoom" was let in, it was because we were "short tempered," just when "long tempered" was called for. William Barclay with his special brand of "know-how" explains how the Greek *makrothumia* "expresses a certain attitude both to people and (significantly, emphasis mine) to events . . . It expresses the attitude to events which never admits defeat, and which never loses its hope and its faith, however dark the situation may be."[7] He quotes R.C. Trench, who describes it as "a

---

7. Barclay, *Flesh And Spirit*, 91.

long holding out of the mind before it gives room to action or to passion."[8] Moffatt says *makrothumia* is "faith (which) holds out." The weakened psychogenic processes worked a "short temper" when the Holy Spirit would have worked a long one. This would have resulted in waiting and watching. "Long tempered" would have resulted in tempering the restlessness, and moderating the anxious impatience which nowadays modern life recognizes as completely normal (metals are much harder when "long tempered").

Not surprisingly, Gay sees the "modern project" to be under the influence of the thinking of Machiavelli, Descartes, Bacon, Hobbes, Locke and Rousseau. These thinkers significantly repudiated:

> the classical philosophical and biblical affirmations . . . This repudiation was based upon their belief that human beings could construct a much more peaceful and prosperous social and political order *more quickly* if left unencumbered by arcane philosophical disputation about "the Good" and invidious theological wrangling about the "kingdom of God."[9]

This means there is no time to wait for those who accede to the claims of the kingdom of God, the rush is on to achieve results, whether that be in the social, political or even the spiritual sphere. Gay's conclusion fits the "disputation" put forward in this book: "Modern, and now 'postmodern' philosophers insist that human happiness is something human beings must construct for themselves and by themselves more or less autonomously *now*."[10] "Zoom" provided the happiness constructed by ourselves for ourselves. Now under the influence of squeeze from the world, patient waiting was no doubt seen as waiting for the night rather than the break of day. Gay thinks our culture has "grown impatient with God."[11] The result—hope is placed in human abilities "God given" provisions such as tech affords us: "Not by might, nor by power but by my spirit sayeth the Lord" (Zech 4:6, KJV) has not just been silenced but appears to have been ripped from the pages of Scripture altogether.

If this impatience is hallowed in the post-Christian culture it looks as though it is also ingrained in the church. This would explain the explosion in the last seventy/eighty years of evangelistic campaigns which have been able to manufacture salvation on the spot, along with our recent experiment with "screen" worship. The "short temper" has taken hold. Much more sinister is that the "short temper" is not zeal to protect God and his glory rather to protect the glory of the church, which has the appearance of those broken fragments of Rome now under the banner of Protestantism.

---

8. Barclay, *Flesh And Spirit*, 91, quoting Trench.

9. Gay, *Way of the (Modern) World*, 309.

10. Gay, *Way of the (Modern) World*, 309.

11. Gay, *Way of the (Modern) World*, 313.

To Church Be the Glory Great Things It Hath Done!

Recently an article came to my attention written by a Christian Minister in the USA, admirably he was attempting to grapple with some of these questions analyzing "screen" worship. Sadly the undertaking was in vain, he became waylaid and entangled, not with a concern for God, but ominously for the church. This is a glaring fundamental error. The glory of God now appears to be overshadowed by the glory of the church, confirming the heart of the problem; we have lost sight of who it is we "church" for. The great writers of the past keep God in focus as does Dr. Reymond in his *Systematic Theology*. He believes church is supremely to be done not for ourselves but God himself. Do we really need constantly to be reminded "that in all things he might have the preeminence" (Col 1:18, KJV)? The Christian may well be justified in asking if there can ever be an "over emphasis" on the church. Surely it is vital to see Christians committed to their church, committed to its health and wellbeing, recalling at all times the centrality of the church in God's eternal purpose? Christ died for it and will return for it, the church is the body of Christ, and a glorious body at that. Understanding the nature and role of the church in the life of a Christian cannot be underestimated and yet it cannot be doubted an underestimation has led to the steep decline of places of worship. Consequently in the UK over the last century we have been blighted by the lack of a living witness in many communities. Evidently over the years a biblical perspective on church has been hemorrhaging from the church itself, it could be Christians are unsure of what it is and what it is for. To be sure a perspective does in fact exist but one drawn up along the lines of church tradition on the one hand and contemporary expediency on the other; both operate on the basis of a "means end" (that which looks advantageous). It will be argued that at all costs we must operate on rational lines, the "advantageous" must always be pursued to extend the kingdom of God. Tragically, it was just such logic which made the liberal church look at Christ and identify him as "the" problem since he is a "stumbling block and a rock of offence" (1 Pet 2:8, KJV) and as such proved to be a major disadvantage. He could be dismissed, jettisoned forever.

Our Social Institutions

Part of the genius of the Reformation was the ability to explain that the individual was to be unhitched from the church (the Church of Rome), since Christ, and not the church, was to be one's only salvation. However, church as an institution was never far away, and as church and state were established, a coalition of thought was imprinted upon the psyche. In England it remains to this day etched upon the social consciousness, meaning there is no removing "the church" as a first cause from the establishment. As remarkable as it may seem, it is the case that uninformed people in the UK labor under the delusion that if they are born in England, christened, baptized as infants in the Church of England, they are in fact Christians with a divine right to heaven. This comes to light when those of apparent faith announce themselves as "Church of England." It is noticeable that these are not first of all Christians, but Roman Catholics, Anglicans, Baptists, Presbyterians, Pentecostalists, meaning "church" not Christ becomes one's identification. It would be preferable if people simply spoke of possessing the Christian faith!

When the Roman Church ruled the lives and hearts of people it was in fact church that was in them and not Christ by the power of the Holy Spirit. The church operated effectively as an overlord, creating a dependency upon itself, especially by its power to wield its own unique brand of magic. We always crave the performance of some form of "institutional" magic, whether from the state or the church, needing someone, something to tell us what to do. The church has always created dependents, either intentionally or unintentionally. In comparison the dependency revealed in Acts 4:32–33 has been one which the church has not wished to practice nor re-create! It is tempting to think that the shift to individualism, born in the Reformation, has sown the seeds in today's church to prevent such a New Testament practice ever seeing the light of day (perhaps because it has the appearance of a notorious "ism"). "They had all things in common, no one called what he had his own!" However, what has seen the light of day is obvious, the church has again taken on the role of providing for dependents. Where ancient magic is no longer needed and New Testament models are deemed unnecessary, the church becomes a "divine support group," a social hub, a place where ironically God looks like the "support act" to the "divine support group."

Our First Love

In more ways than one the church now rises to become the center of people's lives, an act which verges on the sacrilegious. It becomes their devotion, their "first love," not forgetting Christ's rebuke to the church of Smyrna in Revelation 2:4: "they had lost their first love," namely Christ himself. We can be fairly sure the churches which John addressed were unable to act as "divine support groups," yet still some of them had "lost their first love." Nevertheless, particularly in recent times, the church has been happy to operate in this way, ensuring its dependents needed *it* as a panacea. The cornucopia of provision which the church then manages to serve up can have as much or as little of God in it as it likes, depending upon what is most advantageous for the times. In this regard The Church of the Latter Day Saints (The Mormons) is demonstrably impressive, where people, finding succor, fall gladly into its welcoming arms . . . and who can blame them? While not forgetting Christ's church also needs to extend welcoming arms, exhibiting deep compassion coupled with generosity and kindness, at the same time it carefully needs to *wean* people away from the church which might dangerously become "one's life and salvation." This *weaning* is a great skill but we should be under no illusion, there is no room, no latitude for error on this count, lest God and Christ become marginalized by the church.

Demonstrably the apostle Paul had only one life upon which he depended, and upon which others equally were meant to depend. He says: "When Christ, who is your life appears" (Col 3:4, NIV). Clearly beyond this, Paul was unwilling to be followed by anyone as their guru, he was unwilling to be "someone's life." He rebukes the Corinthian Christians "Was Paul crucified for you?" (1 Cor 1:13). He is pointing the early Christians away from himself and to Christ, and Christ alone. Care must always be taken to ensure that commitment is not to the church and its program, however laudable that program may be. Caution is needed so that devotion is not misplaced where affections become easily misdirected, resulting in the church becoming life and salvation itself, exhibiting the look of the cult, even a tragic throwback to the dark ages.

Who or What Is Loved?

In the last ten years as social media has burgeoned and has entered the bloodstreams of us all (astronauts excluded!), by its dominant presence, it has created a dependency which appears to alarm no one, least of all the church. This social is now the new normal and functions like a bedrock in society, which clearly needs it, and seemingly would be lost without it. The social itself becomes a veritable Savior. In truth, society is gorging itself on the social, and the insatiable desire for it shows no sign of abating. It is more than likely that this condition arises out of what Frank Furedi describes as "emotional deficit"[12] and "a one-dimensional preoccupation with the self."[13] Let us picture the people who have gravitated to the church above all exhibiting the need for a social "pick-me-up," of course God may be added to the program but the urgent need is not to be preoccupied with the divine, but with self. The result . . . the church becomes a place of therapy rather than a place of divine worship. Christians need to do some serious soul searching and ask themselves who or what it is they love "with all their heart and with all their soul and with all their strength and with all their mind" (Luke 10:27, NIV). Is it church or is it God?

In the Consulting Room

During the Reformation it is not difficult to both appreciate and visualize how great numbers of churchgoers discovered their business acumen and learned a great deal about commerce, but precious little about the kingdom of God. For many, their souls must have remained completely untouched, but were good churchgoers nonetheless. History reveals that motives at work in churches may be greatly suspect. The church,

12. Furedi, *Therapy Culture*, 26.
13. Furedi, *Therapy Culture*, 25.

with a people desperate for the social, becomes a place for casual "laissez-faire" therapy, a place where feelings are transformed rather than the transformation of one's life by the power of the Holy Spirit to the glory of God.

When lockdown gripped the church, those learning to hone their skills as socialites could not possibly dream of questioning "Zoom," the vast majority would never have read Paul's words about testing (1 Thess 5:21). To turn "Zoom" down would have been quite literally turning down a "fix." The need of church to countless people, especially in the UK, is one drawn along the lines of tradition. The "glue" of village life has always been the public house (the ale house) and the church, these were the places which afforded social adhesion. The people who frequented the "pub" for a social tipple several evenings each week, also attended the Lord's Supper in church on Sunday morning, and many still do.[14] The needs (not insignificant) are in fact one; the institutions exist to meet those needs, one trades in alcohol, the other religion, but it is undeniable that the social is at the center. It is always possible, and more than likely, that the constituency of a large city church will be made up (even within the membership) of those whose chief interest is the self. Interest in God and his worship (why Dr. Reymond thinks we should attend church) may, in truth, play second fiddle to the "desperate" social requirements of the "worshippers." In such an environment where people "attend" in vast numbers, no one sees the need to question what is redolent, the odor is sweet-smelling, so why on earth would anyone think to question it? The draw of the social with God added gives off a most pleasant aroma . . . but the fact is the social is bigger, much bigger than we care to acknowledge.

In the above, worshippers turn out to be, first and foremost dependents upon one another, and this is considered as just fine so long as they do not invoke the dangerous social practices of Acts 4:32–35! The words of the psalmist might be rewritten: "I constantly trust in the Lord, because he is at my right hand I shall not be shaken" (Ps 16:8). Church might be inserted and justifiably so where the Lord appears. "I constantly trust in the church." The church now is rendered a kind of amulet, and the dark ages loom large over our Protestantism. It is true COVID-19 has shaken many people to the core, anxiety levels have been greatly raised, mental ill health is manifest at terrifyingly high levels, (thankfully medication can greatly alleviate this, and we thank God for it, as we do for any other medication). We must never make light of the very real and profound mental health issues which people of all ages face, and more importantly the church needs to be a place where compassion and understanding can be readily accessed.

The obvious danger is the church will send out an incoherent message; mixed messages do nothing to alleviate anxiety. The use of "Zoom" and the requirement of it

14. The author is not an advocate of teetotalism and refers the reader to Professor John Murray, who provides an excellent reasoned argument on the subject. Murray raised the question whether those who are its advocates are in fact imposing their own standards of conduct, thereby dangerously attacking the sufficiency of Scripture. See *Life of John Murray* (1984).

did not testify to a people needing God by entering into the act of worship "together" because this we know is impossible. Instead, it provided vital "one-anothering" which was clothed in the mantle of respectable spirituality, while masquerading all the time as a bonafide act of Christian church worship. It was and is, in truth, a pseudo-event. "Zoom" was the "fix," but entirely the wrong one, and not at all conducive to those who needed to understand and see clearly in very cloudy days. These people were in no position to "test" anything, "the bottom line" for the socially desperate was no different from those who view the church in a mercantile way, and even more, their base requirement of "getting down to business" was just as much "driven." The problem which "Zoom" presents to the church is the unstoppable bleeding of the social into the spiritual, the flesh into the spirit, the kingdom of this world into the kingdom of God and the real into the "make believe."

"Reach Out and Touch Somebody's Hand"

To demonstrate this bleeding, a very helpful contribution has been made by the pastor of a church in the North of England who explains the success rate which "Zoom" has achieved in his church. He says it has enabled the church prayer meeting (an act of worship, emphasis mine) to outperform an "actual," in person, "together" prayer meeting. Far more attend now by "Zoom" where they can pray from the comfort of the lounge sofa. The "Zoom" prayer meeting has seen an increase in attendees and evidence of more willingness to pray. He readily admits that he cannot see the church returning to its former way of "doing prayer" since it cannot compete with the new levels of *success* provided by "Zoom." However, far more enlightening is his observation as to what is taking place in such "Zoom" meetings where he believes "it" works because God is engaged on a vertical plane, whilst by contrast, Sunday worship still needs the church to *actually* come together, enabling us to "reach out and touch" each other. Clearly he makes this distinction, Sunday morning/evening worship in person when *actually* gathered requires the horizontal, with us firmly center stage, whereas the vertical brings the church into contact with God; more enlightening by far, is his observation as to what is occurring in such meetings. In other words he is saying that Sunday is about "one-anothering," the social is the focus, with us firmly "in the frame," the church, not God, is number one. This is what "Zoom" thrives on and this kind of thinking proclaims loudly and clearly that Christians have failed to run any tests in the last decades as to the reason we "do" church at all, and to whom principally it is directed. When Sunday worship is viewed as being less an act of the worship of God than the prayer meeting, it is to be wondered what is being offered in the name of him who says to the angelic host, "Let all God's angels worship him" (Heb 1:6, NIV).

Manipulation

Tragically, this confirms what has been obvious for a long time, the social dimension in much of church life scores very highly with those in attendance. In this the church, like the "pub," is a meeting place where we can get together and "do" the horizontal, where, above all else, the self is satisfied and everyone can go home feeling good about themselves. But the subtle skill of manipulation seems to have eluded us. The book of Acts records the thinking of Simon the Sorcerer who thought that the power of God could be manipulated, purchased for his own nefarious purposes. Even as he "entered into the kingdom of God" he thought he could manipulate, just as he had manipulated people with his magic: "he had amazed (people) for a long time." We discover that even after believing and receiving the truth, his corruption led him to think that the outpouring of the Holy Spirit could be manipulated to his own ends like that of his former magic act. Peter both rebukes and informs him that his heart is not right before God (Acts 8:9-24). Acceptable Christian worship must have hearts which are upright before him, manipulating it by our own creative means, renders it, to use Reymond's words, "bankrupt."

Bereavement

Obviously this assessment of the social dynamic in the church as it touches on "Zoom" worship was not alone in its influence; it is not beyond reason that many other features are just as applicable. What is surely self-evident is that when government regulations closed the doors of the churches, people experienced a bereavement of kinds. Nor is this implausible, indeed it would be entirely understandable and particularly felt by those for whom the church has developed into a dependency. With the "smell of death" in the air we should not be at all surprised that in the gathering gloom, "Zoom" worship became their refuge. In an instant people were cut off, cut off not from God, but a "life" and "institution" where many find their "all-in-all," their acceptance, meaning, belonging, even the place where the most meaningful friendships and cordial relations have been forged. For some, the church may have become the only place that could be trusted, the place which felt safe and secure, a place to depend upon. In this, the church is often a wonderful "lifeline" to people, and in many ways it should be. However, the Achilles Heel is that it easily takes on the appearance of an ark, and even operates dangerously as one, either by stealth or default, doubling as salvation itself. Church in this way becomes family, it is a kind of second home and for some even a first. This is not to decry the concept of the church as a family or to deprecate it in any way. On the contrary, all true Christians are brothers and sisters adopted into God's family with Christ as their elder brother and God as their heavenly father (Rom 8:15-17). When understood biblically, this is the blessing of heaven on earth . . . a part of the Lord's Prayer is realized. Yet our first relation must always be toward God, and then towards one another.

When the lockdown came hearts were broken at the sight of church closures, the loss was immense, working a kind of bereavement . . . the loss was comparable to death. People were cut off, marooned in a sea of uncertainty, locked up in a place beyond imagination, no-man's-land. Such an encounter, never experienced before, probably brought on emotional and psychological deprivation (in the UK some churches were closed for over a year). Assessing the anatomy of "online grief," the Counseling Psychologist, Elaine Kasket, identifies what is a common response when we encounter loss: "It's not coincidental, then, that unpredictability and uncontrollability are two of the main ingredients in the mix when we experience stress and trauma."[15] She observes how digital technologies are now playing a significant role in coping with death, not surprisingly this is not to everyone's liking. She highlights the painful case of a grieving mother in Brazil, who discovered a memorial page on Facebook after the tragic loss of her daughter. The mother had to endure what she described as "This Wailing Wall" which exacerbated her suffering so much that she took the matter to court. Evidently the way some were coping with this death was through the visual mechanism of Facebook, and no doubt some will say: "Why not?" Digital technologies are after all capable of delivering anything (worship included), so why not memorial and grief?"

Where Does My Help Come From?

It is not asking too much to suggest the church suffered grief at the lockdown and found no coping mechanism in God himself. Mourning and melancholia would not require divine medication, rather the church could just as well deliver this medicine. Instead of the cure being dispensed from heaven, it would be found in "one-anothering" which would alleviate the emotional pain of separation, the screen being the "tool" to deliver it. If the writer to the Hebrews had been consulted in the first place he would have been heard to say "The Lord is my helper I will not be afraid" (Heb 13:6). We now know in reality (though reality was only an illusion) "Zoom" would be the helper to enable the lost contact to be regained, the dead could be reached after all! This scenario brings us back to Saul, desperate as he was in his loss to "see," to go beyond death, to cheat that which had shut him out. In his bereaving unpredictability he was determined to lay his eyes once more on Samuel, even if it meant doing the unthinkable, employing a medium.

Desperation will make one do the most outrageous and silly things, which in the end, might endanger our souls. It is possible that this "unprecedented" moment in our modern church history owes much to the feeling of bereavement, resulting in

15. Kasket, *All The Ghosts In The Machine*, 40.

unpredictability leading as it has to our uncontrollability. With stability gone, and the ship sinking fast, "screen" worship was the stabilizing ballast.

The Warrior[16]

In our society, hugely orientated as it is toward the "social," which must be accessed at all costs, we find ourselves in a climate where the church seems powerless, unable to test whether its life in practice is first and foremost for God or for ourselves. In such a climate we are growing in impatience, longing desperately to have our needs supplied. The church (where it still thrives) is in danger of outgrowing God, and "Zoom" is perfectly placed to ensure *we* do not just maintain *our* market share but continue to extend *ourselves*. The voice of John the Baptist echoes down through time to deliver us from ourselves, if we would but listen to him and if, like him, we are prepared to test ourselves, comparing ourselves not with ourselves, but with God (2 Cor 10:12). Only then, can we say "He must increase, but I must decrease" (John 3:30, KJV). "He must become more important while I become less important" (John 3:30, NET). The concern must be that "church" is more important in the lives of many professing Christians, far more important than God himself.

With the social requirements pressing the church, albeit with unspoken demands so as not to give the game away, there was no time for patience, needs must be met immediately, mental fragility especially demanded it! Uncertainty required ministry by the church, the provision of its unspoken therapeutic program, unwittingly this program is depended upon. When the COVID-19 lockdown was enforced the church's over emphasis on church (not God) revealed the brake cable of patience had long since snapped and ran away at some speed. Patience, the strongest of all warriors, had long since laid down his weapons, now looking fatally wounded.

More Haste, Less Speed

We know that when anything picks up speed it can be quite exhilarating, the thrill is a dopamine hit which often requires repetition. On the flip side, speed may result in a crash with fatal consequences. In this speed-driven climate anything which fails to "keep up" is judged by comparison to be glacial, not "moving with the times" as judged by the speed merchants. But may the case not be made that God is also slow? It is inconceivable, when reading the Bible, to trace out God's nature as one characterized by haste ... there is no rush about God. The Son of God was never forced into a frenzy, circumstances never impacted him, compelling him to act rashly. Even when pressed, in what looks like an emergency, regarding Herod's plan to kill him, he simply instructs the anxious religious intelligiencia: "Go and tell that fox [Herod] I

---

16. "The strongest of all warriors are these two—Time and Patience" (Leo Tolstoy).

do this today and that tomorrow ..." (Luke 13:31–32). Clearly, situations never mastered him. The church of today would do well to recall the words of the apostle Peter: "Christ also suffered for you, leaving an example for you to follow in his steps" (1 Pet 2:21, NET). William Barclay observes: God's "slowness is not dilatoriness; rather it is patience."[17] The Christian mandate must be to reflect God at all times in the entirety of life, and especially in the church. History, right up to the present day reveals an astonishingly rash haste, which at times has tragically derailed and scarred it. In the winter of 1692 the "godly" Puritans of Salem (colonial Massachusetts) moved swiftly to extinguish their first demoniac, the tragic victim of alleged sorcery. It would take only four months from the first "demonic noises" until Bridget Bishop was hanged in June of that year. This was followed by nineteen others who suffered the same cruelty, still others perished while incarcerated. All these innocent souls were dispatched in haste, in a frenzy, which began in February 1692, concluding in May 1693, confirming church/religious madness often wears a dark ensemble. It would be all too easy to dismiss these examples as irrelevant and extreme. But are we not all children of our time? Quite possibly, future generations may judge church worship conducted through a "screen" as quite deranged. The actions in Salem were almost certainly to ensure the longevity of Christ's church by preserving its purity. History judges their zeal, but not kindly . . . the jury is still out on twenty-first century "spiritual" enthusiasm.

Church history recalls the development of many theological strands, and developing alongside the theology has been the inevitable practices which the theology endorsed and permitted. Thankfully much of it was deeply considered and deliberated over, such as the great confessions. Erasmus must have deliberated over the Greek text to reveal the intrinsic errors which Jerome's Vulgate contained, and which the Catholic church depended upon. Other theological strains like those of the Pentecostal and Charismatic persuasions have tended to lean toward the need of a "quick fix," anxious as those Christians appear to be for prescience, i.e., the need of foresight, especially visual evidence of the power of God (not forgetting Romans 1:16: "The gospel is the power of God"). Despite all this, compulsion cries out . . . "Oh that God would rend the heavens and come down" (Isa 64:1, NIV). This may lead to patience being denied with its effects being thwarted to make way for a form of instant gratification.

Other varieties of this find voice as the church constantly excites itself by every little turn of events, be they local or global, which are a "sure" sign that Christ's *parousia* is imminent. Realms of the outrageously fanciful and extravagant prophetic predictions are "researched," but no matter, it staves off the "short temper." In turn this has the effect of calming the nerves bringing a measure of reassurance which after all, confirms that "something is happening," and by these we can avoid the danger of "growing cold," vis-a-vis "Zoom," thankfully now we have something to look at! But patience would have done this more perfectly, encouraging us to "hold fast," to "endure" and "wait patiently" for Christ's return, "not knowing the day nor the hour."

17. Barclay, *Flesh and Spirit*, 94.

In this we would learn of God who is slow, thankfully slow to anger, merciful and gracious (Exod 34:6, KJV) this will teach something vital about living the Christian life. Jonah learned of God's slowness, God was willing to wait for his disobedient servant so as to be gracious to a "people who could not distinguish their right hand from their left" (Jonah 4:11). We, on the other hand, would have been quite unwilling to wait for Jonah: "Better to be patient than powerful; better to have self control than to conquer a city" (Prov 16:32, NLT). Saul was in a rush to *see* Samuel employing the Witch of Endor, a *medium* so as to meet his immediate need of *seeing* but his tragic loss was profound, the brake of patience, the long temper was dead in the one who stood head and shoulders above the rest,(1 Sam 28:3-25; 1 Sam 9:2).

Daniel Boorstin concludes his book, *The Image*, "We must first awake before we can walk in the right direction. We must discover our illusions before we can even realize we have been sleepwalking."[18] Our age of tech has put us into a trance, and like the magic induced by the shaman we remain mesmerized, becoming dependent upon it. Saul was in a "trance," (at the hands of the shaman) reality had drained from him, he sleepwalked to his doom. What we need is to wake up and discover our illusions. Only as patience does its work on the "short temper," and as we study God, will we learn to do due diligence and rigorously test, test, test everything which our age presents to us as fantastic and credible.

Enquire, Probe and Investigate

If Israel heard about troublemakers in a town who misled the people to worship other gods, they were bound over to make enquiry, to probe and investigate the matter thoroughly (Deut 13:12-15). This was Paul's instruction to the church at Thessalonica: "Test everything, prove all things" (1 Thess 5:21, NIV). Barnes in his notes on this text explains the original word as one applicable to metals i.e.: the assayers test. This would mean the assay office would have the power to give the vital hallmark to a metal. It might have meant a tedious, lengthy process by fire, but the hallmark could only be ascribed when the metal was subject to testing. Barnes says:

> The meaning here (1 Thessalonians 5:21) is, that they were carefully to examine everything proposed for their belief. They were not to receive it on trust; to take it on assertion; to believe it because it was urged with vehemence, zeal, or plausibility. In the various opinions and doctrines which were submitted to them for adoption, they were to apply the appropriate tests from reason and the word of God, and what they found to be true they were to embrace; what was false they were to reject. Christianity does not require men to disregard their reason, or to be credulous. It does not expect them to believe anything because others say it is so.[19]

18. Boorstin, *Image*, 262.

19. Barnes, *Notes on the New Testament*, 61.

It is to be doubted that any church which took up "screen" worship followed Paul's pattern. Furthermore, it might be unthinkable for a humble sheep to raise it with the shepherds of the church, had they done so they would have probably received nothing other than short shrift. Of course many would not have even dared to question this practice, believing its veracity because their leaders confidently, unchallenged, ploughed on, just as the churches did who supported the Graham campaigns, the comparisons are uncomfortable but obvious.

Immediately following prove/test all things we read "hold fast that which is good" (1 Thess 5:21, KJV). Was "Zoom" good for the worship of God? Was it probed and thoroughly examined? An enquiry was needed to search, to question closely, leaving no stone unturned, thus providing the answers.

The British Government has announced that in the future there will be a public enquiry into the COVID-19 crisis. No doubt a senior figure such as a high court judge will be commandeered along with a vast team of lawyers to look at every single aspect of the failures and successes of the Government's handling of the crisis. Their remit will be to amass the evidence and however difficult, ask all the relevant questions. Such enquiries are usually long, drawn out, costly, painful affairs. The problem is they almost always take place after the event/the fact. The hope is that such an enquiry will prevent a similar occurrence. In the case of "Zoom" the tragedy, I fear, is there will probably never be an inquiry because no one will be prepared to acknowledge the fault. This book highlights the need to hold an enquiry, to ask as many of the relevant questions as may be raised with limited resources, to probe the matter as thoroughly as possible. Whatever conclusion the reader reaches from the evidence set out in these pages, it is at least hoped that an acknowledgement will be made that this was an attempt to question a practice, never before seen in the churches, and one thoroughly untested. None of us have New Testament prophetic powers or a crystal ball, but it is not unthinkable that another deadly pathogen will emerge to test the church of the future.

Does "Zoom" pass the test for church worship and gain the divine hallmark? If the answer is "yes" then we must prepare ourselves for anything in the future to present itself as an acceptable medium to be a carrier of the worship of God. Of course some churches will draw the line and unquestionably demonstrate a deep hypocrisy and a confirmation that the church has its own calibrated weighing scales. After all, over the years, many churches have refused even to allow projection of hymns and songs for worship, thus eliminating the need for hymnbooks and song sheets. Presumably in the "actual" worship this was considered a "worldly" step too far. Others will harness the medium and justify its use along with all the other aids and helps to assist "sight" worship. The most precious thing the church possesses will inevitably morph again, and the contorting of it will, in years to come, point more to a "digital art" than to a divine life. Hybrid worship, like cars, will become the new accepted model.

In his book *The Dangers of a Shallow Faith*, A. W. Tozer has a chapter titled "The Irrepressible Law of Consequence" and quotes at its head Haggai 1:7 (KJV): "Thus saith the Lord of hosts; consider your ways." This is plainly what the churches did not do. "Long tempered" would have given a place for considering our ways, to allow for testing, but it was deemed unnecessary. Tozer writes:

> The human mind is so constituted that it must consider something; so it compromises by considering other people's ways. The Pharisees were a class of people who knew the sins of everybody but themselves. They considered the sins of the harlot, the tax collector and the drunkard, but they never considered their own sin at all. A voice is speaking to us in the Word and out of heaven, saying, "Consider your ways"—look closely and consider seriously.[20]

Had the church done this and tested, tested, tested, it would have not only been following a biblical pattern but also it would have reflected the recognized "norms" of the world we live in. Curiously in this the church did not follow the world's example!

Vaccine, Pro or No?

By and large most of us take safety for granted; our modern world has tried to eliminate the contrivance of happenstance from daily life. Consequently, we all tend to be confident of the things we use, assuming these have undergone serious rigorous testing: but cars are recalled for faulty brakes, breast implants have been scrutinized after dangerous failure and in the UK, the domestic water supply has been inadvertently poisoned. All of this adds to the nervousness of multinational companies, who know the potential of damaging lawsuits which can be brought against them. Not surprisingly, when COVID-19 struck, almost immediately the testing mentality was imposed, this time on individuals, failure to test was seen as a matter of life and death.

At the time, life (albeit a broken one), could only proceed with a measure of normality if we were willing to comply with the testing regime. On the horizon though, and emerging at lightening pace, was salvation in the form of vaccines—the race was on to crack the codes of the all powerful pathogen. Quite understandably, some people questioned, dared to doubt even the speed of the enterprise, since the gestation to develop such vaccines ordinarily takes up to a decade. But those who championed the salvation did so by giving comforting reassurances that the testing could be trusted, even if it had been "shoehorned" into place in little under a year. Others drew attention to the very tragic story of "Thalidomide" used in the late fifties and sixties as an antiemetic to treat sickness during pregnancy, which resulted in some birth defects.

Regardless, the desperation for an instant solution, not unlike that seen in the church, saw the roll-out of the vaccine to great effect. Whilst these (thalidomide and the vaccine) are uncomparable, the warning is clear, blind trust in the powers that

20. Tozer, *Dangers of a Shallow Faith*, 71.

be, whoever they may be, can be fatal. The reader should be in no doubt, the author is quite indifferent to the "fors" and "againsts" of this debate, and judges no one for their personal views. Though comic remark might look out of place here, both these new innovations (vaccine/new worship) bring to mind the humorous observations of Warren Buffet (Financial Crisis 2008): "It's only when the tide goes out that you see who is swimming naked!" The nagging thought remains: would Christians have been so willing to receive the alien body into their bodies had it never been tested at all? But then perhaps Christians are far more precious about their own lives, than the life of God in the church, though it might just be that the new "sensible science," which, like the new "sensible worship," meets an age where in-depth scrutiny is denied by the clock.

Albeit this has the appearance of further church demise, and however uncomfortable, it falls to the author to highlight a dreadful retrograde step which will lead, if it has not already, into a state of undress …the tide must go out one day!

Here are the lessons for Christ's church, if it is willing to learn them. Without this blueprint of patiently testing *everything* which kindly suggests itself to help us with our worship, we will see the frightening emergence of more creative chimera, the grotesque product of our worst imagination, the likes of which many of us thought we would only ever see in the confines of the darkest religions.

Once again we should recall Francis Bacon's words: "It is better to begin with doubts and end in certainties," and this strikes a vital note of humility. We do not know until we know, and that only when we have rigorously, thoroughly subjected matters to deep scrutiny. Under the spotlight of testing, uncomfortable as it may be, we may have our doubts confirmed, but from a biblical perspective, our worship can never be an experiment, it must always be clothed in certainty, because only then may we call it what scripture demands . . . acceptable (Heb 12:28).

CHAPTER 12

CONCLUSION

*Technology . . . the knack of so arranging the world
that we don't have to experience it*

MAX FRISCH

*I have striven not to laugh at human actions, not to weep at them
nor to hate them, but to understand them.*

BARUCH SPINOZA

*Do not be deceived. God will not be made a fool.
For a person will reap what he sows*

GALATIANS 6:7 (NET)

Final Thoughts From Outer Space!

TO EXPERIENCE ZERO GRAVITY IS obviously something "out of this world" and very
few have tasted it (to date around five hundred), perhaps in the future those with sufficient funds, along with the help of Messrs Branson and Bezos, will be able to indulge
their desire for the trip of a lifetime. At least for now, my own outer space adventure is
confined to my imagination, but clearly not mine alone. As the year 2021 progressed,
it has been illuminating and gratifying to observe others who have also decided to
ascend to the same vantage point, so as to scrutinize what we on planet Earth have
willfully inflicted upon ourselves. I can thoroughly recommend the advantage I have
gained (elevation of course does not imply superiority), though in my writing I have
never intended to persuade anyone to give up their technology, the only design has
been to "clip the claws" of modern tech as I saw its dangerous impact upon God's
civilisation. Resistance is to a technologically dependent life, one which is proving to

be dangerously addictive, and now one which impacts the church. Let no one ever forget the apostle Paul will not permit anything to master him (1 Corinthians 6:12). Essentially, I have only sought to examine the one issue, whether God may be acceptably worshipped by his people *together* through a medium, a television screen, a computer monitor or a mobile telephone. This approach is not at all dissimilar from Owen's examination of a single issue explored in depth in the "Death of Death"—one subject, many layers! Necessarily this has led to iteration, but in turn, this hopefully enables the reader to access the main argument in every chapter.

The Fog

Since most Christian people in the UK decided to engage in "screen" worship (apparently 80 percent of churches), I acknowledge I am in the significant minority, but not quite a minority of one. A dear, old, departed friend often gave the reassurance: "One plus God is a majority." In undertaking this work, I could only put pen to paper because I believed "God was in this place." From the outset, my observations convinced me that Christians, with very good intentions, were genuinely uncertain about the emergence of the new worship, but participated nonetheless. This critique is written with those uppermost in mind, in anticipation that it may help to chart a way through the self-imposed fog. When Charles Dickens opens his classic, *Bleak House*, he does so by comparing the Chancellor's Court (a place where justice might be found) to a thick London fog. Lincoln's Inn Fields was the court where legal London was in a fog: "Fog up the river . . . fog down the river . . . Fog on the Essex marshes, fog on the Kentish heights . . . fog all around them."[1] I wonder, if Dickens wrote today, would he, with his powerful descriptive turn of phrase, see us exposed to the same? My two assistants, unashamedly with candid honesty, admit that when lockdown "screen" worship was presented to them they felt somewhat in a fog, which had descended without a moment's notice, no one appeared to have light to penetrate it. Ordinarily clear thinkers, they were not derailed in their faith, but, to coin a phrase, "sat on the fence," believing this to be a *grey* area. No doubt the behavioral scientist could instruct us as to the "whys" and "wherefores" of this, but for now we must settle for the obvious—the fog had descended.

In conclusion, it is hoped that the reader who has dared to encounter the "loving resistance fighter" also understands the sympathy he feels for anyone led astray into new, but obscure paths. If the "loving resistance fighter" appears strident, it is not from an elevated perch of supercilious superiority, rather, it is the recognition that a life-long immersion in the visual arts has enriched his cognition and erudition, giving to him the sensitivities of the canary in the coal mine, used to warn of noxious gases. Thankfully, for now, the air in the church is just about breathable, but for how much

1. Dickens, *Bleak House*, 3.

longer? As I witness more and more *actual* congregational loss, my conviction grows, we need to engender more and more depth in *actual* worship . . . our civilization is crumbling fast. Finally what is written, I believe is needed more than ever as we try to dispel this unpleasant fog which still lingers, preventing Christians from *seeing* true worship, this will, by its very nature, cause fatal accidents in Christ's church.

I take for granted not everyone is enamored by space travel and the virtue of exploration on distant shores; meaning the work of the astronaut can sometimes appear irrelevant, and a total waste of time to those earthbound in their imagination. For a little while longer I must go on breathing a different atmosphere to draw together the final threads of this work. My hope is that it may be possible to dispel this unpleasant fog which, by its very nature, lingers and causes dreadful accidents.

The Millennial Experience

Oscar Wilde said (as only he could) "Experience is the one thing you can't get for nothing." Experience costs us! In 1999 David Bowie was interviewed by the BBC flagship news program "Newsnight," and when speaking about the new emerging tech he said, "We are on the cusp of something exhilarating and terrifying," dismissing the idea that the new tech was merely a "tool," describing it instead as an "alien life form," one which might reach the rank of apotheosis (emphasis mine). Regrettably, the church did not share Bowie's opinion and mistook the "alien life form" for just another "benign tool." Some, recognizing the size of Bowie's remarks, saw it as a "prophetic" contribution, something very difficult to argue with. It is said that one of the traits identifying millennials, is that they have little interest in the way their forebears did in "possessing," "owning," and "investing" in *things*, but instead are committed to buying experiences. It has to be said all of us in some measure thrive on buying an encounter, we crave experiences of one kind or another, exhilarating ones if possible. In the introduction to his book *Stuffocation*, James Wallman explains how in a later chapter he will show: "why experiences are better than material goods at making us happy."[2] Almost certainly this is because we often find life tedious, becoming exasperated by its irksomeness. Like a panacea, holidays come to the rescue, and are able to eat into our so-called drudgery. The desire for experience(s) of an exhilarating kind is nothing new, being common to most of us, and as the exhilaration of experience continues to grow, it breaks new ground, not being confined, not in the least restricted, always evolving. Alien life forms are enormously popular!

My heart veritably leaps at the prospect of standing in the National Gallery (London) to gaze at Giovanni Bellini's (1435-1516) Doge Loredano, which in my opinion is one of the greatest paintings ever made. I never tire of the experience, returning again and again, having a thirst to repeat the same. A casual observer might be forgiven

2. Wallman, *Stuffocation*, 28.

for asking how this is possible, yet as a matter of fact I have been in awe, studying the masterpiece for fifty years, never being wearied by it. As Oscar Wilde observes: "Experience is the one thing you can't get for nothing," meaning there must be a price attached, which for me is an eight hour expensive round trip to London to gaze at a painting. This example confirms the truth seen in many experiences: we are willing, more than willing to pay for them, thereby revealing how much they are valued. Bungee jumping, roller coaster riding, opera-going and church-going are all experiences which cost. In a way it seems appropriate that they do cost so that a value may be placed upon them. Love and to be loved is an experience upon which we place a high value, but when we no longer have a value for love, the experience is lost.

Costly But Free

Wilde's appreciation meets its match when we consider the experience of knowing God. The gospel is free. The grace of God costs nothing . . . "Nothing in my hand I bring simply to thy cross I cling."[3] The experience of coming to faith in Christ is entirely a free gift (Eph 2:8), nor dare we detract from it as an experience. The Christian faith is not only one of knowing through the revelation of scripture, we do not receive it in purely propositional terms but thankfully we also experience it. The one who has faith in Christ has encountered him personally. The *knowledge* of acquittal, being declared "not guilty" by justification, in turn brings peace, and this peace with God is an experience (Rom 5:1). The hearing of one's divine acquittal lifts the roof on the soul, producing an experience, as must the reality of Rom 8:1 (NIV): "Therefore there is now no condemnation for those who are in Christ Jesus," and equally "If the Son shall set you free you shall be free indeed" (John 8:36, NIV). What an experience! If this is not true then we are mere automatons, making, for example, the glorious riches of our hymnology (courtesy of Newton, Charles Wesley, Horatius Bonar and others) the product of miracle working rather than the heartfelt experience arising from faith. Ultimately the indwelling of the Holy Spirit, who is the Spirit of Christ, is not only the knowledge of him, but a living experience of him. Knowing him in this way (if words are to mean anything) must exhibit the reality of experiencing him. This means the spiritual life which he actually imparts is not, nor can it be, *real* apart from the experience of it being *real* which in turn must be corroborated not by the church, not by any human being, but by God's word alone in the power of the Spirit.

Taste and See . . .

In writing this critique of "screen" worship I have chosen to reference my encounter with cancer, hoping that it would be useful as an example, and in turn that it might

3. Toplady, "Rock of Ages," hymn.

speak to some who have also made this journey. Only those who have experienced cancer can possibly speak about it in a personal way. Those who "walk the walk" can "talk the talk," the rest is theoretical knowledge. We know life is never short of experiences, some of which we wish we had never encountered, but thankfully God invades our lives with his Spirit, delivering the most remarkable of experiences. "My cup runneth over" (Ps 23:5, KJV) is one of them. "O taste and see that the Lord is good" (Ps 34:8, KJV) is an invitation to an experience, an encounter with the beneficence of almighty God. The seeing (not literal) is the result of the tasting, and since such an encounter is offered, the one who dares to taste personally will discover for themselves the promise is not vain, because it always lives up to its billing. Nothing of this kind can ever be offered by the world since "all the promises of God in him are yea, and in him Amen" (2 Cor 1:20, KJV).

Seduction

Seduction comes in all shapes and sizes, and usually one way or another delivers up some new experiences, of which we may have previously been unfamiliar. The promise which the serpent laid before Eve was a brutally, seductive experience, which enticed, beguiled and captivated her, ensuring she was completely ensnared. If, "ye shall be as gods" (Gen 3:5, KJV) was to work its deep magic and be capitalized upon, it would require some kind of visualization. After all, what other way do we suppose she could apprehend or comprehend the disfiguring, rapine promise? The offer was one of an entirely new experience, and therefore had to be persuasively of a seductive nature. The suggestion to Eve was an introduction to something new, something hitherto outside of her experience, confirming the unknown is not always frightening. Since that day we have shown how easy and prone we are to seduction by new experiences. In fact it is alarming, so little seduction is needed to secure our interest, our desire then for experience becomes a quest, rendering us pliable in the extreme.

Quite possibly when this seduction is analyzed it demonstrates what is really at stake, we are on a journey in search for the "ideal," the "ideal" being perfection. What could be more "ideal" to the mind's eye than the offer to become gods (not forgetting Adam and Eve, despite their perfection, were human)? The serpent offered an unknown experience to Eve which would be gained through her eyes being opened. In this way she and her husband might reach beyond the "limited" confines of the serpent's suggestion, providing an open door to a new world of new experiences. Daniel Boorstin, subjecting "the image" to his unique brand of analysis, points out the merger of the ideal with the synthetic: "'Ideal-thinking' and 'image-thinking' are the differences between our thinking before and after the Graphic Revolution."[4] Without any reference whatsoever to the events in the Garden, Boorstin thinks the first great

---

4. Boorstin, *Image*, 201.

seduction in history was where the seducer's appeal was increased by disclosing his art. For anyone to vainly attempt to defend "screen" worship as if it was not an art form, would be trying to stand on the point of a pin. The seduction of the screen in itself is an art form, quite apart from what appears on it. The screen is an experience, a seductive one at that, where we ourselves may even become "as gods." The thrust of this book has been toward the fact that "Zoom" cannot deliver worship, but it can deliver art (albeit of a very poor quality). In our quest for the "ideal" (a different ideal) and one which has nothing to do with perfection, our precious, priceless goods will have been plundered right from under our noses.

Alternative Facts!

Following in Eve's footsteps, the church seems unable to comprehend the seduction, captivated and hypnotized by the promise of the "new ideal." The neon god convinces the church that the "world can be its oyster." While Eve contemplated the possibilities of the "new ideal" through the opening of her eyes, in her vain imagination she failed to grasp that an increase in knowledge does not necessarily result in greater wisdom. Today we labour under this delusion: More knowledge does not of necessity make us more wise. "The fear of God is the beginning of wisdom" (Prov 9:10, NIV). Indeed the experience of the fear of God should be instrumental in driving out of us the futile pursuit of the "ideal" experience which is always presenting its seductive offer. It not only provides the winning ticket for the lottery, but also the "ideal" man or woman, the "ideal" holiday of a lifetime. The truth is we are not unlike our first parents, prone to the lure, the *subtle* lure (Gen 3:1, KJV). "Zoom" worship is not "ideal" i.e.: as in perfect worship, but for the bereaved church it was the "perfect fit" for the circumstances. Even if it could not deliver the experience of "real," "actual" worship, the tech could lure us, deceive us, into believing the lie . . . we were not there *together*, oh but we were! In the last fifty years tech has undoubtedly delivered breathtaking, even life changing experiences at such lightning speed, therefore we should not be surprised if we feel we now belong to the gods. Like the world in a spin, the church has been unable to catch its breath, with its heart racing at the "possibilities," caught (blinded) in the headlights, the potential new experiences clinched the deal. It did not occur to the church that this "tool," which had taken its breath away, might in the end leave it gasping. The thirst for the experience of "worship" via a screen obscured the unpredictability and unreality of the exercise. Boorstin's observations apply once more: "We fill our lives not with experience but with the images of experience."[5] The saying is true: "The first step in any journey is the largest one," and in this experiment it was the largest, most unpredictable one. The bungee jump is always somewhat unpredictable, but the lure of the experience shuts out the voice which cries "unpredictable and dangerous." Dr.

5. Boorstin, *Image*, 218.

Susan Greenfield makes the same connections: "Anyone who eats knows the consequences of eating too much, and anyone who gambles is always aware of the possible outcome. But the thrill of the moment, be it the sensation of the taste of the food or the excitement of the roll of the dice, trumps the consequences."[6]

The desire for the experience gets the better of us. If in our times we are conditioned by image, being certain of its rewards, it is obvious we will struggle when the "ideal" in this form of image is presented to us. Boorstin thinks the image is "always exaggerating expectations,"[7] trading in alternative facts. Perhaps this is what Eve bought into, at least in her mind's eye, the exaggerated expectations which she must have visualized. Furthermore Boorstin sees our deep fascination with the "process of fabricating and projecting the image"[8] (recall the young woman with her camera photographing art in the Pergamum Museum in Berlin, in Chapter 5), which Camille Laurens describes as that "two-dimensional death."[9] "We are all interested in watching a skillful feat of magic,"[10] creating what Kellyanne Conway infamously called "alternative facts"! Magic, what an experience . . . "Zoom" magic, wow!

To the would-be worshipper, no matter the unpredictability, the need for experience shuts down any dialectical discourse. As Robert K. Merton observes as far back as 1964, "the conflict of propaganda takes the place of the debate of ideas."[11] The lure of a new ecclesiastical experience was not simply a "new way to worship" but, more significantly, to experience oneself and others via the screen in "worship." It leaves us wondering whether with the click of the fingers, as Ian Lesley very astutely remarks about social media, "a switch was flicked which said be human in a different way."[12] Experience par excellence! Did Christians bending over a screen need to be human in a different way as they attempted to worship? I believe they did, because the medium demands it. The medium refuses to allow us to be ourselves, it will not permit natural. Watch the Oscar winners every year on the "red carpet" performing, receiving their accolades as they stand in front of the camera, but this time for the reporting news channels, the actors just go on acting, the medium demands a different way of being human.

Were the "Zoom" worshippers exactly the same in front of a screen as they were in *actual* worship, or was the switch flicked? Perhaps we need to ask what it means to be human before God's presence. If we are uncertain, and even reticent to countenance such an awesome thought, let us consider the medium of warfare and its power to alter the mind. Countless former combatants give testimony to this, as in the field

6. Greenfield, *Mind Change*, 95.

7. Boorstin, *Image*, 198.

8. Boorstin, *Image*, 199. viii

9. Laurens, *Little Dancer Aged Fourteen*, 136.

10. Boorstin, *Image*, 199.

11. Merton, Ellul, *Technological Society*, Foreword.

12. Lesley, "BBC Documentary," David Baddiel, Dec 2021.

of conflict they were altered, this experience changed their lives forever. It was one thing to fire live rounds at an inanimate target, a straw dummy or such-like, in basic training, but to fire a red hot projectile at living tissue in war would prove for many to be an experience which made them less than human, leaving them scarred. They were now required to be human in an entirely different way.

The sight of oneself on the screen in "worship" is something which thankfully none of us ever experience in *actual* worship, but "Zoom" changed this allowing for the seduction of the instant opinion poll to work its captivating power by inevitably bringing the "worshippers" themselves into sharp focus. The churches which were quick to boast of their increased numbers attending "worship" via "Zoom," were evidently well aware of the instant opinion poll, and by announcing it, they confirmed that "lockdown was not that bad after all."

The world of church worship had now been so arranged that we did not have to experience it in reality. Caught in the headlights, with our breath taken away by the wonder of it all, Christians failed to realize their experience was fake, it was not one of church worship at all. Frisch was right: "tech can so arrange the world that we don't need to experience it." Picture the flight simulator providing the opportunity to fly a great commercial aircraft or fighter jet, of course useful for training but not the real thing, as everyone using the simulator knows, and would never describe it as *actually* flying an aircraft. At this very late hour, and at the risk of sounding condescending, is it too robust to point out the obvious? The simulator does not *actually* have wings, nor Rolls Royce engines. It does not *actually* have cabin crew nor a hold for baggage. Why? Because it is *actually* not an aeroplane! This can only be confused with reality as we live in a make-believe world of illusion and alternative facts! It seems no matter the impossibility, the desperate search for the ideal can deceive us by taking our breath away.

Following Christ's words in John 4, the one who went up to Jerusalem to worship by accessing the "Holy City" (as a medium through which to go to God), was in fact deceived, just as those who make this same pilgrimage today. These worshippers are as much in the fog as the one exiting a flight simulator believing that he had *actually* flown a 747.

True worship is the jewel in the crown of the church when rendered to God by the power of the Holy Spirit *alone*. Only this will supply the genuine experience of a "living" encounter with God. Great care must always be taken in God's service, worship must be true in every part, it must be the "ideal" lest the experience turns out to be synthetic. "It is impossible to use God and worship him at the same time,"[13] and "worship that costs us nothing is worth precisely what it costs."[14]

Since experience is the focus of this final chapter it seems fitting to reference King David's dark experience of God's wrath, a display of his displeasure arising from

13. Blanchard, *Sifted Silver*, 329.
14. Blanchard, *Sifted Silver*, 330.

David's self-confidence and lack of faith (2 Sam 24). The prophet Gad had informed him of God's wishes in the wake of the census disaster: "So David went up as Gad instructed him to do according to the Lord's instructions" (2 Sam 24:24). Historically churches often followed this very principle in worship, namely to do *only* what God had *actually* prescribed, often called the regulative principle. Now a new challenge faced David: Should he respond positively to Araunah's "freebie" . . . was it just a generous "provision" of the Lord? It was being "handed to him on a plate," he would certainly have saved himself some inconvenience and unnecessary expense (to worldly thinking—a no-brainer!). What was not to like about this provision? With reference to the earlier chapters, the genius of pragmatism/rationalism would suggest this was looking a "gift horse in the mouth"! But despite the temptation of convenience, David realized there was only one way to please God, the short-cut was out of the question. "I will not offer to my God burnt sacrifices that cost me nothing." The answer to the external had to come up from the heart, the heart overpowered him. As cited earlier, the very idea of worshipping God through a "screen," comfortably sat at home with the cat on one's lap, and a hot cup of coffee, has the appearance of the caricature about it, but caricature has a way of bringing home the truth with particular force. The worship service offered to God as a sweet smelling savor must be true, it must be ideal, in some measure it must be sacrificial.

The Echo Chamber

That a new church acolyte should emerge in the form of the neon god really ought to be no surprise, the church has always displayed the need to keep moving on exploring new frontiers, especially expanding *itself*. Of first importance, it must be noted, this is not the much needed, ongoing, continuous spiritual reforming which the church always needs. Little wonder that the church has often fallen into the arms of "kind benefactors" who wished to give it a generous "helping hand," from "state support"[15] to powerful backers with "deep pockets." Luther, as we know, had his Friedrich the third (the Wise) the elector of Saxony, where politics played a major role in enabling the Reformation to become established. For a variety of reasons the wealthy and influential have played their part, and continue to do so in the establishment of church civilisation. The Lady Huntingtons and Lord Shaftesburys of this world, not to mention William Wilberforce, the politician, have lent their not insubstantial hand to the cause of the gospel. In my native Yorkshire, Titus Salt, of Saltaire fame, not only built a model town but also an extraordinarily impressive Congregational church in its midst. When an average Yorkshire church building might have cost the princely sum of £800, his contribution was nearer £16,000. Although his wife desired and obtained an elevated

---

15. Most churches in the UK register as charities so as to maximise tax breaks on their income. Joining hands with the world is not so bad after all! Christ, unlike the church, would brook no confederacy with the world: John 18:36.

box so as to oversee the Sunday proceedings, separating herself from the other Sunday worshippers, he resisted her wishes with great stealth, insisting upon them both sitting each Sunday with the rest of the congregation. An important thought: what pressure on the people to express vital faith in God whilst being beneficiaries, not of the riches of heaven, but those of the earth.

God's Unusual Friends and Allies from History

Coming up out of the echo chamber are some very strange noises which can only be described as both romantic and novel in the extreme . . . "Zoom" is a provision from God! "Zoom" users in the church might like to inform the multibillion dollar company of the divine mantle which it can now proudly wear. The same romantic notions proliferate in Christian circles, revealing God's remarkable preferences for certain world leaders, where, depending on which side of the political fence you sit, you can decide for yourself where God "casts his vote." Similarly, many of us (thanks to church history) have gleaned identical notions about King Henry VIII, and God's endorsement of him. This is a lesson in life explaining the very real dangers which we face regarding something like "Zoom." After all anything can look untouchable, charmed with the divine stamp of approval on it!

A more comprehensive reading of history, beyond just the evangelical, is vital if we are to gain an accurate picture providing balanced working models which we so much seek. Tracy Borman in her epic work on the life of the Polymath Thomas Cromwell, quotes the critic: "William Cobbett, who denounced Henry VIII as a "tyrant" king and his chief minister (Thomas Cromwell) as "the brutal blacksmith" . . . a Machiavellian schemer."[16] John Foxe of *Foxe's Book of Martyrs* fame, writing a full twenty years after Cromwell's death: "credits the minister with spearheading the English Reformation,"[17] whilst others are less fulsome in his praise and speak of his "ruthless" hypocrisy. Picking one's way through the historical minutiae may never bring up a successful nor satisfactory conclusion about Cromwell. Was he in fact God's man, or God's man and the king's man, or neither, just his own man? We may never fully know. The Tudor king on the other hand is hardly a character about whom we need to speculate, being married (so-called) six times, probably (according to Archibald Robertson) syphilitic, and neither Catholic nor Protestant, who in the end "threw" his friend Cromwell "to the wolves." Notwithstanding all this, a Bible was printed in 1535 at Zurich, dedicated to the king presumably in recognition of his association and close proximity to the God of truth. Like the digital royalty of our day he must have been seen as "God's provision," regardless of the fact that his life bespoke more of the Prince of Darkness than the Prince of Peace. During the upheavals of his reign there were those in the South of England who had good economic reasons to give thanks

16. Borman, *Thomas Cromwell*, 390.
17. Borman, *Thomas Cromwell*, 389, quoting Foxe, *Foxe's Book of Martyrs*.

to God for his beneficence, no matter how dreadful, how pernicious, how malevolent a benefactor, but a benefactor all the same. The aforementioned people always have good reason to thank God for thinking upon them. From within their own sixteenth century echo chamber, we can easily imagine those who were able to personally benefit from this brutally, sexually deviant king, anxious as they must have been to recognize his divine qualifications. None of his malevolence mattered if he was the "tool" to deliver his subjects from the tyrant of Rome, even if he achieved it by his own tyrannical, evil machinations. It is tempting to think that the people of the mid-sixteenth century possessed, just as we do today, the same rigged calibrated weighing scales, which always suit our personal preferences and purposes. Weighed on these scales, Henry was a divine provision in an exceptional "time of need" (not dissimilar from our own) in which anything goes, in which anything may be endorsed for the greater good and the glory of God. However, it is hardly likely that Anne Boleyn thought of Henry in this way, but then it depended upon which side of the axe you fell! It must be admitted God has some extraordinary friends!

What is more, it is very unlikely that the one in such an "echo chamber" will ever venture outside to hear another voice . . . there would be so much to lose. If they did, they might just get a *sight*, not only of our growing dependencies, but also where friendships and associations might lead in the future. Once committed to Henry's cause it might have proved impossible to retreat, the very real possibility of loss of limb or life would certainly have educated the would-be dissenter, as Cromwell found to his cost.

In retrospect it might be easy to laugh at some of the outlandish claims of God's so-called "provisions" for the church, or even to weep over them and possibly, as some have done when recalling the outrages of the church, to respond and develop a root of bitterness. Throughout the writing of this critique I have endeavored to be led by Spinoza's spirit of wisdom. It is better to gain understanding about church pragmatism and rationalism and highlight them, attempting the same by understanding our new idolatry and social dependency. These are worthy of effort to gain deeper understanding as to just why we are being shaped the way we are.

The Loving Resistance Fighter

God's word directs us to "speak the truth in love" (Eph 4:15, NIV). Paul did so with the Galatian Christians, but it engendered a spirit towards him which forced the question: "Have I now become your enemy by telling you the truth?" (Gal 4:16, NIV). What has been written in these pages is not at all out of kilter with the history of good criticism, which will always have its place, and, as suggested in the preface, will always be needed. Hopefully what has been written will not be discarded as perfunctory, nor as pedantic. It may appear that there is a surfeit of criticism, or even a caviling spirit, be that as it may, the issues dealt with needed a thorough examination to reveal the sheer size of the complexities of matters considered. C. S. Lewis thought criticism was important enough to write a book on the subject, *An Experiment in Criticism*, worthy of anyone's time who cares to assess literature beyond personal likes or dislikes. A healthy dose of constructive criticism can do us all good . . . "Let the righteous smite me; it shall be a kindness: and let him reprove me; it shall be an excellent oil which shall not break my head" (Ps 141:5, KJV).

Constructive Criticism

Criticism is in itself a difficult tool, none of us know how to perfectly use it. I have attempted to avoid being unduly vitriolic and should anyone doubt this, for a sight of vitriol in its "perfection," I point the reader to the "Two Attestations" provided in the opening of John Owen's *Death of Death in the Death of Christ* (1647).[18] Stanley Gower and Richard Byfield can school us well in the art of invective, as they were used to warfare "in" and "out" of the church, where we, by contrast, might be described as more of the "snowflake" variety! In view of this and Spinoza's maxim, I have endeavored to use the language which would best fit the seriousness of the case set out, and upon this I make no apology. By virtue of the fact that I consider "screen" worship to be an act of naked inveiglement, a profound act of seduction, I have not resisted the criticism which it clearly deserves. All Christians who read this may like to make themselves familiar with Paul's words: "*All* scripture is given for correction, for rebuking," to the end that we might be "thoroughly furnished unto every good work" (2 Tim 3:16–17, KJV). This should help any would-be vitriolic critics of this book, to stop and count to ten, or at least listen to the warning words of the author David Berlinski, "The Devil's Delusion." He opens with a quote from Sam Harris' *Letter to a Christian Nation*. Sam Harris writes that, "His fiercest and most 'disturbed' critics are Christians who are "deeply, even murderously, intolerant of criticism."[19] It is to be hoped that those who take issue with this book, do not follow in the footsteps, to quote Scripture: of those who are "swift to shed blood" (Rom 3:15, KJV).

I have referenced Dr. Billy Graham and his approach to employing the "Invitation System," his "tool" to bring seekers to Christ. To many he may be the exemplar of the twentieth century evangelical success story, but I find fault with his methods (as I am at liberty to do). Does this suggest in any way that I could hold a light up to the evangelist who clearly loved people and longed for them to know his Savior? Certainly not! My comments regarding him are specifically about his techniques and practices which I find reprehensible, questionable, ditto . . . the new "screen" worship! To highlight Dr. Graham in this way is not to say that others were not as excited as he was by these methods, yet to steer clear of the "leading light," as a new expression of

---

18. Owen, *Death of Death*, 35.
19. Berlinski, *Devil's Delusion*, xiii, quoting Harris, *Letter to a Christian Nation*.

evangelism, would have been an adroit move on my part to avoid stinging criticism, and a failure to drive home the truth.

The Watchman's Voice

"So I do not laugh, I do not weep unduly, nor do I hate, but I try to understand." If Spinoza's words have been an accompaniment, then so have those of Alexander Solzhenitsyn: "Crimes should be exposed not when they are being talked about but while they are being committed." What is more I observed this practice of "screen" worship fitting into the abrasive, but incisive voice of R.C. Trench who said bluntly, "Win men with honest trifles to betray them in deepest consequence."[20] Does this mean I am bereft of hope? No, and I offer some at the end of this chapter. Do I believe the church can be prevailed upon to come to its senses, I very much doubt it since the "die is sadly cast." Nevertheless, the role of the watchman must still find a voice in the church of the future (Ezek 3:4-9). When Ezekiel anticipated the coming of Israel's true shepherd, he contrasted him with the shepherds of Israel who in fact only cared for themselves: "Should not shepherds take care of the flock" (Ezek 34:2). At his conclusion he promises: "They will know that I am the Lord when I break the bars of their yoke and rescue them from the hands of those who enslave them." God's people have the unfortunate habit of enslaving themselves all over again, and no less so in the twenty-first century.

It is expected that the warnings which abound in these pages will arouse opprobrium. So be it. If they rouse some to exit the "echo chamber," and think again, my work of love will have been done! Some will argue that all this does violence to catholicity and excludes amity, in truth it is "screen" worship which is the violator of these excellent virtues.

Not Fit for Process

If worship is in fact a *process,* then it stands to "reason" that any part of it, at any time, might be treated as such. Merely chalking off, and "ticking the boxes" that "it" was conducted, that a given number were in attendance (verifying success), that the requirements were all met and signed off, fits perfectly into *process. Process* lives and breathes the oxygen of duty. When worship is mechanical a criminal act is performed before God, because *process* cares nothing for the artificial, the manufactured, and the result . . . God is a mere appendage. The "systematically organized" often requires automatons who cleave to the system. The church, collaborating with "Zoom" demonstrated all of this. What must be true is that in some degree, this condition had to have been already established or otherwise the experiment would never have been entered into. This confirms that "Zoom" did not have to struggle to overcome the church,

20. Trench, *Westminster and Other Sermons.*

rather it was a most willing compliant, being already sold to worship as a mechanism. Surely it must be acknowledged that Christians/churches are always extremely vulnerable to just "going through the motions," this we know keeps the *business* nicely ticking over. Worship offered in Spirit and in truth is more than a simple crossing of "t's" and dotting of "i's," rather it is the Spirit interceding with our spirit in prayer so as to deliver groanings which cannot be uttered (Rom 8:26). This hardly has a military look about it!

The danger must be admitted, any professing Christian at any time might fall foul of *process*, so that worship becomes a "thing" of just "nuts and bolts." The Quakers clearly "felt" something of this condition in the church, and in their own day reacted against it, as a result they chose to express their worship in an entirely different way from that which was perceived to be the "acceptable way." The Pentecostal and Charismatic churches have also assessed this, and come to their own and very different, demonstrative conclusions. Without endorsing their conclusions it is nonetheless easy to see why they have arrived where they have, their "genie will never go back into its bottle." Our militaristic approach to "getting the job done," ticking the boxes of *process* is frankly no better than so-called "ecstatic worship," where one *appears* dead and the other very much alive. The remaining question, which matters above all else, must be: Are these fit for *process*? If the answer is "yes," logic says we must "get down to business." This may well be due to our overarching view of technique, speaking of this technical civilization Ellul sees an "irreversible rule of technique is extended to all domains of life. It is a civilization committed to the quest for continually improved means to carelessly examined ends."[21]

Ellul adds: "Technique turns means in to ends. "Know-how" takes on an ultimate value."[22] Paul appears to be quite otherwise (albeit we may adjudge this not to be a strict church setting) when we see him at a place of prayer by the river, an occasion which led to Lydia's conversion (Acts 16:11-13). What of the unfortunate incident with Eutychus which resulted in the young man's death because "Paul talked on and on" (Acts 20:9, NIV)? Obviously he was not keeping his eye on the clock! Human commands and regulations have never been far away from the church, directing and influencing it, enabling the designated objective to be achieved; Paul could hardly be described as "The Technical Man (is) fascinated by results."[23] Yet none of this diminishes or suggests that we may not freely make plans for the offering of our worship *together*, only that we must ask at all times whether we are being enslaved by times and seasons of our own creating, which in turn threaten the *life* of the church.

21. Ellul, *Technological Society*, vi.
22. Ellul, *Technological Society*, vi.
23. Ellul, *Technological Society*, vi.

The Lord's Table—A Parody

This inbuilt concept of *process* afforded the church the latitude to experiment with "screen" worship, just so long as the meeting went ahead, nothing else mattered, even though we were not *actually* in attendance at any meeting. Nevertheless, those "sticklers" for *process* could feel a sense of accomplishment, with the added certainty that God was satisfied with such devotion. All the while superstition (which COVID-19 had exploited), was being extracted and raised to the surface. This would also need to be satisfied. What a relief to see the *process* intact and functioning still! The result, the worshippers believed all was well in the spiritual world. Accompanying this would also be the comforting confirmation that thankfully, they were not as others who were ostensibly disobedient, who had fallen into the habit of not "gathering themselves together" (Heb 10:25), or even worse, were willing to break the law by continuing to meet *actually* in person. With this kind of thinking all forms of worship had to be on the "table." The prayer meeting (an act of worship) could now be televised, watched like any other show. The morning and evening worship also brought under the same umbrella, and naturally as one thing follows another . . . The Lord's Table, Communion, the Eucharist would also have to bend to *process*. In these circumstances the one loaf of bread, (showing that we are one body) (1 Cor 10:17, NIV) was easily manipulated to becoming hundreds of loaves, and consequently hundreds of bodies. Did Christians realize that by this practice they had entered the ultimate world of magic and make believe? Geoffrey Wilson, commenting on this passage, calls upon Fausset who says, "Believers thus receive this cup from the Lord with thanksgiving, and "we bless" shows that this "consecration is the *corporate* (emphasis mine) act of the church"[24] (*NB*: the *corporate* act; The *one* body joining in the *one* loaf obviously in *one* location). It is very interesting to observe how the Church of England is able to take the communion (the bread and wine) out into homes so as to enable housebound parishioners to participate around the kitchen table, the ultimate in superstition. "Screen" communion was following in well-worn footsteps.

When Hodge comments on these verses he does so in this way: "The design of the apostle is to show that everyone who *comes* (emphasis mine) to the Lord's Supper enters into communion with all other communicants. They form one body in virtue of their joint participation of Christ. This being the case, those who *attend* (emphasis mine) the sacrificial feasts of the heathen form one religious body."[25] They were *actually* in attendance. When Paul was reasoning with the Corinthians on these matters he tenderly acknowledges that they are *reasonable* people (emphasis mine). (Therefore) "decide for yourselves if what I am saying is true" (1 Cor 10:14-17, NLT). These were *reasonable* people who needed the warning that if they thought they were standing firm they should watch out, they might experience a dreadful fall (1 Cor 10:12).

---

24. Wilson, *Commentary of 1 Corinthians*, 147, quoting Fausset, *Commentary on 1 Corinthians*.

25. Wilson, *Commentary on 1 Corinthians*, 147, quoting Hodge, *Commentary on 1 Corinthians*.

Pauline Diagnosis

When assessing the considerable challenges which the technical society presented, Ellul recognized that to tackle them a "distinction be made between diagnosis and treatment. Before a remedy can be found, it is first necessary to make a detailed study of the disease and the patient."[26] He says, "Technique presents man with multiple problems . As long as the first stage of analysis is incomplete, as long as the problems are not correctly stated, it is useless to proffer solutions."[27] Should Christians attempting to celebrate the Lord's Supper through a television screen really be thought of as *reasonable* people? Are they not playing God for the fool? It is tempting once more to say that Christians, overly excited by the spirit of the age in this unprecedented, febrile moment, in desperation lost their minds and senses. Following this line of thought, in the future, we might expect to see baptisms in private bathrooms, accommodating Baptists, and in the shower for Presbyterians! Presumably all of this would be perfectly legitimate, as worshippers gather around the screen "together" to witness the event. Even marriage could be shaped for the screen but will attendance, to use Hodge's words, be required? If all this seems quite ridiculous and ludicrous, the truth is, it is just that . . . ridiculous and ludicrous. Who knows what might yet be encountered in the descent down this rabbit hole? The race to the bottom in this digital experiment already includes the attempt to remember Christ in his death through a screen. In reality this was no remembrance at all, but in every way the act of a superstitious and extremely vulnerable people, giving the impression that their own light, might somehow be in danger of being extinguished if they do not participate, and that with great urgency.

This all looks strange, odd in the extreme and the words of 1 Corinthians loom large over us. In the early church those abusing the Lord's Table appear, in some remarkable way, to have been struck down. "Now in giving the following instruction I do not praise you, because you *come together* not for the better but for the worse!" (1 Cor 11:17, NET). At least we may applaud them as they *actually* came *together*, yet it proved detrimental to them, and had dire consequences. "God is not made a fool, he is not mocked, what a man sows that shall he also reap" (Gal 6:7). "For the one who eats and drinks without careful regard for the body eats and drinks judgement against himself. That is why many of you are weak and sick, and quite a few are dead" (1 Cor 11:29-30, NET). The New Testament church was born bearing witness to occurrences of a unique kind, which even though these bore witness to God's displeasure as with Israel in their disobedience (1 Cor 10:1) the people of the church were still willing to risk their very lives. Common sense might have instructed them that they could not just "do their own thing," they could not play the creative card with the Lord's Supper. Paul's conclusions carry a particular force and point to "treatment" of their

26. Ellul, *Technological Society*, xxxi.
27. Ellul, *Technological Society*, xxxii.

condition, "But if we were more discerning with regard to ourselves we would not come under such judgment" (1 Cor 11:31, NIV). His final comment is a tragic judgment upon the "screen" celebrating communicants via "Zoom." "So then, my brothers and sisters, when you gather to eat, you should all eat together" (verse 33) Yet no doubt, amongst the ongoing participants, there will still be those who remarkably insist, laboring under the delusion that they are *actually* meeting together. At this very moment, Metaverse (Facebook, WhatsApp, Instagram) in its current promotion is targeting its audience with the tantalizing revelation: "Metaverse may be virtual but the impact will be real." Even in this, the business world appears to grasp the reality, the "screen" encounter is not *real*, it is the technology: "so arranging the world that we don't have to experience it." This recognition is plainly what churches cannot grasp. The so-called worship *together* is virtual, it can never be *real*.

All Together Now!

This entrapment by the "screen" has succeeded in deceiving people from across the Christian and non-Christian world: Roman Catholics, to the Church of England, Baptists, Charismatics, Methodists, Muslims, Jehovah's Witnesses, all strangely coagulated as one in the desperate attempt to reach higher. It has been quite instructive to observe the practices of the Catholic church as it faced the problems of lockdown. In particular, the Mass being as it is at the center of Catholic "worship," was bound to be an issue. What is apparent, but not at all surprising is that even within that church hierarchy, no single authoritative position on the subject, nor any opinions and practices are available. It looks like a case of "Hobson's Choice," but true to form, the "calibrated weighing scales" exist within the Roman church, just as much as elsewhere. Even Jehovah's Witnesses have expressed their deep misgivings regarding their own "Zoom" worship, but in that organization as elsewhere . . . relativism rules!

One priest says: "Some sacrament laws are flexible others aren't." Presumably the priest will decide for the flock who will gladly follow his example and wisdom. Another priest identifies what he sees to be the problem (something expressed by Protestant nonconformists) "the rules (for worship) were created before the technology, and the church is not attuned to changing those regulations because of emerging technology." His pragmatism then delivers the inevitable, "The important thing is that your congregation receives forgiveness, not the way they deliver their confession." Based only on this kind of rationalism, the Catholic and Protestant, very uncomfortably, join hands in agreement. This man sees the *process,* whichever way it is carried out, to be the most important thing, "getting the job done" is what essentially matters. This must appear to many as quite normal, leaving the historical church worship looking rather tardy!

An entirely different approach is set out by Mark Weismer, the pastor of St. Augustine's Catholic Church in Pleasanton, California. "All of the Catholic Church sacraments must happen in person." Dominic Longerin, OP, Dominican priest and professor of theology in Washington, bluntly states the truth: "Electronic communication is not enough. And there is a reason why those watching Mass on TV know that it is not the same thing as physically being at Mass." Well said that man! It is not the same thing! If this observation were transferred across the divide from Catholicism to Protestantism, it carries with it a cruel ring and a cutting judgement on Christian worship in every aspect, including the Lord's Table. The reason: the worship offered to God does not have the privilege of "not being the same thing." Worship must always be the same thing, that is in Spirit and in truth, offered personally and directly to God himself, with the absence of any kind of medium. When the church meets "together" "actually" it must always be the ideal and never the synthetic. Real and fake can never be joined in worship, and must never drop somewhere between the two. Christians must never forget they are not playing games, the stakes are far too high. Such worship is not fit, nor ever can be fit for purpose, even if it is fit for *process*! God may not be taken for the fool.

Jack Need Not Be a Dull Boy!

Christianity has many prerequisites, confirming the God who has revealed himself is true. The God and father of Jesus Christ is the true God. Accordingly then, he makes demands upon his subjects which must reflect this, not least in acts of worship. All Christians without exception feel the weight of Paul's words "Let God be true and every human being a liar" (Rom 3:4, NIV). Guarding the truth then becomes a Christian/church responsibility and overwhelmingly so when joined *together* in corporate acts of worship. "God's household, which is the church of the living God, the pillar and foundation of the truth" (1 Tim 3:15, NIV). This alone outlaws any pretensions of illusion; worship cannot slip between reality and misleading reality. Mark Twain said, "The best thing about telling the truth is you don't have to remember what you said!" Pilate, in uncertainty, asked: "What is truth?" (John 18:38, NIV). Jesus on the other hand affirmatively announced: "the truth is able to set us free" (John 8:32). *NB* the difference between the two could not be greater, one trapped, uncertain, locked in, unable to do the right thing, whilst the other opening the door to liberation. The psalmist, knowing God intimately, informs us of God's desires . . . yes God has desires! As I have repeated throughout, he "desires truth in the inward parts" (Ps 51:6, KJV). By contrast, the prophet comments on the fact that "truth is fallen in the street" (Isa 59:14, KJV). Evidently theory and doctrine in various wings of the church appear to prosper; yet a cursory glance at the practice of church worship confirms its impoverishment, and dissolute worship may have taken another new turn—just when some of us thought we had seen everything . . . along came "Zoom" worship.

The so-called clean, pure, "God given" science based tech has not finished with us yet, meaning, with "truth fallen in the streets," our natural allegiance to tech renders us vulnerable to future assaults, as already virtual reality worship is making significant inroads. I expect many people to continue vaguely asking Pilate's question, but sadly discovering that the church, lost in the fog, will be unable to provide the correct answer.

Historically, the church rejecting the injunction of scripture, but buoyed by confidence, looks to construct great things for itself, even having a "name," "Seekest thou great things for thyself seek them not" (Jer 45:5, KJV). Neil Postman, like a true seer, highlights the "tyranny of the present"[28] and then goes on to offer a life-saving antidote to arrest the deadly poison. Postman calls for an "historical study"[29] of past things of extraordinary merit "humanities artistic roots" (Had Jeremiah been speaking of culture he might have described this as the *old paths*). Postman evidently saw the need for the art of literature, music and painting to lift us from the strictures of the present, taking us deeper beyond being "mere functionaries," confirming now Postman's observations are not at all dissimilar from those of John Calvin as referenced in Chapter 2, "all the arts come from God and are to be respected as Divine inventions." And as Postman continues: "their subject matter contains the best evidence we have of the unity and continuity of human experience and feeling."[30] For this reason he states the need for the "humanities" to be taught: "We should emphasize the enduring creations of the past."[31] He thinks (as I do) that our knowledge of the form and content of the arts displays a cavernous ignorance. Having become obtuse, a vacuum is created, a soulless emancipation of the creative world. From his perspective, hope lies in the works of Beethoven, Milton, Keats, Dickens, Whitman, Twain, El Greco and Goya, and to which I gladly add a host of others, not least Vermeer, Botticelli, Mozart, Turner, Van Dyck, Degas, Egon Schiele, D. H. Lawrence, Laurie Lee, Verdi, Vivaldi, Berlioz, and Wordsworth. Very ominously he sees: "The culture (our culture) tries to mute their voices and render their standards invisible."[32] He implies we are being emptied out. By and large, in Christ's church, culture may have been killed off (if it has ever been given birth) and as a result we are held hostage, slaves to our times . . . "Jack has indeed become a very dull boy!"

May we take it for granted that Christians, along with everyone else, are inquisitively gorging themselves almost relentlessly on the "provisions" of Twitter, Facebook, TikTok and other social platforms. Perhaps aided in their "research" by social video assistance. All this making an undoubted contribution to the "Blitzkrieg"! Unquestionably, world and church are harmoniously joined in this new world order, but being reshaped by their voracious appetite. As a consequence of living at close proximity (though quite unaware of this), the beautiful melodious voices from the past

28. Postman, *Technopoly*, 196.

29. Postman, *Technopoly*, 196.

30. Postman, *Technopoly*, 196.

31. Postman, *Technopoly*, 196.

32. Postman, *Technopoly*, 197.

(Postman) are drowned out. These are voices which would call us "higher" but they need mental space and time to do so, of which there is evidently precious little.

It comes as no small providence[33] at the close of this book to observe the rapid developments which are emerging around TikTok. The reader may recall in a previous chapter how cyber security journalists were referenced revealing a concern relating to "Zoom" content being sold on to China. Will Christians now share government angst about popular platforms and their alleged associations? And if they are distressed, will this essentially reflect the disaffection for the flag of the five stars, which TikTok may have wrapped itself in? It hardly seems likely that Christians would care less about the ethic of the fashionable platform, or "Zoom" or any of the others for that matter ... watch this space!

The author is of a different persuasion, and sees these provocations of all shapes and sizes, political or otherwise, profiting from a blasé attitude: Namely a blind confidence placed in those who kindly tell us what is good for us ... an Orwellian lesson if ever there was one; a lesson for every nation, for every family and every church and every Christian. Postman analyzing these changes draws on Orwell and Huxley: "Orwell feared that the truth would be concealed from us. Huxley feared that the truth would be drowned in a sea of irrelevance. Orwell feared we would become a captive culture. Huxley feared we would become a trivial culture."[34] We are drowning in that sea of "captive irrelevance," without a life preserver in sight.[35]

Zoom Worship ... Not Now, Not Ever!

If the builders of the "Tower of Babel" had halted construction for a moment, no doubt they would have observed an existing, glorious creation, i.e., God's creation, which could not fail to put their puny efforts into perspective. Perspective was the missing link, but, in a race to the top, the ivory tower could not be put on hold, it had to be erected *now*. Being willfully blind to the past, these people saw only the present, and the possibility to "make a name for themselves." Assuredly, "Zoom" will go down in church history as a turning point, and the modern church will be able to take all the plaudits.

---

33. What is providence? Except: The one who ordains the end also ordains the means to that end. Psalm 139:16 (NIV): "All the days ordained for me were written in your book before one of them came to be." Confirming the biblical declaration on personal salvation, far from being a mere human contrivance/decision, is in fact locked into God's gracious eternal purpose (Acts 13:48, KJV, NIV). John Newton's analysis of Gods dealings with Joseph leading to the coming of Christ is probably the most succinct and accurate Scripture explanation revealing this most comforting doctrine. It can be found in the preface to Jerom Zanchius, *Doctrine of Absolute Predestination*.

34. Postman, *Amusing Ourselves to Death*, foreword.

35. Huxley's *Brave New World* may be unknown to most Christians but quite possibly in the near future one of its own making might well emerge, confirming Charles Dickens' great perception: the affectionate parasite Hedera helix (ivy) overcomes the parent tree (Bleak House).

This building of new worship via the "screen" is not only a breach with the past, but a break with tradition, a glorious, biblical tradition, as it touches upon our worship of almighty God. At its inception I believed it to be an egregious act, and that while ever it is practiced, it will forever be recondite, an obscure remodeling of worship at the hands of the *new god*, which has so powerfully brought us under its esoteric spell. At the conclusion of his book *Strange Fire* John MacArthur's analysis of counterfeit worship encourages, "All who are faithful to the Scriptures must rise up and condemn everything that assaults the glory of God."[36] . . . Everything. If counterfeit worship is seen in what MacArthur exposes, what should be our response to "screen" worship and its assault on the glory of God? Courageously, and in a restless pursuit, every church and every true Christian is tasked with this noble first cause. G. I. Williamson wrote: "There is no safeguard to purity of worship except conscious and persistent adherence to this (regulative) principle: What is commanded is right and what is not commanded is wrong."[37] While I tend to lean towards J. I. Packer's persuasion that the "regulative principle" is a Puritan innovation, nonetheless, the rule of Scripture regulation and not our own, can be the only safe directive. And so to direct us to our conclusion: the final Scripture text comes up from the wisdom of Qoheleth . . . the words of the teacher:

> Not only was the Teacher wise, but he also taught knowledge to the people; he carefully evaluated and arranged many proverbs. The Teacher sought to find delightful words, and to write accurately truthful sayings. The words of the sages are like prods, and the collected sayings are like firmly fixed nails; they are given by one shepherd. Be warned, my son, of anything in addition to them. There is no end to the making of many books, and much study is exhausting to the body. Having heard everything, I have reached this conclusion: Fear God and keep his commandments, for this is the whole duty of man. For God will evaluate every deed, including every secret thing, whether good or evil (Ecc 12:9-14, NET).

For those of us who admired A. W. Tozer, the title "twentieth-century prophet" may have looked out of place, but surely the mantle was intended to be worn metaphorically. The distinction was bestowed with good intentions, after all, he was certainly a unique voice. The church both in his day, and right up to the present has shown itself to be resistant, impervious to his timely warnings. It is hardly surprising then, that he failed to ingratiate himself with those who ostensibly at least, shared his faith. He was an outspoken critic of much that had become "acceptable Christianity," and his objectionable remarks almost certainly still rancour. What Tozer discovered is that the evangelical paradigm must not be disturbed.

---

36. MacArthur, *Strange Fire*, xvii.

37. Reymond, *New Systematic Theology*, 872.

Wearing his metaphorical, prophetic mantle he followed in the line of genuine "bonafide prophets," not unlike Ezekiel, whom God inspired as a voice to his people. His challenge: he was pitted against a constituency which was "obstinate" and "hard-hearted" (NET), "impudent" (KJV). The proverbial bell tolls upon our contemporary scene, when these words are read: "Whether they listen or not—they will know that a prophet has been among them" (Ezek 2:5, NET). The prophets often met an obdurate and unyielding public, in fact the passage of time does not diminish this. Unfortunately the hostile terrain has not deterred the self-styled prophets of our day, attributing to their own powers "what should not once be mentioned among us." Impressively though, Tozer and others wear a very humble mantle. Neil Postman is one such "seer." The final chapter of his book, *Amusing Ourselves To Death*, would go a long way to save every humble Christian from what he calls "a vastly overrated technology."[38]

Postman has been at my side throughout the duration of this endeavor, he has helped me to ask questions which I thought others should consider. He is dead but still speaks, and it would be gratifying if Christians discovered this wonderful "loving resistance fighter" and his reasoned provocations. "Prophet" that he was, he deserves the final word: "Our youth must be shown that not all worthwhile things are instantly accessible and that there are levels of sensibility unknown to them."[39] The sensibilities of worship which the youth of the future need to see are not in the small print of Scripture but writ large for all to see, meaning there is no room for "Zoom," not now . . . not ever! If there is an acceptable worship (Heb 12:28) then most obviously there is an unacceptable worship, "Zoom" worship, corrosive as it must be, fulfils the latter. A discovery of these sensibilities alone will enable future generations, when contemplating "screen" worship, to press the "off" button. Only by doing so can we do honor to the triune God, God the Father, God the Son, and God the Holy Spirit for whose cause this has been written.

My namesake, Ernest Hemingway, counseled, "Only write when you have something to say." I have had something to say, which is now said. It remains with others to decide whether it was worthwhile saying it at all. I hope so, and in this hope that the church in its worship service to God will be *civilized*.

---

38. "Postman, *Amusing Ourselves To Death*, 166. "Prophets" like Postman, Huxley, and Orwell have been in the vanguard of "breaking spells" by simply "asking questions."

39. Postman, *Technopoly*, 197.

BIBLIOGRAPHY

Barclay, William. *Flesh and Spirit*. Edinburgh: Saint Andrew, 1962.

Barnes, Albert. *Notes on the New Testament*. 11 vols. London: Blackie and Son, 1878.

Barth, Karl. *Protestant Theology in the Nineteenth Century: Its Background and History*. Valley Forge, PA: Judson, 1973.

Beeke, Joel R., and Mark Jones. *A Puritan Theology: Doctrine for Life*. Grand Rapids, MI: Reformation Heritage, 2012.

Bell, Martin. *War and the Death of News: Reflections of a Grade B Reporter*. London: One World, 2017.

Beniger, James R. *The Control Revolution: Technological and Economic Origins of the Information Society*. Cambridge, MA: Harvard University Press, 1986.

Berlinski, David. *The Devil's Delusion: Atheism and Its Scientific Pretensions*. New York: Basic, 2009.

Betz, Hans Dieter. *Galatians*. Fortress Press, an Imprint of Augsburg Fortress.

Blanchard, John. *Sifted Silver: A Treasury of Quotations for Christians*. London: Evangelical, 1995.

Boice, James Montgomery. *The Gospel of John: Vol 1 The Coming of the Light John 1-4*. Grand Rapids, MI: Baker, 1938.

Boorstin, Daniel J. *The Image: or What Happened to the American Dream*. New York: Penguin, 1962.

Borman, Tracey. *Thomas Cromwell: The Untold Story of Henry VIII's Most Faithful Servant*. London: Hodder and Stoughton, 2014.

Brown, Colin. *Philosophy and the Christian Faith: An Introduction to the Main Thinkers and Schools of Thought from the Middle Ages to the Present Day*. London: Tyndale, 1969.

Bruce, F. F. *The Epistles to the Colossians, to Philemon and the Ephesians: The New International Commentary on the New Testament*. Grand Rapids, MI: Eerdmans, 1984.

Buber, Martin. *I and Thou: A New Translation, with a Prologue and Notes by Walter Kaufmann*. New York: Scribner's, 1970.

Bunyan, John. *The Holy War: Made by Shaddai upon Diabolus for the Regaining of the Metropolis of the World or The Losing and Taking Again of the Town of Mansoul*. Grand Rapids, MI: Baker, 1977.

Calvin, John. *Genesis. The Geneva Series Commentary*. Edinburgh: Banner of Truth, 1965.

Carr, Nicholas. *The Shallows: How the Internet Is Changing the Way We Think, Read and Remember*. New York: W.W. Norton, 2011.

Carson, Donald A. *Christ and Culture Revisited*. Grand Rapids, MI: Eerdmans, 2008.

———. *Intolerance of Tolerance*. Grand Rapids, MI: Eerdmans, 2012.

Chadwick, Henry. *The Early Church*. Great Britain: Penguin, 1967.

Cunningham, W. *The Moral Witness of the Church on the Investment of Money and the Use of Wealth: An Open Letter addressed to His Grace the Archbishop of Canterbury, President of the Convocation of the Province of Canterbury.* Leopold Classic Library: Cambridge University Press, 1909.

Dickens, Charles. *Bleak House.* Hertfordshire, UK: Wordsworth Editions Limited, 1993.

Eire, Carlos M. N. *War Against the Idols: The Reformation of Worship from Erasmus to Calvin.* Cambridge: Cambridge University Press, 1986.

Ellul, Jacques. *The Technological Society: A Penetrating Analysis of Our Technical Civilization and the Effect of an Increasingly Standardized Culture on the Future of Man.* New York: Vintage, 1964.

Furedi, Frank. *Therapy Culture: Cultivating Vulnerability in an Uncertain Age.* London: Routledge, 2004.

Gay, Craig M. *The Way of the (Modern) World: Or, Why It's Tempting to Live As If God Doesn't Exist.* Grand Rapids, MI: Eerdmans, 1998.

Gilley, Gary. *This Little Church Omnibus Edition: Went to Market, Stayed Home, Had None.* UK: E.P., 2014.

Greenfield, Susan. *Mind Change: How Digital Technologies Are Leaving Their Mark on Our Brains.* New York: Random House, 2015.

———. *Tomorrow's People: How 21st-Century Technology Is Changing the Way We Think and Feel.* London: Penguin, 2004.

Guinness, Os. *The Dust of Death: A Critique of the Counter Culture.* London: InterVarsity, 1973.

Harris, Michael. *The End of Absence: Reclaiming What We've Lost in a World of Constant Connection.* New York: Penguin, 2014.

Harris, Tristan. *The Social Dilemma.* Neflix Film, 2020.

Hendriksen, William. *Matthew New Testament Commentary.* Edinburgh: Banner of Truth, 1973.

Jenkins, Simon. "If the Church of England Worships Online, How Can Its Historic Buildings Survive?" *The Guardian,* December 26, 2020. https://www.theguardian.com/commentisfree/2020/dec/26/church-of-england-worship-online-historic-buildings-congregations-churches.

Johnson, Paul. *A History of the American People.* London: Weidenfeld and Nicolson, 1997.

Jurassic Park, Film, 1993

Kasket, Elaine. *All The Ghosts in the Machine: The Digital Afterlife of Your Personal Data.* London: Robinson, 2019.

Korn, Peter. *Why We Make Things and Why It Matters: The Education of a Craftsman.* London: Vintage, 2015.

Koestler, Arthur. *The Sleepwalkers: A History of Man's Changing Vision of the Universe.* London: Hutchinson, 1959.

Kuyper, Abraham. *Lectures on Calvinism.* Grand Rapids, MI: Eerdmans, 1931.

Lanier, Jaron. *Ten Arguments for Deleting Your Social Media Accounts Right Now.* London: Vintage, 2019.

———. *The Social Dilemma,* Netflix Film, 2020

Laurens, Camille. *Little Dancer Aged Fourteen: The True Story Behind Degas's Masterpiece.* Paris: Editions Stock, 2017.

Lembke, Anna. *The Crime of the Century.* Netflix film, 2021.

———. *Dopamine Nation,* Headline Publishing Group, London, 2021

Lesley, Ian. *BBC Documentary David Baddiel*. December 2021.

Lewis, C. S. *An Experiment in Criticism*. Cambridge: Cambridge University Press, 1967.

Lloyd-Jones, Martyn. *Preaching and Preachers*. London: Hodder & Stoughton, 1976.

MacArthur, John. *Strange Fire: The Danger of Offending the Holy Spirit with Counterfeit Worship*. Nashville: Nelson, 2013.

MacCulloch, Diarmaid. *Reformation: Europe's House Divided 1490-1700*. London: Penguin, 2003.

————. *All Things Made New: Writings on the Reformation*. London: Allen Lane, 2016.

McFadyen, Alistair I. *The Call to Personhood: A Christian Theory of the Individual in Social Relationships*. Cambridge: Cambridge University Press, 1990.

McLuhan, Marshall. *The Medium Is the Massage: An Inventory of Effects*. London: Penguin, 1967.

Mangalwadi, Vishal. *The Book That Made Your World: How the Bible Created the Soul of Western Civilization*. Nashville: Nelson, 2011.

Marlowe, John. *The Puritan Tradition in English Life*. London: Cresset, 1956.

Mecklenburg, R. W. *The Philosophy of Size and the Essence of Enough: A Minimalist Treatise*. USA: Morelia of Santa Fe Press, 2020.

Miller, Graham. *Calvin's Wisdom: An Anthology Arranged Alphabetically by a Grateful Reader*. Edinburgh: Banner of Truth, 1992.

Mumford, Lewis. *Technics & Civilization*. Chicago: University of Chicago Press, 1934.

Murray, Iain H. *Evangelism Divided: A Record of Crucial Change in the Years 1950 to 2000*. Edinburgh: Banner of Truth, 2000.

————. *The Life of John Murray*, Edinburgh, Banner of Truth, 1984.

Murray, John. *The Epistle to the Romans*. Grand Rapids: Eerdmans, 1997.

New Dictionary of Theology. Edited by Sinclair B. Ferguson, David F. Wright, and J. I. Packer. Downers Grove: IVP, 1988.

Noll, Mark A. *The Scandal of the Evangelical Mind*. Grand Rapids, MI: Eerdmans, 1994.

Orlowski, Jeff, dir. *The Social Dilemma*. Netflix film, 2020.

Owen, John. *The Death of Death in the Death of Christ: A Treatise in which the whole controversy about Universal Redemption is fully discussed*. London: Banner of Truth, 1959.

Packer, J. I. *A Quest for Godliness: The Puritan Vision of the Christian Life*. Wheaton, IL: Crossway, 1990.

————. *God's Words: Studies of Key Bible Themes*. London: InterVarsity, 1981.

Pink, Arthur W. *Exposition of the Gospel of John*. Grand Rapids, MI: Zondervan, 1945.

————. *Gleanings in Genesis*. Chicago: Moody, 1922.

Postman, Neil. *Amusing Ourselves to Death: A Public Discourse in the Age of Show Business*. York: Methuen, 1987.

————. *Informing Ourselves to Death*, Speech at German Informatics Society, 1990.

————. *Technopoly: The Surrender of Culture to Technology*. New York: Vintage, 1993.

Reinke, Tony. *12 Ways Your Phone Is Changing You*. Wheaton, IL: Crossway, 2017.

Reymond, Robert L. *A New Systematic Theology of the Christian Faith*. Nashville, TN: Thomas Nelson, 1998.

Roberts, Vaughan. *Transgender*. London: Good Book, 2016.

Robertson, Archibald. *The Reformation*. London: Watts, 1960.

Robinson, Andrew. *The Story of Writing: Alphabets, Hieroglyphs & Pictograms*. London: Thames and Hudson, 1995.

Rolston, Holmes, III. *John Calvin Versus the Westminster Confession*. Richmond, VA: John Knox, 1972.

Rosling, Hans. *Factfulness: Ten Reasons We're Wrong About the World - And Why Things Are Better Than You Think*. London: Sceptre, 2018.

Ryken, Philip Graham. *Art for God's Sake: A Call to Recover the Arts*. Phillipsburg, NJ: P&R, 2006.

Saxton, David W. *God's Battle Plan for the Mind: The Puritan Practice of Biblical Meditation*. Grand Rapids, MI: Reformation Heritage, 2015.

Schaeffer, Francis A. *The Great Evangelical Disaster*. Wheaton, IL: Crossway, 1985.

Smith, Charles Saumarez. *The Art Museum in Modern Times*. London: Thames and Hudson, 2021.

Spielberg, Steven, dir. *Jurassic Park*. Universal Pictures, 1993.

Strate, Lance. *Amazing Ourselves to Death: Neil Postman's Brave New World Revisited*. New York: Peter Lang, 2014.

Taylor, Fredrick Winslow. *The Principles of Scientific Management*. London: Harper, 1911.

Tawney, R. H. *Religion and the Rise of Capitalism*. London: Pelican, 1938.

Thomas, Hugh. *The Slave Trade: The History of the Atlantic Slave Trade: 1440-1870*. London: Papermac, 1998.

Tozer, A. W. *The Dangers of a Shallow Faith: Awakening from Spiritual Lethargy*. Minneapolis: Bethany, 2012.

———. *That Incredible Christian*. Harrisonburg Pa: Christian Publication, 1964.

Trench, R. Chenevix. *Westminster and Other Sermons*. London: Paul, 1888.

Valley of Vision: A Collection of Puritan Prayers and Devotions. Edinburgh: Banner of Truth, 1975.

Vanhoozer, Kevin J. *Pictures at a Theological Exhibition: Scenes of the Church's Worship, Witness and Wisdom*. London: InterVarsity, 2016.

Wallman, James. *Stuffocation: Living More with Less*. London: Penguin, 2015.

Watson, Thomas. *A Body of Divinity: Contained in Sermons upon the Westminster Assembly's Catechism*. Edinburgh: Banner of Truth, 1965.

Wengrow, David. *What Makes Civilization? The Ancient Near East and the Future of the West*. Oxford: Oxford University Press, 2010.

Weber, Max. *The Protestant Ethic and the Spirit of Capitalism*. Mineola, NY: Dover, 2003.

Wilson, Geoffrey B. *1 Corinthians: A Digest of Reformed Comment*. Edinburgh: Banner of Truth, 1978.

Zanchius, Jerom. The Doctrine of Absolute Predestination. Translated by Augustus M. Toplady. Grand Rapids: Baker, 1977.